Merleau-Ponty and Buddhism

Merleau-Ponty and Buddhism

Edited by
Jin Y. Park and Gereon Kopf

LEXINGTON BOOKS
A division of

ROWMAN & LITTLEFIELD PUBLISHERS, INC.
Lanham • Boulder • New York • Toronto • Plymouth, UK

Published by Lexington Books
A division of Rowman & Littlefield Publishers, Inc.
A wholly owned subsidary of The Rowman & Littlefield Publishing Group, Inc.
4501 Forbes Boulevard, Suite 200, Lanham, Maryland 20706
http://www.lexingtonbooks.com

Estover Road, Plymouth PL6 7PY, United Kingdom

British Library Cataloguing in Publication Information Available

Library of Congress Cataloging-in-Publication Data

The hardback edition of this book was previously cataloged by the Library of Congress as
follows:

Merleau-Ponty and Buddhism / edited by Jin Y. Park and Gereon Kopf.
    p. cm.
  Includes bibliographical references and index.
  1. Merleau-Ponty, Maurice, 1908–1961. 2. Buddhism. I. Park, Jin Y. II. Kopf, Gereon.
B2430.M3764M467 2009
  194—dc22   2009017070

ISBN: 978-0-7391-1825-2 (cloth : alk. paper)
ISBN: 978-0-7391-1826-9 (pbk. : alk. paper)
ISBN: 978-0-7391-4077-2 (electronic)

Printed in the United States of America

Contents

Abbreviations   vii

Credits   ix

Introduction: Philosophy, Nonphilosophy, and
Comparative Philosophy   1
Jin Y. Park and Gereon Kopf

Part I: Body: Self in the Flesh of the World   15

  1   Merleau-Pontean "Flesh" and Its Buddhist Interpretation   17
     Hyong-hyo Kim

  2   Merleau-Ponty's Theory of the Body and the Doctrine
     of the Five Skandhas   45
     Yasuo Yuasa with translator's introduction by Gereon Kopf

  3   How the Tree Sees Me: Sentience and Insentience in
     Tiantai and Merleau-Ponty   61
     Brook Ziporyn

  4   The Human Body as a Boundary Symbol: A Comparison
     of Merleau-Ponty and Dōgen   83
     Carl Olson

Part II: Space: Thinking and Being in the Chiasm of Visibility   95

  5   The Double: Merleau-Ponty and Chinul
     on Thinking and Questioning   97
     Jin Y. Park

6   The Notion of the "Words that Speak the Truth"
       in Merleau-Ponty and Shinran   113
       Toru Funaki

7   Self in Space: Nishida Philosophy and Phenomenology
       of Maurice Merleau-Ponty   133
       Bernard Stevens

8   Merleau-Ponty, Cézanne, and the *Basho* of the Visible   141
       Gerald Cipriani

9   "Place of Nothingness" and the Dimension of Visibility:
       Nishida, Merleau-Ponty, and Huineng   155
       David Brubaker

Part III: The World: Ethics of Emptiness, Ethics of the Flesh   181

10 The Flesh of the World Is Emptiness and Emptiness Is the
       Flesh of the World, and Their Ethical Implications   183
       Glen A. Mazis

11 Merleau-Ponty and Nāgārjuna: Enlightenment, Ethics,
       and Politics   209
       Michael Berman

12 *Ki*-Energy: Underpinning Religion and Ethics   229
       Shigenori Nagatomo

13 Merleau-Ponty and Asian Philosophy: The Double
       Walk of Buddhism and Daoism   241
       Jay Goulding

Notes   255

Glossary of East Asian Characters   283

Bibliography   291

Index   301

About the Contributors   309

Abbreviations

BC	Kuang-ming Wu, *The Butterfly as Companion: Meditations on the First Three Chapters of the Chuang Tzu*
BL	Nobuo Kazashi, "Bodily Logos, James, Merleau-Ponty, and Nishida"
BS	Edward Conze, ed. and trans., *Buddhist Scriptures*
C.	Chinese pronunciation
EB	Steve Odin, trans., "An Explanation of Beauty: Nishida Kitarō's 'Bi no Setsumei'"
EM	Maurice Merleau-Ponty, "Eye and Mind," in *The Merleau-Ponty Aesthetics Reader: Philosophy and Painting*
ERE	William James, *Essays in Radical Empiricism*
FP	Nishida Kitarō, *Fundamental Problems of Philosophy: The World in Action*
IF	David Dilworth, "The Initial Formations of 'Pure Experience' in Nishida Kitarō and William James"
IG	Nishida Kitarō, *An Inquiry into the Good*
J.	Japanese pronunciation
K.	Korean pronunciation
KS	Bernard Faure, "The Kyoto School and Reverse Orientalism"
LEM	Stephen T. Katz, "Language, Epistemology, and Mysticism"
LW	Nishida Kitarō, *Last Writings: Nothingness and the Religious Worldview*
NKZ	Nishida Kitarō, *Nishida Kitarō zenshū*
PG	Nāgārjuna, *The Precious Garland and the Song of the Four Mindfulnesses*
PhP	Maurice Merleau-Ponty, *Phenomenology of Perception*
Pp	Maurice Merleau-Ponty, *Phénoménologie de la perception*
PR	Maurice Merleau-Ponty, *The Primacy of Perception*
PW	Maurice Merleau-Ponty, *The Prose of the World*

RM	Jean Smith, ed., *Radiant Mind: Essential Buddhist Teachings and Texts*
S	Maurice Merleau-Ponty, *Signs*
SN	Maurice Merleau-Ponty, *Sense and Non-Sense*
T	*Taishō shinshū daizōkyō*
TPC	Geraldine Finn, "The Politics of Contingency: The Contingency of Politics—On the Political Implications of Merleau-Ponty's Ontology of the Flesh"
TPP	Eleanor Godway, "Toward a Phenomenology of Politics"
VC	Stephen Batchelor, *Verses from the Center: A Buddhist Vision of the Sublime*
Vi	Maurice Merleau-Ponty, *Le Visible et l'invisible*
VI	Maurice Merleau-Ponty, *The Visible and the Invisible*

Credits

Chapter 4, "The Human Body as a Boundary Symbol: A Comparison of Merleau-Ponty and Dōgen" by Carl Olson, appeared in *Philosophy East and West* 35 (April 1986): 107–20.

Chapter 11, "Merleau-Ponty and Nāgārjuna: Enlightenment, Ethics, and Politics" by Michael Berman, appeared in *Journal of Indian Philosophy and Religion* 7 (October 2002): 99–129.

Chapter 12, "*Ki*-Energy: Underpinning Religion and Ethics" by Shigenori Nagatomo, appeared in *Zen Buddhism Today* 8 (October 1990): 124–39.

Introduction

Philosophy, Nonphilosophy, and Comparative Philosophy

Jin Y. Park and Gereon Kopf

In the introductory essay to the anthology *Les Philosophes célèbres*, Maurice Merleau-Ponty writes: "Putting together an anthology about famous philosophers may seem to be an inoffensive undertaking. Yet one does not attempt it without reservations. It raises the question of what idea one should have of the history of philosophy, and even of philosophy itself."[1] Merleau-Ponty further observes that an effort to create "a history of philosophy" would be "unfaithful to what they [great philosophers] were greatly concerned with, a truth which rises above opinion." Interestingly enough, the anthology begins with discussing four Asian philosophers, the Buddha and Nammalvar in the section "Two Indian Philosophers," and Xunzi and Zhuangzi in the section "Two Chinese Philosophers." In his section introduction to "The Orient and Philosophy," Merleau-Ponty discusses philosophy's relation to the "Orient," and the position of "Oriental" philosophy in the "museum of famous philosophers." Merleau-Ponty contends that Hegel was the one who "invented the idea of 'going beyond' the Orient by 'understanding' them," but also who "contrasted the Western idea of truth as the total conceptual recovery of the world in all its variety to the Orient, and who defined the Orient as a failure in *the same understanding*" (italics in original).[2] In Hegel's world of philosophy, the Orient remains in its "childishness." Merleau-Ponty asks whether the Hegelian approach to the boundaries of philosophy in which the West claims absolute authority in and "right" to philosophy can still be justified. Merleau-Ponty did not fail to note that the problem that divides Eastern and Western philosophies runs deeper than geopolitics. That is so because "[p]ure and absolute philosophy, in the name of which Hegel excluded the Orient, also excludes a good part of the Western past."[3] Identifying Husserl as one who could have overcome the limits in the understanding of philosophy's relation to the East but who fell short of it, Merleau-Ponty emphasizes, "If Western thought is what it claims to be, it must prove it by understanding all 'life-worlds.'"[4]

This volume inherits Merleau-Ponty's legacy of challenging the border that compartmentalizes philosophy and groups it into different camps of philosophy and nonphilosophy, Eastern and Western philosophies, or childish and mature philosophies. An investigation of the life-worlds, to be faithful to its meaning, should include all factual realities of life before a division between philosophy and nonphilosophy is created and before such a division hinders our philosophical investigation. To think "about" philosophy and its outside, then, as Merleau-Ponty proves, is not one topic of philosophy but directly related to philosophizing itself. And for Merleau-Ponty, phenomenology is philosophy's way to go back to its original promise.

MERLEAU-PONTY'S PHENOMENOLOGY AND BUDDHIST PHILOSOPHY

"Phenomenology is . . . a philosophy which puts essences back into existence, and does not expect to arrive at an understanding of man and the world from any starting point other than that of their 'facticity,'"[5] Merleau-Ponty writes at the beginning of his *Phenomenology of Perception*. He further states: "It is a transcendental philosophy . . . but it is also a philosophy for which the world is always 'already there' before reflection begins—as an inalienable presence; and all its efforts are concentrated upon re-achieving a direct and primitive contact with the world, and endowing that contact with a philosophical status."[6] These passages note where Merleau-Ponty positions himself in the evolution of contemporary continental philosophy, i.e., what he inherited from his predecessors and where he diverges from them. As is well known, G. W. F. Hegel (1770–1831) was one of the first European philosophers to use the term "phenomenology" to identify a philosophical method. Edmund Husserl (1859–1938) developed phenomenology into a full-fledged philosophical discipline. Not unlike Hegel, Husserl attempted to resolve the Kantian legacy that postulated an infinite abyss and insoluble dichotomy between the *noumena* and the *phenomena*. Hegel sought absolute reality and certainty at the end of an infinite process in which the philosopher investigates "being" (*Sein*) as it is *given* to consciousness only to realize that it is not what it seems to be. However, Husserl proposes to establish a first philosophy that is grounded in a return to the "things themselves" (*Dinge an-sich*) and thus unmasks the essences behind the *phenomena*. As the method of such a return Husserl identifies a threefold reduction, also referred to as *epoché*. Through the process of *epoché*, Husserl attempts to suspend false presuppositions (*doxae*) and reveals the "transcendental ego" as the foundation. He also wants to demonstrate the ambiguity of the act of constitution (*noesis*) and the meaning it posits (*noema*) as the structure of human experience and knowledge in general. In his later work, Husserl shifts the focus of his reduction from the "transcendental ego" to the "life-world" (*Lebenswelt*) of the *cogito*. Nevertheless, Merleau-Ponty was dissatisfied with Husserl's phenomenology; he felt Husserl erred on the side of the subject. For Merleau-Ponty, transcendental phenomenology favors the subject over the object, and, at the same time, reduces the world in which the subject lives to abstract meaning. To remedy the ills of Husserl's approach, Merleau-Ponty suggests a brand of phenomenology he developed under the influence of Martin Heidegger's belief that human existence—in Heidegger's term, *Dasein* ("being-there")—constitutes a "being-in-the-world" (*in-der-Welt-sein*).

Merleau-Ponty fundamentally believed that a philosophy had to be grounded in the notion of the "life-world" instead of the "transcendental ego." This commitment to make the "life-world" the pivot of his phenomenology had far-reaching consequences. Such a phenomenology is interested in "all the living relationships of experience,"[7] and not simply in abstract essences or disembodied meanings. The subject that engages in this "life-world" does not constitute an intellectualized consciousness, but rather is the somatic self that interacts with other subjects and concrete objects. Merleau-Ponty's approach is a phenomenology of the *body*, not of the *cogito,* which is Husserl's view. The body constitutes the individual subject that interacts with the physical environment as well as other embodied subjects. In its engagement with the environment and the other, the embodied subject transgresses the boundary of what has traditionally been conceived of as body, person, and self. In this context, "intentionality," an important concept in phenomenology, acquires a new meaning with Merleau-Ponty.

For Merleau-Ponty, intentionality does not compose an intramental act of constitution, but destabilizes the preconceived boundary between mind and body, inside and outside, and self and the world. Merleau-Ponty refers to this intentionality of the somatic self as "intentional arc" (*l'arc intentionel*). The somatic self reveals a structure of ambiguity insofar as "I apprehend my body as a subject-object, as capable of 'seeing' and 'suffering.'"[8] This means that the "intentional arc," by means of which the somatic self engages with the world, cannot but be bilateral; perception requires action and vice versa. Merleau-Ponty observes that "[w]e experience a perception and its horizon 'in action.'"[9] Ultimately, Merleau-Ponty's emphasis on the "life-world" over the "transcendental ego" is not simply a modification of Husserl's phenomenological method but, more fundamentally, indicates a paradigm shift. Revisioning Husserl's phenomenology, Merleau-Ponty overcame what he perceived to be the stalemate between intellectualism and empiricism, and articulated a third philosophical position. In this process, Merleau-Ponty abandoned the Cartesian quest for certainty that was at the basis of Husserl's attempt to reveal the essences underlying the phenomena, and embraced the ambiguity between body and mind, self and the world, and sensor and the sensible.

Merleau-Ponty's phenomenology resonates well with some of the basic doctrines of Buddhist philosophy. Despite the diversity that has evolved in the history of Buddhism, most Buddhist schools share the basic doctrine known as dependent co-arising (*pratītya-samutpāda*).[10] The classical definition of the concept appears in early Buddhist texts as "Because this arises, that arises; because this ceases, that ceases." Dependent co-arising at its bottom is a theory of causation, but it negates a mechanical causal theory in which causes and effects are clearly separable and identifiable. Dependent co-arising is a theory of conditioned causality. The theory of dependent co-arising demonstrates the nonidentity of identity in the sense that an entity is at all times already a matrix of diverse causes and conditions that contribute to the existence of a current event. The seemingly same cause on a surface will produce diverse results based on the conditions under which an action takes place. Multilayered elements involved in the generation of a current event will, in their turn, make contributions to the occurrence of future events. The designation of past, present, and future in this sense has significance only provisionally and in linguistic and commonsense convention. That is so because when an event is understood as an occurrence in the nexus of multilayered causes, none of which has an independent identity, the temporal separation of past, present, and future is not tenable. In order to demonstrate the lack of one fundamental locus of identity that constitutes one's self, the Buddha explains a self through the theory of the five aggregates (skandhas) of form, sensation, perception, mental formation, and consciousness. By understanding the self as a combination of these five impersonal categories, the Buddha claims that there is no center in a self. Also, by rejecting the idea of existence either as anchored in a soul that exists permanently or in a body that perishes upon one's death, the Buddha separates his philosophy from both metaphysical eternalism and materialist annihilationism, and claims the "middle path." The "middle path" is not a meridian point attained by balancing two extremes; it is the third space, which is fundamentally different from either extreme of binary postulations. It demonstrates the impossibility of sustaining dualistic opposites that require identities independent of those being opposed.

In his later works, Merleau-Ponty explains this intertwining of opposites through the concepts of chiasm and the flesh (*la chair*). Merleau-Ponty's early works have already laid out this chiasmic understanding of the traditionally binary oppositions. In his *Phenomenology of Perception*, he maintains that in perception, "[t]he sensor and the sensible do not stand in relation to each other as two mutually external terms."[11] To explain the dissolution of the boundaries of what seems to be mutually external objects in sensory perception, Merleau-Ponty describes a perceptual experience that seems reminiscent of Zen Buddhism's account of the nonduality of the body and mind as a microcosm. Merleau-Ponty writes: "I am the sky itself as it is drawn together and unified, and as it begins to exist for itself; my consciousness is saturated with this limitless blue."[12] In its intentional engagement with the "life-world," the somatic self reaches out across space and time, drawing the external world—be it an other, an object of perception, the past, or the future—into its own horizon and into the "interworld,"[13] as well as the "mutual harmonizing and overlapping of past and future through the present."[14] The boundary between self and the world of objects is to be eliminated and the separation between self and others overcome. As one notes in the theory of the five aggregates, and later development of Buddhist theories, many Buddhist texts work off the fundamental assumption that consciousness is inherently somatic. Buddhist scholar David Shaner refers to this embodied consciousness as "bodymind,"[15] directly translating the Chinese characters *shenxin* into English. In the canon of Buddhist scriptures, these characters are generally employed to express the conviction that human existence is always embodied. In other words, body and mind constitute the two marks of the "self" and they are inseparable. Also as in Merleau-Ponty, in Buddhism, the self's engagement with its world is much related to the idea of intentionality. Volition (or mental formation, C. *xing*), one of the five aggregates, is the modality of human interaction with the world, and the concept is stratified and developed in terms not unlike Merleau-Ponty's "intentional arc." The self engages with the environment by means of volition; it is also the activity of volition that creates the self's own future.

When a self is perceived as the "bodymind," the concept of the self is inherently ambiguous; it can be identified as neither entirely active nor solely passive. This "bodymind" is devoid of an essence or a self; it relates in a chiasmic relationship with other "bodyminds" and to the cosmos as a whole; and it possesses an ambiguous structure. Buddhist thinkers, such as Chinese Tiantai thinker Jingxi Zhanran (711–782) or Japanese Zen master Dōgen (1200–1253), identify the individual "bodymind" as the place in which the entire cosmos is reflected and manifested. Zhanran claims that the "three thousand quiddities" are manifested in a "single moment of experience" (C. *yinian sanqian*). Dōgen defines the "bodymind" as "the whole world pervading the ten directions" and as the "total body,"[16] and compares the "bodymind" to a "bright pearl" that reflects all of nature and, ultimately, the entire cosmos.

In discussing consciousness in relation to Buddhist awakening, Buddhist scholar Shigenori Nagatomo makes a distinction between two types of consciousness: first, everyday consciousness and, second, "samadhic awareness."[17] "Everyday consciousness" is the trope of the "unenlightened" or "ordinary person" that occurs frequently in the Buddhist canon. Samadhic awareness, on the other hand, is characteristic of the various goals of Buddhist practice, such as the cessation of karma, awakening, or the attainment of Buddhahood. Everyday consciousness discloses a specific center, the *cogito*, and engages the environment by means of a "unilateral intentional arc."[18] Samadhic awareness, on the contrary, is devoid of a center, and discloses an infinite number of centers like Indra's net, a representative symbol of interconnectedness in Huayan Buddhism. Its modality of engagement is a "bilateral intentional arc."[19] Thus defined, both forms of awareness utilize a specific modality of engagement. Everyday consciousness is necessarily thetic and demonstrates a "positional attitude."[20] Samadhic awareness, on the other hand, is nonthetic and discloses a "nonpositional attitude."[21] Samadhic awareness does not engender any private world *for itself* and, therefore, must be devoid of thetic consciousness: None but "nonthetic awareness" unlocks the "horizon *in toto*."[22]

Part I of this volume, "Body: Self in the Flesh of the World," explores Merleau-Ponty's phenomenological understanding of body and its implication in various realms of philosophical discourses including mind, self, and the world, with Buddhist notions of dependent co-arising, the five aggregates, the subject-object relationship, and the problem of mind-body dualism.

In chapter 1, Hyong-hyo Kim offers an extensive discussion of Merleau-Ponty's concept of the flesh and contends that the concept is comparable to the Buddhist doctrine of dependent co-arising. Kim further expands his comparative study into the realm of Huayan Buddhism, bringing in the Huayan Buddhist concept of nature-origination (K. *sŏnggi*). Kim notes that, whereas Buddhist nature-origination offers the state of salvation as demonstrated by the Buddha or bodhisattvas, Merleau-Ponty's existential phenomenology does not contain the concept of salvation. It is debatable whether the relation of dependent co-arising (or dependent origination) and nature-origination in Huayan Buddhism is as dualistic as Kim presents in his chapter. However, with that claim, Kim underscores Merleau-Ponty's refusal to make a recourse to any discourse that might risk deviation from the factuality of the phenomenological reality of existence.

In chapter 2, Yasuo Yuasa argues that the theory of the five aggregates in Buddhism assumes an inherent inseparability of mind and body and rejects the dichotomy of self and the world; thus, in fact, it proposes something akin to Heidegger's "being-in-the-world." He also contends that the activity of this embodied self must be conceived of similarly to Merleau-Ponty's "intentional arc." Yuasa finally suggests that such a nonsubstantial conception of the embodied self is best illustrated with the Daoist conception of the human body as "vital energy" (*qi*).

Brook Ziporyn (chapter 3) explores the threefold truth of a Chinese Buddhist school known as Tiantai Buddhism in conjunction with Merleau-Ponty's conception of subject-object relationship. In Tiantai, Ziporyn writes, "[r]eality means, by definition, phenomenal reality, for any putative nonphenomenal reality is conceived in Tiantai as another local coherence, which serves, as it were, as the Ur-structure of phenomenality." Ziporyn further contends: "It is not just a fact that something is 'insentient': to say something is insentient is to say that it is seen as insentient from some perspective, that it is seeable AS insentience." Likewise, in Merleau-Ponty, one's experience of perception always exceeds what one perceives. In the Merleau-Pontean world of "the flesh," as in the Tiantai concept of a "single moment of experience" which contains three thousand quiddities, the seeing and the seen, the perceiver and the perceived, and the me and the non-me are always chiasmically intertwined.

In chapter 4, Carl Olson discusses the nonduality of body and mind in Merleau-Ponty and thirteenth-century Japanese Zen master Dōgen. For both thinkers, Olson argues, existence is embodied experience: "No one can be absolutely certain where one's body terminates and where precisely the world begins, and vice versa." Olson contends that, for Merleau-Ponty, the nonduality of body and mind is based on his phenomenological approach to beings, whereas Dōgen's nondualism is based on Buddhist practice of *zazen* (meditation). Olson contends, as Hyong-hyo Kim does, that Merleau-Ponty's interrogative approach "does not provide final answers." For Olson, however, Dōgen's Buddhism "enables one to realize Buddha-nature, reality itself."

SPACE: THINKING AND BEING IN THE CHIASM OF VISIBILITY

As the divide between mind and body, self and other, sentience and insentience becomes blurred, the form of philosophizing also changes. One way of describing this change is to understand it as a movement from temporal to spatial imagination. In this context, language has been a major tool to conceptualize the seemingly counterintuitive idea that traditionally exclusive binaries are in fact mutually inclusive.

From its beginning, Buddhism was aware of the problem associated with linguistic convention and that the nonsubstantial nature of Buddhist doctrine would conflict with the function of language that bases itself on a fixed identity. The tradition thus contains a list of anecdotes and incidents in which the Buddha allegedly claims that he did not say a word in his lifelong teaching,[23] or that he kept silence as a response to questions raised by his followers. The problem of language in Buddhist tradition reached an apex in Zen Buddhism. The classical definition of Zen Buddhism attributed to Bodhidharma, the alleged founder of the school, symbolically demonstrates the conundrum of language in the Zen tradition. Bodhidharma is reported to have defined Chan/Zen as a "special transmission outside scripture/without relying on words and language/directly pointing at human mind/looking at the nature [of the mind] and attaining Buddhahood."[24] The negation of language articulated in this passage serves a symbolic rather than a literal function. Despite the seeming negation of language in this passage, Zen Buddhist tradition has generated a sizable number of texts to be added to the existing corpus of Buddhist canons. More importantly, Zen Buddhism introduced unique ways of working with language. One notable practice in this regard is known as "encounter dialogue" (C. *gong'an*) between Zen masters and students. These dialogues became a ground for later development into a form of meditation known as *huatou* meditation (or meditation on critical phrases). The creation of the genre known as "records" (C. *yulu*) of Zen masters' teaching also demonstrates a new approach to language in the Zen tradition. In working with language, Zen Buddhists deal with not only the issue of the representation of Buddhist philosophy through a linguistic medium, as was usually the case with the previous Buddhist schools, but also its embodiment in each individual practitioner. Especially for the purpose of the latter, one frequently finds that language is used against itself in Zen Buddhist literature, challenging the fixed identity embedded in a linguistic system and in one's mode of thinking. This process becomes possible by creating a third space in which the identity of an entity is both preserved and violated.

In recent continental philosophical tradition as well, discussions on language have been at the core of philosophical investigation. In the essay "On the Phenomenology of Language" (1952), Merleau-Ponty notes that "[i]n the philosophical tradition the problem of language does not pertain to 'first philosophy.'"[25] The development of philosophical discourse since his work testifies to a change in this tradition. It is not difficult to identify predecessors of the current concern for the role of language in continental philosophy. For example, Montaigne believed that our understanding is always interpretation, without the guarantee of an unshakable truth, foreshadowing the problem of language in the search for truth. The violence of language is understood as a disease in Rousseau, who, as Derrida fully explicates, has to maintain the purity of language and the self through the condemnation of writing. In the Kierkegaardian idea of indirect communication, faith is obtained only in that place where the logic of language breaks down. At another level of indirect communication, achieved by using a pseudonym, the Kierkegaardian speaking subject keeps a distance from the textualized subject. For Nietzsche, language is accused as an accomplice that supports the fictional authority of the self. The Lacanian dictum "the unconscious is structured like a language"[26] demonstrates that the pendulum made a full swing in our understanding of the relationship between the subject and language.

Merleau-Ponty's way of seeing language sheds light on the ontological bearing of language, which has a direct connection to his concept of perception. His ontology of language is comparable to the Heideggerian way of seeing language on the one hand and, on the other, to Kristeva's vision of language articulated in her discussion in *Revolution in Poetic Language*. To Merleau-Ponty, our relation to language is similar to our relation to things in perception. Merleau-Ponty thus writes: "[The phenomenology of speech] teaches me a new conception of the being of language."[27] As the transversity of one's body connects the person and other beings in perception, signification in language has what he calls "quasi-corporeality" through which "the spoken word . . . is pregnant with a meaning which can be read in the very texture of the linguistic gesture . . . and yet is never contained in that gesture."[28] As in perception, in speech as well, its consequences always exceed its premises because, as with perception, speech already stylizes. Stylizing in both perception and speech, however, does not exclusively rely on the act of the speaking or the seeing subject. When speech takes place, through the "coherent deformation" of styles, not only the hearers but also the speaking subject herself go through "a decisive step"[29] to know herself as she learns about the other whom the speaking subject addresses. The mutual transformation of the speaking subject and the spoken object occurs in the "third space" created through the chiasmic intertwining of the two.

Part II of this volume examines this third space by discussing language in Merleau-Ponty and Buddhism and language's relation to thinking. Jin Y. Park (chapter 5) investigates Merleau-Ponty's chiasmic space of interrogation with the Zen Buddhist *gong'an* tradition, focusing especially on twelfth-century Korean Zen thinker Pojo Chinul's (1158–1210) *huatou* meditation. Bringing together Merleau-Ponty's concepts of "sedimented language" (*le langage parlé*) and "speech" (*le langage parlant*) with Chinul's live words (K. *hwalgu*) and dead words (K. *sagu*), Park identifies the projects of Merleau-Ponty's and Chinul's philosophy as a turning from substantialist to nonsubstantialist philosophy.

In chapter 6, Toru Funaki examines the use of language in Merleau-Ponty and Shinran (1173–1262), the founder of Japanese True Pure Land Buddhism (J. *Jōdō shinshū*). Funaki focuses his discussion on a comparison between the Buddhist invocation of Amida Buddha, *namu amida butsu*, and the notion of the *tacit cogito* in Merleau-Ponty. While acknowledging differences in context and scope between these two notions, Funaki identifies three fundamental similarities. First, both thinkers highlight the inherent ambiguity of language as it simultaneously discloses and conceals meaning. Second, they agree that language is always performative. Finally, in both cases, the agent of a speech act is no longer the *cogito* or self-conscious self but rather a transcendent function, namely Amida Buddha in the case of Shinran and the *tacit cogito* in the case of Merleau-Ponty.

Three chapters in part II discuss Merleau-Ponty's thought in connection with Japanese philosopher Nishida Kitarō (1870–1945). In his early works, Nishida demonstrates idealistic tendencies, focusing his philosophy around conceptions such as the "pure experience" (J. *junsui keiken*) and the "dialectical universal" (J. *benshōhōteki ippansha*). Starting with his essay "Acting Intuition"[30] published in 1938, Nishida's writing makes a transition from the idealistic to spatial imagination and begins to explicitly integrate Buddhist texts and ideas into his writing. During the same period, Nishida elevates the "body" to one of his foundational concepts. To Nishida, the "body" functions as the "place" (J. *basho*) in which the subject engages the environment by means of a bilateral modality of intentionality that Nishida calls "acting intuition" (J. *kōiteki chokkan*). Nishida's definition of the body echoes many of the themes characteristic of Merleau-Ponty's early philosophy. It also reflects Nishida's exposure to phenomenology, albeit Husserlian, and Buddhist philosophy, in particular the philosophy of Dōgen, and thus functions as a conceptual bridge between both philosophical traditions.

In chapter 7, Bernard Stevens explores Merleau-Ponty's notion of "flesh" with Nishida's notion of "active intuition." Stevens tells us that, for Nishida, as for Merleau-Ponty, the ambiguity of the body is "reducible neither to interiority nor to exteriority"; it "possesses both objectivity and subjectivity." Stevens further examines Nishida's spatial understanding of self in his discussion of the "locus of beings" (J. *yū no basho*) and "locus of oppositional nothingness" (J. *tairitsuteki mu no basho*). These are the space, or the locus, from which "the constituting subjectivity and the world it constitutes can be mutually understood because it transcends both."

Gerald Cipriani (chapter 8) examines Nishida's concept of *basho/logus* with Merleau-Ponty's discussion of Cézanne's paintings. For Merleau-Ponty, Cipriani writes, the paintings of Cézanne were testimonies about one's way of relating to the world through sensory perception and, by extension, of one's embodied way of being in the world. Cipriani reads Merleau-Ponty as one of the first to understand painting through the ontology of the visual. Artistic experience is based on the experience of the conversion of conventionally dualistic worlds of the body and mind, the subject and the object, and thus this experience is comparable to the experience of what Nishida calls *basho*.

In chapter 9, David Brubaker utilizes Nishida's concept of the place of nothingness, Merleau-Ponty's concept of visibility, and the seventh-century Chan master Huineng's dicussion of "self-nature" in his challenge to the dualistic approach to philosophy and religion. Brubaker contends that the concepts that have been considered as nonphilosophical by some thinkers, such as "nothingness," "suchness," or "emptiness" can be used for philosophical investigation and that philosophical examination of these concepts help us articulate some of Buddhist concepts such as wisdom and compassion in particular and religious experience in general.

THE WORLD: ETHICS OF EMPTINESS, ETHICS OF THE FLESH

What kind of ethics does one envision in the chiasmic third space? The blurring demarcation between self and other, or the subject and the object, could be understood as a hindrance to our ethical imagination. If there is no specific subject to identify, how does one define the agent for ethical actions? If things are intertwined in reality, how does one distinguish right from wrong and good from evil? In this context, one might even question whether ethics is possible in Merleau-Ponty's chiasmic world and in the Buddhist world of no-self. In order to answer these questions, let us first consider the following question: Does ethical behavior necessarily require extraordinary efforts, or does it occur naturally in one's daily life? In his discussion of ethics in Merleau-Ponty's world, James Hatley considers one's relation to ethics through the concept of "ethics as usual." He notes:

> The very urgency of ethical comportment, that it *ought* to be done, rather than merely *is* to be done, suggests that living an ethical life puts the agent at odds with the usual situation, the normal turn of events, or the course of nature as it would run unimpeded within the given world (emphasis original).[31]

By setting ethical obligation as a categorical imperative that is unconditional and context-free, the deontological ethical vision takes the position of the former, that is, the position of *ought*. One can draw the same conclusions about utilitarian ethics, if not for the same reasons. Buddhist tradition, especially the Mahāyāna Buddhist tradition, has long taken pains to explain the relation between "ought" and "is" in one's ethical behavior in the discussion of the bodhisattva path. From the perspective of Mahāyāna Buddhism, the idea of "ought" presupposes one's separation from others. Furthermore, when one says, "I ought to help you," the obligation of "ought" already sets the position of the "self" higher than the other, unto whom the self exercises its "ought." From the Mahāyāna Buddhist perspective, establishment of an independent ethical agent and the implicit hierarchy involved in this structure deprive the possibility of ethics instead of being its foundation. That is because such an ethical paradigm violates the ontological reality of a being.

The difference between "ought" and "is" in ethical imagination is not merely a matter of one's approach to ethics. The difference bases itself on the fundamental difference in the understanding of the ontological and existential realities of an entity. For Merleau-Ponty, a being is not a fixed entity; a being is a biological organism, which is constantly and consistently being embodied through interactions with its environment. Ontological ambiguity, which is engendered through the chiasmic existence of a being, also implies ambiguity in relation to one's ethical thinking. In a similar way, the Buddhist concept of ethics anchors itself on the basic ontological position of Buddhists, who claim a fundamental lack of any unchanging substance in a being. Conceptions of no-self and emptiness, which arise from the Buddhist worldview of dependent co-arising, nullify the concept of categorical imperatives. This, however, does not denote that ethics is not possible in Buddhism. Instead, as in Merleau-Ponty, ethical imagination also begins in Buddhism with one's awareness of or encounter with the ontological reality of intertwinement.

In the introduction to *Signs*, Merleau-Ponty writes: "Evil is not *created* by us or by others; it is born in this web that we have spun about us—and that is suffocating us. What sufficiently tough new men will be patient enough to really re-weave it?"[32] He further states: "The remedy we seek does not lie in rebellion, but in unremitting *virtù*. A deception for whoever believed in salvation, and in a single means of salvation in all realms."[33] These passages are representative of two significant issues in Merleau-Ponty's conception of ethics. First, for Merleau-Ponty, ethics and ethical categories are not unchanging universal forms as such, but exist within the intertwining web of existence. Second, ethical behavior cannot be understood through a teleological program that can be completed at a certain point. Like an organism, whose existence is possible only through the incessant movements of various biological organs and simultaneously through the constant exchanges between its internal and external environments, the ethical life of that organism requires nothing less than "unremitting *virtù*." Ethics for Merleau-Ponty comes from our existence itself, our way to "be."

In Mahāyāna Buddhist tradition, bodhisattvas' activities to help sentient beings are to be done without making a distinction between the two—that is, between bodhisattvas (enlightened beings) and sentient beings (unenlightened beings)—and this action is endless. The well-known bodhisattva vow thus states that bodhisattvas' works will not end until the suffering of the sentient beings comes to an end. It further states that, since there will be no end to the suffering of the sentient beings, there will be no end to bodhisattvic activities. This statement does not indicate that there will always be unenlightened beings in need of the help of bodhisattvas, nor does it envision a teleological time when all the suffering will eventually disappear. Rather, it indicates the necessity of unceasing activities of bodhisattvas in the life-world, by virtue of the very nature of the existence of beings. Being-in-the-world-with-others, when the other is already in the web of "my" intersubjectivity and when "my" existence is possible in the flesh of the world, indicates that ethics is not just "ought," but "is," which, however, also requires incessant effort to "be." This "to be" is not a static existence, which is distinct from the state, of becoming; "is" in this case is "ought" as it is.

In chapter 10, Glen A. Mazis offers a comparative discussion of Buddhist emptiness and Merleau-Ponty's concept of the flesh that is based on the concept of "ego," and considers their ethical implications, which he contrasts with ethics. Mazis contends that, unlike rational reasoning, which is at the bottom of this concept of ego and an ethical paradigm emerging from the self-sufficient self, Merleau-Ponty's ethics becomes possible through the exercise of sympathy, which "does not presuppose a genuine distinction between self-consciousness and consciousness of the other but rather the absence of a distinction between the self and the other." By the same token, at the core of the Buddhist ethical paradigm lies compassion, which is "the functioning of an interconnected, interdependent reality."

Michael Berman (chapter 11) further explores the nature of ethics and politics that are offered in the philosophies of Merleau-Ponty and Mādhyamika Buddhism (Buddhism of the Middle Way), founded by the second-century Indian Buddhist monk-thinker Nāgārjuna. Challenging the essentialist approaches to ethics and politics, Berman focuses on the nonrigid and open form of ethics that is aware of intersubjectivity, contingency, and ambiguity as fundamental conditions of human existence, and points to a *style* of politics that involves responsible and compassionate governance. Neither a priori categories nor context-free rules would be capable of putting such an ethics and politics into practice. Berman argues that only "unremittingly vigilant" efforts to realize *virtù* will take us closer to the practice of an ethics that honors these differences instead of silencing them. Berman relates the practice of Buddhism with Merleau-Ponty's position on freedom and states that "the attainment of *nirvāna* (enlightenment) is not necessarily an *apolitical* act," an account that offers a valuable point of departure for the contemporary discussion of Buddhist ethics and political theory.

The two final chapters in the volume locate Merleau-Ponty in the context of broader East Asian philosophical paradigms, in addition to Buddhism. Shigenori Nagatomo (chapter 12) discusses Merleau-Ponty's "intentional arc" as "a third term," with which he also identifies *ki* in the theory of *ki*-energy. This third term is a space "which is neither in-itself nor for-itself, neither the physiological nor the psychical"; it is reminiscent of Plato's third space, *khōra*. Nagatomo considers

Merleau-Ponty's intentional arc the "diffusion" of invisible energy "whose working is more subtle than the physical." Since this energy is the third term, Nagatomo contends, it facilitates a "mutual interfusion . . . between the subject and the object as a condition for the subject-object dialogue to take place."

In chapter 13, Jay Goulding explains three Chinese bodies—the heavenly body of Confucianism, the earthly body of Daoism, and the Buddhist body of the Void—and considers Merleau-Pontean flesh as "the double walk" of Daoist and Buddhist bodies. Goulding also reads Merleau-Ponty's spatial image and phenomenological body in the literature of the floating world of Qing China and Togukawa Japan, demonstrating the "thickness" created by multilayered significa-tion through Buddhism, Daoism, literature, and philosophy.

In his discussion of Merleau-Ponty's legacy in continental philosophy, Hugh J. Silverman emphasizes the "limits of philosophy," about which Merleau-Ponty was concerned and whose philosophy attempts to overcome. Silverman writes: "Philosophy had in certain respects undermined its own opportunity to fulfill its mission, to enter into the texture of things, to interrogate them, to understand the workings of brute being."[34] For Merleau-Ponty, phenomenology is the way by which philosophy could overcome its own demise, which is processed through essentialist positions of subjectivism and scientific objectivism. Phenomenology, according to Merleau-Ponty, means "the whole truth" without the divide of the subject and the object, the East and the West, philosophy and nonphilosophy, phenomena and noumenon. The nonduality of the binary opposites that Mer-leau-Ponty persistently demonstrates, from his early works on perception to later works on the chiasm of visibility, demands that philosophy radically challenge the conventional wisdom and go "beyond" the philosophy to embrace "nonphiloso-phy." This is not to promote nonphilosophy, but to negate the boundary that cre-ates this division. The Buddha describes this third space, in which both the inside and the outside are negated, as the middle path, which denies both metaphysical eternalism and materialist annihilationism, but understands the world through simultaneous double negation and double affirmation. Ethics, in this world of Merleau-Ponty and the Buddha, begins not through the awareness of the "ought," but through the awareness of the fundamental ontological and existential realities of coexistence and its effect.

I

BODY: SELF IN
THE FLESH OF THE WORLD

1

Merleau-Pontean "Flesh" and Its Buddhist Interpretation

Hyong-hyo Kim

HOW BUDDHIST IS MERLEAU-PONTY'S PHILOSOPHY?

How Buddhist is Maurice Merleau-Ponty's philosophy? If his philosophy does not envelop the idea of saving the world, there is a distance between his philosophy and Buddhist thought. Given that Buddhism is a religion, as much as it is a philosophy, with the idea of salvation, Buddhism and Buddhist practitioners have a strong desire to transcend this world of suffering. Buddhist thought is, in a word, a soteriology. Merleau-Ponty's philosophy, on the other hand, does not have a sense of saving this world from suffering. The idea of salvation is lacking in his thought. Human beings are born with a body, and this body is the ground of primordial limitations of human existence, which one cannot leave until death. Because this body cannot be separated from the world, Merleau-Ponty takes the position that the idea that human beings can save this body and the world (while both of them belong to this world) is only an imagination, something that is existentially impossible. Seen from this perspective, Merleau-Ponty's philosophy is distant from the Buddhist thought of salvation.

However, the salvation that Buddhist philosophy develops does not take the form of idealistic discourse, which attempts to transform radically this world through normative rules. Instead, Buddhist salvation is none other than a liberation that becomes possible through an awareness of the original reality of the world, which has evolved in its suchness from the beginningless beginning, and by transforming this awareness into wisdom. In this sense, Buddhist soteriology is not a theory of revolution based on an idealistic concept of "should"; instead, it is an awareness of the aspect of life in which the world and human beings are originally and mutually interconnected. Because Buddhist soteriology does not distance itself from such an original aspect of

human life, one may say that Merleau-Ponty's philosophy shares some nuance
with Buddhism.

Merleau-Ponty's philosophy can be Buddhist in that sense, but the situation
does not seem that simple. Ambiguity, which Merleau-Ponty understands as the
phenomenon of the original reality of the world, suggests similarities with the
Buddhist concept of "the nature of dependent arising" (K. *ŭita'gi sŏng* 依他起
性) on the level of "conventional truth." However, the "ultimate truth" of Buddhism, which asserts the truth of true suchness and emptiness of all things, does
not seem to be found in Merleau-Ponty's philosophy. As pointed out by a Belgian
philosopher, Alphonse de Waelhens, and a French philosopher, Ferdinand Alquié,
"ambiguity" is the original reality to Merleau-Ponty. This ambiguity takes the
form of double affirmation. Good does not have its own castle to be secured in the
name of goodness, but is ambiguously mixed with evil. Merleau-Ponty's ambiguity
tells us of the impossibility of drawing a clear boundary between good and evil in
many cases in history, and it thus emphasizes the irony that on the other side of
good lies evil. Not only in the case of good and evil, but also the concepts of right
and wrong, or of medicine and poison, are mutually interconnected as well. Such
an idea shares the Buddhist concept of interdependency in which arising and
ceasing (or life and death) are different but, at the same time, cannot exist independently. We can say that what Merleau-Ponty suggests by ambiguity is close to
the mutual dependency in the dependent co-arising of Buddhism. Ambiguity, like
dependent co-arising, implies double affirmation of mutual dependency.

In Merleau-Ponty's philosophy, the law of dependent co-arising is described as
the reality of the origin of the world; however, the law of emptiness as ultimate
truth is not found. Merleau-Ponty's philosophy deals with the double-affirmative
law of dependent co-arising, but he does not point out that on the other side of
this double affirmation exists double negation, which is the law of salvation. Since
Merleau-Ponty claims the nonsubstantialist and nonatomist idea that good and
evil are mutually inscribed, and that right and wrong cannot exist independently
from one another, he is denying the logic of the binary opposites of good and evil
and right and wrong. This refusal of the logic of binary opposites contends that
the theory of self-identity, which maintains an independent identity of an entity,
is not the ground of the world. It denies the Aristotelian logic of identity and the
excluded middle.

Merleau-Ponty's philosophy of ambiguity declares that the self is not an entity
that maintains identity completely separate from others; instead, self and others
are simultaneously and mutually interdependent. Hence, the concept of self, like
that of others, cannot have a clear demarcation but relies on others; both self
and others come to be and cease together. The nature of one's self cannot exist in
separation from one's reaction to that which has been inscribed in oneself latently
by others with whom one is acquainted. Though it is called "self," it is impossible
to know how much of the identity of "self" genuinely belongs to the self. Because
the self is a product of its relationship with others, the identity of the self is always

preconditioned by the existence of others. This is why Merleau-Ponty's ambiguity takes the position of double affirmation. This double affirmation can be seen also as the simultaneity of the nonsimultaneous. Because there is a difference between self and others, they are nonsimultaneous; however, identity of self is already inscribed in the identity of others. When self is understood, others come along. The differences between them, then, coexist simultaneously—hence, the simultaneity of the nonsimultaneous.

Merleau-Ponty's ambiguity of the double affirmation is strictly focused on the conventional level of the secular world. That is because his philosophy is based on the existential phenomenology that denies the possibility of a "high-altitude thinking" (*la pensée de survol*),[1] which looks down at the world from an idealist position, flying above the reality of body and the world that is related to the body. For Merleau-Ponty, human existence can be identified only by its existential existence in the body and the world. Merleau-Ponty thus declares the original existential condition of human being as "being-in-the-world," borrowing from Heidegger. This should mean that human existence is equivalent to "being-in-situation." Such an existentialist tendency in Merleau-Ponty's thought seems to lead him to deny the concept of a sage, which Asian philosophy takes as being at the center of the philosophical endeavor. From his perspective, a sage is a perfect human being. Perfection, however, to Merleau-Ponty is understood as an illusion of ideation that deviates from the situations of the world and thus distances itself from the existential reality of life. The sage in Asian philosophy, however, is not the product of the nonsituational idea, as Merleau-Ponty criticizes it. A sage in Asian tradition—be it a Buddhist sage or a Confucian one—is a person who realizes the principle of the world and embodies the principle through the unity of knowledge and praxis. A sage, then, is not someone who positions herself outside of the world and looks down at it by projecting a neutral and idealistic vision. Such a being can be at best a bystander who does not get hurt by and who feels no pain about the tragic reality of the world. The one who looks at the world from the position of the high-altitude thinking is no more than an idle spectator. Sages, especially in Buddhist tradition, are not onlookers who remain indifferent to the affairs in the world.

A Buddhist sage is one who has experienced the existential pain and suffering innate in the situations of the world and who has discovered the ontological salvation to liberate herself from such existential pain. Hence, the Buddhist concept of ontological salvation is not the same as what Merleau-Ponty identified as a high-altitude thinking about the world and existence. Through the ultimate truth of suchness, Buddhism offers ontological salvation derived from the awareness of the existential reality of the world. Such a truth cannot be obtained by leaving the conventional truth of the secular world; instead, it is a truth rediscovered as one finds existential meaning from the existential reality of the secular world. What is meant by existential truth is equivalent to what Merleau-Ponty frequently calls the attitude of natural lifestyle. The natural attitude is what he also identifies as the "ante-predicative life of consciousness" (*la vie ante-prédicative de la conscience*), which is included in the phenomenon of perception that humans feel in their relationships in the daily life-world as they live with the sense organs of their bodies. Existential truth can be taken as a synonym of original facts that function in the prepredicative consciousness. By the same token, what Merleau-Ponty calls "ambiguity" is an expression indicating the facts of which the prepredicative consciousness becomes aware. This, I believe, has similarities with the Buddhist theory of dependent co-arising on the conventional level. Merleau-Pontean ambiguity tells us that a phenomenon X does not come to exist through a single cause, but is already mixed with others that distinguish themselves from the phenomenon X. In such logic, the traditionally emphasized idea of a truth that contains a clear identity and division cannot be sustained. Merleau-Ponty's concept of ambiguity contends that truth does not have an identity to be clearly distinguished from others but is a combination with others. Ambiguity, in this sense, contains the logic of double affirmation.

Existential reality of ambiguity is sensual and based on the feelings of one's body. The feelings of the body, however, do not rely on the subject-object dualism on which the traditional rationalist idealism and empiricist realism declared its position. Nor is it a part of the seemingly objective mode of thinking that is based on substantialist and atomist philosophy. Merleau-Ponty claims that the traditional interpretation of feelings was not faithful to the feelings themselves; instead, they were one's thoughts about feelings (*la pensée de sentir*), which reinterpret original facts about the feelings. The original phenomenon of the feeling is so ambiguous, Merleau-Ponty contends, that even when we simplify it to its utmost, it contains dual affirmation. Merleau-Ponty, however, does not address the issue of salvation as to how human beings might liberate themselves from the sufferings and constrains that the feelings of humans inevitably contain in themselves. In this sense, I believe that Merleau-Ponty's philosophy does not lead to any type of salvation.

The Buddhist concept of liberation as presented in the law of emptiness is in accord with the logic of double negation. The double affirmation of the theory of dependent co-arising leads an individual to an awareness of reality when one frees oneself from the subtantialist and essentialist thought of being attached to divisions. The double negation of the theory of emptiness offers the vision that enables individuals to reconsider the existential reality that they attained through the double affirmation into the ontological awareness. Ontological vision is related to the reflection on the invisible and intangible essence of a being, which one reaches through the visible and tactile phenomena of the sensual world. The existential reality is related to the sensible and visible phenomena. On the other hand, the ontological reality is related to the invisible essence of a being, which is not separated from the visible phenomena, but which is also not the same with the visible phenomena. In *The Visible and the Invisible*, the major work in his late period (as the *Phenomenology of Perception* represents his early period), Merleau-

Ponty greatly emphasizes the meaning of the invisible phenomena. In *The Visible and the Invisible*, Merleau-Ponty's emphasis is on the mode of nondual thinking through which he explores how the essence of the invisible is existent in the visible phenomena and how they are mutually related. However, in this work, he rarely addresses the issues of how a phenomenon overcomes its phenomenality and represents the essence of being.

Merleau-Ponty rejects Satre's strict dualism of being in itself (*l'être en soi*) and being for itself (*l'être pour soi*), which represent being and nothing, respectively. Instead of identifying the invisible as nothingness (*le néant*), the invisible, for Merleau-Ponty, is understood as the hollow (*le creux*), the concave, or the Heideggerian unconcealment of the concealed (*Unverborgenheit der Verborgenheit*), which reveals the diverse dimensions of the visible. The invisible in this sense is significantly different from the Sartrean nothingness of consciousness whose function lies in the nullification (*la néantisation*).

Merleau-Ponty's philosophy describes the path through which the invisible essence descends to the visible, but does not deal with how the reality in the visible phenomena transcends its phenomenality and ascends to obtain the meaning of the invisible. This probably is why one finds it difficult to see the double negation of the philosophy of nothing and the concealment of essence (*Abwesen*) in nothing, as one finds in Heidegger, and the subsequent lack of the philosophy of liberation in Merleau-Ponty. The truth on the level of the ultimate truth in Buddhism is pregnant with the desire for the truth in the conventional level to be liberated from the pains caused by one's body and consciousness. Gabriel Marcel names such a desire ontological *exigence* (*l'exigence ontologique*).[2]

At this point, we need to elaborate on the concepts of the existential truth of the conventional level and the ontological truth of the ultimate level. We also need to reflect on whether it is legitimate to develop a hypothetical thesis in which we introduce Buddhist philosophy into the Heideggerian concept of essence. We have identified the ultimate truth of suchness with the law of emptiness (or emptiness of all beings); if we are to interpret the law of emptiness by using the ontological concept, are we not facing here a self-contradiction? The law of emptiness is the other side of the law of dependent co-arising. Nāgārjuna has already pointed out that because the law of dependent co-arising is based on nonsubstantiality of beings, the phenomena of the dependent co-arising are nothing but the traces of emptiness. If we transform Nāgājuna's Mādhyamika philosophy into the concepts in the Yogācāra, the provisional being (K. *kayu* 假有) that exists through the nature of dependency according to the law of dependent co-arising is nothing but the skillful means through which emptiness without self-nature manifests itself. Hence, the provisional being, or the almost being (K. *sayu* 似有), is also called the functional being (K. *sisŏlyu* 施設有). The functional being returns to the state of non-being when those temporary functions of being disappear. Why then do we identify the essence of nothing and emptiness ontologically? To introduce essentialism to Buddhism may create misunderstanding because such an attempt could be associated with essentialism of Abhidharma, which Nāgārjuna criticized. However, if we understand essence in Heideggerian sense, we will save ourselves from falling into the substantialist essentialism of the Abhidharma because essentialism is directly related to an illusion that the essence exists ontically. In other words, essentialist illusion contends that an entity (*das Seiende*) contains something permanent.

Let us look more in detail into what Merleau-Ponty indicates by the existential reality of ambiguity. Clarifying this point not only directly connects the understanding of the core of his philosophy but also clarifies the relationship of his philosophy with Buddhism. To put it in a nutshell, what Merleau-Ponty identifies with the consciousness is completely different from Sartre's consciousness, and it is indistinguishable from body. For Sartre, body is the realm of unclear fact to which things as being-in-itself cannot penetrate, whereas consciousness is the realm of pure idea and ultimate freedom. For Merleau-Ponty, however, body is neither a pure entity nor pure consciousness; it is an ambiguous middle point. He thus understands body as being equal to behaviors of one's body. This is the leading concept that prevailed in his first publication *The Structure of Behavior*. The behaviors of body are comprehensive biological reactions that appear as one's consciousness of perception and *Gestalt* of things ambiguously mingled into each other. For example, the reactions of one's body when one climbs up a rough cliff and when one walks through a field covered with wild flowers are definitely different. This is possible because one's bodily movements are the reflection of the reciprocal relations that take place in one's body between the sensory motors and the *Gestalt* (or form) of a thing at hand. This further suggests that it is virtually impossible to draw a clear line between the psychological realm and physical reality of one's behavior.

By the same token, social life in the life-world is an ambiguous interweaving of coexistence and battle. If we take a bystander's position in our life, struggle and mutual conflict that are common in our social life will never occur. The sense of conflict and struggle arises because we feel the sense of living together. Struggle and coexistence, then, are not two separate entities, but symbolize the dual nature of social consciousness of being separate but at the same time being together. The intertwining (*l'entrelacs*) of love and hatred of social consciousness indicates that human society is a phenomenon with dual faces, rather than one characterized by either pure love or pure hatred. According to Merleau-Ponty, the intertwining of "me" seeing others and others seeing "me" makes it impossible for one to be a complete loner in human relationship. By the same token, a community of pure love is not possible either. In the phenomenon of the life-world, for Merleau-Ponty, to find clarity of complete reduction of being into an independent identity is not possible.

The human relationship in social life is not the only example of such an intertwining ambiguity. The same logic applies to the act of perceiving things. In critique of Sartre's dualism, Merleau-Ponty writes: "Then I am no longer the pure negative, to see is no longer simply to nihilate, the relation between what I see and I who see is not one of immediate or frontal contradiction; the things attract my look, my gaze caresses the things, it espouses their contours and their relief, between it and them we catch sight of a complicity."[3] The complicity that the body feels in this world applies to both human relationship and one's perception of things, and, in both cases, it is similar to the textuality of the coexistence of difference and identity. Merleau-Ponty calls this relation of complicity "flesh" (*la chair*), an expression that is uniquely his own. Flesh indicates the range of the horizon on which the feelings of body function, and, at the same time, it is another name for the boundary of the incarnated consciousness (*la conscience incarnée*). If there were no flesh, one would not be able to act in complicity with others as well as with the world.

Because the flesh refers to the perceivable—that is, the intertwining of phenomena sensibly perceived—it indicates existential dimension; however, because it sensiblizes the invisible aspect of phenomena, it cannot be understood in separation from the flesh of one's existence. Hence, the "flesh," as Merleau-Ponty indicates, is a philosophical term unique to Merleau-Ponty, a term that indicates that visible phenomena do not exist in separation from the invisible essence. In this context, one can see that Merleau-Ponty's thought is close to Huayan Buddhist philosophy. Fazang, the third patriarch of Chinese Huayan Buddhism, discusses how the visible form in the factual world and the essence of the invisible emptiness are mutually interpenetrated. He states: "By relying on emptiness, form establishes itself; by relying on form, the emptiness reveals itself; when both are negated, the meaning of both disappears; when both are affirmed, both come to appear."[4] The meaning of this statement is not far from Merleau-Ponty's claim. However, it should also be acknowledged that the two modes of thinking locate themselves on different levels.

Merleau-Ponty's philosophy centers on the description of existential reality. Because of this, as we noted earlier, it lacks the theory of salvation. His philosophy focuses on the phenomenology of dependently co-arising reality, and, as a result, lacks the desire to liberate people from the suffering and pain caused by the reality of living in this world. This lack is one of the reasons why his philosophy was not able to transcend into the Huayan vision of nature-origination (K. *sŏnggi* 性起). The nature-origination and the dependent origination (or dependent co-arising) share similarities, but whereas dependent co-arising aims toward existential phenomena, nature-origination is equivalent to truth-suchness itself. Nature-origination suggests that once one looks at the world from the perspective of ontological reality, the world is as it is, always already saved, and thus is suchness. Fazang's above-cited passage reveals similarities with the law of dependent co-arising, which is also Merleau-Ponty's concept of ambiguity. However, the two—nature-origination and dependent origination—are different in terms of the position they are taking. Buddhist dependent co-arising and Merleau-Ponty's concept of ambiguity are not different from Heidegger's concept of difference and Jacques Derrida's *différance*. Dependent origination and nature-origination are similar in terms of structure in the sense that both concepts demonstrate the difference (or *différance*) of visible form and invisible emptiness. However, the position they take is different. The *différance* of dependent origination is the reality felt through body and, thus, is accompanied by the defilements and suffering of the world, whereas the *différance* of nature-origination is the happy state of dharma-nature in which one forgets both body and self and practices bodhisattva spirit with no constraints whatsoever.

Let us examine more in detail Merleau-Ponty's concept of the flesh. Because the flesh is the horizon of the perception of the body as the embodied consciousness, it cannot be just an object standing in front of us. It is a world in which the visible body and things and the invisible human mind and meanings of things are mixed together. The flesh is the life-world in which humans inhabit. This does not mean that another world exists for humans. Merleau-Ponty exclusively focuses on this existential reality of our existence; he seems to have completely forgotten the soteriological and ontological desires of humans. He does not want to go beyond the "perceptual faith" (*la foi perceptive*), which our body senses. Terminologies in his philosophy, such as the body subject, intertwining, perceptual faith, and chiasmus, are all interchangeable with the concept of the flesh. Because the human world is flesh as it is, and because a distanced view of that world is not possible, the world of the flesh, for Merleau-Ponty, is the only limit on the possible and unified horizon.

The only possible unity of the world, however, is not that which can be obtained through the logical conclusion of abstract thinking. It is only a tentative presumption that the perceptual faith originally entails in it. Hence, the world cannot be completely closed, but always open in its incompletion and possibilities. Merleau-Ponty explains this point as follows:

> If the synthesis could be genuine and my experience formed a closed system, if the thing and the world could be defined once and for all, if the spatio-temporal horizons could, even theoretically, be made explicit and the world conceived from no point of view, then nothing would exist; I should hover above the world, so that all times and places, far from becoming simultaneously real, would become unreal, because I should live in none of them and would be involved nowhere.[5]

EXISTENTIALITY OF THE FLESH
AS SENSED THROUGH PERCEPTUAL FAITH

Perceptual faith does not present the world as material for the objective judgment of the perceiver, which becomes possible when one's perception voluntarily and ideationally takes distance from the world. Instead, it symbolizes the fact that the perception of the body and the world are in the relationship of acquaintance (*l'accointance*) or copulation (*l'accouplement*) in the state of predivision of the subject and object, which Merleau-Ponty calls the "prepredicative" understanding of the world. Merleau-Ponty calls the state of "acquaintance" or "copulation" "faith" because that is the state the body believes to be most natural; this is the state before the objectification of the world takes place. Merleau-Ponty frequently calls the copulation of acquaintance the flesh. The primary reality of perception of sensation erases the dualistic division between consciousness and things, or between one's consciousness and others'. One's activity in terms of seeing things is a voluntary action of one's body toward its outside world, but such a voluntary action cannot be separated from passivity in that the action takes place because of the existence of the *Gestalt* (or form) of others, which makes one's action of seeing that object possible. In this sense, one's perception is the locus of the chiasm of passivity and activity of one's action, which Merleau-Ponty calls the flesh. Merleau-Ponty writes: "The flesh = the fact that my body is passive-active (visible-seeing), mass in itself *and* gesture"(Vi 324/ VI 271, italics original). He further states: "The essential notion for such a philosophy is that of the flesh, which is not the objective body, nor the body thought by the soul as its own (Descartes), which is the sensible in the twofold sense of what one senses and what senses" (Vi 313/ VI 259).

It is not difficult to understand the above-cited passages. The flesh is the dimension before the divide between passivity and activity takes place; it is a sign that some material quantity expresses itself through the movements of one's body. For Merleau-Ponty, the flesh cannot be an objective entity and thus cannot be the possession of the soul as projected by the soul. The flesh is sensed by the body, but, at the same time, the body is itself sensible as well; hence, there is the dual sensibility in the flesh, which is the world of textuality in which the one who senses and that which is being sensed mutually intertwine.

According to Merleau-Ponty, such intertwining texture occurs because humans have upright bodily structures: "Thus the body *stands* before the world and the world upright before it, and between them there is a relation that is one of embrace. And between these two vertical beings, there is not a frontier, but a contact surface" (Vi 324/ VI 271). That humans have upright body structures indicates that they transcend their bodies when confronting the world. Crawling beings or flying birds would not experience such transcendence. In this sense, the beings crawling on the ground and birds flying in the air cannot sense the existential reality created by the flesh through the body's relationship to the world.

The flesh in Merleau-Ponty's philosophy is also the realm of Being in which the perception (or sensation) which is visible and meaning which is invisible exist together. One can say that the Being (*l'Être*), with a capital "B," according to Merleau-Ponty, indicates manifestation through the sense in the existential world of the invisible, whereas the being (*l'être*), with a small "b," or beings (*les êtres*), refers to the various forms of existence. Beings also seem similar to Heidegger's concept of beings (*das Seiende*). However, unlike Heidegger, Merleau-Ponty does not assume a clear difference between the Being and a being. Since Merleau-

Ponty's philosophy is centered on the existence of the body, existence as the Being
is none other than the sensational appearance of the Being.

The flesh indicates the promiscuity (*la promiscuité*) of the body as the corporeality of the mind with the outside world. This means that in order for the flesh to
take form, the promiscuous activities of the body with the world are prerequisites.
Merleau-Ponty describes such activities as encounters between the body and the
world in their upright positions. Since the corporeality of the body as the subject
is facing the world, each of which is in a vertical position, both hostility and the
sense of bonds always exist in the flesh. The flesh is like a communication or communion of the senses with the outside world, which Merleau-Ponty calls "transcendence." This concept of transcendence is comparable to *Dasein*'s care (*Sorge*),
as Heidegger discusses in his *Being and Time*. The existence of upright position
indicates that the body is projecting something in its relationship with the world.

The transcendence is also comparable to the concept of subjective aspect,
which is the act of the mind in terms of revealing its concern for the world. In this
case, the objective world is none other than a painting drawn by a subject. The
objective world does not remain as completely passive reality in relation to the
subject but reacts to the body which the subject projects to the world. The world
suggests something to the body, attracts its attention, and enthralls it. This also
suggests that the world, as much as the body, is standing upright and talking to
the perceptions of the body. To make a reference again to Yogācāra concepts, it is
said "The seed is giving a birth to the current action" (K. *chongja saeng hyŏnhaeng*
種子生現行) and "the current action is shaping the seed" (K. *hyŏnghaeng hun
chongja* 現行熏種子). The mutual influence and bridge-making of the transcendence and projection of the body to the world, and the world's introjection to the
body, are what Merleau-Ponty refers to as the flesh. Hence, the transcendence,
which constructs the flesh, is "the identity within difference[s]" (*l'identité en différence*), as Merleau-Ponty writes in *The Visible and the Invisible* (Vi 279/ VI 225).
Even though Merleau-Ponty uses the expression "identity" as to the difference
between the world and the body to refer to the flesh, "identity" does not seem
to be a well-selected term. Instead of "identity," which is very charged with the
meaning of traditional logic, expressions such as "promiscuity" or "encroachment" (*l'empiètement*) as he used them in *The Visible and the Invisible* seem to be
more fitting to the concept of the flesh as a vertical Being (*l'Être vertical*). That is
because the concept of encroachment fits well with the concept of ambiguity. It
also can be connected with "the idea of chiasm and *Ineinander*" (Vi 322/ VI 268),
the latter borrowed from Heidegger.

Merleau-Ponty also calls the vertical Being "the wild Being" (*l'Être sauvage*)
(Vi 306/ VI 253). "The wild Being" must refer to the natural mode of existence
before it is damaged by artificial and objective presentation and discriminatory
thinking. The mode of existence of the flesh as the vertical Being is also described
as "overdetermination" (*la surdétermination*) or circularity (*la circularité*) (Vi 323/
VI 270). Overdetermination indicates that the flesh is created through dependent

co-arising of the body and the world, which is the phenomenon of reversibility in the body and the world that mutually reflect each other. As to overdetermination and circularity, which also involve the world of *différance* or the in-between, Merleau-Ponty further states: "The flesh is *a mirror phenomenon* and the mirror is an extension of my relation with my body" (Vi 309/ VI 255; italics original). The dependent co-arising of the flesh is the reality which explains the "wild Being" as the original mode of existence of the world and of humans. Hence, the world of arising and ceasing of Buddhism in the context of the dependent co-arising offers the prototype of how humans and the world live together.

Since the flesh is the thickness of sensation of the coexistence and coitus of the body and the world, no activities of consciousness or subjectivity can be understood as independent voluntary actions separated from tradition and the habitual energy of the world. For Merleau-Ponty, the Kantian idea in which the subject is understood as the voluntary activity and the world as passivity cannot represent the original nature of the world. By the same token, Cartesian dualism cannot explain the natural state of the world. Such a dualistic manifestation is possible only when one artificially erases the meaning that is represented with the reality of humans as vertical beings. As mentioned, there is a reversible circularity between the body and the world in that the former reflects the latter, and vice versa. This mirror phenomenon might give the impression that the law of dependent co-arising is applied only to the spatial dimension. However, the dependent co-arising of the flesh also functions in the temporal dimension. The most visible aspect in which the temporal dimension of the dependent co-arising of the flesh reveals its existential being is the duet of freedom and destiny.

We often say that character is destiny. There is some truth in this. One's character is the style of one's actions and way of speaking and thinking that have been formed in oneself through accumulation in the continuation of time. This is called karma in Buddhism. Karma might be understood as destiny. However, according to Merleau-Ponty, karma as destiny exerts its value simultaneously with choice of freedom.

Let us further examine this thought. Suppose someone likes music very much. Since it is not through external forces that this person likes music, we can consider that her liking of music is based on choice. However, in this choice, there is no indifference that lets her dislike music. In other words, that choice the person made is already related to the person's personal tendency of liking or disliking. Personality is the result of accumulated karma. The personality of liking music was not known to the person until she made the choice of liking music. If we understand this personality of karma as a manifestation of some fixed *thing*, we would think that the person's action is completely dominated by external conditions, which leads one to fall into the trap of absolute determinism. On the other hand, if one does not consider karmic tendency, and understands that the person's moment-to-moment decision making is exclusively based on her choice, we are led to the opposite trap, which is a theory of absolute freedom.

Merleau-Ponty negates both extremes of absolute choice and strict determinism and contends that, in the realm of the flesh, the two are ambiguously intermingled. Each and every moment, we make efforts to change our given situation
by making free choices. Such efforts for changes are already limited by "previous
acquisition[s]" (*un acquis prealable*) (Pp 501/ PhP 439). Since freedom is not
enslaved by karma, it attempts to open a new dimension by correcting karmic
results, but the act of freedom does not occur in separation from the habitual energy of karma that exists in the body. The moment a choice is made to exercise the
act of freedom, the destiny of karmic results also appears. The flesh is the in-between dimension of the *différence* in which karmic energy and one's freedom are
intermingled ambiguously; it is the inscription of destiny and, at the same time, a
distancing from it. If we consider the destiny not as the karmic result of individual
activities but as karmic activities that are socially and historically related, then
the existential reality of one's flesh cannot be separated from social and historical
implications. Merleau-Ponty writes that "all explanations of my conduct in terms
of my past, my temperament and my environment are therefore true, provided
that they be regarded not as separable contributions, but as moments of my total
being, the significance of which I am entitled to make explicit in various ways,
without its ever being possible to say whether I confer their meaning upon them
or receive it from them" (Pp 519/ PhP 455).

In this sense, the existential mode of the flesh is comparable to *différance*: the
flesh which the flesh has received from the world in its preconscious state and that
with which it is to return toward the world in its conscious state are intertwined.
Merleau-Ponty explains this as follows: "We choose our world and the world
chooses us" (Pp 518/ PhP 454). He further states:

> To be born is both to be born of the world and to be born into the world. The world
> is already constituted, but also never completely constituted; in the first case we are
> acted upon, in the second we are open to an infinite number of possibilities. But this
> analysis is still abstract, for we exist in both ways *at once*. (Pp 517/ PhP 543; italics
> original)

Not in the mathematical sense, but in the rhetorical sense, half of our existence in existential reality has already been constituted, and the other half is
still open for possibilities. The body is not completely determined, nor is it absolutely free; as Merleau-Ponty writes: "There is, therefore, never determinism
and never absolute choice, I am never a thing and never bare consciousness"
(Pp 517/ PhP 453).

We can try to imagine the "bare consciousness" (*la conscience nue*) as the consciousness at degree zero at which the body is completely free of any influence
of karmic habitual energy. Even from the Buddhist perspective, consciousness in
such a complete zero state is not possible. Perhaps Buddhism takes the position
that such a consciousness is possible only to the Buddha or bodhisattvas who have

completely cleaned up karmic results from previous lives. However, to sentient beings in the secular world, absolutely pure consciousness is not possible. In this sense, Merleau-Ponty's philosophy meets Buddhist thought. The differences also need to be addressed. Buddhism contends that moving toward the ultimate truth of suchness (K. *chinyŏje* 眞如諦) and original enlightenment (K. *pon'gak* 本覺) is possible through practice and meditation. The ultimate truth of suchness and original enlightenment is at a distance from what Merleau-Ponty considers high-altitude thinking. The original enlightenment of true suchness is a transcendental liberation and freedom in which the body is forgotten. As far as humans cannot leave the condition called the body, humans cannot help being constrained by the drama of existential reality, as Merleau-Ponty contends. As far as humans live in the constraint of sensations and perceptions of the body, the field of the flesh is the only situation in which the truth of the world is understood in terms of dependent co-arising. Merleau-Ponty's philosophy leads us from the illusions of a discriminatory representational mode of thinking and substantialist views to the realm in which the world is viewed from the perspective of dependently co-arising reality. In this sense, Merleau-Ponty's philosophy is no doubt comparable to the law of dependent co-arising of the conventional truth.

However, the law of dependent co-arising is not the only truth of the world to which one is awakened. The law of emptiness at the ultimate level of truth in Buddhism is the other side of the double affirmation of the law of dependent co-arising. It expresses the idea of no-self indicated in dependent co-arising in terms of double negation. The meaning of the ultimate truth emerges along with the need for a higher stage of awakening in the midst of awakening to the conventional truth of the dependent co-arising. This need for the higher truth is comparable to Marcel's "ontological *exigence*" (or ontological need) that demands moving from the realm of existential reality to that of ontological reality. According to Marcel, the existential awareness that "I am my body" leads one to the next stage of awareness that "I am not just my body." The ultimate truth of suchness envisions the stage of liberation in which individuals become oblivious of their body. However, Merleau-Ponty would not want to have room for ontology of no-self that is based on the awakening to "true emptiness and marvelous existence." Without the existential reality in the conventional truth, the need for the ontological reality in the ultimate truth might not arise. That is because the ultimate level of truth emerges in response to the need for absolute freedom in the midst of conventional truth. In this sense, the structure of the ultimate truth and conventional truth cannot be different. Both liberate us from delusional attachment and representational discrimination. However, the truth of dependent co-arising at the conventional level of truth and the truth of the emptiness of all beings in the ontological reality of conventional truth are different: the former awakens one to the first level of freedom, whereas the latter leads one to the absolute freedom of a higher stage. To return this higher stage to the law of dependent co-arising so that one can understand the reality of the world anew is the Huayan Buddhist doctrine of "nature-origination."

Even though I said "to understand the reality of the world anew," this is only an expression for the sake of convenience. The world is always already in the state of nature-origination. Because of "ignorance," humans fail to realize it in that way. A Heideggerian expression for the reality of the world as nature-origination could be *Ge-wesen-heit*, that which has always already been, in the present perfect tense. Heidegger's *Ge-wesen-heit* has its philological origin in essence (*wesen*), and this essence is similar to what Huayan Buddhism calls "dharma nature." Some might think that the concept of dharma nature contradicts Nāgārjuna's doctrine of emptiness that he proposes in criticism of Abhidharma theory. Like Nāgārjuna, in the Zen Buddhist tradition, the sixth patriarch Huineng declares in his *Platform Sūtra* that the self-nature is the Buddha nature. The nonsubstantialist theory of emptiness that claims a no-self nature of things and the ontological theory of the dharma nature, however, do not contradict each other, because the doctrine of "true emptiness and marvelous existence" explains the relationship between the two. We will not get into a discussion of this theory, since it deviates from our topic. Suffice to say that both dependent co-arising and nature-origination explain the fundamental reality of the world; the former does it from the perspective of existential reality, whereas the latter from that of ontological reality, which produces a difference in nuance. One can also say that the existential conventional truth is related to the initial awakening (K. *si'gak* 始覺), and the ontological ultimate truth, original awakening.

In this sense the conventional truth of the existential realm and the initial awakening explains the truth of form, whereas the ultimate truth of the ontological realm and original awakening explains the truth of emptiness. The truths of form and of emptiness share a similar structure with regard to double affirmation and double negation, respectively; the differences lie only in the level of these truths. Merleau-Ponty's philosophy of the flesh is a phenomenology from the perspective of form. Since his phenomenology of visible form is pregnant with manifestations and implications of the invisible emptiness, one can fairly identify his philosophy as existential ontology. From the perspective of existential ontology, the difference between the Heideggerian Being and beings does not offer significant meaning. And Merleau-Ponty does not understand the existential and visible beings as an object of representational thinking as Heidegger does. Instead, Merleau-Ponty understands beings as visualization or corporeality of the Being. Merleau-Ponty states, "Any entity can be *accentuated* as an emblem of Being (= character)" (Vi 323/ VI 270; italics original). Hence, the Being with a capital "B" never leaves beings with a small "b," which is sensual and existential. The following statement supports our view: "Say that the things are structures, frameworks, the stars of our life: not before us, laid out as perspective spectacles, but gravitating about us. Such things do not presuppose man, who is made of their flesh. But yet their eminent being can be understood only by him who enters into perception, and with it keeps in distant-contact with them" (Vi 273/ VI 220).

This passage contains significant meaning. Since among the phenomena in the world of the flesh is constructed a certain thickness of the flesh, things as phenomena in the world are not objects that can be investigated through mathematical distances, but structures of the flesh or even its framework. Merleau-Ponty even calls them "the stars of our life." Just as the stars in the night sky send us twinkling signals, things in our life-world are talking to us, instead of being simply located there as neutral entities. The philosophy of the flesh shares its thought with the idea of union between things and self, which Asian philosophy has emphasized since ancient times. Things being one with our body, they are not different from the whispering of stars that exist together with us. The whispering of stars is audible only when one understands the relationship as mutual: one looks up the stars in the sky and the stars speak to him in return. Humans are not the creator of those things, but unless one senses their existence through perception—unless one understands the intertwining of contact with and distancing from one's body—they will not come to us with any significance. We humans are not the ruler of the world, but without humans, signification will lose its meaning.

I just mentioned that because of the function of perception, signification of the world is possible. Perception in this case is comparable to the Buddhist concept of consciousness or *vijñāna*. Without consciousness, to talk about even the facts of the world is not possible. The sixth consciousness in Buddhist Yogācāra School refers to the totality of consciousness. Merleau-Ponty's body as the corporeality of consciousness is similar to the sixth consciousness. The body as the sixth consciousness is not a separate and isolated atom. It is a history of one's karma that has had a relationship with the world since the beginningless beginning. Karma is one's action in the past, but since it still has its function in the present, it has the form of the present perfect tense. This relationship of the karma is what Merleau-Ponty declares to be sexuality:

> Sexuality has, so to speak, an interior (that it is lined throughout with a person-to-person relationship), and that the sexual is our way (since we are flesh, our carnal way) of living our relationships with others. Since sexuality is relationship to other persons, and not just to another body, it is going to weave the circular system of projections and introjections between other persons and myself, illuminating the unlimited series of reflecting reflections and reflected reflections which are the reasons why I am the other person and he is myself.[6]

The passage indicates that as far as one has sexual desire, to free oneself from the constraint of karma is not possible. The karma of the body is that of human relationship represented by sexual desire.

Sexual desire cannot be said to be everything of human relationship, but Merleau-Ponty suggests that human relationship is everything for humans, because karma is nothing other than the history of human relationships that one has created consciously or unconsciously. It is significant to note that Merleau-Ponty cites a passage from Antoine de Saint-Exupéry's *Flight to Arras* (*Pilote de guerre*) at the end of *Phenomenology of Perception*: "Man is but a network of relationships, and these alone matter to him" (Pp 520 / PhP 456). In other words, one's karma reflects the history of dependent co-arising. In *Signs*, Merleau-Ponty defined this human relationship as sexual; in his posthumous work *The Visible and the Invisible*, he replaces a "person"—who is a coproducer of the network in the dependent co-arising—with "complementary roles":

> The I-other relation to be conceived (like the intersexual relation, with its indefinite substitutions . . .) as complementary roles one of which cannot be occupied without the other being also: masculinity implies femininity, etc. Fundamental polymorphism by reason of which I do not have to constitute the other *in face of* the Ego: he is already there, and the Ego is conquered from him. Describe the pre-egology, the "syncretism," indivision or transitivism. What is it that *there is* at this level? There is the vertical or carnal universe and its polymorphic matrix. Absurdity of the *tabula rasa* on which *cognitions* would be arranged: not that there be cognitions before cognitions, but because there is the *field*. The I-other problem—A *Western* problem. (Vi 274/ VI 220–21; italics original)

For Merleau-Ponty, the relationship between self and other is polymorphism in that self is not an entity that exists separate from other but happens simultaneously with other. By the same token, the difference between self and other is not that between two different entities but that of their role. The self does not have an independent and self-sustaining unique identity but is constructed through different roles that result from the network of relationships with others. The concept of karma that is dependent co-arising can be understood through the concept belonging to the realm of the "pre-egology," and can be understood through the "syncretism" or "indivision" of identity and difference, or "transitivism" of exchanging identities of self and other. For Merleau-Ponty, one's body at no occasion exists in the state of the *tabula rasa*, and this idea confirms his position that the pure consciousness of degree zero does not exist in the world. The notion of flesh, which is so important in his philosophical project, suggests that living in the life-world is, phenomenologically speaking, a sharing of the existential field with others, and this is the indivisible state of dependent co-arising.

Identity plays its role as identity because of differences that exist in contrast to identity, and vice versa. Since mutual relatedness of roles constitutes a field, for Merleau-Ponty, intersubjectivity is not a result of relationship between the two poles that have already had their fixed consciousness; instead, the thickness of the flesh (*l'épaisseur de chair*) between identity and difference has already been established. In this sense, Merleau-Pontean intersubjectivity needs to be understood in relation to his notion of the flesh, instead of consciousness. Intersubjectivity in its concrete and existential implication is interchangeable with the idea of intercorporeality (*l'intercorporéité*). Since human relationship is the field of the flesh, sexuality is the basic structure in which the flesh is understood in the context of dependent co-arising. Sexuality in this sense cannot be limited to mere biological instinct. The flesh as an existential reality is to be understood by its role, but a role by nature cannot serve its function when there is only one person. A role has a meaning only when it exists with others playing different roles, hence the mode of existence of a role is intersubjectivity par excellence. If we understand others from the perspective of intersubjectivity, we can rather easily understand the meaning of the following passage by Merleau-Ponty:

> The other is no longer so much a freedom seen *from without* as destiny and fatality, a rival subject for a subject, but he is caught up in a circuit that connects him to the world, as we ourselves are, and consequently also in a circuit that connects him to us. . . . And this world is *common* to us, is intermundane space. . . . And there is transitivism by way of generality. . . . And even freedom has its generality, is understood as generality: activity is no longer the *contrary* of passivity.
>
> Whence carnal relations, from below, no less than from above and the fine point Entwining. (Vi 322–23/ VI 269; italics original)

When karma is examined from the outside, it seems to take a form of destiny. By the same token, when others are understood from the outside, they appear as subjects with their own individual freedom, different from me and competing with me. However, I and others are not two separate subjects, but intersubjective corporeality that is mutually connected through dependent co-arising. Since the flesh that connects "me" and others is commonly a shared field, the idea that "I" have freedom unique to "my" own that cannot be understood by others is an illusion. As the flesh is a shared aspect of our life, so is freedom. Freedom is not the antonym of destiny, nor is activity the antonym of passivity. They coexist in the relation of textual intertwining. Merleau-Ponty's expressions such as circularity, chiasm, or overdetermination, explain this. When two people are embracing each other, who can distinguish who is playing the active role of embracing and who is being passively embraced? Such a distinction itself loses meaning.

Merleau-Ponty's philosophy never leaves the existential and sensational phenomena. To leave them is refused by Merleau-Ponty as distance taking. However, one can distinguish early and later phases in his short life. His philosophy in the early phase centered on his work *Phenomenology of Perception* and is within the boundary of existential phenomenology, whereas in his later phase, as revealed in his *Visible and the Invisible*, Merleau-Ponty introduced an ontological mode of thinking. His ontology does accept the Being with the capital "B," but his Being in no circumstances takes the form of a transsensual being that leaves concrete and perceptual reality. In other words, he does not refuse the perceptual world in order to accept the philosophical thesis that there is the Being. To abandon phenomenon in order to maintain the Being, for Merleau-Ponty, is like taking a mummy for a living being. Ontology in his philosophy, hence, is allowed only as far as sensational and existential reality is related to it.

Let us take a more in-depth look at the nature of Merleau-Ponty's existential ontology. The bottom line of his existential ontology is that thinking which does not embody the flesh of our existence is considered to have no significance. No signification is possible if it is not already autochthonous to each individual's existentiality. This might sound like a contradiction of our definition of freedom as being communal. The communal in this sense, however, is not an abstract concept, but indicates its common sharedness among the bodies registered in the field of the flesh. If we are not careful, there might arise some contradiction between the notions of the communal and the autochthonous: "There is an autochthonous significance of the world which is constituted in the dealings which our incarnate existence has with it, and which provides the ground of every deliberate *Sinngebung*" (Pp 503/ PhP 441). There already exists, as we read in this passage, a certain shared syncretism between our existence and the outside world. We received the umbilical cord from the world into which we were born, and at the same time we maintain a centrifugal distance from it. In this relationship of neither one nor two emerges what Merleau-Ponty calls "an autochthonous significance" between the world and us. The world or the Being that is not in such a relationship with our existence is no longer the world or Being. In this sense, in order for the Being to have meaning, it needs to be existentially autochthonous.

In other words, the Being comes to have meaning only through our existential sensation. As Merleau-Ponty states, "sensation is literally a form of communion" (Pp 246/ PhP 212). The "communion" originally indicates sacrament in Catholicism. The communion does not mean a romantic transcendence into one through the union of two existences. Merleau-Ponty considers such a romantic human relationship to be naïve illusion. Sexual desire and expression of love between man and woman, for Merleau-Ponty, is not a romantic beatified lyrical verse. Nor does it indicate dialectical synthesis of the two. Merleau-Ponty interprets communion as a communication between the one who senses and that which is being sensed, which he further compares to the Catholic sacrament: "[T]he sacrament not only symbolizes, in sensible species, an operation of Grace, but is also the real presence of God, which it causes to occupy a fragment of space and communicates to those who eat of the consecrated bread, provided that they are inwardly prepared" (Pp 245/ PhP 212). Like the sacrament in which the invisible God is present in the sensible, the Being comes to exist in the reality of the flesh.

Appearance of the Being in this case is not the result of one's logical inference but a natural symbol that appears in one's perceptual vision. Merleau-Ponty does not deny logic per se, but he considers artificial any logic that is not based on perceptual faith. Hence, on the grounds of perceptual faith, he discusses the invisible reality of the logical, metaphysical, and intellectual world. The invisible world of signification has meaning in the limits of the existential horizon of perception. From the Buddhist perspective, the invisible principle (K. *li* 理) does not exist separate from visible phenomena (K. *sa* 事). The coexistence of the principle and phenomena in its nonduality creates the existential realm of the flesh. Merleau-Ponty also calls this the hinge in which the visible and invisible encounter. In the flesh coexist the metaphysical Being and physical material in their differences.

Since the flesh and the autochthonous world cannot be clearly distinguished from each other, in order for principle and phenomena, spirit and body, sensation and mind to coexist, they together become communion as sacrament in which metaphysical principle, soul, or spirit comes down to be present in each small fragment of material. Each goes through its own experience in the flesh to which it belongs. This is the existential experience.

We have mentioned that such existential experience and perception cannot be something belonging to "me." There obviously exists a realm that others do not understand. Hence, solitude is an inevitable part of the world of the flesh. Solitude, however, does not justify solipsism. Solitude is an inevitable instance that occurs when what is experienced as total to "me" is experienced as partial to others. What each individual senses cannot be shared with others in its entirety (*le tout*), but only as one instance of entirety (*un tout*), and solitude is an inevitable companion in the communication of the flesh. Since solitude itself exists in the sensation of the flesh that one shares with others, solipsism cannot be a factual phenomenon in the world. It is a countereffect of sharedness of one's life in the state of difference. The Being that presents itself in the autochthonous world—the interworld of hinge between the visible and the invisible—cannot be the perfect whole that humans have speculated. The world of concrete reality that exists in the historical, political, and existential context cannot be "a certain totality." The nature of existential being is always incomplete, always in a state of delaying, and pregnant with possibilities of chiasmic relations with the autochthonous world of others. In sum, it is always open.

As a word contains signification, the essence of an existential being cannot exist beyond visible phenomena. Merleau-Ponty declares:

> No longer are there essences above us, like positive objects, offered to a spiritual eye; but there is an essence beneath us, a common nervure of the signifying and the signified, adherence in and reversibility of one another—as the visible things are the secret folds of our flesh, and yet our body is one of the visible things. (Vi 158/ VI 118)

Because of this, we say that Merleau-Ponty's philosophy shares some aspects with Buddhism, but at the same time differentiates itself from it. Merleau-Ponty emphasizes that the essence of the invisible emptiness can never be separated from the visible forms, but the form cannot transcend its form-ness to be empty. In this sense, he does not leave the realm of phenomenology. For him, the path to the transphenomenological, in the sense that Marcel suggests it, does not seem possible.

This also has to do with the different understanding of nothingness in Heidegger and Merleau-Ponty. The difference lies in that Heidegger's thought proposes ontological salvation, whereas, for Merleau-Ponty, the role of his philosophy is to present an honest understanding of the facts of the world based on existential ontology. For Heidegger, nothingness is the clearing (*Lichtung*) in which the Being appears, but he also does not deny the possibility of the Being concealing itself, hiding itself in nothingness, covering itself with the thinness of a veil. And this concealing and appearing are nonsimultaneously a simultaneous happening. Nothingness and emptiness, for Heidegger, remain behind the Being because he considers that ontological thinking without nothingness has degraded itself to "ontical" thinking, in which the notion of the Being becomes equivalent to ownership, as humans own the Being. Heidegger understands nothingness and emptiness as the groundless ground (*Ab-grund*) that lets the Being be as the Being instead of as beings. Nothingness in this sense cannot be nihilism; it is the ontological groundless ground. This understanding of nothingness is reminiscent of the ultimate truth of emptiness. In Merleau-Ponty, nothingness is understood as the invisible. The invisible nothingness comes down to be present amid the visible phenomena of the flesh. The "presence of absence" in which the invisible nothingness becomes visible is emphasized, but the "absence of presence" in which the presence of the Being returns to nothingness and thus transcends itself is not mentioned in Merleau-Ponty. This can be said to be the basic difference between the two philosophers.

CHIASMIC TEXTUALITY OF THE VISIBLE
AND THE INVISIBLE AND THE *DIFFÉRANCE*

I have mentioned Marcel's "transphenomenological ontology." It suggests the idea that "I am not just my body." For Marcel, the statement that "I am my body" refers to the truth at the level of existential phenomenology. However, when one realizes that one's existence cannot be limited by the corporeality of body, the "ontological *exigence*" emerges to individuals. In Merleau-Ponty, the ontological *exigence*, which is also connected with the ultimate truth, cannot be found, and the path to Huayan Buddhist nature-origination and dharma nature is closed. This distinguishes his thought from Heidegger's philosophy. Huayan doctrines of nature-origination and the dharma nature transcend the dependent co-arising in the conventional truth and further confirm that the ultimate truth does not exist in separation from the facts in the conventional world. Nature-origination becomes possible when the dependent co-arising as understood by sentient beings is transformed into that understood by Buddhas and bodhisattvas. The essence of existence, in this sense, is immanent in the flesh, but not just immanent. It transcends the flesh but does not fly in the air of ideas beyond the flesh. The transcendence is none other than the ontological *exigence* to overcome the suffering of the flesh.

As Merleau-Ponty states, "[t]he dimension of philosophy cuts across that of the essence and the [fact]" (Vi 161/ VI 121). Here he indicates that the visible facts and the invisible essence are not the same. Since they are not the same, to "cut across" is possible. The essence of the Being and the facts of phenomena are neither one nor two, and in the relationship of *différance*, they are in an ambiguous relationship like relatedness in the dependent co-arising. Ambiguity in this sense is not limited to the relationship between the essence of the Being and facts of phenomena. Ambiguity for Merleau-Ponty is the most fundamental and original truth for human beings living their lives as sentient beings. Merleau-Ponty writes:

> This does not mean that there was a fusion or coinciding of me with it [the world]: on the contrary, this occurs because a sort of dehiscence opens my body in two, and because between my body looked at and my body looking, my body touched and my body touching, there is overlapping or encroachment, so that we must say that the things pass into us as well as we into the things. (Vi 165/ VI 123)

What Merleau-Ponty refuses to include in his philosophy is the complete monistic idea of fusion or coincidence as well as complete dualistic distancing through the concepts like pure essence. Instead of expressions reflecting either monistic or dualistic positions, Merleau-Ponty prefers to use ambiguous expressions that reveal the double nature of truth. Expressions such as "being in dehiscence," "proximity in distance," "auscultation or palpation in thickness," "a torsion of self upon self" (Vi 170/ VI 128), and "a coinciding from afar" (Vi 166/ VI 125) demonstrate the nature of his ontology. These expressions tell us that Merleau-Ponty's philosophy takes the form of "indirect ontology": "One cannot make a direct ontology. My 'indirect' method (being in the beings) is alone conformed with being—'negative philosophy' like 'negative theology'" (Vi 233/ VI 179). What he calls an "indirect ontology" is not too different from what we call "existential ontology," which we can further identify with ontology of the flesh. The mode of existence of the flesh being ambiguous, it is intertwined like the involutedness of the logic of neither the same nor difference. Merleau-Ponty's chiasmic intertwining is comparable to Heideggerian and Derridean concepts of difference. In this sense, Merleau-Ponty's philosophy already reveals the postmodern mode of thinking while still remaining anchored in existential phenomenology.

The truth in existential phenomenology is not the only realm where truth reveals its ambiguity; for Merleau-Ponty, the ontological truth is ambiguous as well. The former refers to the truth in factuality, whereas the latter indicates the truth in principle. In *The Visible and the Invisible*, Merleau-Ponty uses the expression "in principle" as often as he does "in fact." This can be read as an indication of his metaphysical interest through the principle of ontological truth together with the factuality of existential phenomenology. His ontology, however, is not in a realm totally different from his phenomenology, as has been pointed out. Hence, the Being in his philosophy as the invisible is understood in the textuality with the visible. Merleau-Ponty describes the nature of the Being as follows: "What there is is not a coinciding by principle or a presumptive coinciding and a factual non-coinciding, a bad or abortive truth, but a privative non-coinciding, a coinciding from afar, a divergence, and something like a 'good error'" (Vi 166/ VI 124–25). As existence is ambiguous, so is difference. As existence cannot be understood in separation from phenomenology of perception, nor can the Being be understood in separation from reflection and distancing in vision.

The reflection in this case does not indicate total reflection of consciousness as in the case of Cartesian *cogito*, which verifies the complete transparency of consciousness. The reflection in this manner is what Merleau-Ponty denies as a view from a distance. His notions of reflection and vision include distancing from the world, but this distancing is not staying away from the world. Rather, it is related to the awareness of the body that one received through the umbilical cord from the world in the preconsciousness and ante-predicative state. As we have already cited, "[t]o be born is both to be born of the world and to be born into the world." This indicates that existential perception has a dual structure; the body is not different from the world in that it has already embraced the world on its preconscious level on the one hand, and it is not the same in that it returns to the world on the other. Merleau-Ponty explains this as follows: "Everything comes to pass as though my power to reach the world and my power to entrench myself in phantasms only came one with the other. . . . The world is what I perceive, but as soon as we examine and express its absolute proximity, it also becomes, inexplicably, irremediable distance" (Vi 23/ VI 8). Reflection about the world made science possible, but as science objectifies the world, Merleau-Ponty contends, it erases the perceptual faith. In science, the world is reduced into the objective world, which is the only world worth knowing in science, while it treats perceptual faith as nothing but a subjective view of the world. Merleau-Ponty denies such an objectivist reduction of the world. For him, even science cannot be free from the domain of perception. Since the double meaning of existential perception is equivalent to finding meaning in the original world, the phenomenology of existential perception, for Merleau-Ponty, is already pregnant with ontology that recognizes the appearance of the invisible. The phenomena already embraces the Being. In other words, existence already embraces essence.

Merleau-Ponty concretizes the essence, or the Being, in *The Visible and the Invisible* as *Gestalt*. The *Gestalt* in this case obviously has to do with *Gestalt* psychology, but we should not interpret it completely in the context of *Gestalt* psychology. In his early work *Structure of Behavior*, Merleau-Ponty is critical of American behaviorism and is in favor of German *Gestalt* psychology. But he also warns about *Gestalt* psychology's conception of *Gestalt* as a physical and independent entity. The concept of *Gestalt*, for Merleau-Ponty, is comparable to that of the flesh, in which the invisible Being is immanent in the visible phenomena. In Buddhist terms, the world of form, or phenomena, contains emptiness or the principle. In Merleau-Ponty, the world of form, or phenomena, is more active than that of emptiness or principle, and the former weighs more than the latter in his philosophy. This offers a clue for our claim on the difference between Merleau-Ponty and Buddhism. Merleau-Ponty's philosophy aims only at the conventional level of truth but excludes the ultimate level of truth from the boundary of his philosophy.

We have yet to fully explore the ontological meaning of the invisible in Merleau-Ponty's philosophy, which we will take up now as the last topic in this chapter. This will enable us to show how the Being in the invisible is directly connected with emptiness, or nothingness, in his philosophy. To address the conclusion first, the concept of the invisible, which is nondual with the visible in Merleau-Ponty's philosophy, is closer to the Buddhist notion of "empty form" (K. *kongsang* 空相) rather than "empty nature" (K. *kongsŏng* 空性). Merleau-Ponty writes:

> [T]he force of being is supported by the frailty of the nothingness which is its accomplice, that the obscurity of the In Itself is for the clarity of the For Itself in general, if not for that of "my consciousness." The famous ontological problem, the "why is there something rather than nothing" disappears along with the alternative: There is not something *rather than nothing*, the nothing could not *take the place* of something or of being: nothingness inexists (in the negative sense) and being is, and the exact adjusting of the one upon the other no longer leaves room for a question. Everything is obscure when one has not thought out the negative; everything is clear when one has thought it as negative. For then what is called negation and what is called position appear as accomplices and even in a sort of equivalence. (Vi 92/ VI 64; italics original)

The above passage needs elaboration. In the translation above, both French *rien* (nothing) and *néant* (nothingness) were translated into "nothingness" (K. *mu* 無).[7] The difference in nuance is that the former is the negation of "something" (*quelque chose*), whereas the latter is the opposite of being. On a practical level, they could mean the same thing. Merleau-Ponty considers in the above passage that the force of being coexist with that of non-being (or nothingness). Hence, being and nothingness for Merleau-Ponty are not mutually exclusive as they are in Sartre. Unlike Sartre, for Merleau-Ponty the pitch darkness of being-in-itself is not in conflict with my consciousness as a being-for-itself; they are in a complementary relationship. The traditional ontological question posed by Leibniz, "Why are there beings and not rather Nothingness?" ("Warum ist überhaupt Seiendes und nicht vielmerh Nichts?"), is also a question that Heidegger takes with seriousness in his *Introduction to Metaphysics*. According to Merleau-Ponty, however, the question asking whether the being/Being exists instead of "nothingness" is representative of the mode of thinking that understands being and nothingness in a contradictory relationship. Instead of taking being and nothingness as binary opposites, Merleau-Ponty contends that, since nothingness by nature does not exist, to ask whether nothingness exists or not is not possible. One should say "something" does not exist, but one cannot say that nothingness does not exist. Since nothingness is not replaceable with somethingness, one can say that nothing exists, but one cannot say that nothingness does not exist. The clarity in understanding an affirmative statement that something exists is possible because of the assumption of a negative statement that something does not exist. Since the presence of something cannot be understood without its absence, being and nothingness, affirmation and negation are accomplices for each other.

Passages in *The Visible and the Invisible* further support this idea. Unlike Sartre, Merleau-Ponty does not contrast being and nothingness. Nothingness for Merleau-Ponty does not have the same value as being but is the invisible side of being. In his philosophy, only beings exist. Merleau-Ponty writes, "what is primary is not the diffuse 'consciousness' of the 'images' . . . it is Being" (Vi 304/ VI 251). His ontology does not deal with the Being in general. When he discusses Being, what worries him most is the logical statement that turns it into an abstract Being based on high-altitude thinking. In order to avoid the path to abstract ontology, Merleau-Ponty offers us the following:

> Our point of departure shall not be *being is, nothingness is not* nor even *there is only being*—which are formulas of a totalizing thought, a high-altitude thought—but: there is being, there is a world, there is *something*; in the strong sense in which the Greek speaks of τὸ λέγειν, there is cohesion, there is meaning. One does not arouse being from nothingness, *ex nihilo*; one starts with an ontological relief where one can never say that the ground be nothing. (Vi 121/ VI 88; italics original)

Being for Merleau-Ponty is not Being in general; there exist only concrete beings like the world, something, cohesion, meaning.

Since Being cannot be understood in separation from concave and convex relief structures, being and nothingness for Merleau-Ponty need to be understood as two concrete aspects of Being: the positive visible and the negative invisible. Hence, "the positive and the negative are two 'sides' of a Being" (Vi 278/ VI 225). The concave, for Merleau-Ponty, represents the visible, which reveals depth; it takes the form of, as Merleau-Ponty says, "Being doubled with nothingness" (Vi 290/ VI 237). Since nothingness as the negative cannot be separated from sensation of the visible, the visible offers to us the occasion to understand the invisible nothingness. As he states, "[n]othingness is nothing more (nor less) than the invisible" (Vi 311/ VI 258). Hence, he mentions that "the invisible . . . is what exists only as tactile or kinesthetically" (Vi 311/ VI 257). This suggests that the invisible nothingness is sensed inside the existential body; the invisible is corporeal. This could be why he prefers the expression "non-being" (*le non être*) to "nothingness" (Vi 249/VI 196). And he contends that nothingness as non-being is not a hole (*le trou*), as Sartre sees it, but should be understood as hollow (*le creux*). The invisible hollow appears in the background of the visible; the visible in this case is the incarnation of the invisible idea and signification. The idea related to the invisible adds depth to the visible. Merleau-Ponty considers that Marcel Proust has demonstrated this relationship better than anyone else. In Proust, Merleau-Ponty contends, the invisible as the idea acutely reveals itself as the lining and the depth of the visible.

Our discussions so far should suffice to support our earlier claim that seen from a Buddhist perspective, Merleau-Ponty's philosophy is more focused on the "empty forms," which is nondual with form in the conventional world, instead of the "empty nature," which is transcendental. Merleau-Ponty discusses nothingness but not emptiness, which Heidegger takes up in his philosophy. However, since Merleau-Ponty's nothingness is related to the invisible and appears in the concrete forms of being—like the world, something—we can interpret this as empty form that is the phenomenal appearance of the nature of emptiness. And the visible is equivalent to forms. Empty-form represents the visible phenomena as a representation of the invisible, and empty-nature refers to the essence of the invisible, which transcends the visible. From the perspective of Huayan nature-origination, the essence of the invisible dharma nature cannot be separated from the phenomena of the visible things, and the essence of the dharma nature is not different from nature-origination, which is the dependent co-arising of the essence of dharma nature. This vision of the Huayan world is the world seen from the position of the Buddha or bodhisattvas. Merleau-Ponty's philosophy, however, is not intended to present the world as seen by the Buddha and bodhisattvas; it presents the world from the existential reality of sentient beings. Hence, in his philosophy, the path of the Buddha or bodhisattvas that transcends the body cannot be found. We have already pointed out that this transcendence is different from what Merleau-Ponty calls high-altitude thinking.

There is another reason we contend that the invisible in Merleau-Ponty's philosophy is equivalent to the Buddhist empty-form. Merleau-Ponty writes:

> Meaning is *invisible*, but the invisible is not the contradictory of the visible: the visible itself has an invisible inner framework (*membrure*), and the in-visible is the secret counterpart of the visible, it appears only within it, it is the *Nichturpräsentierbar* which is presented to me as such within the world—one cannot see it there and every effort to *see it there* makes it disappear, but it is *in the line* of the visible, it is its virtual focus, it is inscribed within it (in filigree). (Vi 269/ VI 215; italics original)

It should not be too difficult to understand this passage. The invisible does not present itself by itself but does so indirectly through the visible phenomena of the sensible flesh on its existential level. This is why Merleau-Ponty calls his ontology "indirect ontology." All the artificial efforts disrupt the meaning of the invisible nature of emptiness. The visible form, in other words, is always pregnant with the invisible emptiness. The invisible, in principle, is "the *Nichturpräsentierbar*" but in reality is given through the flesh. The invisible, described as "the lining," is not visible, but through the shape and rhythm of the visible clothes informs of its existence. The negativity of the invisible nothingness is also described by Merleau-Ponty as absence in contrast to the presence of the form, but this absence "counts in the world" (Vi 281/ VI 228).

In conclusion, Merleau-Ponty's philosophy does not go beyond the horizon of the flesh from beginning to end. Since his concept of the flesh is the dimension of the existential reality in which the visible form and invisible emptiness are chiasmically intertwined, the invisible forms of emptiness also weave nondual textuality with the flesh. This absent presence of the empty-form is sometimes referred to by Merleau-Ponty as spirit, or soul, which is the other side of the flesh. Both spirit and soul are comparable to the lining of clothes:

The "other side" means that the body, inasmuch as it has this other side, is not describable in *objective* terms, in terms of the in itself—that this other side is really the
other side *of the body, overflows* into it (*Ueberschreiten*), encroaches upon it, is hidden
in it—and at the same time needs it, terminates in it, is *anchored* in it. There is a body
of the mind, and a mind of the body and a chiasm between them. (Vi 313/ VI 259;
italics original)

He also states: "[T]he bond between the soul and the body is not a parallel-
ism. . . . It is to be understood as the bond between the convex and the concave,
between the solid vault and the hollow it forms" (Vi 286/ VI 323).

Let us dwell on the above two passages for a moment. On the surface, Merleau-
Ponty seems to make an essentialist claim for the reality of the soul and the spirit
when he insists that the soul and the spirit are the other side of the body. Looking
at them in detail, we find that Merleau-Ponty describes the spirit and the soul as
negative hollow images instead of being positive existence per se. The image of
hollow in the concave is playing the role of lining the visible body in the image
of the convex to come into being. Since the flesh entails the trace of the absence
in the concave, the flesh becomes three-dimensional in its vertical meaning and
embraces the perfuming of the depth. The flesh without the depth of the concave
cannot but be shallow. The visible and the invisible, then, each play a role for the
other. As has been discussed, in Merleau-Ponty, the self and others exist dependently, like the complementary functions of male and female.

The visible form and the invisible emptiness, the positivity of being and negativity of nothingness, the concave of meaning and idea and the convex of sensible
Gestalt, the hollow of the spirit and the soul and the thickness of the body—the
chiasmic intertwining of these is the weight of the flesh which is comparable to
the relatedness of the law of dependent co-arising. The intertwining of differences
is at the center of his philosophy. Merleau-Ponty explains this as follows: "The axis
alone given—the end of the finger of the glove is nothingness—but a nothingness
one can turn over, and where then one see *things*. . . . The only 'place' where the
negative would really be is the fold, the application of the inside and the outside
to one another, the turning point" (Vi 317/ VI 263–64). This somewhat confusing passage suggests that for Merleau-Ponty, the axis of his philosophy lies in the
crossroads in which a glove or item of clothing turns inside out. Nothing can be
found at the end of fingers of a glove, but when the nothingness is turned inside
out, there exist fingers as something. The only place where one can find the real
existence of negativity like nothingness is not different from the place where one
finds the fingers by turning a glove inside out. This is the place of the fold in
which different existences like being and nothingness lean against each other; it is
also the application in which inside and outside exchange a different nature with
each other, or it is the suture in which grafting takes place. Because there exists a
boundary between different things like the fold as the "interworld," this and that
are mutually enclosed; the end of the glove where one finds nothing is the point

of departure for the fingers when the glove is turned inside out. The doubling and pairing nature of inside and outside, being and nothingness, enable us to identify this paired relationship as the law of dependent co-arising.

In sum, for Merleau-Ponty, the reality of the world takes the form of chiasm. Merleau-Ponty describes the dependent co-arising of chiasm as follows:

> Chiasm my body—the things, realized by the doubling up of my body into inside and outside—and the doubling up of the things (their inside and their outside). Start from this: there is not identity, nor non-identity, or non-coincidence, there is inside and outside turning about one another. (Vi 317/ VI 264)

The flesh is the textuality created through the intertwining of the invisible spirit and the visible body and things. Textuality here suggests the idea of difference, which is frequently mentioned in postmodernism. Merleau-Ponty's philosophy does not go beyond the realm of phenomenological existentialism, but his philosophy is already at the door that opens to the space beyond existential phenomenology. However, his philosophy never leaves phenomenology of body. As a result, the liberation of the ultimate level of truth is not part of it, even though he gets through the logic of dependent co-arising. By the same token, he fails to see the path to the Huayan idea of nature-origination, which is the same in its structure with dependent co-arising but is located on a different level. For Merleau-Ponty, philosophy is the most honest mode of thinking that tries to understand the facts of the world, including the original fact of suffering. In this sense, even though his philosophy lacks the sense of necessity of salvation, one cannot but express respect for his honesty and at the same time acknowledge what is lacking in his philosophy. Needless to say, salvation here is not the kind of outmoded salvation advocated by Marxists.

Translated by Jin Y. Park

2

Merleau-Ponty's Theory of the Body and the Doctrine of the Five Skandhas

Yasuo Yuasa with translator's introduction by Gereon Kopf

Yasuo Yuasa (1925–2005),[1] one of the most innovative Japanese philosophers of the past century, made a name for himself as a philosopher who tried to bridge the gap not only between various intellectual traditions—most notably the East Asian and European intellectual and religious traditions—but also between religion and science.[2] He was particularly interested in constructing a comparative philosophy of the body that took as its sources Buddhist and Daoist theories of self-cultivation, continental philosophy, *qi* (J. *ki* 氣) theory, analytical psychology, and physiology. While his work may be, at times, susceptible to the accusations of orientalism and methodological naiveté, Yuasa's is a compelling vision of a cross-cultural and interdisciplinary dialogue on the human body, which seemed, for the most part, ahead of its time. His writing not only reveals the erudite mind of its author, but, most of all, introduces a dual-layered conception of the body that is capable of serving a variety of disciplines such as scientific medicine, religious studies, traditional Chinese medicine, and psychology.

At the basis of Yuasa's philosophical system lies the concept of "self-cultivation," which grounds his metaphysics, epistemology, ethics, and philosophy of religion.[3] Yuasa defines "self-cultivation" simply as "the performance of a practice that facilitates a somatic experience involving the totality of body and mind";[4] in other words, the term "self-cultivation" designates religious practices that engender a psychophysical transformation. Yuasa cites examples as diverse as Buddhist and Daoist meditation, martial arts, shamanistic experiences, out-of-body experiences, and the so-called Zen arts ranging from *Nō* theatre to *waka* poetry as the primary examples of self-cultivation. However, when he sets out to discuss the philosophy of body and mind underlying these theories of self-cultivation, Yuasa usually draws on the writings of the founder of Shingon Buddhism, Kūkai (774–835), and the founder of Sōtō Zen Buddhism, Zen master Dōgen (1200–1253).

From them he inherits the worldview he claims to be characteristic of the theories of self-cultivation that constitutes the foundation of his philosophical system.

Before I commence to outline the metaphysics of self-cultivation Yuasa discovers in the writings of the above-mentioned Buddhist philosophers, I would like to reflect briefly on his methodology. To translate insights of Daoist and Buddhist theories of self-cultivation into contemporary discourse, Yuasa utilizes a heuristic schema that combines insights from both C. G. Jung and Maurice Merleau-Ponty. At first sight, Jung and Merleau-Ponty, the depth psychologist and the phenomenologist, seem to make odd bedfellows. However, they share the central paradigm Yuasa sees at work in all theories of self-cultivation: the dual-layered conception of the human mind and, admittedly to a more obvious degree in Merleau-Ponty, the deep conviction that mind and body cannot be separated. As is well known, Jung divides the human psyche into the fields of the conscious and the unconscious, while Merleau-Ponty distinguishes between the "actual body" (*le corps actuel*) and the "habit body" (*le corps habituel*). Yuasa then clearly, and probably not unfoundedly, identifies Merleau-Ponty's "actual body" as the conscious dimension and the "habit body" as the unconscious layer of our somatic existence. The former he sees embodied by what he calls the "bright *cogito*" (J. *akarui cogito* 明るいコギト), the latter, following Merleau-Ponty's terminology of the "silent *cogito*" (*cogito tacite*), as "dark *cogito*" (J. *kurai cogito* くらいコギト). Yuasa identifies as the pivotal insight of theories of self-cultivation this dual conception of what David Shaner calls the "bodymind,"[5] identifying a conscious dimension at the surface as well as an unconscious layer at the depth of human existence.

Yuasa finds the prototype of the dual-layered "bodymind" in the writings of the medieval Japanese Zen master Dōgen, specifically in a passage in the *Shōbōgenzō Genjōkōan* in which Dōgen explains the difference between practice and actualization. Here, Dōgen introduces, according to Yuasa, two fundamental, existential attitudes toward the world: a self-conscious one and one in which the self is attuned with the totality of the cosmos, internal and external. In Dōgen's words: "To practice the ten thousand dharmas while carrying the self is delusion, to approach the ten thousand dharmas while practicing the self is awakening. The Buddhas are awakened about delusion, sentient beings are deluded about awakening."[6] A few lines later he continues: "To study the Buddha-way is to study the self, to study the self is to forget the self, to forget the self is to be actualized by the ten thousands dharmas."[7] Yuasa interprets these two observations to indicate a dual-layered conception of the self. One layer is egocentric and involves an intentional act—in Dōgen's language, the act of "studying the self." The other layer, indicated by Dōgen's "forgetting the self," is devoid of a center, self or otherwise, and is not readily accessible from the standpoint of the *ego-cogito*. The words "self," "learning," "ten thousand dharmas," and "forgetting" provide clues to correlate the two attitudes Dōgen identifies as "delusion" and "awakening" with the everyday consciousness personified as *ego* on the one hand, and with an awareness that includes even what Jung calls the "collective unconscious" (*Kollektive Unbewusste*), on the other. Since Dōgen assumes the inseparability of what we call "body" and "mind," Yuasa interprets these two dimensions of human existence—self-consciousness and world-awareness—as two aspects of the "bodymind." While it is certain that Dōgen in all probability did not intend the psychological spheres Jung had in mind or the phenomenological analysis of Merleau-Ponty, I think Yuasa offers here a helpful if not important heuristic device. He suggests interpreting "delusion" as a self-centered attitude that generalizes and absolutizes the standpoint of the self-conscious individual self and obscures other aspects of human existence as well as the world, while "awakening" indicates an awareness of self and world that acknowledges that self-consciousness does not constitute the center of human existence and eschews the dichotomies constructed by the intentional activities of the *ego-cogito*. In other words, self-cultivation engenders an existential transformation of the self-conscious existence that bifurcates the world into self-world, mind-body, and conscious-unconscious to an attitude of attunement that can be paraphrased in the language of phenomenology as "body-in-the-world." This transformed modality is embodied by the self that manifests the "ten thousand dharmas" and the attitude Dōgen refers to as "casting off body and mind," which eschews dichotomies yet does not melt the world of phenomena into a mass of oneness.

Yuasa suggests that the metaphysical structure of the psychophysical depth layer of human existence Dōgen describes in his writings discloses a "correlative dualism of body and mind" (J. *shinjin sōkanteki nigenron* 心身相関的二元論).[8] Such a worldview poses, of course, a considerable if not insurmountable challenge to the "disjunctive dualism" (J. *bunriteki nigenron* 分離的二元論)[9] characteristic of the modern worldview. This conception of the "bodymind" in which mind and body are conceived to be neither separate nor identical reverberates the Buddhist notion of "body-mind oneness" and what the Daoist thinkers call the vital energy *qi*, which constitutes the basis of the psychophysical complex and flows between as well as integrates the two polarities of *hun* (魂), the yang dimension of the self, and *po* (魄), its yin dimension.[10] The insistence of modernity on privileging the epistemic subject resulted in the isolation of the self on three basic levels: The self-conscious self posits itself as separate from the world on the vertical axis, from the other, on the horizontal axis as well as from itself, to be exact, from its own unconscious, thus dichotomizing its own internality. This threefold dichotomization of the phenomenal world, and the subsequent isolation of the self, is alien to the worldviews of Dōgen and Kūkai. But rather than duplicating the pantheism of the myths developed in antiquity around the world,[11] theorists of self-cultivation like Dōgen and Kūkai propose such a "correlative dualism." Dōgen and Kūkai apply, not unlike other Buddhist as well as Daoist thinkers, this "correlative dualism" to the relationship between sentient beings and "all Buddhas" as well as self and others. Buddhist thinkers like Dōgen usually articulate this worldview by means of the doctrine of "no-self." The term "no-self" here does not indicate a negation of selfhood but rather a rejection of the conception that the self constitutes an

independent and unchanging essence. While what we call the self can be identified as an individual phenomenon, it is not separate or different from the cosmos.
Yuasa finds this correlative dualism expressed more sophisticatedly in Kūkai's
esoteric Buddhism. Kūkai suggests that in the esoteric ritual, most prominently
the "meditation on the character 'A'" (J. *ajikan* 阿字観), the practitioner manifests
her/his original oneness with the cosmic principle, the "cosmic sun Buddha," or
Mahāvairocana, without losing his/her individuality and dissolving in an undif-
ferentiated mass. Thus, Yuasa calls Kūkai's philosophy a "theory of the great self"
(J. *daigasetsu* 大我説)[12] rather than one of "no-self."

According to Kūkai, the human body constitutes the microcosmic embodiment
of the cosmos personified as *Mahāvairocana* itself; in the words of Shaner, "the
horizon experience is thus a microcosm of the macrocosmic Dharma-kāya."[13]
Thus conceived of, the individual body constitutes the location where the "six
elements" (J. *rokudai* 六大) and the "ten worlds" (J. *jikkai* 十界) reside. While
the former claim may be palatable even to skeptics insofar as all living beings
are made out of the same chemical elements, the second assertion seems to be
harder to swallow since it challenges our metaphysical presuppositions about the
world. However, Kūkai deliberately eradicates the delineation between individual
and cosmos, sentient beings and Buddhas. In his own words, "[t]he term 'body'
signifies my body, Buddha's body, and the bodies of all sentient beings . . . that
body is this body and this body constitutes that body. The body of Buddha is that
of the sentient beings and the bodies of the sentient beings comprises the body of
Buddha."[14] Philosophically, this means that the body is individual and universal
at the same time. Yuasa interprets these statements to suggest that "we constitute
the condition in which the absolute itself and the universe itself exist."[15] In this
experience of the "self-fulfilling samādhi" (J. *jijuyōzanmai* 自受用三昧), the human body is simultaneously individual and universal. Such an awareness, which
David Shaner refers to as the experience of the "horizon in toto,"[16] discloses to
the practitioner the totality of the cosmos in the "oneness of the dharma-kāya."[17]
The philosophical implications of this statement are far-reaching. Kūkai, and by
association Yuasa, renounce any possibility to clearly identify individuals and
demarcate them from other individuals or the world *in toto*. At the same time, he
does not reject the notion of the individual itself but only that of discrete essences.
In other words, the "self-fulfilling samādhi" reveals that individual bodies embody
the cosmos, do not possess determined boundaries, and are devoid of unique and
unchanging characteristics.

Another issue at the heart of theories of self-cultivation is the process of self-
cultivation itself. As Yuasa suggests in his analysis of Kūkai, self-cultivation does
not constitute just any transformation, but comprises the sublimation of *libido*.
Like most of Buddhism, Shingon Buddhism, which is Kūkai's form of esoteric
Buddhism, identifies as the cause of all evil, the "defilements" and most prominently among them the "three poisons" of desire, hatred, and ignorance. Through
the practice of self-cultivation, these passions are to be transformed into "wis-

dom." In esoteric Buddhism, the latter is embodied in the shape of *Acalanātha* (J. *Fudō myōō* 不動明王). In Japanese depictions, *Acalanātha* does not make a very inviting impression. He usually holds a sword and a rope in his hands, sports a rather grim expression, bares two long and pointed teeth, and is surrounded by a halo of fire. Yuasa remarks that "[s]een from the standpoint of psychology, [this depiction] symbolizes the struggle with the dark passions at the bottom of the human heart."[18] Ultimately, *Acalanātha* embodies the "mind of enlightenment" (*bodhicitta*; J. *bodaishin* 菩提心) insofar as he is victorious over his own passions and assists sentient beings in their struggles as well. What is important to Kūkai's esoteric Buddhism, however, is that this sublimation does not imply an escape from the body, but an awakening to the original nature of human existence. To Kūkai this is the *dharma-kāya* (J. *hōshin* 法身) within the somatic existence; Kūkai refers to this awakening as "becoming a Buddha in the present body" (J. *sokushinjōbutsu* 即身成仏). In the practice of Shingon Buddhism, the practitioner manifests the body, speech, and mind—also referred to as the "three mysteries" (J. *sanmitsu* 三蜜)—of *Mahāvairocana* by enacting the *mudrās*—meticulously prescribed hand positions, repeating the sacred *mantras* (sacred syllables), and visualizing the Buddhas and bodhisattvas that inhabit the various regions of the *Garbha-maṇḍala* (J. *Taizōkai mandara* 胎蔵界曼荼羅). To the Shingon practitioner, the most important among the Buddhas is *Mahāvairocana*, who resides in the center of this particular *maṇḍala* where he is surrounded by four Buddhas and bodhisattvas each. Yuasa explains that "the many Buddhas in the outer rim of the *maṇḍala* embody the form of us ordinary people, but the closer we get to the center, the more we reach *Mahāvairocana*."[19] The practice of esoteric Buddhism does not only transform desire into *prajñā* but, moreover, the body of the practitioner into the body, the *dharma-kāya* so to speak, of *Mahāvairocana*. Yuasa uses Jungian terminology to elucidate Shingon practices and suggests that by means of practices such as the *Ajikan* meditation the practitioner integrates the collective and individual unconscious elements into the "self-fulfilling samādhi."

Having explored the theories of Dōgen and Kūkai, we can now turn to Yuasa's theory of self-cultivation. To Yuasa, the term "self-cultivation" refers to any systematized practice that employs the repetition of simple physical exercises and has two primary goals: the discovery and integration of the unconscious and the transcendence of the "disjunctive dualism" characteristic of everyday consciousness. Yuasa observes: "From the perspective of depth psychology, this [continuous practice of meditation] sublimates the repeated activities, appeases the mind, and enters the world of the psyche or the soul."[20] For this reason, Yuasa treats theories of self-cultivation as an example of the *individuation* process discussed in the work of Jung,[21] during which an individual overcomes his/her alienation from the world, others, and itself and thus manifests his/her true individuality. In addition, phenomenologically speaking, the practice of self-cultivation engenders the habit that reveals body and mind in, as the translator of many of Yuasa's works into English, Shigenori Nagatomo, would say, "attunement."[22] This attunement, to Yuasa, constitutes a bidirectional modality of engagement[23] that involves the external as well as the internal worlds and describes a process from everyday consciousness to a self-awareness that includes the depth layers of human existence. The former is characterized by a binary structure that is reflected in theories of mind-body dualism; the latter Yuasa finds in the nondual worldview frequently found in Daoist and Buddhist meditation and martial arts manuals. Everyday consciousness is characterized by an egocentric, in the literal sense of the word, attitude by means of which the self defines itself as different and apart from the external world. In other words, on the level of self-consciousness, the self conceives of itself as the epistemic subject and the world as the object of its knowledge. Employing such an attitude, however, the self not only objectifies the world it encounters but also itself. In the act of self-consciousness—that is, the self's consciousness of itself—the self divides itself into the self that knows, the Cartesian *cogito*, and the self that is known. While the latter self is comprised of the body-qua-subject, the objectified self is usually reified as either the images the self has of itself or externalized as the body, the Cartesian *res extensa*. In the practice of self-cultivation, the mind of the practitioner is brought into an attunement with the objects of the external world and the internal world alike and thus overcomes the binary structure of everyday consciousness and the various dualisms it creates. Nagatomo describes this process as one from the modality of "tensionality" to that of "nontensionality."[24] During the process of self-cultivation, the tension in which subject and object oppose each other in self-consciousness gives way to a coexistence of both aspects in the "self-fulfilling samādhi." The process of self-cultivation results in a transformed awareness—Nagatomo refers to it, borrowing Buddhist terminology, as "samadhic awareness"[25]—in which the alienation characteristic of everyday consciousness is overcome and which discloses, to use Yuasa's terminology, a "correlative dualism of body and mind."

The most central element of these theories of self-cultivation, however, is the belief that the human body constitutes a "living body"[26] (*le corps vivant*), which defies the dualisms of mind and body, self and environment, subject and object. In *Shūkyō keiken to shintai* (Religious Experience and the Body*)*, Yuasa introduces a three-layered model of the body that provides more clues about his conception of the "living body." Particularly, he suggests that while a "third-person perspective" renders the "object body" (J. *kyakkanteki shintai* 客観的身体) of biology[27] and a "first-person perspective" the "subject body" (J. *shukanteki shintai* 主観的身体) of psychology,[28] a "second-person perspective" discloses the "oneness of body and mind" (J. *shinjingōitsu* 心身合一) indicative of the interpersonal encounter.[29] This three-layered model reveals a couple of interesting presuppositions underlying Yuasa's notion of the "living body": First, Yuasa seems to imply that any worldview that differentiates between mind and body or self and environment reflects, to some degree, the dichotomy between subject and object. In addition, the various conceptions of the body as "subjective body," "objective body," and "living body" are constituted by particular vantage points. Finally, the former two perspectives are indicative of everyday consciousness, while the latter one signals "samadhic awareness." This means that a "first-person" or a "third-person perspective" is limited and insufficient, whereas a "second-person perspective"—that is, a perspective transformed in the process of self-cultivation—provides access to the true condition of the body. In other words, while everyday consciousness dichotomizes the body and conceives of it either as a "subject body" or an "object body," the practice of self-cultivation discloses the "living body," which embraces and "overcomes"[30] the ambiguity of subjectivity and objectivity as well as self and cosmos. This notion of "living body" qua "body mind oneness" comprises the key to Yuasa's theory of the body.

In his *Ki, shugyō, shintai* (*Ki*-energy, Self-Cultivation, and Body), Yuasa develops this notion of the dual-layered body into a more sophisticated model, his fourfold body schema. Specifically, he identifies as the basic information systems of the human body the "external sensory-motor circuit" (J. *gaikaikankaku-undōkairo* 外界感覚-運動回路), the "holistic circuit of coenestesis" (J. *zen-shinnaibu–kankakukairo* 全身内部-感覚回路), the "emotion-instinct circuit" (J. *jōdō–honnōkairo* 情動-本能回路),[31] and the "unconscious quasi-body" (J. *muishikiteki junshintai* 無意識的準身体).[32] The "external sensory-motor circuit" corresponds to the peripheral nervous systems that organizes the body's interactions with the external world through perception and motion; the "circuit of coenestesis" to the central nervous system that organizes the cerebral cortex's interaction with internal organs and the limbs; the "emotion instinct circuit" to the autonomous nervous system that connects the internal organs to the brain stem. The "unconscious quasi-body" does not correspond to any element or region of the anatomical map but rather to the *qi*-energy that has been introduced by Chinese medical treatises and Daoist meditation and martial arts manuals. In the context of Yuasa's body-scheme, *qi* is best understood as the matrix that connects and grounds the preceding three circuits. The former two circuits correlate to Merleau-Ponty's "actual body" and the latter two to his "habit body."[33] What is of interest for the current discussion is neither the relationship between the various models Yuasa employs nor the scientific viability of Yuasa's body scheme, but its philosophical implications. To be exact, this model of the human body constitutes the concrete if not medical application of the philosophy of the body rendered by the Buddhist and Daoist theories of self-cultivation. It is in this model that Yuasa sees the contribution of physiology, *qigong* (J. *kikō* 氣功) theory, and philosophical reflections on practices of self-cultivation to our systematic understanding of the human body converge.

Philosophically speaking, this model advances the conception of the body characteristic of theories of self-cultivation; it eschews essentialism insofar as each circuit has to be understood as a bilateral intentionality and as "action-perception"[34] or "acting intuition"[35] (J. *kōiteki chokkan* 行為的直観) respectively rather than an object. It also challenges the dualisms of mind and body as well as of activity and passivity insofar as each circuit constitutes a somatic or embodied awareness and discloses the "correlative dualism of body and mind." This model furthermore subverts the notion that the body or the self has a center since the four different circuits are characterized by four varying conceptions of inside and outside; the four circuits outline a path of transformation which is characterized by increased awareness and a shifting sense of internality. The "external sensory-motor circuit" renders as internal what is inside the skin, the "circuit of coenestesis" what is inside the brain, and the "emotion instinct circuit" what is inside the brain stem. At the final stage of the transformation when the practitioner is aware of the "unconscious quasi-body," there exists neither a center nor a sense of inside and outside since the "unconscious quasi-body" pervades the whole body. It is called "unconscious" since most self-conscious subjects are not aware of this fundamental dimension of the somatic existence of human beings. Of course, the term "unconscious" does not imply a spatial model of the human psyche as is indicated by Sigmund Freud but simply indicates that the "unconscious quasi-body," which reveals itself in "samadhic awareness," escapes everyday consciousness. Dōgen describes this final state as the "realization of the ten thousand dharmas" and Kūkai as "becoming Buddha in the present body." Behind Yuasa's language, which borrows heavily from physiology and phenomenology alike, one can easily detect the central Mahāyāna Buddhist belief that the human body is without an essence or center and is yet connected to the universe. Or, as Yuasa points out, the essence of the human body is the "truth body" (*dharma-kāya* 法身), which does not constitute a substance in either the Aristotelian or in the Spinozan sense, but rather indicates that the human body reveals the ambiguity of subjectivity and objectivity, inside and outside, particular and world. While a dualistic metaphysics attempts to dissolve this tension, Yuasa's "correlative dualism" suggests that the process of integrating and transforming these polarities is necessary for a healthy existence.

It is on the background of this philosophical project that Yuasa wrote the current essay only months before he passed away on November 7, 2005. The paper constitutes his attempt to examine to what degree his model of the body was already present in the early Buddhist texts, particularly in the "five skandhas." While Yuasa does not indulge in an in-depth study of the "five skandhas" and at times seems to superimpose concepts alien to the Abhidharmic texts onto this theory, he does uncover exciting connections between the Abhidharma, Merleau-Ponty's phenomenology, and Daoist theories of *qigong*. All these philosophies share a skepticism toward essentialist models of body, insist that the body constitutes an "intentional arc" rather than an object, emphasize the bilateral nature of this form of intentionality, and, subsequently, suggest a metaphysics that substitutes a dualism of essences with a "correlative dualism." Such a philosophy not only eliminates the artificial boundaries between self and environment, inside and outside, and stratifies a philosophy that envisions the body as simultaneously subjective and objective, private and public, but moreover develops a philosophy of the body that involves insights from medical science and psychology. This and nothing less we owe to the lifework of Yasuo Yuasa.

MERLEAU-PONTY'S THEORY OF THE BODY
AND THE DOCTRINE OF THE FIVE SKANDHAS

Yasuo Yuasa

Whenever we look for ideas akin to Merleau-Ponty's theory of the body ("somatics") in the writings of Buddhist philosophers, the question of methodology arises. In this paper, I would like to use the doctrine of the five skandhas as developed in early Buddhism to facilitate such an exploration. The Japanese philosopher Watsuji Testurō (和辻哲郎 [1889–1960]), who explored early Buddhism, borrows the notion of intentionality from Husserl's phenomenology[36] in order to investigate the philosophical ramifications of the theory of the five skandhas. Such an examination of the five skandhas renders an understanding of human subjectivity as "being-in-the-world" (*in-der-Welt-sein*). At the same time, it strives to conceive of the relationship between human beings and the world as an intentional engagement of the subject with the environment.

In his *Sein und Zeit* (Being and Time), Heidegger describes human beings as "being-in-the-world" and conceives of their relationship to the environment in terms of temporality. He calls the existential modality of the subject with regards to the temporal dimensions of past, present, and future *Dasein* (literally, being-there). *Dasein* has the meaning of living in the here and now. In short, to say that one lives means to acknowledge that we exist here in the present. This means, according to Heidegger, that the subject synthesizes past and future in the present. In the here and now, that is, by living in the present, the subject grasps past and future in the modality of being ready-to-hand (*zuhanden*). To put it simply, when the subject thinks about its past and future, it exists in the here and now. This is the meaning of its existence.

However, by defining *Dasein* in such a way, Heidegger overlooks the fact that the subject possesses a body. This is ironic because is it not our body which experientially verifies the fact that we live in the here and now? In Europe, Merleau-Ponty was the first philosopher to pay attention to this fact. Again, Heidegger refers to human existence as "being-toward-death" (*Sein zum Tode*). This terminology strongly suggests that *Dasein* possesses a passive and emotive attitude toward the environment. The temporal dimensions of past, present, and future manifest themselves in the psychological states of "care" (*Sorge*) and "anxiety" (*Angst*); it is by means of these two modalities that the present self reflects retrospectively on the past. Merleau-Ponty, on the contrary, first points to the fact that, as a body, the subject is rooted inside the world itself. In addition, his conception of time places an emphasis on the future and puts into focus the subject's active engagement with the world.

In contrast to Heidegger, Merleau-Ponty grasps the relationship between subject and the environment in terms of the subject's future intentional attitude. At the same time, Merleau-Ponty pays attention to the fact that the concept of intentionality as it was framed by Husserl's phenomenology, which Heidegger neglected, is important to describe the relationship of the subject to the environment. What we call environment does not simply comprise the objective condition of the subject, which is given to it from the outside. Rather, the subject repeatedly apprehends the environment in an active engagement simultaneously as its objective condition as well as the content that is expressed by its own intentional activity. This intentional activity is projected from the body onto the environment. What I call the "condition" constitutes the environment that has to be understood as the place wherein the somatic subject itself acts. In other words, "being-in-the-world" signifies the subject that acts under such circumstances; the body embraces the world in a bundle of intentional activities.

The five aggregates central to early Buddhist philosophy are signified by means of the difficult word "skandha." It is an old word that is best translated as "aggregate" or "element." The theory of the five skandhas, subsequently, can be said to be a theory that understands the relationship of the subject to the world in terms of five structural elements.

These five elements are (1) *rūpa*, (2) *vedanā*, (3) *saṃjñā*, (4) *saṃskāra*, and (5) *vijñāna*. If we translate these terms into contemporary language, the term *rūpa* (J. *shiki* 色) has the connotations of "color" as well as "form" and indicates what surrounds the subject. I would like to point out that the term "environment" does not refer to a pile of objective material, but signifies what the subject apprehends in the visual experience as color and form. On the other hand, the subject that opposes the environment constitutes the fifth skandha, *vijñāna* (J. *shiki* 識). We can say that *vijñāna* corresponds almost completely to the contemporary concept of consciousness. In other words, the terms *rūpa* and *vijñāna* map out a spatial relationship that is based on our visual experience wherein subject and environment engage. This form of engagement can be most appropriately described by means of the concept of intentionality as it has been developed and provided by phenomenology.

The three elements between *rūpa* and *vijñāna* comprise the activities that connect the subject to the environment. The second and third elements, *vedanā* (feelings; J. *ju* 受) and *saṃjñā* (perception; J. *sō* 想), constitute a pair of passive and active modalities. The term *vedanā* designates the perception facilitated by our sense organs but it is not limited to sense perception; it also includes psychological activity usually identified as perceptive judgment such as the feeling of pleasure and displeasure. In short, *vedanā* constitutes the passive modality of the body's totality. *Saṃjñā*, on the other hand, has to be understood as the mental activity that creates psychic phenomena such as images, concepts, and thought. It comprises the imagination and emotion that is born from within the subject.

The fourth element, *saṃskāra* (J. *gyō* 行), constitutes the activity of engagement. If we compare the theory of the five skandhas to Merleau-Ponty's philosophy of the body, the notion of *saṃskāra* is especially important. This is so because the concept of *saṃskāra* reveals an idiosyncrasy of many Buddhist theories of action. This concept played a central role in the evolution of early Buddhism from the philosophical debates among the eighteen schools of early Buddhism to the Mahāyāna Buddhist theory of representation-only (S. *vijñapti-mātra*; J. *yuishiki* 唯識).[37] Etymologically, the term *saṃskāra* is designed to indicate the causal relationship of "that by which something is created" and "that which is created." Consequently, the term *saṃskāra* simultaneously evokes the active meaning of "that which creates," "the creating," and "the power of formation" as well as the passive meaning of "that which is made" and "the result of the formative process." In this sense, *saṃskāra* should be translated as the "potential formative power."

Saṃskāra arises together with human action, that is, karma. The term "karma" was assigned a plethora of meanings by later Buddhist philosophers. However, in the phase of early Buddhism, it was a concept that evoked the combination of what is known as the three psychophysical functions. These three functions are usually identified as bodily movement, linguistic expression, and mental intention. In the later development of Buddhism, esoteric Buddhism called these three functions the "three mysteries" (J. *sanmitsu* 三蜜) of body, speech, and mind.[38] Early Buddhist psychology thus suggests that when the subject engages with the environment, the activity of *saṃskāra*, which emerges together with karma, is at work and produces a definite effect.

If we continue to investigate the theory of action in early Buddhism further, it becomes evident that while action is externalized in the three functions of movement, verbal expressions, and intention, there exists an internal impetus toward action at the root of the will. Early Buddhism refers to this force as "defilements." "Defilement" designates the central mental activity of the self that is connected to physical instincts. In Freudian terms, *kleśas* (defilements) may be understood along the lines of the concept of *libido*. In short, the operations of the psyche are driven by the central instinct of the self in the depth of human actions. For this reason, *saṃskāra*, which arises together with action—that is, the formative power of potentiality—engenders a definite effect insofar as the "defilements" trigger a causal process.

Merleau-Ponty developed his body-schema to articulate the dual condition of the human body, which comprises the "actual body" that can be seen from the outside and the "habit body" that is felt from the inside. The former constitutes the body that is understood from a third-person perspective; it is conceived of from the standpoint of biology as that which provides the structure and function common to all human beings. However, people know their body from the first-person perspective as that which belongs to themselves. Consequently, to think about the unity of body and mind it is necessary to combine both the standpoints of objectivity and that of subjectivity. It is significant to his overall philosophy that Merleau-Ponty called the subjective dimension of the "habit-body" the "lived body" (*le corps vécu*).

When it engages the environment in activity, the subject projects its intentional acts toward the environment and, at the same time, apprehends the environment continuously as its own condition and as the place of motion wherein it is located.

Merleau-Ponty refers to this intentional activity as "intentional arc" (*l'arc intentio-nel*). To illustrate this concept, I would like to use the example of a bow. In this example, the arrow symbolizes the bundle of intentional activity, which penetrates and engulfs the environment. Does not this image evoke the notion of *saṃskāra* that I have expounded earlier? However, many contemporaries reject the idea that psychological activity can be projected outside of the human body. The reason for this lies in the fact that the Cartesian mind-body dualism and the dichotomy between the physical and the psychological or some version thereof has become mainstream ideology. Even Husserl believes that intentionality constitutes, if we examine his original thought, an activity that possesses a logical character but does not comprise a psychological function. The thinkers of antiquity, by contrast, neither distinguished clearly between the material and the psychological nor had the habit of differentiating between the logical and the psychological. In the same way, the term *saṃskāra* is designed to signify the psychological function of inten-tionality that is projected into the environment at the time of movement and ac-tivity; at the same time, it refers to the potential power of formation that produces a definite effect equally on the psychological and the material level.

Merleau-Ponty's philosophy is diametrically opposed to the dualism character-istic of modern thought and points toward an approach that discloses new levels of understanding. It defines the intentional activity that is projected from the body "as a third term between the psychological and the biological or, in other words, between the in-itself and the for-itself."[39] In short, Merleau-Ponty says that intentional acts connect the psychological activity that is born at the inside of the subject with objective biological activity; in other words, the psychological and the biological constitute two essential aspects of intentionality. This implies, of course, that any philosophy of body schema (*le scheme corporéal*) that is grounded in the experience of and reflects on the subjective body discloses an ambiguous structure. The British physiologist Henry Head presupposed that the concept of the body scheme constituted the foundation of internal sensation. However, Merleau-Ponty expanded this idea and suggested that the body schema comprised the center that projects intentional acts into the external world outside of the body. Therefore, intentionality as conceived of by Merleau-Ponty does not remain purely at the level of psychological activity that is determined from the inside of the subject; on the contrary, it constitutes an essential activity whose nature has to be thought to reach the horizon of the perceptual field and penetrates even the physiological and material dimensions of the environment.

I would like to point the reader to the fact that this way of thinking has been de-veloped in many philosophical traditions of the body in Asia from ancient times. One example of a philosophy that maintains such a conception of the body is the theory of *qi*-energy. It has been transmitted in Chinese and Japanese manuals on medicine, martial arts, hygiene, and meditation theory until today. For example, the famous *Inner Classic of the Yellow Emperor* introduces the notion of the merid-ian along which *qi* flows inside the body. It is thus a perfect example of a work that identifies *qi* as the source and essence of various affects and emotions. *Qi*-theory, in general, addresses phenomena akin to what clinical psychology refers to as complexes or stress. In recent years, attention has been given to medical practices and psychological hygiene such as *qigong*. For example, researchers have started to quantify the *qi*-energy that is projected from the body to the outside and measure its effects. However, the idea of such a vital energy is not unique to East Asia. In South Asian traditions of self-cultivation as well, there exists a concept that is similar to that of *qi*—namely, the notion of *prāṇa* (literally, breath), which has been transmitted from antiquity. Moreover, these traditions identify and develop the notion of a network along which *prāṇa* flows inside the body. It is called *nadī* and exhibits similarities to the system of meridians in Chinese medicine.

These conceptions of body presuppose a philosophical paradigm that cannot be reconciled with the dualism characteristic of modern philosophy and science. Therefore, can we not say, using Merleau-Ponty's words, that they suggest a new concept that indicates a time of transition as well as a paradigm shift in science and philosophy? Instead, his ideas disclose an inherent ambiguity because they emerged during a time of transition and indicate a paradigm shift in science and philosophy. I thus think that the Asian philosophical traditions are able to provide a new conception of the body to the contemporary philosophical discourse and to support Merleau-Ponty's observations.

In addition, there is a second, deep connection between Merleau-Ponty and Buddhism that is frequently overlooked: Merleau-Ponty's philosophy of the body not only thematizes the direction from the body toward the external environment but also provides a theoretical approach that is directed toward the inside of the self-consciousness of the subject. Examining Descartes' methodological skepticism, Merleau-Ponty maintains that at the bottom of the "spoken *cogito*" (*cogito parlé*) a "silent *cogito*" (*cogito tacite*) is latent. "If the spoken *cogito* did not meet the silent *cogito* inside myself, I could not find the meaning of either '*cogito*' or '*sum*.' . . . What Descartes aimed at when he wrote the Meditations, was the silent *cogito*; this *cogito* vitalizes and guides all expressive activity."[40] Merleau-Ponty maintains that this "silent *cogito*" constitutes the presence of the self to the self (*la presence de soi à soi*). This means that inside the self, there exists a latent self that is deeper than that which arises from the inside. He thus seems to suggest that, at times when the self confronts the fear of death or the gaze of other, the "silent *cogito*" is experienced in the feeling of limitation as if the existence of the self itself is negated. The contention that the "silent *cogito*" and the *cogito* are inextricably intertwined may be hard to understand, but I would like to emphasize the fact that Merleau-Ponty cites from the *Meditations* (*Meditationes Prima Philosophia*) in this context. It is generally agreed that, in the *Meditations*, Descartes introduced and explained his famous *cogito ergo sum* and developed his mind-matter dualism on the basis of this concept. However, do those who talk about Descartes' dualism not ignore the fact that this book intends to prove the existence of the soul and God? His methodological doubt was designed to explore a realm of the soul that is separate from the realm of the body. Merleau-Ponty said that doubt is simply based on logical presuppositions. This means that the "silent *cogito*" facilitates and indicates the emergence of the self from its own depth within and thus functions as the structure and basis of the self itself. If we look at it from a psychological standpoint, what Merleau-Ponty calls the "silent *cogito*" can be understood to signify the basic realm of the deep unconscious that is found inside the consciousness of the self. Employing the language of Freud's psychoanalysis, Michel Henry argues that the unconscious discloses the structure of auto-affection.

I would like to alert the attention of the reader to the fact that Merleau-Ponty's reflections on the "silent *cogito*" correspond to the later philosophical elaboration of early Buddhist ideas. The concept of *saṃskāra*, which can be found in early Buddhism, was inherited and developed by the Abhidharma theory of Theravāda Buddhism and the Vijñapti-mātra theory in Mahāyāna Buddhism. The concept of *saṃskāra* occupied a central role in the subsequent philosophical expositions. The passive form of *saṃskāra*, *saṃskṛta*, signifies an effect that is being formed and being produced. Abhidharma theory focuses on classification systems of *kleśa*, defilements. As such, it discloses an analysis of, speculation about, and understanding of the psychological working of the deep layer underlying consciousness. This analysis led to the theory of the *kleśas*, which is based on meditation and self-cultivation as it has been practiced and experienced in early Buddhism. In early Buddhist texts, "dharma" is a generic term for the psychological activity that is experienced during meditation. This psychological content of meditation can be divided into two categories: the psychological activity that gives rise to definite effects called "conditioned dharmas" (S. *saṃskṛta dharma*) and the psychological activity that produces no effect whatsoever, namely the "unconditioned dharmas" (S. *asaṃskṛta dharma*). The Chinese translation of "conditioned dharmas" is *youweifa* (J. *uihō* 有為法) and that of "unconditioned dharmas" is *wuweifa* (J. *muihō* 無為法). The former constitutes the psychological activity that arises when the practitioner is motivated by self-centered defilements. If this is the case, the *saṃskāra* that accompanies activity certainly produces *karma*, that is, a definite effect. *Asaṃskṛta-dharma*, on the contrary, constitutes the psychological activity that does not engender any effect. This corresponds to the psychological activity that accompanies the experience of samādhi, the highest meditative state according to early Buddhism. In his *Abhidharmakośa*, Vasubandhu contrasts the relatively low number of three classes of *asaṃskṛta-dharma* to seventy-two types of *saṃskṛta-dharma*. The reason for this is that, even psychological activities that are experienced during meditation still belong to the self-centered defilements for the most part. In short, at the bottom of self-consciousness there are various layers and structures of "defilements." From the inside of the self a deeper self emerges. In the extreme case, that is, in the case of the experience of samādhi, the self is extinguished and the no-self emerges. At this time, the *saṃskāra* that gives rise to all effects also disappears.

The "bright *cogito*" that occupies a place in self-consciousness constitutes the center of the subjective body and in its activity makes the environment the field of intentional action. In this way, we can find similarities between Merleau-Ponty's philosophy of the body and the five skandhas, especially the *saṃskāra-skandha*, in early Buddhism. Merleau-Ponty inquires into the structure of the "silent *cogito*" that supports the "bright *cogito*." His inquiry is not complete but it indicates a direction where we can find a common ground shared by phenomenology and the philosophical elaborations of early Buddhist thinkers.

Translated by Gereon Kopf

3

How the Tree Sees Me

Sentience and Insentience in Tiantai and Merleau-Ponty

Brook Ziporyn

I see. I can be seen. For these two seemingly innocuous commonsense claims to stand together, the meaning of the terms "I," "can be," and "seeing" must be teased out. Depending on how this is done, certain much less commonsensical claims may come to light. Even where a dualistic conception of spirit and matter, or of sentience and insentience, has been left behind, there are many theoretical loopholes that can allow one that both seeing and being seen pertain to the same being, or level of being here; the question rests on what type of being is claimed for the "I" here, and how "seeing" is understood. But I would like to argue here for the reasonableness of the far stranger claim emerging from the reconfiguration of the understanding of seeing explicitly put forth in the doctrines of Tiantai Buddhism, in particular as developed by Jingxi Zhanran (711–782) and Siming Zhili (960–1028), and arguably defensible in the works of Maurice Merleau-Ponty (1908–1961), rooted in his early work *Phenomenology of Perception*, but reaching its fruition in his posthumous work *The Visible and the Invisible*. The stranger claim concerns the status of not only the "I" and of "seeing," but also the seen object. I see. I can be seen. But is it the case that I am *necessarily* seen? And may I reverse this proposition? May I say that being seen necessarily entails seeing? Commonsense materialism says that, while I, this animal being, see and perhaps, but not necessarily, am also seen, the inanimate cup before me is only seen, and does not see. On the other hand, an animist or pantheist might assert that the cup sees as well as being seen, in that it embodies a mind or spirit of some kind: the spirit of the cup, or the universal spirit as manifest in the cup, looks back at me. Metaphysical dualists, of course, would simply say that I see and the cup is seen, not vice versa. The two doctrines I want to discuss here, those of Tiantai and Merleau-Ponty, are distinctive in that, while asserting unequivocally the abyss between the animate and the inanimate, they nonetheless also assert the sentience necessarily pertaining to the insentience and, indeed, the insentience of the sentient. The cup I see sees me. The cup is seen. The cup sees. What must be stressed is that for both Tiantai and Merleau-Ponty, these claims are compatible with the claims, say, that seeing is the by-product of a central nervous system, and that this can only exist in an organic animal being. Nonetheless, the cup is looking at me. How? In this chapter I will try to work through what this kind of claim can mean in these two streams of thought, how they differ, and what their convergences imply.

Tiantai Buddhist doctrine rests on two intimately related foundations: the doctrine of the Three Truths, and the doctrine of "opening the provisional to reveal the real." The Three Truths are an expansion of the traditional Nagarjunian idea of the Two Truths. In Nāgārjuna's system, these are Conventional Truth, which includes ordinary language (everyday descriptions of selves, causes, effects, beginnings and ends, and so on, as well as traditional Buddhist statements about value and practice—for example, the Four Noble Truths, the Eightfold Noble Path, the marks of suffering, impermanence, and no-self), and Ultimate Truth, which is in the first place Emptiness as the negation of the absolute validity of any of the terms accepted as conventional truths, and finally also the Emptiness of Emptiness, which extends this same critique to the concept of "Emptiness" itself; in the end, Ultimate Truth is indescribable—it refers to the lived experience of liberation, and thus even "Emptiness" is relegated to merely conventional truth. It is to be noted that in this theory there are really three categories: (1) plain error (metaphysical theories which take ordinary speech terms to be designations of absolute realities; statements about the beginning and end of the universe, God, ultimate reality, etc.); (2) conventional truth (ordinary speech and Buddhist speech); and (3) ultimate truth (the experience of liberation, for which even the term "Emptiness" is insufficient). The criterion for what counts as conventional truth is pragmatic: whatever is conducive to the comprehension of ultimate truth—that is, statements that can serve as a means to lead beyond themselves, to the negation of themselves, and hence to ultimate truth—is conventional truth. Whatever cognitive claims obstruct this pragmatic goal falls into the category of falsehood. Note also that "Emptiness" has a double status here: as the direct negation of the literal reality of conventional truth, it is the privileged description of ultimate truth. But as a concept in its own right, it too is a conventional truth only.

This is how it stands with Indian Mahāyāna, particularly in the writings of Nāgārjuna. Tiantai alters this picture decisively by speaking of not two but three truths. These are Conventional Truth, Ultimate Truth, and the Center. This reconfiguration has two direct consequences. First, the hierarchy between conventional and ultimate truth is canceled; indeed, even the difference in their content is effaced: according to the Tiantai tradition, provisional and ultimate truths are equal in value and ultimately identical. Second, the category of "plain falsehood" that was implied by the Nagarjunian idea of Two Truths is here eliminated entirely; all claims of whatever kind are equally conventional truths, and thus of equal value to and ultimately identical to ultimate truth, or the conception of Emptiness, and its self-overcoming.

The Tiantai term for conventional truths is "provisional positing" (*jia* 假). Ultimate truth is simply emptiness (*kong* 空). We may better understand the Tiantai position by retranslating these terms as "local coherence" and "global incoherence" respectively. Provisional truth is the claim that some qualium X has a certain discernible, coherent identity. Ultimate truth is the revelation that this coherent identity is only provisionally coherent, that it fails to be coherent in all contexts and from all points of view. X is analyzable exhaustibly into non-X elements, non-X causes, non-X antecedents, and non-X contexts, which are revealed not to be external to X, but to be constitutive of it. No X is discoverable apart from the non-X elements, causes, antecedents, and contexts, which are present here, we may say, "as" X. This "as" may be taken as a shorthand way of indicating what is meant by the "third truth," Centrality, the relation of contrast/identity between X and non-X, between this qualium's identity as X and the effacing of that identity. These non-X elements which are present here as X are revealed simply by closer attention to X itself; they are not brought in from outside. X appears exclusively as X only when our field of attention is arbitrarily narrowed to exclude some of the relevant ways it can be considered; attention to its constitutive elements, antecedents, and contexts reveals this very same item, X, is also readable as non-X. Hence the two seemingly opposite claims of the Two Truths turn out to be two alternate ways of saying the same thing: to be identifiable is to be coherent, to be coherent is to be locally coherent, and to be locally coherent is to be globally incoherent. With this move, the third category, "plain error," from the Two Truths theory drops out of the picture: all coherences, even alternate metaphysical claims, are in the same boat; all are identities which are locally coherent/globally incoherent. The truth of a statement consists simply in its coherence to some given perspective, which is always the effect of arbitrarily limiting the horizons of relevance. When all considerations are brought in at once, X has no single consistent noncontradictory identity.

In addition, the old pragmatic standard of truth is applied more liberally here: all claims, statements, and positions are true in the sense that all *can*, if properly recontextualized, lead to liberation—which is to say, to their own self-overcoming. Conversely, none will lead to liberation if not properly contextualized. This fact, that conventional and ultimate truths are synonymous, is what is meant by the Center. This is also taken to mean that this coherence, X, is the center of all other coherences in the distinctively Chinese sense of being their source, value, meaning, end, and ground, around which they all converge and into which they are all subsumed. All entities are locally coherent, globally incoherent, and the center of all other coherences. X subsumes all the non-X qualia that are appearing here as X: they are instantiations of X, which serves as their subsuming category. X is, as it were, the overall style of being that is expressed by its various aspects, which is now seen to include all non-X elements without exception. X is, let's say, like a song: all non-X elements are aspects or moments of this song, which make it what it is—the rhythm, the melody, the arrangement, even the surrounding context, are present here as this "song." The "song" as such, as a totality, is present as a style of being in each of these elements, and yet there is no song outside of the elements. But this one-way relation between subsumer and subsumed does not apply here; each element is itself a center. It is as if we could further say that "the song itself," as well as the rhythm and the arrangement and the context, are also present here AS the melody. Because they are all in the position of being the subsumer, they are also all in the position of being subsumed. To be X is to be locally coherent (X), globally incoherent (non-X), and intersubsumptive asness (X expressing itself in the form of [AS] all non-Xs, and all non-Xs expressing themselves in the form of [AS] X).

The second pillar of Tiantai doctrine is the concept of "opening the provisional to reveal the real." This is a way of further specifying the relation between local coherence and global incoherence, which are not only synonymous, but also irrevocably opposed, and indeed identical only by means of their opposition. Provisional truth is the antecedent, the premise, and indeed in a distinctive sense the *cause* of ultimate truth, but only in its relation of strict exclusion of ultimate truth. I have suggested elsewhere that the everyday example of the joke could serve as a helpful model for understanding this structure, with the provisional as the set-up and the ultimate as the punchline, thus preserving both the contrast between the two and their ultimate identity in sharing the quality of humorousness that belongs to every atom of the joke considered as a whole, once the punchline has been revealed. The setup is serious, while the punchline is funny. The funniness of the punchline depends on the seriousness of the setup, and on the contrast and difference between the two. However, once the punchline has occurred, it is also the case that the setup is, retrospectively, funny; we do not say that the punchline alone is funny, but that the whole joke was funny. This also means that the original contrast between the two is both preserved and annulled; neither funniness nor seriousness means the same thing after the punchline dawns, for their original meanings depended on the mutually exclusive nature of their defining contrast. Each is now a center that subsumes of the other; they are intersubsumptive.

We can restate the above somewhat more formulaically as follows. Every phenomenal object is a coherence. That is, it is a joining (cohering) of disparate elements—either the factors that comprise it, its internal parts, or its temporal antecedents, or its conceptual contexts. Context and content are in the same boat on this view, in that for this object to appear phenomenally—to be "coherent" or legible, discernible—requires the coming together of multiple factors: figure and ground, elements in a structure, causal conditions. What is crucial here is that these factors are heterogeneous, and phenomenally differ in some discernible way from the object they come to constitute.

Every coherence is a local coherence: it remains coherent as such and such only within a limited horizon of relevance. That is, its legibility depends on the fixing of a certain scale, frame, or focal orientation; its identity as this precise thing depends phenomenally on restricting the ways in which it is viewed, or the number of other factors which are viewed in tandem with it.

Every local coherence is globally incoherent. When all contexts are taken into account at once, and all applications and aspects brought to bear, the original coherence vanishes.

Every globally incoherent local coherence subsumes all other coherences.

Every subsuming is an intersubsumption.

In the Tiantai classification of teachings, we find on this basis a fourfold interpretation to be given to any fact and its negation, a gradual unfolding of the full implications of the intimate intertwining of any X and its own constitutive non-Xness. This applies most directly to the relation between sentience and insentience, as follows, giving us four levels of understanding of this relation:

1. To be sentient will always lead to, emerge from, and involve insentience. There is a necessary and inescapable connection between the two, but one that allows that the two phases are determinately separate: sentience is impermanent and conditional, so that when there is sentience here and now it implies that there is insentience there and then. Sentience, like every other determinate entity, is impermanent. This simply means that, given sentience, there are necessarily other times and places where sentience does not occur.

2. Precisely where there is sentience there is always already also insentience itself. The two are not really separable, and every instance of sentience proves, upon examination, to be pervaded with insentience. Sentience is composed entirely of insentient elements, causes, and contexts. The contexts are shown, in the Tiantai analysis, not to be external to that which they contextualize, although ultimately they cannot be construed as internal to it either. This is done through an examination of the relation between an arisen object and its causes, antecedents, elements, and conceptual contrasts; all of these are necessarily "not" the entity that arises, and yet, according to the Nagarjunian analysis, this entity cannot arise from itself, from another, from both, or from neither. Sentience is identifiably sentience due to its contrast with insentience. Is the interface between sentience and insentience sentient or insentient? Does the contrast between sentience and insentience occur within sentience or within insentience? Neither answer will work; in either case, the same question must be posed again. This leads to a reconfiguration of what both sentience and insentience actually mean. They can be neither the same nor different. They must be mutually entailing, copresent, reducible to each other, and emergent from one another. Here we have moved from a relation of necessary linkage to a simultaneous copresence or even a certain type of identity; right in the sentience itself, there is also insentience, and vice versa. The wave is wet, the wetness is wavy, not in part, but in every single locus. At this stage reversibility is not yet explicit. Focusing on an existing instance of sentience, we here see it as inseparable from or identical to insentience that could still, at

this point, be construed as a sort of substratum. It is not yet obvious that this will entail the reversed claim that insentience is always already also sentience itself. A reductive reading is still possible at this level, whereby sentience is an epiphenomenon, an emergent quality of insentience, such that sentience is entirely composed of insentience, but not vice versa.

3. There is sentience because there is insentience, and vice versa. Both sentience and insentience are two sides of a single fact, grounded in a totality that is itself neither sentient nor insentient (either this structure itself or some transcendent *tertium quid*). Here we make explicit the interfusion of identity and casual necessity. An equilateral triangle is also an equiangular triangle, and wherever one is present, the other is present. Both equilaterality and equiangularity are aspects, ways of describing, this third thing, the triangle, applying to the whole triangle, forming a logically necessary relation to one another, but remaining two distinct claims about the triangle. Given the inseparability established in levels 1 and 2, the totality of sentience and insentience is a single entity. This totality can be described neither as sentient nor as insentient, and indeed both characteristics pervade its entirety. Sentience and insentience are both aspects of the Middle Way, which transcends both. The technical Tiantai term for this position is "The Exclusive Center": the center transcends and includes the two extremes, but not vice verse. The notion of reversibility enters here with respect to the two opposed extremes, but not between the levels of "extremes" versus "center"; since insentience is incoherent in isolation from sentience, we can say not only that insentience is present wherever sentience is present, but also that sentience is present wherever insentience is present.

4. Sentience per se is insentience per se, and vice versa. This is the "Nonexclusive Mean," and indicates more than merely identity in the sense of two aspects of a single entity. It signifies that either aspect, taken in itself, is always already both, and hence that either of the extremes is also always the center and the other extreme, and vice versa. Reversibility pertains to the two extremes, and also between levels, between the center itself and the extremes. Each extreme is itself the center, and centers the other two terms. Equiangularity itself is equilaterality, because the full meaning of equiangularity involves equilaterality; each is merely a shorthand way of saying both. Furthermore, "the triangle" is itself equiangularity, is itself equilaterality, and vice versa; just thinking through what "equiangularity" means already includes the meaning of the subject to which this predicate pertains, "the triangle." Concrete and abstract, subject and predicate, are here explicitly reversible. Each term, taken in itself, is a way of describing all phenomena without exception, focused here and now so as to appear "as" this particular entity. There is, in the cosmos, only form, only sound, only fragrance, only flavor, only tactile sensation, only mind. There is only sentience. There is only insentience.

This fourth position is what Tiantai writers describe as the Integrated Teaching (*yuanjiao*). It should be noticed that the all-pervasion of a qualium—for example, sentience—is premised on, and indeed finally identical to, its limitedness, its nonpervasion (level 1). It is because it is not everywhere that it turns out to be everywhere. To spell this out more clearly, it is because it is not everywhere that it is a qualium at all: a local coherence. Only because it is not everywhere can it be something or somewhere. To be determinate is to have termini, boundaries. But these boundaries, separating the this from the not-this, turn out to be impossible. This is composed of not-this, the outside is in the inside. To be distinguishable from one another, this and not-this must be copresent. But they can be neither literally copresent nor literally distinct. They can exist only AS one another. Without the separation, there is nothing for the "this" to exist AS. But if the separation were ultimate truth, there would also be no "this" appearing. So the only coherent possibility is the mutual pervasion of Asnesses, conceived in terms of the Three Truths.

Insentience may not seem to be the same thing as "being seen." But in the Tiantai view, the positing of a coherence that has any property (for example, in this case, insentience) is a way of describing the fact that it appears that way to some sentient being. Reality means, by definition, phenomenal reality, for any putative nonphenomenal reality is conceived in Tiantai as another local coherence, which serves, as it were, as the Ur-structure of phenomenality. It is not just a fact that something is "insentient": to say something is insentient is to say that it is seen as insentient from some perspective, that it is seeable AS insentience. The Asness structure is a rejection of any privileged perspective, and on this view "brute fact" is merely a concealed form of a God's-eye-view, of a privileged way-of-seeing. The rejection of *simpliciter* objectivity is a consequence of the rejection of the "view from nowhere." Being is appearing-as, which always implies a perspective; and a perspective always implies the possibility of alternate perspectives. What we explicitly describe as "being seen" is a kind of special case of the relation of Xness to its constitutive non-Xness, its "outrunning of itself," as Merleau-Ponty puts it, into its moretoitivity—that is, there is always more to discover—its constitutive elements, antecedents, and contexts. Not-seeing means "being seeable as not-seeing." This is what Merleau-Ponty will refer to as the immanence of phenomenal perception, one side of the paradoxical nature of perception to be addressed momentarily. Hence, we can elaborate the above chart to apply to seeing and being seen as follows:

1. Seeing will always lead to and come from being seen.
2. Seeing is always already being seen.
3. Seeing and being seen cause each other, or together derive from and express a single cause.
4. Seeing is being seen. Being seen is seeing.

In *Phenomenology of Perception* and other early works, Merleau-Ponty steers a middle course between intellectualism and empiricism. This methodological approach reflects a parallel ontological insight avoiding the extremes of both idealism and materialism. The phenomenal is the real, and the characteristics of phenomenal perception are neither those of the material "thing" nor those of the intellectual "idea." Neither abstract bodies nor abstract minds can pertain here. Neither mind nor object (sentience nor insentience) are predetermined, fully constituted entities; we cannot speak of minds as mirroring prior determinations existing on their own in the world, nor of mind projecting its own contents onto the world in accordance with its own autonomous schemata. Rather, mind is at best the word for the phenomenal process of disambiguation itself, a continuation of an always preexistent tradition of possibilities and evocations, which could then be called the world. As Merleau-Ponty states, perception is thus paradoxical when looked at in terms of either empirical or logical standards, the standards of nonparadoxicality derived from either the pure mental realm of ideas or the pure material realm of things. He puts the point succinctly as follows:

> The perceived thing itself is paradoxical; it exists only in so far as someone can perceive it. I cannot even for an instant imagine an object in itself. As Berkeley said, if I attempt to imagine some place in the world which has never been seen, the very fact that I imagine it makes me present at that place. I thus cannot conceive a perceptible place in which I am not myself present. But even the places in which I find myself are never completely given to me; the things which I see are things for me only under the condition that they always recede beyond their immediately given aspects. Thus there is a paradox of immanence and transcendence in perception. Immanence, because the perceived object cannot be foreign to him who perceives; transcendent, because it always contains something more than what is actually given. And these two elements of perception are not, properly speaking, contradictory. For if we reflect on this notion of perspective, if we reproduce the perceptual experience in our thought, we see that the kind of evidence proper to the perceived, the appearance of "something," requires both this presence and this absence.[1]

This simultaneous presence and absence brings us, through another route, close to the Tiantai notion of "Asness" discussed above, to some degree. As Merleau-Ponty nails it, "What enables us to centre our existence is also what prevents us from centring it completely."[2] Coherence can exist only as local coherence, as not completely centered coherence. There is always more to it than is immediately perceived, the phenomenal object "outruns" my perception of it, but nonetheless it is only my perceiving of it that makes it appear, and is inseparable from its presence. Moreover, these are not two entirely separate facts about it, but derive from the same principle; the transcendence and the immanence are necessary to one another. It is because it is never completely given (the transcendence of the perceived) that it can be given at all, but it is also because it is given only as inseparable from the perceiver (the immanence of the perceived) that it can never be given completely. But this formulation, in terms of "that which centers (gives coherence)" and "that which prevents complete centering," asserting that the agent of both is one and the same, and hence that the two (centering and failure to completely center, emergence as X and failure to be completely X) are two aspects of one and the same thing, does not go far enough from a Tiantai perspective; it falls into what we have characterized as the third of the four ways of understanding the relation between any quiddity's being X and its not being X. In this formulation, these are still two distinct facts about X, which derive from a single source, rather than restatements of a single fact, as in the fourth way, espoused by Tiantai doctrine. But in Merleau-Ponty's posthumous work *The Visible and the Invisible*, he seems to be working his way toward the fourth position.

We can find seeds of this move to the fourth view even in Merleau-Ponty's earlier work, which perhaps reveal the direction from which he later comes to approach it. We may think here of Merleau-Ponty's description of what he calls the "anonymity of perception." In describing the relation of "subject" and "object" in sense experience, and the implications close observation of this relation will have for understanding the relations between the *a priori* and the *a posteriori*, on the one hand, and *natura naturata* and *natura naturans*, on the other—all these relationships are disclosed as forming intertwining chiasms. Merleau-Ponty writes:

> The sensor and the sensible do not stand in relation to each other as two mutually external terms, and sensation is not an invasion of the sensor by the sensible. It is my gaze which subtends colour, and the movement of my hand which subtends the object's form, or rather my gaze pairs off with colour, and my hand with hardness and softness, and in this transaction between the subject of sensation and the sensible it cannot be held that one acts while the other suffers the action, or that one confers significance on the other . . . a sensible datum which is on the point of being felt sets a kind of muddled problem for my body to solve. I must find the attitude which *will* provide it with the means of becoming determinate, of showing up as [e.g.] blue; I must find the reply to a question which is obscurely expressed. . . . I do not possess it in thought, or spread out towards it some idea of blue such as might reveal the secret of it, I abandon myself to it and plunge into this mystery, it "thinks itself within me," I am the sky itself as it is drawn together and unified, and as it begins to exist for itself; my consciousness is saturated with this limitless blue . . . of the sky, as it is perceived or sensed, subtended by my gaze which ranges over and resides in it, and providing as it does the theatre of a certain living pulsation adopted by my body, it can be said that it exists for itself (i.e., as aware of itself), in the sense that it is not made up of mutually exclusive parts, that each part of the whole is "sensitive" to what happens in all the others and "knows them dynamically." . . . Every perception takes place in an atmosphere of generality and is presented to us anonymously. I cannot say that *I* see the blue of the sky in the sense in which I say that I understand a book or again in which I decide to devote my life to mathematics. . . . So, if I wanted to render precisely the perceptual experience, I ought to say that *one* perceives in me, and not that I perceive. Every sensation carries within it the germ of a dream or depersonalization such as we experience in that quasi-stupor to which we are reduced when we really try to live at the level of sensation. . . . By means of sensation I am able to grasp, on the fringe of my own personal life and acts, a life of given consciousness from which

these latter emerge, the life of my eyes, hands and ears, which are so many nature selves. Each time I experience a sensation, I feel that it concerns not my own being, the one for which I am responsible and for which I make decisions, but another self which has already sided with the world, which is already open to certain of its aspects and synchronized with them.[3]

Here we find an indistinguishability of subject and object, of sensor and sensed, in each individual act of sensation, each inextricably operative in the other, to the point of undecidability. We have here a precursor of Merleau-Ponty's later idea of "the flesh," the intertwined chiasm of the visible and the seeing, of the sensed and the sensing. In the perceived world there is already self—a self who is more me than me, which has already "sided with the world," and in the self there is already world. This other self who is me perceiving, this non-me who is more intimately me than me, brings us close to the Tiantai "single moment of experience" as "three thousand quiddities," and that moment of experience is also where there is no way to disentangle the agent from the patient, the seer from the seen, the doer from the done. As Zhanran says: "Since both the environment and the person are present as a single moment of experience, they cannot be divided into agent and patient. Although there is neither agent nor patient, the environment and the person are clearly present as always."[4] For Zhanran, all three thousand quiddities, of matter and mind, environment and person, pertaining to every possible subjectivity and objectivity, are identical to the moment of experience, present as this moment of experience. For Tiantai, this unreservedly implies that we may reverse the creator and the created, the subject and the object: mind creates matter, matter creates mind, I am performing the world, the world is performing me, I am thinking myself in the sky, the sky is thinking itself in me; the intersubsumption of self and other allow us to see how we can claim that any single quiddity in this simultaneous three thousand can be singled out as the center, as the unifier, as what is expressing itself as all the others.

Merleau-Ponty clearly recognizes the "self-awareness" that applies to, say, the sky when "I" see it: "it sees itself in me." But here he contrasts this I of perception to the I of knowing and understanding on the one hand ("I who understand a book") and the I of willing and action ("I who decide to devote my life to mathematics"), the one who understands ideas and concepts, or even the "things" in the world as identifiable entities, and the one who "commits himself" and wills his own projects. Here, the implication would seem to be, as opposed to what takes place in the realm of pure sensation, I am indeed the real agent of my actions, the one who makes myself. But the fundamental tangling of subject and object in any act of disclosure rooted in perception, as all acts of disclosure can be seen to be, their reversibility and intersubsumption, pushes us beyond this clear-cut distinction, even in the realm of volition. Merleau-Ponty himself moves in the same direction. First he notes the correlativity of this incompletion of the self with the necessary incompletion of any quiddity that is appearing to me: "Sensation can be anonymous only because it is incomplete. The person who sees and the one who touches is not exactly myself, because the visible and the tangible worlds are not the world in its entirety"[5] (i.e., because any quiddity we perceive is always inherently "moretoitive"—that is, there is always "more-to-come"). Because the object is not quite itself, I am never quite myself.

But he goes on to connect perception with a kind of impersonal *action*:

> My first perception and my first hold upon the world must appear to me as action in accordance with an earlier agreement reached between x and the world in general, my history must be the continuation of a prehistory and must utilize the latter's acquired results. My personal existence must be the resumption of a prepersonal tradition. There is, therefore, another subject beneath me, for whom a world exists before I am here, and who marks out my place in it. This captive or natural spirit is my body, not that momentary body which is the instrument of my personal choices and which fastens upon this or that world, but the system of anonymous "functions" which draw every particular focus into a general project.[6]

Here we have an acute phenomenological description of the temporal presituatedness of all our *actions*, which makes each of them more than it conceives of itself to be and more than any single act of intention can be determined, which corresponds closely to the Tiantai reading of the revelation of everyone's prehistory in the *Lotus Sūtra*. It is not just the I who perceives is more me than me, and the world as perceived is more than it is; the I who knows and acts and undertakes projects is also not just me, and its objects, world, and goals are also constitutively moretoitive.

And the full fruits of this advance come to light in the discussion of time in the same work, where the active/passive dichotomy is fully broken through: "We are not in some incomprehensible way an activity joined to a passivity, an automatism surmounted by a will, a perception surmounted by a judgement, but wholly active and wholly passive, because we are the upsurge of time."[7] Here Merleau-Ponty moves beyond the possibility of reading his chiasm as a kind of "always part X and part non-X" position (equivalent to level 3 above) to a more fully Tiantai "both completely X and completely non-X" (level 4) type of claim. We find this more explicitly when Merleau-Ponty says of time itself: "We shall be obliged to say of [time] what we have said of other objects; that it has meaning for us only because 'we are it.' . . . It discloses subject and object as two abstract 'moments' of a unique structure which is *presence*."[8] This is so because, among other things, "[t]he world is inseparable from the subject, but from a subject which is nothing but a project of the world, and the subject is inseparable from the world, but from a world which the subject itself projects."[9] Here we are more than halfway to the omnicentric intersubsumption characteristic of the Tiantai position.[10]

Looked at from a Tiantai perspective, then, Merleau-Ponty seems to be wavering between the third and fourth levels in his understanding of the relation between the sentient and the insentient. It is in his later work that he moves decisively toward the fourth level, in his notion of the chiasmic flesh, which is not just an inseparability or intertangling of the seeing and the seen, but implies actual reversibility of perspective, where subject and object can switch places, so that the seer becomes also the seen and the seen the seer, without losing the everpresent distinction between them. Seeing is never disembodied; it is always from a certain perspective, and to see means to be outrun by what is seen; it is always seeing-as. This means to be susceptible to alternate perspectives, other ways of seeing, other seeings-as. In that case, to see installs me in a world of visibility which, by virtue simply of seeing, already establishes myself, the viewer, as also visible, as also viewable from other perspectives. Seeing then is synonymous with showing, which is making oneself seen. Thus the very act of seeing already makes me seen, and the disclosure of the seen object is also the disclosure of my seenness. This is the groundwork for the thesis that, in a certain sense, the object sees me: in seeing it, I am being seen. But the agent of this seeing remains for Merleau-Ponty the anonymous flesh of "the world," undecideably shifting between its subject and object poles so that they cannot be definitively distinguished. Some ambiguity remains here as to how far this claim can be taken. Would it therefore be as correct to say that "the object" is the agent of the seeing that sees me, as to say that "I" am the agent who does the seeing of the object? After all, "I" am ultimately not the seer of the seen; it is rather the anonymous flesh itself that sees in me. How far can this reversibility be taken for Merleau-Ponty?

In *The Visible and the Invisible*, Merleau-Ponty states that reversibility is "the ultimate truth." It should be noted that reversibility is neither pure identity nor pure difference; in the reflections on the body's attempts to touch itself while touching in *The Phenomenology of Perception*, Merleau-Ponty asserts that "the two hands are never simultaneously in the relationship of touched and touching to each other. When I press my two hands together, it is not a matter of two sensations felt together as one perceives two objects placed side by side, but of an ambiguous set-up in which both hands can alternate the roles of 'touching' and being 'touched.' . . . [But] in passing from one role to the other, I can identify the hand touched as the same one which will in a moment be touching."[11] This is the consideration that will blossom in Merleau-Ponty's last works into the reversibility thesis, and we see here as there is both the identity and the difference embedded in this claim. There too, reversibility is always a possibility, never an accomplished coinciding of the two sides. In *The Visible and the Invisible*, Merleau-Ponty states: "[I]t is a reversibility always imminent and never realized in fact. My left hand is always on the verge of touching my right hand touching the things, but I never reach coincidence; the coincidence eclipses at the moment of realization."[12] The subject and object sides are not reversed in fact, but always reversible. There is a fission between them which is nonetheless always on the verge of reverting, or capable of reverting, without ever coming to complete simultaneous self-coincidence. But this is not a difficulty for the reversibility thesis, but rather its very premise. Indeed, this fission is necessary even to the unity of the two sides, since if they ever wholly fused they would simply form a single abstract subject or object, one or the other. The intertwining of the subject and object, seer and seen, requires both an inseparable unity and an irreducible difference. It is the constant *possibility* of reversion that is the flesh, and that makes it nether object nor subject. Hence Merleau-Ponty states that this noncoincidence of the two reversible sides is not a failure or an ontological chasm between the two sides, but rather a clearing within the totality of flesh, serving as a hinge for its opaque zones. This pivoting clearing is "spanned by the total being of my body, and by that of the world," which Merleau-Ponty describes metaphorically as "the zero of pressure between two solids that makes them adhere to one another."[13] It is precisely this intercorporeity that defines the flesh, which is not self, not world, not both, not neither, but rather the hinge, reversibility, the ultimate truth.

This reversibility is the litmus test for the final and distinctively Tiantai position. But we must still make the distinction between "reversibility as ultimate truth," the "Exclusive Center" of the tertium quid position of level 3 in the Tiantai analysis (reversibility has a greater ontological ultimacy than either of the two reversible terms), and the "Nonexclusive Center" of level 4, which in Tiantai terms would mean that "seen," "seer," and "reversibility between seen and seer" are each equally the ultimate term, each reducible to the others, each equally a shorthand way of saying all three. This would require Merleau-Ponty to also be capable of saying "the Visible alone is the ultimate truth," "the Seeing of the Visible alone is the ultimate truth," and "reversibility between the two is the ultimate truth." In practice, it appears that Merleau-Ponty rather grants ultimacy to the very undecidability between the two sides, which thus serves as the transcendent tertium quid, the sole ultimate truth. The Tiantai position would be rather that "The Visible" per se, properly understood, already means "the reversibility between the visible and the seer," and vice versa. The test of this claim must be: Can we say that the object sees me? Or is it only "the world," "the flesh," or "reversibility" itself that can be validly described as the agent of the seeing?

This question comes to prominence in Tiantai writings especially in Zhanran's works, in particular in his *Jingangpi* (金剛錍), where he argues for the "Buddha-nature of the insentient." The modifier "Buddha" in the term Buddha-nature, Zhanran tells us, is a term used to indicate, initially, awareness, or sentience itself. "The Nature" means unchangeably present in all occurrences, and unmodified it is neither aware nor unaware, neither sentient nor insentient. "Buddha-nature" is thus a deliberate combination of opposite terms, meaning "the sentience of the neither-sentient-nor-insentient (or both-sentient-and-insentient)":

> Object means the unaware. Buddha means the aware. Ordinary sentient beings possess the principle of unawareness, but lack the wisdom to become aware of the unaware, which is why we temporarily make a distinction between the two, to make them aware of the unaware. But once they are aware of the unaware, it is no longer still unaware. How could the object of awareness be separated from the agent of

awareness? . . . Originally the two are not different, but the ordinary sentient being regards them as separate. Hence we reveal this to sentient beings, to make them aware of the unaware, making awareness and unawareness converge into a single suchness. Hence we know that awareness without unawareness cannot be called the Buddha-nature (subject), and unawareness without awareness cannot be called the dharma-nature (object). If there were no unawareness within awareness, how could it be called the Buddha-nature (subject)? Hence the idea of a dharma-nature (object) without the Buddha-nature (subject) belongs to the lesser vehicle, but in the great vehicle, the dharma-nature (object) is precisely the Buddha-nature (subject).[14]

Here we have moved only as far as the inseparability, perhaps identity, of sentience and insentience. Zhanran presses further toward reversibility in the same work, through a consideration of the intersubjectivity implicit in the Tiantai notion of Asness, the simultaneity of multiple interpretative perspectives on each token of experience. This is taken to imply that the environment too will achieve Buddhahood, eliminating any one-way subjective/objective relationship between the self and things. The subject is as much environment to the things as the things are environment to the subject, so that their mutual regard is always going in both directions. The work more or less opens with the thenceforth oft-repeated formula, "The organisms of the lowest hell, and their entire environment, is located completely within the ultimate sage's own mind, and the body and land of the Buddha do not exceed a single moment of the experience of the lowliest unenlightened being."[15] The specific, qualitative nature of these terms is to be noted. It is not just "the world" that subsumes "the subject," and vice versa. Just as there is no single self, there is no single "world." Rather, each apparently single subjectivity and objectivity entails a multiplicity of alternate worlds, qualitatively distinct from one another. Hence, in this passage, Zhanran indicates the mutual inclusion of the highest value as a token in the constitutive environmental field of the experience of the lowest value, and vice versa. The two value opposites are placed in a mutual regard and embrace where each side completely absorbs the other without remainder. The unenlightened are part of the world of the enlightened, and hence a part of enlightenment, which in omnicentric terms means they *are* enlightenment. Conversely, the enlightened are part of the world of the unenlightened, and hence *are* unenlightenment. At the climax of the same work, in explanation of the *Avatamsaka Sūtra*'s claim that "there is not the slightest difference between one's own mind, all sentient beings and Buddha," Zhanran writes:

My own mind, and each and every sentient being, in every moment of experience without exception, interpenetrates with and mutually enters into the virtues of the Buddha's enlightenment, body and mind, living being and environment, self and others, in perfect equality. I and all other sentient beings equally possess this nature, which is thus called the Buddha-nature. This nature creates everywhere, transforms everywhere, subsumes everywhere. . . . Once it is understood that this nature pervades everywhere without exception, it becomes clear that the result of Buddhahood includes the causal nature of self and other, and equally that my own mind possesses the virtues of the result of Buddhahood. From the point of view of the result, the Buddha-eye and Buddha-wisdom contemplate me, and see only the Buddha's own beginningless self. In the position of the cause (sentient beings), if we see things in occult correspondence with this true vision and true wisdom, we also see that all sentient beings are nothing but Buddha, and there is no other resultant Buddha than this. Thus outside of sentient beings there is no Buddha. . . . Thus when one Buddha attains enlightenment, nothing in the entire Dharmadhatu is not part of this Buddha's constitutive environmental field. The same is true for all Buddhas. Sentient beings are from the beginning within the Buddha's own constitutive environmental field, and yet they give rise to views of difference such that joy and sorrow alternate, and each one thinks it is his own body and environment alone.[16]

Note how the proposition "there is no Buddha but sentient beings" here again hinges on the putative fact that at least one sentient being has attained Buddhahood, on a being initially conceived as "outside" us—indeed, as our most thoroughgoing negation. It is the nonempirical assertion of the existence of Buddhas that itself accounts for the superfluity of Buddhas. We are Buddhas because somewhere, someone attained Buddhahood, which meant seeing us as Buddhas. The Buddha sees us as identical to himself. Casting his eye over the entire universe, he perceives nothing but himself, his own unborn essence, his own constitutive environmental field. He and his environment are not two, and we are part of his environment. By being deluded, we posit the negation of delusion, enlightenment. This is intrinsic to delusion because it is outside it, negates it, as explained above in the exposition of the Three Truths. This perfect negation of delusion that is posited by that delusion has the character of viewing that delusion as an aspect of itself (also because our delusion *lacks* this ability). Ergo, we are the Buddha.[17] Because of the Tiantai doctrine of the nonduality of provisional and ultimate, this proposition is reversible. There is no Buddha but sentient beings, no sentient beings but Buddha. The Buddha sees that we all have the Buddha nature, which means also that each of us shall become a Buddha. What we are doing right now is a *cause* of our future Buddhahood. But Buddhahood is the kind of result that includes its cause (nonduality of cause and effect). From the perspective of that result, we shall look back and see this other who is the sentient being we are right now, and identify with him, and realize that the ignorant karmic activities we are currently engaging in actually turn out, via "opening the provisional to reveal the real," to be stimulus/response acts of the Buddha we have eventually become (who is identical to all the Buddhas of past, present, and future). Hence, there is no Buddha outside the sentient beings who are struggling toward Buddhahood in ignorance and karma-creating confusion.

What must be noted here is that this does not amount to a psychologizing reduction whereby we therefore no longer need any Buddha, since our own mind is Buddha; the fact that our own mind is Buddha, that there is no Buddha outside our own mind of this moment, is constituted by the view of the Buddha—the

Buddha we will become and all the other Buddhas, with whom, needless to say, he is identical. It is indeed true that both mind and Buddha are mind, but it is equally true that both mind and Buddha are Buddha. By being regarded by this Other as identical to that regarding Other, we are constituted as not needing any Other, for this Other is inherent in our own being, as is our being-viewed-by-the-Other. Indeed, there is no self of ours prior to this; we have been intercorporeal from the beginning, and all our self-practice was also interactive. Zhanran's point is to make this intercorporeity irreducible to any one side; as he says earlier in the same work, "Every speck of dust and every mental act anywhere are precisely the nature of the mind of every sentient being and every Buddha. There is no question of any of them belonging to anyone's own mind alone, since all together create them, all together become them, all share in being the same objects of liberative transformation, and all share in performing the same acts of liberative transformation."[18] Each slightest token is a presence in every interpretative world, and indeed is the "center" of each, fully expresses the quiddity of each. This includes being on both sides of every liberative action performed everywhere, and on both sides of the Buddha/deluded sentient being relationship. The Buddha-mind we are to realize, then, is not the one looking out of our eyes at the world, but the one which is looking at us, seeing us as itself, and seeing that we are looking out at the world and also thinking of the Buddha who is thinking of us. The intersubjective moment is crucial and never dispensed with, as is the concept and name "Buddha" as looker who sees us this way, existing in our own minds.[19] It is the thought "Buddha" within our own mind that makes this situation possible. We are to experience the world through the mediation of our being experienced by a Buddha, to see as one who is seen by a Buddha, one who sees himself in what is seen, even in the deluded seeing of others, including their deluded seeing of himself seeing. To a certain degree, then, the use of the word "Buddha" is a self-verifying performative utterance; by entertaining the idea of the existence of such a being viewing us, we see ourselves as seen as he would see us, and our actions thereby become tokens in that alternate semiotic network, which is precisely that in which our own Buddhahood consists.[20]

The full extent of reversibility to which Tiantai writers are willing to take this can be seen in the following passage from Zhanran, where the claim is made that the object sees the subject, just as the subject sees the object:

Q: The *Fahuaxuanyi* says that the object is able to contemplate the subject. Although many scriptures are quoted to prove it, this principle is hard to understand.

A: If we follow the merely upayic teachings, this principle is incomprehensible. But from the point of view of the ultimate teaching, the principle is quite easy to integrate. We take mind itself as the object, while mind is also the subject that is doing the contemplating. Thus subject and object are both mind, and the essence of mind pervades everywhere. Each state of mind reflects on another state of mind—the principle of this is quite clear. Thus at the beginning of the section on the Inconceivable Object it says, "The inconceivable object is itself precisely the subject doing the contemplating." From this we can derive four different but equally accurate descriptions: the object is aware of the object, the object is aware of the subject, the subject is aware of the object, the subject is aware of the subject. As soon as there is any awareness, it is beyond description. But the awareness should be described, and this is beyond what can be completely comprehended by the awareness. Conversely, as soon as there is any description, it is beyond awareness. But the description should become an object of awareness, and this is beyond what can be completely comprehended by the description. Thus it is different from what people of the world normally think of, namely, an inert object as that which we are aware of, and also differs from the idea of a partial, small mind as the subject that contemplates. Nor is it the same as the idea of artificially setting up Suchness as the object of contemplation. These differences applying to the object also apply to the subject—let there be no confusion on this.[21]

We have here another affirmation of the ontological primacy of the phenomenal. Note that it is equally valid to say that the object perceives the subject, the subject the object, the object the object, or the subject the subject; that is, none of these are really final or adequate (globally coherent) descriptions (hence, "As soon as there is any awareness, it is beyond description"), but the distinctively Tiantai move is not to therefore disallow all four descriptions, but rather to allow all four. This is due to the Three Truths ontology outlined above, for which *all* coherence without exception is local coherence/global incoherence. This entails an affirmation of the globally incoherent/locally coherent descriptions; each of this is adequate to different soteriological situations. This is why Zhanran says not only that the experience is beyond description, but also that the description is beyond experience; this is how Tiantai differs from the standard Mahāyāna epistemology that privileges experience over description. Experience is in the same boat as description: both are locally coherent/globally incoherent, necessarily outrunning themselves into the other, verging toward reversibility. At the end of the passage Zhanran again rejects the idea of a pure subject, a pure object, or a pure tertium quid (Suchness) that subtends both; this is the level 4 position, where each and any of the reversible terms is reversibility itself.

Zhanran elaborates on the implications of this position as follows:

Q: The external matter that makes up inanimate beings is not endowed simultaneously with mind. How can it have replete within it the Three Meritorious Properties [Liberation, Wisdom, Dharmakaya], such that you say the Three Meritorious Properties pervade all places?

A: It is not only the external matter that is not simultaneously endowed with mind; the matter inside one's own body is just the same as grass, trees, tiles and bricks. But if we are talking about the inherent entailment of the Meritorious Properties, it is not only the internal mind that is a transformation of the mind. Thus it is said of both the internal mind and external matter that, *because mind is neither internal nor external, matter too is neither internal nor external.* Thus each is both internal and external. Following the purity of the mind, the Buddha-land is pure, and following the purity of the Buddha-land, wisdom is pure. Because both mind and matter are pure, all dharmas are pure. Because all dharmas are pure, mind and body are pure. How can we say only that the external matter lacks mind?[22] (emphasis added)

Both mind and matter are omnipresent—not just the reversibility between the two, not just the chiasmic flesh as a tertium quid, but each of the extremes is itself omnipresent. Each is neither within nor without; each is the entire dharma-realm. However, it will be noted that Zhanran privileges the position of mind in these descriptions. This is done for a purely pragmatic reason. In Buddhist praxis, Zhanran thinks, we begin with the contemplation of our own minds. When that mind—the deluded, temporally arising mind of intentionality—is seen to be neither inside nor outside, this allows for the realization that the same is necessarily true of the object. In terms of praxis, mind is privileged; ontologically, there is equal ultimacy to subject, object, and the chiasm between the two. The Tiantai approach here is in close accord with Merleau-Ponty's understanding of the Husserlian eidetic reduction. As he puts it, "The most important lesson which the reduction teaches us is the impossibility of complete reduction."[23] The phenomenological praxis of the reduction calls for a necessarily doomed attempt to reduce all experience to mind; in fact, the goal of the practice is to show its impossibility, and in the process lead to a reconfigured understanding of what mind itself is, disclosing its inescapable intertwining with world, and finally "wonder in the face of the world." As Zhanran puts it:

Q: All the texts say that mind and matter and nondual. But if we want to contemplate this, how do we set up our contemplation?

A: Mind and matter are one substance; neither precedes the other. *Each is the entire dharma-realm.* But in the sequence of contemplation, we must start with the internal mind. Once the internal mind is purified, this pure mind can encounter all dharmas, and naturally meld with them all perfectly. Moreover, we must first understand that all dharmas are mind-only, and only then begin contemplating the mind. If you can understand all dharmas, you will see *that all dharmas are nothing but mind, and that all dharmas are nothing but matter.* You must understand that everything comes from the mind's own differentiations. When have the dharmas themselves ever declared themselves to be same or different?[24] (emphasis added)

What all this boils downs to is stated succinctly and explicitly by Zhanran's latter-day disciple, Siming Zhili:

Thus we can say that all the sentient beings and all the Buddhas of the past, present and future, throughout the ten directions of space, and also their constituent environments, are the object being contemplating, and also that all the sentient beings and all the Buddhas of the past, present and future, throughout the ten directions of space, and also their constituent environments, are the wisdom as subject doing the contemplating (*neng guan zhi* 能觀智). The object and the wisdom are two names for the same entity. Thus subject and object are two and not two.[25]

It is the world, the self, the intercorporeal flesh that contemplates itself. But even this description is not privileged here: rather, we can equally say *for any experience of anything occurring anywhere or anywhen* that *any* sentient being, *any* object is the contemplator, any is the contemplated; for any of these terms, by the Three Truths, means the whole and the fission of the whole. Zhili further makes clear that even this fact, the "ultimate truth," itself is not exempt from this reversible intertwining. It too is not an inert object to be contemplated, but is another member of the totality of chiasmic entities, simultaneously the contemplated and the contemplator. Reversibility contemplates itself. Reversibility is itself reversible:

> The Real-mark is the Principle of the Middle Way. The entirety of this Principle of the Middle and the Real is the active wisdom that is doing the contemplating, the contemplating wisdom, and this is what is called the Wisdom of the Real-mark. The Real-mark itself is the wisdom; it is not that there is some other wisdom that is given this name because of the object that it reflects upon.[26]

This is why Tiantai writers can assert the absolute reality not only of the whole, not only of the intercorporeal body-world itself, not only reversibility or undecidability as such, but rather of each and every particular thing. Zhanran puts it this way:

> The Real [i.e., Absolute] mind connects to the Real [Absolute] object.
> The Real [Absolute] conditionings are thereby produced in sequence.
> Real pours into Real one after another,
> And naturally one enters the Real Truth.
> To explain this, I say: If the mind connects to the object, then the object necessarily connects to the mind. When mind and object are connected, this is called the Real conditioning. And then again this is done by the following moment of mind, so that one mental event follows another mental event uninterruptedly. This connection between these mental events is called "[One Real after another Real] pouring into one another." This means also the mind pouring into the object, the object pouring into the object, the object pouring into the mind. Each mind, each object, each thought pours into all the others.[27]

Looking back to Merleau-Ponty from the Tiantai position, then, we find a certain hedging in his reversibility thesis. Merleau-Ponty is willing to say, in the famous description of the experience of the painter in "Eye and Mind": "Inevitably the roles between him and the visible are reversed. That is why so many painters have said that things look at them. As Andre Marchand says, after Klee: 'In a forest, I have felt many times over that it was not I who looked at the forest. Some days I felt that the trees were looking at me, were speaking to me. . . . I was there, listening . . . I think that the painter must be penetrated by the universe and not want to penetrate it.'"[28] Merleau-Ponty quotes Marchand's comments approvingly, as an instantiation, it would seem, of his reversibility thesis, at least in the special experience of the painter, who appears here as a kind of spontaneously accomplished phenomenologist, and whose experience is therefore indicative of a larger fact about phenomenal reality as such, even if inaccessible to ordinary experience. But Marchand's formulation seems to privilege one side of the relation—"penetrated by the universe, and not want to penetrate it"—which snags the full sense of reversibility here, granting ultimacy rather to the world-side, which serves as active agent to the passive painter. Merleau-Ponty's own comments cancel this one-sidedness, but only to the point of reverting to his tertium quid, the undecidability of passive and active, of seer and seen: "There really is inspiration and expiration of Being, action and passion so slightly discernible that it becomes impossible to distinguish between what sees and what is seen, what paints and what is painted."[29] This only takes us so far: who is doing the painting may be undecidable, intercorporal, or anonymous, but the *content* of the painting is nonetheless still the object, not the physical body of the painter. One could argue that the painter's embodiment is present in the painting of the trees, but this is still a far cry from the explicit appearing of the body seen by the trees, the body of the painter standing there. This objecthood and visibility is indeed present in Marchand's figure of being penetrated, of being watched; but it remains an abstract visibility, rather than a complete affirmation of this body standing here with a paintbrush, as we would expect on a Tiantai reading. Merleau-Ponty therefore rejects as an absurdity "color that sees itself, surface that touches itself," putting in its place "this paradox: a set of colors and surfaces inhabited by a touch, a vision, hence an *exemplar sensible*, which offers to him who inhabits it and senses it the wherewithal to sense everything that resembles himself on that outside, such that, caught up in the tissue of the things, it draws it entirely to itself, incorporates it, and, with the same movement, communicates to the things upon which it closes over that identity without superposition, that difference without contradiction, that divergence between the within and the without that constitutes its natal secret."[30] This passage is rather obscure, but it appears to be once again granting a sort of ultimacy to "touch, vision, the tissue of things"—that is, intercorporeal flesh itself as "an element," as Merleau-Ponty says elsewhere—as a whole, albeit an open whole, rather than to each individual element of this flesh. We are still wallowing in level 3, the unicentrism of the tertium quid, rather than the omnicentrism of level 4, which would be equally comfortable with "world sees itself," "I see world," or "world sees me," and, more importantly, not just "the world," but "this tree sees me." For the tree, in the Tiantai reading, is simply the world as this tree, the entire reversibility which is the flesh present as this tree—and outside of this tree, there is no other, abstract single "flesh." Merleau-Ponty understandably wants to avoid the implication of the world as subject and the world as object, seeing itself or thinking itself, because he has shown that these terms are untenable. Hence, he wants to replace them with better terms—flesh, reversibility, and chiasm—which allows us to do without these questionable concepts. The Tiantai position is that all conceptions are questionable, some more so and some less so *for any given situation* but none *globally* more so or less so, and thus is able to affirm absolutely the value of the individual percept, the individual perception, the individual perceiver, the individual subject, object, thing, self, and world, *as well as* the neither-nor/both-and that is their intercoiled flesh.

This means that the Tiantai engagement with the tree would suggest that when I see the tree, my seeing discloses not only my preinstallment in the world of the visible, not only the fact that I am visible, and not only the fact that I am perceived; it is not just that seeing is intercoiled with being seen. It is furthermore that seeing the tree is intercoiled with being seen *specifically by this tree*. This is no more transparently knowable or completely fathomable than my own seeing of the tree; it is an invitation to the vague way in which this tree intuits my own body, as whatever blob of warmth and shadow I might imagine a tree might intuit. The reversibility of positions puts me on the other side, usually only for an anonymous split second, in what Merleau-Ponty described as "that quasi-stupor to which we are reduced when we really try to live at the level of sensation," being the tree as it encounters the strange presence of this other, my body. Here Tiantai would take exception to Merleau-Ponty's claim that "I am always on the same side of my own body."[31] Seeing the tree is being the tree, because neither the being nor the seeing are ever completable. Seeing the tree discloses the view of myself from the side of the tree, the specific clearing in the flesh of the world that stands over there as tree. This groping apprehension of how a tree might see me is strictly correlative to my own groping apprehension of the tree, which is my own never-completable seeing of the tree—and indeed, my own groping and incomplete apprehension of myself. This means that seeing the tree puts me in the position of the tree, which at the same time calls forth an unendable series of other specific views on my own body, on the tree, on trees, and on the flesh itself—what Tiantai writers call "the three thousand." The difference is that for Tiantai seeing, since it is by definition seeing-as, discloses not just visibility in general, but an expanding dissemination of every possible "visible-as," how I, in my seeing, am seeable from every other possible perspective. My visibility is exposed not just to the all, but to the all and also to each, and these singularities, although never separable, are also never collapsible into an overarching synordinate oneness that would be described in one way, even in an artfully intertwined manner as a multifarious flesh. The centering of all being, coincident with the incompletion of this centering, is going on everywhere, not just in the overarching theoretical apprehension of the flesh; for each converging center, I am a different periphery. My own multifariousness is revealed by the multifariousness of the world I see, the multifariousness of the perspectives from which I am always being seen. It is not just the flesh that sees me, just as it is not just the flesh that I see. I see specifically this tree, and it is specifically this tree that sees me. This tree is the flesh, and, for Tiantai omnicentrism, there is no flesh outside this tree.

However, the editors of Merleau-Ponty's manuscript indicate that he has inserted a passage that seems to indicate some wavering on this question of whether a color can see itself and so on: "One can say that we perceive the things themselves, that we are the world that thinks itself—or that the world is at the heart of our flesh."[32] Here, in the bold affirmation of the full implications of the reversibility thesis, and the second-order reversibility between various levels of description, we find Merleau-Ponty perhaps moving closer to the Tiantai position—and it is gratifying to think that these were perhaps the last words he ever wrote on the subject, showing a greater willingness to embrace this absurdity. But for a Tiantai thinker, it is still not enough to say that the world thinks itself in us; this is still too unicentric, and privileges one description over all others. The multifariousness pertains not only to seeing, but also to saying, calling forth all beings not only as all incompletable experiences but as all incompletable descriptions. Each thing thinks the world in me, each thing thinks each thing in me, each thought makes the being of each thing in that thing and in each thought, each thought makes the being of each thought in each thought and each thing, and so on. I see. I say. I am seen. I am said. The world sees me. The world says me. Each thing in the world not only sees me, but says me. The lamp on the table sees me. The lamp on the table says me.

4

The Human Body as a Boundary Symbol

A Comparison of Merleau-Ponty and Dōgen

Carl Olson

In the Pali texts of the Theravāda Buddhist tradition and in many Mahāyāna Buddhist texts, one can find numerous negative references to the human body. There are, of course, exceptions in the Buddhist tradition, especially if one takes into consideration Buddhist Tantra and the significance of the body in Buddhist meditation. Western philosophy, on the other hand, is infamous for its mind/body dualism. Dōgen and Merleau-Ponty tend to be exceptions, although not necessarily the only examples, to the prevalent tendencies of their respective philosophical traditions. The human body, for Dōgen, is not a hindrance to the realization of enlightenment; it rather serves as the vehicle through which enlightenment is realized by the aspirant. Dōgen argues that those aspiring to become enlightened strive with their bodies, practice seated meditation with their bodies, understand with their bodies, and attain enlightenment with their bodies. Thus the body attains a metaphysico-religious status in Dōgen's thought.[1] Using the phenomenological method in his earlier work, Merleau-Ponty wants to deliver a fatal blow to the historical tradition of philosophical dualism and overcome it.

The intention of this chapter is to bring these two thinkers together to engage in a philosophical dialogue on the human body. A comparative philosophical dialogue has several benefits. It can help us to see not only the similarities and differences in the respective positions of philosophers, but it can also enable us to comprehend the value of philosophical insights foreign to our own tradition. It thus involves us in a comparative realm of meaning, places us spatially between Eastern and Western traditions, transcends the historical time that separates philosophers, provides us with a possible common ground on which to understand each other, and sets us on the path to truth, which emerges in the dialogic exchange between thinkers who share similar human problems and concerns. If the philosophical dialogue retains a posture of expectant openness, the dialogic participants can teach us, for instance, something about the human body. As the comparative dialogue unfolds, each thinker should be understood to be engaged in a mutual search for the truth. When thoughts are compared they must not become isolated, static intellectual concepts. They must rather remain alive, open, dynamic, and potentially creative ideas. A comparative dialogue possesses the advantage of widening our own horizons by enabling us to participate in the philosophical tradition of another culture. By means of comparative dialogue, the subjects and ourselves are drawn together into a common human culture, which enhances the opportunities for authentic dialogue, sharing of common roots and problems, and new agreement and understanding about a common problem.

This chapter will bring together Dōgen and Merleau-Ponty on the problem of the human body in a comparative dialogue. With relation to the latter thinker, I will concentrate my attention on his earlier work *The Phenomenology of Perception* and his later work *The Visible and the Invisible* only to the extent that it throws light on his understanding of the body. Due to Merleau-Ponty's extensive discussion of the human body a certain amount of selectivity seems necessary in a brief chapter.

BODY AND WORLD

When discussing the body, Merleau-Ponty is not referring to an object or a mere physical entity.[2] The body cannot be comprehended by measuring its properties, the causal relations among its parts, or its causal relation to other such entities, nor can it be reduced to an object, which is sensitive to certain stimuli. If it is not a thing that can be measured, is it a thought? It is neither object nor subject. It is, however, subject and object. The human body is a lived body; it is mine. Since the body is primarily my body, it is personal, subjective, objective, and inhabited by an intentionality that enables it to express meaning.

For Dōgen, the body is both subject and object, and more. What does Dōgen mean by more? Dōgen answers: "What we call the body and mind in the Buddha Way is grass, trees and wall rubble; it is wind, rain, water and fire."[3] Since the mind is all things and vice versa, everything represents a single and total body. There is an important consequence of Dōgen's position: "If your own body and mind are not grass, wood, and so on, then they are not your own body and mind. And if your own body and mind do not exist, neither do grass and wood."[4] Therefore, the body and mind represent the entire world. Consequently, human beings are not separated from the world by their bodies. In fact, no one can be absolutely certain where one's body terminates and where precisely the world begins, and vice versa.

To have a body means, for Merleau-Ponty, that one is involved in a definite environment, because our body is our vehicle for being in the world.[5] Although the body is to be distinguished from the world it is our medium for having a world and for interacting with it. If to be a body means to be tied to a certain world, being a body involves being in the world, a primordial form of existence, which is preobjective. The body is not in space in the same sense that water is in a vase, because the body is a point from which space radiates and around which things arrange themselves in an orderly way. Since the body is both being-in-itself and being-for-itself, the spatiality of the body indicates that it is itself the author of space, the low and high, the far and near. If the world possesses spatiality for me, it is because I inhabit it by means of my body, which involves a dynamic, living relationship and not a conceptual relation. The spatiality of the body is not a position; it is rather a situation, because existence includes space and time in this primordial relation to the world.[6]

Dōgen agrees that the body includes space and time and occupies a situation. Somewhat analogous to what Merleau-Ponty intends to state in his philosophy is Dōgen's use of the image of a bright pearl to express reality.

> One bright pearl communicates directly through all time; being through all the past unexhausted, it arrives through all the present. Where there is a body now, a mind now, they are the bright pearl. That stalk of grass, this tree, is not a stalk of grass, is not a tree; the mountains and rivers of this world are not the mountains and rivers of this world. They are the bright pearl.[7]

Dōgen, like Merleau-Ponty, states that the human body participates in the external world. In fact, the mind, body, and things of the world interpenetrate one another without the possibility of a lucid demarcation among them. As we will see, this nondualistic position is similar to what Merleau-Ponty calls the flesh.

According to Merleau-Ponty, the human body and the perceived world form a single system of intentional relations;[8] they are correlations, which implies that to experience the body is to perceive the world and vice versa. Since the body is the medium of things, its presence to the world enables things to exist.[9] Thus the body and world are an inseparable, internal relation.

The body and world are also inseparably interconnected for Dōgen. Like everything else, the body is dynamic, a position with which Merleau-Ponty would concur. For Dōgen, life is analogous to riding in a boat in which the voyager uses its sails and tiller to guide and move one to his destination. Although the sailor can perform certain tasks to assist him in his journey, it is the boat that carries him. Even though the boat is the sailor's mode of transportation, it is he who makes it a boat, which becomes a world for the sailor: "It is for this reason that life is what I make to exist, and I is what life makes me. In boarding the boat, one's body and mind and the entire surrounding environment are all the boat's dynamic working; both the entire earth and all space are the boat's dynamic working."[10] Thus the body, mind, and world are nondual and dynamic.

When I experience my body, according to Merleau-Ponty, an ambiguous mode of existing is revealed to me because the traditional distinctions between object and subject are called into question. I can, for instance, touch an object with my right hand, and my right hand can be touched by my left hand. Ceasing to be a sensing subject, my right hand becomes a sensed object. Thus the body possesses the ability to turn back on itself and take itself for its own object, manifesting its ability to be for itself (subject) and in itself (object). Thus the body can be both touched and touching.

Since the experience of one's body reveals an ambiguous mode of existing, which is especially true in sexual experience,[11] Merleau-Ponty attempts to overcome this ambiguity of the body by turning to ontology in his later work. *The Visible and the Invisible* represents an attempt, although it is an incomplete work, to discern the metaphysical structure of the body. What Merleau-Ponty calls the flesh, an opening of being or wild being, is not a fact or a collection of facts; it is neither matter nor spirit. The flesh represents an element,[12] an essential element, which enters into the composition of everything and thus appears in everything; it makes everything be what it is. As an element, flesh is the style of all things and appears in everything and everywhere, but it does not itself appear. Thus there is an underlying unity between an individual, a lived body, and the world because both are flesh.[13] In other words, beneath the apparent duality of consciousness and object lies "wild being," which entails that humans are mixed in with being and gathered up with things into a fabric of being.

BODY AND CONSCIOUSNESS

The body and consciousness, for Merleau-Ponty, are interrelated because the latter is dependent on the body, although consciousness is not reducible to the body. Thus consciousness is incarnate for Merleau-Ponty, a position with which Dōgen agrees because he affirms that the body participates in an individual's inner world. Merleau-Ponty refers to the tacit *cogito*, a prereflective, silent consciousness, an intentional operative, which supports reflective consciousness, forming the basis of all evidence and certainty that originates in the act of perception and not the prior correspondence of consciousness with itself.[14] In other words, the certainty of perception is the certainty of being present to the world, to be conscious that something appears to me. This beginning consciousness represents a primitive self-consciousness, which is simultaneous with the consciousness of the world. Consciousness, an opening upon the world, mutually implies the world because its ultimate correlate is the world and vice versa.[15] Due to the fact that consciousness is conscious of something other than itself, it is able to be conscious of itself. Thus, consciousness can possess itself only by belonging to the world.[16]

This line of reasoning is a trap or a dead end for Dōgen. Rather than a consciousness of the world and rather than an intentional consciousness, which originates in perception, Dōgen wants to go beyond intentional thinking to nonthinking (J. *hishiryō*), a simple acceptance of ideas without affirming or denying them.

Nonthinking is more fundamental than the prereflective, silent consciousness of Merleau-Ponty. It unites thinking, an intentional weighting of ideas, and unthinking, a negation of mental acts, and possesses no purpose, form, object, or subject. Nonthinking, the pure presence of things as they are, is realized in *zazen* (seated meditation)[17] and is a "thinking" of the unthinkable or emptiness. There is importantly, however, no bifurcation of the body and mind in the state of nonthinking.

Communication between consciousness and the world is possible, according to Merleau-Ponty, due to the body, the third aspect of the dialectic of existence. The body functions as the mediator of consciousness and world; it opens them up to each other in the sense that the body forms the immediacy of the world by placing consciousness in direct and immediate contact with the world.[18] Thus there is a dependency of consciousness on the body and expression in speech, a means by which consciousness stabilizes itself. If thought, the product of consciousness, is dependent on perceptible expression grounded in a lived body, then it is fundamentally temporal and historically conditioned.[19]

Dōgen argues that the human body is the ground from which consciousness evolves. Since the body and consciousness penetrate each other and are inextricably interwoven, they are nondual: "You should know that the Buddha-dharma from the first preaches that body and mind are not two, that substance and form are not two."[20] Although the mind ultimately transcends them, it is both subject and object; it is consciousness and nonconsciousness.

BODY AND PERCEPTION

A theory of the body presupposes, for Merleau-Ponty, a theory of perception. If one presupposes that to see the world means to be situated so that objects can show themselves, and that to perceive the world one must dwell within it, then one perceives an object when one inhabits it. Merleau-Ponty writes: "My body is the fabric into which all objects are woven, and it is, at least in relation to the perceived world, the general instrument of my 'comprehension.'"[21] Human perception of world and its objects is contingent upon the lived body. Therefore, perception is embodied for Merleau-Ponty and also for Dōgen, who writes about seeing forms and hearing sounds with the body and mind.[22] Merleau-Ponty states that one perceives with one's body, which implies that the position and movement of one's body not only allows one to see, but also determines what is accessible to one's view, since one can see no more than what one's perspective grants.[23] If one loses an arm or a leg, not only is one's world altered, but one's perception of the world is changed due to the contingency of one's perception on one's body.

In contrast to Merleau-Ponty, Dōgen emphasizes what is important to perceive is not simply objects that appear, but rather Buddha-nature, which represents both beings and being itself. The individual does not necessarily have to do anything special to perceive Buddha-nature because he should simply be attentive to ordinary temporal condition. However, what is to be perceived does not refer to the perceiver or that which is to be perceived. There is neither a correct nor an incorrect way to see. It is just *seeing*. This type of perceiving refers neither to my own seeing nor to the seeing of another: "It is 'Look! temporal condition!' It is transcendence of condition."[24] It is simply seeing Buddha-nature in a flash without conditions, without intention, and without duality.

As a perceiving being, one finds oneself, according to Merleau-Ponty, in a particular situation, which entails being intertwined with a body, an object, and other individuals within a general milieu. A given situation refers to a sedimented situation, "which enables us to rely on our concepts and acquired judgments as we might on things there in front of us, presented globally, without there being any need for us to resynthesize them."[25] The result enables situations to become immediately familiar to us, which means that sediments are closely interrelated in the form of a schema of sedimented structures.[26] This fact possesses three important implications: (1) since a sensation can be sensed only by means of a structure, a sensation is only possible if it is a certain type, (2) every type of sensation is closely related to every other type of sensation to form a unified schema of sensory structures, and (3) if sensations are structural, they are meaningful.[27]

In his later work, Merleau-Ponty argues that the body can prevent perception, even though one needs it to perceive. It is not entirely one's body that perceives because it is built around a perception that dawns through the body. Thus perception emerges in the recess of a body.[28] The body is a perceptible reality, which can perceive itself, become visible for itself, and become tangible to itself because it can touch itself. For the body to actualize the possibility of becoming a perceiving perceptible is to realize a potentiality, which is inherent in the being of the world.[29] Beneath the perceiver and perceived or toucher and touched—a crisscrossing—is a shared, preestablished harmony, which takes place within the individual forming an underlying unity of perception.

The body actualizes itself and achieves a preestablished harmony, for Dōgen, in the process of *zazen*, which is not entering into realization, but is already realization even when one begins to sit.[30] *Zazen* is a fundamental form of spiritual life; it represents the nonthinking mode of consciousness where body and mind are cast off[31] and one takes a leap to enlightenment. By casting off body and mind, one severs one's defiled thoughts, which originate in one's discriminating consciousness.[32] To advocate casting off body and mind, Dōgen does not mean that one should reject one's body. He wants to affirm that one should not be attached to the body. He still recognizes that the path to realization is through the body.

An assertion that Merleau-Ponty does not make because he adheres to his phenomenological convictions[33]—even though he recognizes that the body is material and spiritual—is that the body can manifest the absolute. Even though Dōgen acknowledges the impermanent nature of the body and the necessity of the aspirant for enlightenment to become detached from his body, he asserts that the body manifests Buddha-nature, beings and being itself. Dōgen writes: "The

Buddha-body is the manifesting body, and there is always a body manifesting Buddha-nature."[34] This revealing is at the same time a concealing, because Buddha-nature eludes the grasp of knowledge. By the power of the Buddha-nature to subsume and transcend existence and nonexistence, the manifesting of Buddha-nature by the body negates the body and transcends it. Thus, to grasp the essence of the body truly is intuitively to grasp emptiness, the dynamic and creative aspect of Buddha-nature.

TIME AND BODY

Just as the body inhabits space, it also dwells in time for Merleau-Ponty. Like a work of art that is indistinguishable from the existence that expresses it, the body inhabits time, and its temporality is indistinguishable from it.[35] In a sense, within my body I am time: "My body takes possession of time; it brings into existence a past and a future for a present; it is not a thing, but creates time instead of submitting to it."[36] The primordial significance of the body is to be discovered on the preobjective level of experience—not as a mere object among other objects, but rather as radically temporal. Thus the essential intentionality of the body is its temporality, which is also its being.[37]

Dōgen's position on this point is remarkably similar to that of Merleau-Ponty. Our body and mind are time, for Dōgen, just as all dharmas (things) are manifestations of being-time (*uji*): "Entire being, the entire world, exists in the time of each and every now."[38] Thus the mind, body, being, world, and time form a unity. Not only are entities time, and not only is time in me, but activities are time: "As self and other are both times, practice and realization are times; entering the mud, entering the water, is equally time."[39]

The unity of time is manifested most lucidly for Dōgen, when applied to Buddha-nature, whose being is time itself, a position diametrically opposed to that of Merleau-Ponty: "As the time right now is all there ever is, each being-time is without exception entire time."[40] Within the Buddha-nature, both future and past signify the present. Dōgen emphasizes the now moment because there is never a time that has not been or a time that is coming. Dōgen writes: "[A]ll is the immediate presencing here and now of being-time."[41] Thus time is a continuous occurrence of "nows." This position has important consequences for Dōgen's philosophy, because Buddha-nature is not a potentiality to be actualized in the future, but it is a present actuality. In other words, every moment of illusion and enlightenment contains all reality.[42] Therefore, Buddha-nature is both illusion and enlightenment.

Time, a transitional synthesis of the world, is literally, for Merleau-Ponty, the presence of the world in which the multiple ways of being in the world are gathered together and dispersed. The present moment contains both past and future; although they are never wholly present, past and future spring forth when one reaches out toward them. In fact, the body unites time. Merleau-Ponty writes: "In every focusing movement my body unites present, past and future, it secretes time, or rather it becomes that location in nature where, for the first time, events, instead of pushing each other into the realm of being, project round the present a double horizon of past and future and acquire a historical orientation."[43] Just as space enables one to be present to others, time makes it possible to be mutually present to other beings. In contrast to Merleau-Ponty's position, Dōgen denies the continuity of time because each instant of time is independent and distinct of every other moment of time.[44] The discontinuity of time means, for Dōgen, that each point of time is independent of each other moment of time.[45] Present time, for example, cannot be conceived as a linear, evolutionary process. Each moment of time—past, present, or future—is distinct from every other, whereas Merleau-Ponty argues that past and future are supported by an objective present. Since each moment of time constitutes a discrete reality for Dōgen, all moments are lived times. Dōgen asserts that time does not pass because in one moment all time is viewed simultaneously.[46] Consequently, the past is retrievable, the future is not beyond grasp, and the present is not merely transient. Rather than being a form of bondage, time becomes an opportunity for human creativity and transformation. Merleau-Ponty agrees with Dōgen by referring to the ecstatic character of temporality, which implies that one can reach out beyond the present into the past and future time.

To inhabit space and time, according to Merleau-Ponty, is to encounter other bodies in a common world. My body and other bodies form a system of competing or cooperative intersubjective beings. My body perceives the body of another person and recognizes that it possesses the same structure as my body: "Henceforth, as the parts of my body together comprise a system, so my body and the other person's are one whole, two sides of one and the same phenomenon, and the anonymous existence of which my body is the ever-renewed trace henceforth inhabits both bodies simultaneously."[47] Dōgen would be sympathetic to Merleau-Ponty's position to a certain extent. Just as there is no separation between body and mind for Dōgen, there is no division between oneself and others in the state of nonthinking, since isolation from others only arises upon reflection.[48] Dōgen expresses the unity of being and time as follows: "[T]he *time* has to *be* in me. Inasmuch as I am there, it cannot be that time passes away."[49] Again, "'Time being' means time, just as it is, is being, and being is all time."[50] The common denominator of being and time is impermanence,[51] which is characteristic of all existence. Dōgen argues that Buddha-nature is impermanent; it is that aspect which eternally comes into being and passes out of being. Dōgen's nondualistic equation of being and time results in a radical temporalization of existence and a radical existentialization of time.[52]

Although time is immeasurable, intangible, and elusive, both thinkers radically temporalize being, oppose a quantitative view of time, see time as a lived reality, and propose a nondualistic equation of being and time and body and time. Merleau-Ponty disagrees, however, with Dōgen's contention that things and events of the universe are time. This position leads Dōgen to a nondualistic assertion that mountains, oceans, pine trees, and everything else are time.[53] The universe, for Dōgen, is not something fixed and motionless; it is a being in time.

METHOD AND REALITY

To alleviate any possible mistaken impression that Merleau-Ponty and Dōgen are in total philosophical agreement with respect to their thinking about the lived body, it could prove useful to indicate briefly some of their major distinctions with respect to their methodology and understanding of reality, since there are considerable philosophical differences between them.

The phenomenological method of Merleau-Ponty is an attempt to grasp what is or what appears to be one's perception. By attempting to grasp what is fundamental to one's experience of the world, the phenomenologist is akin to an archeologist, who must often dig deep to discover the artifacts of a civilization. Just as the archeologist returns to the artifacts of a civilization in order to understand it, so the phenomenologist returns to the things themselves, which is to return to that world that precedes knowledge.[54] Once the phenomenologist makes a discovery, or once something appears to one, it is essential that one describes what appears to one without constituting it. "The real has to be described, not constructed or formed," Merleau-Ponty writes.[55] When a thing appears, there must be something to which it appears. This something is consciousness, which for Husserl is the fundamental structure—intentionality—of consciousness, but its major function, for Merleau-Ponty, is to reveal the world as present. Thus Merleau-Ponty widens the concept of intentionality to include consciousness, the world, and our relationship to others. For Merleau-Ponty, intentionality constitutes a preconscious, preobjective, and dialectical ontological relationship. When we penetrate into our existence we discover our fusion with the world and others.

When things appear to our consciousness we must stand back and not prejudge these appearances. This does not mean that we bracket out the world or refrain from any judgment, because nothing would appear to consciousness if the world were held in suspension: "The world is not an object such that I have in my possession the law of its making; it is the natural setting of, and field for, all my thoughts and all my explicit perceptions."[56] The world and the one who perceives it cannot be separated from each other. Thus reflection is not an introspection accomplished by an isolated self; it represents an extrospection, a reestablishing of one's direct contact with the world in which one finds oneself and things interrelated in the world, a system in which all truths cohere. Therefore, Merleau-Ponty does not find a place in his thought for Husserl's eidetic reduction, a method used to capture the facts in their primordial uniqueness, a provisional character imposed on us by the nature of language,[57] but is rather trying to grasp the living stream of existence. One does not think the world; rather, one lives through the world, is open to it, does not doubt one's communication with it, and recognizes that one does not possess it.[58]

In contrast to Merleau-Ponty, the primary method for Dōgen is *zazen* (motionless sitting in meditation). The practice of *zazen* is one's passport to freedom: "To sit crosslegged is to make a leap straightaway transcending the entire world and find oneself exceedingly sublime within the quarters of the Buddhas and patriarchs."[59] Thus *zazen* is not a practice prior to enlightenment; it is rather practice based on enlightenment: "It is entering into realization."[60] Since there is no distinction between acquired and original enlightenment and since practice and realization are identical, *zazen* is not the cause of enlightenment. *Zazen* enables one to cast off body and mind. Thereby one is able to sever disordered thoughts emanating from one's discriminating consciousness.[61] Egoism is overcome, and all is emptiness.

It does not necessarily follow, for Dōgen, that an aspirant should cease practicing *zazen* upon gaining enlightenment. On the contrary, *zazen* must be continued because awakening must continually be confirmed in seated meditation.[62] When the moment of enlightenment dawns for the aspirant, there is a simultaneous attainment of the way (J. *dōji-jōdō*). An important implication of this position is that once one gains enlightenment, everything in the universe attains enlightenment simultaneously.[63]

The essential art of *zazen* consists of thinking of not-thinking, which is accomplished by nonthinking.[64] One must cease the following: involvement in worldly affairs, all movements of the conscious mind, and making distinctions. The aspirant must simply sit silently and immobile and think of nonthinking, which is the essence of *sammai* (S. *samādhi*: concentration). Nonthinking, a mode beyond thinking and unthinking, functions by realizing both thinking and unthinking.[65] It is thinking of emptiness, a thinking of the unthinkable, which implies that nonthinking is objectless, subjectless, formless, goalless, and purposeless. There is nothing comparable to Dōgen's position in Merleau-Ponty's philosophy.

The methods of both thinkers are radically different, although their methods share an experiential emphasis and foundation. The method of Merleau-Ponty enables him to elucidate a bodily scheme that operates within its own field of existence. In a more radical way, Dōgen's method, which leads to a state of nonthinking, involves somatic transformations of one's body, enabling one to achieve a true human body (J. *shinjitsu nintai*), which is an expression of Buddha-nature. Furthermore, for Merleau-Ponty, philosophy, an interrogative approach to problems grounded in history, does not provide final answers. Dōgen's method does provide final answers because it enables one to realize Buddha-nature, reality itself.

Buddha-nature, for Dōgen, is neither a process nor an entity. It is not something to be achieved; it already is. Dōgen modifies a famous passage from the *Mahāparinirvāṇa Sutra*: "All sentient beings possess the Buddha-nature without exception." The Buddha-nature is not a potentiality possessed by sentient beings.

It is rather all-inclusive in the sense that it includes both sentient and insentient beings. Since Dōgen equates all existence and sentient beings, the Buddha-nature includes plant life, animal life, and the inanimate world.[66] The Buddha-nature is, however, the possession of neither sentient nor insentient beings; it is beings and being itself. The absolute inclusiveness of the Buddha-nature does not imply that it is immanent in all existences; rather, all existences are immanent in it.[67]

Although Buddha-nature already exists for Dōgen, in contrast, Merleau-Ponty thinks that philosophy is an act of bringing truth into being and not a reflection on some preexisting truth or reason, because the only preexistent *Logos* is the world itself.[68] It is the duty of philosophy to bring the world into visible existence. Thus philosophy, for Merleau-Ponty, is the art of relearning to perceive the world. Philosophy must reject any idea of eternal truths, refuse to speculate about the absolute, and acknowledge that it cannot become an absolute knowledge. Since rationality is contingent, and since we cannot experience nor have access to eternal truths, we must refuse to strive to know that which is impossible to grasp, although it can be admitted that we, as lived bodies within the world, are condemned to meaning.

BODY, LIMITATION, AND BOUNDARY SYMBOL

In conclusion one can ask: What does the philosophical dialogue on the body by Merleau-Ponty and Dōgen teach us? These thinkers help us understand that the individual is capable of expressing himself in language, exercising freedom, intuiting, and thinking; none of these activities of the individual are possible without a body. Therefore, to be a human being is to be embodied, which entails being pretheoretically and precognitively "with" things and others or in the midst of objects and other embodied beings. Even though we may experience the body as a biological and physical organism, it is fundamentally the locus for one's life and experience. Without reviewing the significant differences of their respective positions, we can say that both thinkers arrive at very similar positions at several points, using, oddly enough, very different methodologies: phenomenology for Merleau-Ponty and seated meditation for Dōgen. Although their methods are different, both thinkers have placed us in a comparative realm of meaning concerning the human body.

In order to avoid a static result for our dialogue, I want briefly to take the problem of the body in a slightly different direction without claiming that Merleau-Ponty or Dōgen would necessarily agree with the following comments. I not only experience the body as mind, but, just as fundamentally, I recognize my body as radically other than me.[69] If I can recognize that I am both my body and that I am also not my body, this realization expresses that I am radically limited by my body, which irrevocably determines my life by its limitations. In the sense of potential frustration, anguish, pain, fear, dread, and death, I am at the mercy of my body.[70]

One does not have to be a medical student to know that there are bodily processes over which I have no control, which indicates that the body possesses a biological life of its own. Since my body is a temporal and biological process, it can proceed without my being aware of it, although Merleau-Ponty and Dōgen want to make us aware of our bodies and their philosophical significance.

Dōgen would agree to some extent with Merleau-Ponty when he states "the body can symbolize existence because it brings it into being and actualizes it."[71] The body, although it is observable, is the hidden form of our being. As an expression of total existence, the body expresses a unity. Bodily actions are gestures of humans which are not mere signs; they are symbols of themselves and express significance and meaning beyond themselves.

Even though human beings are rooted in time and the world, their bodies symbolize transcendence of biological and natural existence. To be in the world and to be at the mercy of unseen biological forces of the body represents a human limitation. Although humans experience their incarnation as a limitation, this experience is already an overcoming of this limitation.[72] Thus the body restricts our freedom and affirms it.

Just as the dialogue between Merleau-Ponty and Dōgen takes place on the boundary of Eastern and Western philosophy, our body is a boundary symbol, which expresses that we are on the border of freedom and bondage. Our incarnation points to our ambiguous situation. As embodied beings, we are not totally free nor are we entirely bound. Our embodiment affords us the possibility of freedom, an absence of inhibiting coercion, and a capacity for continual creativity. A person on the boundary eludes normal classification and structure. Such a person overcomes, at least potentially, sexual distinction, the cosmic rhythms of life and death, the spatial polarities of here and there, the temporal polarities of past and future, the ethical opposition between good and evil, the dichotomy of human relationships, and the ordinary distinction between body and self. Such a boundary person seems to be an ideal candidate for an intercultural, philosophical dialogue. One's "betweenness" affords one the freedom to listen to both sides and decide for oneself.

II

SPACE: THINKING AND BEING IN THE CHIASM OF VISIBILITY

5

The Double

Merleau-Ponty and Chinul on Thinking and Questioning

Jin Y. Park

The last lecture course Maurice Merleau-Ponty taught before his death in 1961 was titled "Philosophy and Nonphilosophy since Hegel." In the opening paragraph of the lecture notes for the course, Merleau-Ponty wrote: "No battles occur between philosophy and its adversaries. Rather what happens is that philosophy seeks to be philosophy while remaining non-philosophy. . . . True philosophy scoffs at philosophy, since it is aphilosophical."[1] This short passage raises a series of questions regarding the nature of philosophy Merleau-Ponty had in mind at the time. Who or what are the adversaries of philosophy to which Merleau-Ponty refers in this passage and what kind of philosophy is it that becomes true to itself only by being the other of itself? The inside of philosophy is moving toward its outside in search for its true self, and, through self-denial, philosophy comes to be its own. In the notes, Merleau-Ponty identifies this "nonphilosophy" as "negative philosophy" in the sense of "negative theology." He further states, "'Negative philosophy' has access to the absolute, not as 'beyond,' as a positive second order, but as another order which must be on this side, the double—inaccessible without being passed through."[2]

The paradoxical definition of philosophy is indicative of Merleau-Ponty's proposal for a new direction for philosophy, the nature of which is well articulated in his later works, but which is also laid out in his early works. In his posthumous publications, *The Visible and the Invisible* and *The Prose of the World*, Merleau-Ponty repeatedly returns to the theme of the dichotomy between body and mind, subject and object, and transcendental idealism and empirical realism as they are expressed in the philosophy of reflection and the objectivism of science. Reflective philosophy envisions a subject who plays a purely active role in his understanding of the world. The subject in this case is understood as a meaning-giving entity to a passive reality. Scientific objectivism, on the other hand, espouses a passive role for the subject in an inquiry into the world and being. Merleau-Ponty rejects both essentialist subjectivism and scientific objectivism and proposes a philosophy that reveals the inevitable intertwining of binary opposites. For Merleau-Ponty, the "intertwining" of the opposites is the "double" that philosophy needs to "pass through," not "go beyond," in order to reach truth. This double, which does not exist as a separate reality, but which is here and now, is, for Merleau-Ponty, the phenomenal reality through which, and only through which, the absolute appears; "the absolute would not be absolute if it did not appear as absolute," writes Merleau-Ponty.[3] This appearance is "not an effect of the absolute, but the absolute itself," declares Merleau-Ponty.[4] Phenomena, which can be reduced to neither the reflection of subjectivism nor the objectivism of science, are "the whole truth" for Merleau-Ponty. This horizontal reality, which is the double, but which does not allow dualism, leads Merleau-Ponty's philosophy in particular, and what may be called nonsubstantialist philosophy in general, to a search for a new medium to reach the reality. The major project of Zen Buddhism shares with Merleau-Ponty in its approach to reality and understanding of the nature of reality. The basic Zen promise that the sentient being is the Buddha is a declaration of the "double" as the fundamental reality in the path of one's awakening. How one makes this "double"—of the absolute and the phenomena for Merleau-Ponty, and of the sentient being and awakened reality for the Zen Buddhist—reveal itself and how the subject lives through it, are issues that both Merleau-Ponty and the Zen Buddhist need to clarify.

In *The Visible and the Invisible*, Merleau-Ponty addresses the problem of subjectivism in the sections "Reflection and Interrogation" and "Interrogation and Dialectic." In these sections, he criticizes Cartesian *cogito* for defining existence solely from the subject's analytic reflection. Merleau-Ponty states that in Cartesian subjectivism, the world is transformed into "being-thought" and is speculated upon as a neutral entity which subjectivity, the "I" qua "thought," constructs through reflection. The world and beings, understood in this manner, turn into fixed entities in a vacuum state, and so is time that is put on hold, with no influence on beings that exist in the world. Meaning is constructed through the working of *cogito*, which resides inside a vacuum, or in the Augustinian "inner man" (*l'homme intérieur*), within whom resides the truth of the self, the world, and the real. For Merleau-Ponty, however, there is no inner man; this is because "in the world and only in the world does he know himself."[5] The world, for Merleau-Ponty, is not an object that the subject can possess through the construction of *cogito* but a natural setting that constantly makes contact with beings.

Merleau-Ponty declares that the philosophy of reflection has committed a threefold error by reducing the subject, the world, and others into thought-beings when they are in fact defined by their "openness upon the world" (*ouverture au monde*). The philosophy that negates the fundamental existential reality of the subject, the world, and others, Merleau-Ponty contends, is "untrue to the visible world, to him who sees it, and to his relations with other 'visionaries.'"[6] Merleau-

Ponty writes: "[W]e reproach the philosophy of reflection not only for transforming the world into a noema, but also for distorting the being of the reflecting 'subject' by conceiving it as 'thought'—and finally for rendering unthinkable its relations with other 'subjects' in the world that is common to them."[7] Merleau-Ponty's criticism against reflective philosophy, summarized here, can be put into a broader scope of criticism against substantialism upon which reflective philosophy anchors itself. By substantializing a being as thought that exists independently as an unchanging essence, reflective philosophy forecloses reciprocity in a being's relation with the world and others. Reciprocity, for Merleau-Ponty, however, is not one option in a being's life, but existence itself.

Merleau-Ponty contends that the problem of substantialism and subjectivism in reflective philosophy is visible even in the project of dialectics, despite its initial promise: dialectics identifies itself through multilayered movements of the parties involved in the movements and thus emphasizes their reciprocal and interactive relationship. For Merleau-Ponty, the history of dialectics, however, has shown that its initial promise has never been realized. The line between subject and object has never been erased by the dialectical movement, other than in the movements in which the subject takes the initiative by acting upon the object and conquering it. Instead of allowing for interactions of opposites, and maintaining multilevel opposites and reversals within them, the dialectical movement itself becomes a "pure identity of the opposites."[8] As with reflective philosophy, by substantializing and absolutizing the distinction between opposites, the dialectic makes it impossible to accept the "plurality of the relationships" among the factors involved in dialectical movement. Whether it be that of Hegel or Sartre, Merleau-Ponty contends, in dialectics opposites remain as opposites, as alternatives, instead of being participants in the self-critical movements of the dialectic. By so doing, the dialectic becomes an "explicative principle," "signification," "thesis," or "things said," and eventually "almost someone,"[9] but not reciprocal movements of opposites. A decade later, Jacques Derrida joins Merleau-Ponty and points out the unfulfilled promise of Hegelian dialects and contends that the negative moment in Hegel is simply contradiction. The cancellation of the thesis is there to be cancelled in its turn by the negation of the negation, which reestablishes identity. Contradiction in Hegel is there only "to lift it up . . . into the self-presence of an onto-theological or onto-teleological synthesis."[10] For Merleau-Ponty (as much as for Derrida), both reflective philosophy and the dialectic underestimates and denies interactive and reciprocal activities that constitute the lives of beings. In *The Visible and the Invisible*, against the pure subjectivity of the Cartesian tradition and Hegelian dialectic, Merleau-Ponty proposes "interrogation" as a process through which truth appears, and interrogative investigation is possible through the awareness of the "intertwining" of the traditionally irreducible and irreconcilable opposites. That is so because, when one interrogates things, between the interrogator and the interrogated there arises a relationship similar to the two lines in the Greek letter "chi" ("X"). The interrogator in this relationship has no privilege over the interrogated.

Nor is the interrogated an "empty thing" waiting to be filled with the signification provided by the interrogator. Instead, their relationship is totally mutual, as there emerges a "crisscrossing" or "intertwining" of the two in the act of interrogation.

Merleau-Ponty explains this concept in terms of the chiasm of visibility. Merleau-Ponty tells us that the conventional understanding that "my eyes" see "things" explains only half of the phenomena of visibility. When one sees things, one inscribes one's vision among the visible and this inscription is already a reaction to the visible. The seer not only sees the visible, but at the same time is being seen by the visible. The reciprocal activity between the seer and the seen, and the dual function of the subject and the object, preclude the substantialist attempt to define the relationship as one over the other. Hence Merleau-Ponty writes: "[T]he seer and the visible reciprocate one another and we no longer know which sees and which is seen."[11] This chiasmic visibility, for Merleau-Ponty, represents the synergy through which philosophical interrogation takes place. Philosophical interrogation cannot be the kind of question that passively waits to be filled in by ready-made answers. When a question is raised, between the questioner and the question itself there emerges a relationship similar to the seer and the visible in visibility. The dissonance and disturbance within the questioner designates a gap between the two, and this gap, or this openness, leads the inquisitor toward the ambiguity of existence.

Not all questions necessarily satisfy Merleau-Ponty's concept of interrogation as a philosophical inquiry. However, it is also true that a phrase or a question need not be philosophically charged in order to be qualified as a philosophical interrogation. Unlike the indicative, the positive, or the negative modes of narration, the interrogative is initiated by a discord within a being. When a simple question "What time is it?" arises in the mind of the questioner, it opens up a realm, the nature of which the subject cannot completely identify. What time is it? one asks. As one is checking the time, there arises an inner disturbance within the subject. The subject has already separated herself from the environment of which she has been a part and, at the same time, she is encountering new reality charged with anticipation of the future, placing herself on the fragile boredom of the present; or it could be the anxious longing to hold onto the present, that precious moment, and her checking time is the voice of agitation arising from the reluctance to move into the future. When the subject experiences the questioning of time, as one might do several times a day, she is anything but an island equipped with the capacity to create the external world. Instead, the very ambiguity of the border of the subject, her own existence as a material being and thinking being, and the border between herself and the world overlap through multilayered separation and reconstruction of reality through anticipation, reflection, fear, and pleasure. This is the moment when the parties involved in the interrogation find themselves in the milieu of what Merleau-Ponty calls a chiasmic movement. Meaning emerges, instead of being constructed through the subject's reflection, in this space, in this void that is fully charged with the intertwining web of relation. The fundamental ambiguity of the meaning that emerged through interrogation does not indicate that the query is incomplete and that the ambiguity will be clarified through further investigation.

There are, then, at least two kinds of questions: the question as a temporary absence of signification and the question as an exposure of one's relationship with others. The difference arises through the subject's relation to that which is being questioned, but not because of the intrinsic nature of either the questioning subject or the questioned object. Thus, to Merleau-Ponty, what has been considered as philosophical questions "proper," such as questions regarding essence, time, or space, cannot be more philosophical than questions concerning facts. Nor can philosophical answers, if they are obtained by condensing a variety of factual elements into one essence and thereby seemingly resolving the doubts that have led the subject to those questions, necessarily allow the inquisitor the meaning that the questioner sought after. There is no universal philosophical question whose answer can offer a convenient canopy for the entire life-world. Merleau-Ponty's vision of the relationship between the subject and object, emergence of meaning, and the subject relation to meaning in this chiasmic interrogation is much comparable to that in what is known as *huatou* meditation in Zen Buddhism. Especially relevant to our discussion here is twelfth-century Korean Zen master Pojo Chinul's (1158–1210) rendering of *huatou* meditation.

When Pojo Chinul's *Kanhwa kyŏrŭiron* (*Treatise on Resolving Doubts about Huatou Meditation*, 1215; hereafter *Huatou Meditation*) was posthumously published by his successor Hyesim (1178–1234), it set the direction of Korean Buddhism for the next seven hundred years. In this text, Chinul introduces the interrogative form of *huatou* meditation as the most effective way to attain awakening for Zen practitioners. In so doing, Chinul first laid out the problems of existing Buddhist schools, especially Huayan Buddhism and the Sudden School (K. *tŏngyo*). The ultimate teaching of Huayan Buddhism envisions a world in which various phenomena exist without conflict. Known as the "unobstructed interpenetration among phenomena" (K. *sasamuae*), this final stage of the fourfold worldview of the Huayan school is the doctrinal culmination of the Buddhist concept of "dependent co-arising." Dependent co-arising defines all phenomena as arising through multilayered causation. Its classical definition states: "When this arises, that arises; when this ceases, that ceases." Here, "this" or "that" does not designate one separate entity with essence. The emphasis is in the relation of "this" to "that" without assuming "this" or "that" as an independent entity other than in its provisional status. The existence of "this" is conditioned by non-this, or its other, and the structure and quantity of this other for the occurrence of "this" defies logical calculation; for the happening of one single event, the involvement of multilayered factors is inevitable. Chinese Huayan Buddhist thinker Fazang (643–712) describes this state through the expression "inexhaustibility" (C. *chongchong wujin*), which is reminiscent of Merleau-Ponty's concept of overdetermination (*surdétermination*), by which Merleau-Ponty defines the flesh of the world. The fact that the existence of "this" absolutely relies on "non-this" indicates the ambiguity of the divide between "this" and "non-this." At the same time, the fact that "this" and "that" do not have independent existence does not negate their individual identity on the phenomenal level. As the Buddhist expression "arising" (C. *qi*) (as opposed to "presence" or "existence") indicates, existence itself is kinetic instead of static. By emphasizing the intertwining of different elements for the occurrence of one phenomenon, the Buddhist doctrine of dependent co-arising challenges substantialist approaches in philosophical investigation. Based on this concept of the interconnectedness of all beings, Huayan Buddhism envisions the identity of a phenomenon through its nonidentity, for each phenomenon is always a result of the interconnection of multiple factors. Since all beings obtain their identity of nonidentity through this reciprocal origination, theoretically there should be no conflict among phenomena. Each phenomenon, as it is, is a reflection, or rather immanence of the ultimate reality, and that is because there cannot be the outside, or the transcendence, when the world is viewed through the theory of dependent co-arising. The well-known Huayan dictum that one particle of dust contains the entire universe is the very declaration of this "double" of noumenon and phenomena in phenomenal reality. "One particle of dust" is any man or any thing, not a specific man or specific thing in the world. Fazang explains this all-inclusive vision of phenomena of Huayan Buddhism through his discussion, among others, of counting numbers 1–10.[12] At a given moment at a given reference, each number 1, 2, 3, and so on represents all ten numbers, because without the rest of the nine, number 1, 2, or 3 cannot be 1, 2, or 3. Two implications deserve our attention to summarize this vision: first, each phenomenon, as it is, is an appearance of the absolute itself; second, there cannot be exclusion or exception in this reality of each phenomenal fact being noumenon as it is. These two facts have a significant implication when one considers the ethical dimensions of the Huayan vision.

Huayan Buddhism successfully applied the core of Buddhist doctrine to its interpretation of the phenomenal world and claimed to be the most perfect and complete teaching among the Buddhist schools. In this regard, Huayan Buddhism was recognized as having brought the phenomena back to the center of Buddhist discourse.[13] As Merleau-Ponty demands philosophy to return to the phenomenal reality, Huayan Buddhists also wanted to address phenomenal reality, which is nondually related to noumenon. Dushun (557–640), the retroactively appointed first patriarch of the Huayan school, confirms this idea in his *Huayan wujiao zhiguan* ("Cessation and Contemplation in the Five Teachings of Huayan"). In this essay, Dushun explains: "The scripture states, 'linguistic rendering is different from practice. Truth is divorced from words.' Hence, noticing such phenomena as our eyes' seeing and our ears' listening and so forth is [the very way of] entering into the midst of the dependent co-arising of the realm of reality [*dharmadhātu*]."[14] If the conventional world in which each phenomenon earns individual identity and noumenal level, which Buddhism understands as "empty," are nondual, as claimed by the second-century Buddhist thinker Nāgājuna, who served as the foundation of Huayan Buddhism, then each and every phenomenon is to be understood as the unfolding of the underlying noumenon of the phenomenon, and, more important, the ultimate confirmation of noumenon becomes possible only through the actual happening of each phenomenon. However, despite Huayan Buddhism's efforts to bring together phenomenal and noumenal levels by addressing the phenomenal reality, Chinul feels that it falls short of being complete as Buddhist teaching. For Chinul, Huayan Buddhism does not consider the most important variation in the structure of Buddhist soteriology: the practicing subject. Chinul's reasoning in his criticism of Huayan Buddhism is comparable to Merleau-Ponty's criticism of the philosophy of reflection. The question here is how the appearance of the absolute, or of noumenon, is being "understood" and thus "embodied" by the subject for Merleau-Ponty or by a practitioner for Chinul. Each phenomenon, as Huayan Buddhism states, must be the noumenal reality as it is, and thus "empty," since there is no separable, single essence of an entity. However, a piece of a stone on the street to a sentient being is just a stone, not the reality of emptiness of all things. The sentient being can use a piece of the stone as a paperweight, a decoration for her plant, or a stop-gap to block a hole in her garage, but it is just a piece of stone. How does this simple piece of stone transform into a reality that reflects noumenon, while this piece of stone is always the same, always the double of phenomenon and noumenon? In Sartre's novel *Nausea*, a pebble caused Antoine Roquentin's "nausea" of existential meaninglessness. In order for one to face this, a pebble needs to be encountered as existence in its bare factuality, not as a property that can be owned or an object that has utility function, since ownership or functionality will establish its value in daily life and thus substantialize and concretize the existence of that pebble. Zen Buddhism is an effort to lead a practitioner through this bare reality, or what Merleau-Ponty calls the "brute world." The fact that the phenomena are the noumenon with no "beyond" as dual, and the fact that this noumenon is not a definable substance but is constantly constructed in the intertwining of parties involved in the occurrence of an event makes the job of "understanding" this world and self ironic. As Merleau-Ponty says: "It is at the same time true that the world is *what we see* and that, nonetheless, we must learn to see it" (italics original).[15] The Zen Buddhist challenge to existing Buddhist schools is to make this "learning to see" the major project of the school. Chinul's criticism of Huayan Buddhism addresses this issue.

Chinul understands that the Huayan approach makes an appeal to understanding the theory itself by using a linguistic medium, and the end result of this approach for Chinul is a gap between linguistic expression and the subject's reality. One might wonder, has not Dushun already addressed the issue of the gap created by linguistic rendering in the aforementioned passage? "Truth is divorced from word," said Dushun. Hence, Dushun was pointing the practitioner to experience truth in the happening of each phenomenon such as "our eyes' seeing" and "our ears' listening." Chinul did not think so in his *Huatou Meditation*,[16] and his reasoning for that is once again comparable to Merleau-Ponty's discussion of philosophy's relation to "understanding."

"A philosophy of 'understanding' (whether instrument or medium) destroys itself by placing philosophy and the absolute side by side," writes Merleau-Ponty.[17] For Merleau-Ponty, there exists a fundamental vicious circle in the structure of a philosophy of "understanding," as he points out:

> Philosophy goes "to the thing itself"—but if this movement is established by "understanding" [*Erkenne*], it is conceived either as an instrument or as a medium through which the thing itself is visible to us.—Whence the question of the critique of "understanding": can consciousness acquire *"what is in itself"* by this instrument through this medium?
>
> [. . .]
>
> How does one grasp the absolute? If the instrument is only a trap, like lime for ensnaring birds, bringing the absolute closer to us but without being able to enter into it, then, the instrument becomes a kind of derision. The absolute defies all activities of "understanding."[18]

One notes here that the problem addressed by Merleau-Ponty is at least threefold: the relation between understanding and the absolute, and of the understanding and language, and their relation to the subject. For Merleau-Ponty, phenomenology is the way to challenge this dual stance of philosophy and understanding; thus, noumena, which is not "beyond" the phenomena, is a "double" of the phenomenon to be experienced. In response to a student's question of how one encounters noumenon in phenomena, Chinul offers the example of a magpie's sound:

> There are many points at which to enter the noumenon. I will indicate one approach which will allow you to return to the source.
>
> Chinul: Do you hear the sounds of that crow cawing and that magpie calling?
>
> Student: Yes.
>
> Chinul: Trace them back and listen to your hearing-nature. Do you hear any sounds?
>
> Student: At that place, sounds and discriminations do not obtain.
>
> Chinul: Marvelous! Marvelous! This is Avalokiteśvara's method for entering the noumenon. Let me ask you again. You said that sounds and discriminations do not obtain at that place. But since they do not obtain, isn't the hearing-nature just empty space at such a time?
>
> Student: Originally it is not empty. It is always bright and never obscured.
>
> Chinul: What is this essence which is not empty?
>
> Student: As it has no former shape, words cannot describe it.[19]

To tie this citation with our discussion, some clarification is necessary. For Chinul, the fundamental way to going back to the original reality, or "brute world," is by "tracing back the radiance" of one's mind. The mind, for Chinul, is not a meaning-giving entity as in the Cartesian paradigm; it is the space in which the intertwining of beings takes place. As Chinul advises his student in this passage, the way to get through noumenon does not exist in separation from phenomena. The sound of the magpie is as it is the double of phenomena-noumenon; the phenomena, however, remain as superficial phenomena if the subject is not aware of how this hearing actually takes place. Individual sounds, or the faculty that discriminates different existence, at its root, do not exist as separate reality; hence, they are empty. This, however, does not mean that they do not exist; hence, they are not empty, either. Chinul ends the conversation with the student's acknowledgement that words cannot describe this formless intertwining of beings. In other words, the nonduality or the double of phenomena and noumenon is acknowledged but language remains as a problem of getting through this double, the nonduality.

The Sudden School seems to preclude the problems that arise in the use of language and speculation by emphasizing the "emptiness" of all beings. The Sudden School thus emphasizes: "If even one thought does not arise, that is called the achievement of Buddhahood."[20] Since beings do not have intrinsic nature of their own, and thus are "empty," the arising of thought is evidence that the individual is still holding on to names and forms and treats them as independent substances. The Sudden School encourages practitioners to remove thought and language and utilizes this as the core of its teaching and the grounds for its claim for the suddenness of enlightenment. One notes here that the Sudden School's approach to the subject's identity situates itself on the direct opposite to the essentialist position. The self is not a thinking being; no *ego-cogito* is possible when one understands an entity as an ever-changing locus of chiasmic penetration. However, Chinul raises a question about fundamental assumption of the Sudden School. That is, if practice is based on cutting off one's thoughts and language with the realization of the emptiness of those thoughts, who is cutting off thought and language, and what is being cut off? If everything is empty because things are devoid of self-nature, even the thought that needs to be removed is empty. This means that, in an ultimate sense, "there is neither a thinking subject nor a thought object" (HPC 734b). The concept of subject and object is only a linguistic rendering that functions through a tentative agreement but cannot be validated as a means of substantializing them. Chinul cautions that the idea of cutting off language and thought ironically reintroduces the dualism of subject and object into the Buddhist doctrine of nondualism. As long as one makes a distinction between the destroyer and the destroyed, what should be maintained and what should be removed, one has yet to realize the nonsubstantialistic nature of emptiness. Theoretically speaking, both Huayan Buddhism and the Sudden School faithfully encompass within their systems the concept of "dependent co-arising" and the Buddhist theory of "emptiness." The problem arises from the fact that these Buddhist doctrines by nature defy crystallization and sedimentation with a theoretical system. This also means that their linguistic rendering always presents the danger of violating the very nature of these concepts because the variants that being and the world face in each and every moment would need to be put in a vacuum state in order to validate a clear-cut theory on enlightenment.

Even when we accept the understanding of Huayan Buddhism as the culmination of the Chinese doctrinal school, which focuses on theory, and Zen Buddhism as a meditational school, focusing on practice, the gap between theory and practice that Chinul addresses in his criticism of Huayan and other Buddhist schools is different in nature from the conventional sense of the gap between theory and praxis. In the theory-praxis duo, these two are in a linear relationship. The theory stands by itself; problems might arise in the process of actualizing the theory, and when problems do arise, this does not necessarily indicate flaws in the theory itself. The separation between the theory and praxis in this sense is based on the assumption that ideas can exist in separation from action. Here we need to consider the relationship between linguistic expression and action, which is replaceable with the theory versus praxis paradigm. As in the conventional sense of the theory versus praxis paradigm, action has been understood as opposite to linguistic expression. John Austin's Speech Act Theory brought our attention to the idea that language is not just about making a statement; rather, it "performs." When one says "Now I pronounce you husband and wife," this statement is not just a description but an action that has immediate impact on reality. Applying this idea to the interpretation of Confucius's *Analects*, Herburt Fingarrets states that *ren*, commonly translated into English as humanity, humaneness, and benevolence, is "action."[21] The performative aspects of language then run deeper than Austin's original proposal. When one states "I love you," this is not just a description of one's statement of mind. If someone states "I love you" and hits the person, the person will not believe the statement. The statement becomes real and attains its meaning through various actions, including the action of being together, thinking of the person, various erotic gestures, cooking for the person, and so on. Even a seemingly descriptive statement involves action. When one says "The sky is blue," the statement involves the action of seeing, of believing, and even of feeling the blueness of the sky. Here we find that our interpretation of the performative aspects of linguistic expression is getting close to what Merleau-Ponty describes as "intentional arc." Merleau-Ponty thus writes, to repeat what we cited earlier: "Phenomenology is . . . an appearance which is not an effect of the absolute, but the absolute itself.—In that respect, philosophy is experience."[22] The problem that Chinul addresses, then, is not the traditional concept of privileging experience over linguistic expression. The problem that Chinul's *huatou* meditation and Merleau-Ponty's interrogative philosophy addresses is the issue of reification through institutionalized linguistic convention and established thought system. This is not a problem that exclusively applies to Buddhism but a problem that any nonsubstantialist mode of thinking has to deal with. If the world is the flux of constant happening and the texture of these happenings is marked by the interaction of the uncountable number of involvements in the past, present, and future, linguistic convention itself becomes the first adversary of the reality. Resolving the problem by removing language is not a feasible option because language is not an optional element in our existence. Here we can think of Merleau-Ponty's state of philosophy's returning to itself by becoming nonphilosophy. The type of philosophy that has created systems and institutionalized understanding closes out, instead of opening up, one's effort to know the truth and the world. The self-closure of institutionalized philosophy has been allowed for its exchange value in creating a tentative security out of the untamed world.

As opposed to the security and inevitable violence that result from theorization and interpretation, Chinul proposes *huatou* meditation as a way to actualize the Buddhist concept of dependent co-arising. Huatou meditation was proposed as an alternative method to the problems incurred by theoretical rendering of Buddhist doctrines; however, the "theory" of *huatou* meditation and any articulation on *huatou* has to carry the burden of always falling short of what it promises. This is so because, even though the purpose of *huatou* meditation is to overcome the problems created by the theorization and narrativization of "dependent co-arising" and "emptiness," the tools employed in the use of *huatou* will be the same as those used by Huayan Buddhism and the Sudden School as they articulate their systems. In order to resolve this dilemma, *huatou* meditation in particular and the *gong'an* tradition in general introduce two devices: the first is the performative narrative of the interrogative mode, and the second is a dual vision of language.

In *Huatou Meditation*, Chinul provides no definition of *huatou*. Even though Chinul introduces *huatou* meditation with the promise that it will offer a way to overcome the problems left unresolved by Huayan Buddhism and the Sudden School, he claims that the *huatou*, per se, is neither a "healer of diseases" nor "a complete presentation of truth" (HPC 733b). Chinul further states: "The moment one tends toward the slightest idea that the *huatou* should tell something about the ultimate truth or enable one to treat one's defects, one is under the power of the limitations set by linguistic expression" (HPC 733b). *Huatous* like "the oak tree in the garden,"[23] "three pounds of flax,"[24] or "a dog does not have Buddha nature,"[25] obviously offer no clues as to the presence of noumenon in phenomena, as experienced by Chinul's student in the example of listening to the sound of magpie. When the subject encounters these expressions in the context of encounter dialogue,[26] the seeming nonsense (un)intentionally blocks out any further evolution of logical speculation of the subject in his endeavor to interpret these passages. They will remain "flavorless and groundless" (HPC 735b) through and through.

Like Merleau-Ponty's interrogation, the *huatou* begins to function by initiating a discord in the practitioner's mind. "What time is it?" Merleau-Ponty's interrogator asks. The question opens up to the interrogator the unknown space of time, the spatiality of temporality, and the ambiguity of existence. This momentary discord leads the subject to question herself as much as she questions the object of her questioning at hand. In a similar manner, a word or a phrase in a *huatou* creates a chasm in the practitioner's mind since the word or phrase cannot find the ground to anchor itself in conventional logic. Instead, the phrase aimlessly floats around in the practitioner's mind. As the practitioner fails to find a ready-made response to the posed question and is unable to find a language that offers the meaning of the *huatou* phrase, the *huatou* eventually becomes the initiator which opens the door to the abyss of the practitioner's existence. Like Merleau-Ponty's philosopher, who listens to the muteness of things and experiences silence in its contact with Being through interrogation, the practitioner of *huatou* meditation makes his journey into his original nature. If *huatou* functions because it fails to locate itself in the context of conventional language and conventional logic, what kind of language does it speak? Chinul's dual vision of language in *Huatou Meditation* answers this question.

When philosophy turns its direction from the certitude and security of the declarative mode to the openness of the interrogative form, it changes language's relation to the world. In the essay "On the Phenomenology of Language" (1952), Merleau-Ponty examines the Husserlian concept of language and asks whether it is possible to simply juxtapose "language as object of thought" with "language as mine."[27] Merleau-Ponty considers that, in Husserl, language is understood as "one of the objects supremely constituted by consciousness."[28] Thus, language cannot possibly play a role other than that of an accompaniment, substitute, memorandum, or secondary means of communication in respect to thought.[29] In response to Husserl's position on language, Merleau-Ponty states: "As soon as we distinguish, alongside of the objective science of language, a phenomenology of speech, we set in motion a dialect through which the two disciplines open communication."[30] The phenomena of speech, for Merleau-Ponty, do not claim "I speak, you listen." Merleau-Ponty contends that when one speaks, language is not a means to impart one's intention to others; instead, the speaker listens to her own speech, in order to become aware of herself: "Speech does not seek to embody a significative intention which is only *a certain gap* simply in order to recreate the same lack or privation in others, but also to know *what* there is a lack or privation of" (italics original).[31]

Merleau-Ponty calls this language that exceeds the speaking subject's intention the "indirect language," as he develops the idea in "The Indirect Language and the Voice of Silence" (1952) and in his posthumous publication *The Prose of the World* (1969). Language is not a neutral communicative tool in this case. The essentialist position that presupposes a fixed identity of an entity suffocates language, because signification in this case takes place through a sedimented and institutionalized meaning structure. As signification is sedimented and institutionalized through the advocate of the essence within and without, the language employed becomes suffocated. Merleau-Ponty calls this "sedimented language" (*le langage parlé*). The sedimented language effaces itself in order to yield meaning.[32] As opposed to the death or near-death of the language in "sedimented language," "speech" (*le langage parlant*), to Merleau-Ponty, is the language "which creates itself in its expressive acts, which sweeps me on from the signs toward meaning."[33] Sedimented language consists of "the stock of accepted relations between signs and familiar signification."[34] Like the kind of philosophy that confines the being and the world within the realm of the known—dogmatizing and institutionalizing it—sedimented language limits one's experience to ready-made expressions. Merleau-Ponty contends that, unlike "sedimented language," "speaking language" (or "speech") creates a secret meaning out of already existing signs and signification. "Speaking language" does so by listening to the voice of "silence" or "indirect language," the very nascent state of language. The indirect language connects language to "the mute things it interpellates and those it sends before itself and which make up the world of things said."[35]

The dream of sedimented language is the dream of the objective science of language, an endeavor to limit language and to degrade it into a means of communication. This dream is nonsensical, Merleau-Ponty argues, for, like *chora* in Julia Kristeva's account of poetic language, the silent voice of the indirect language always works in our use of language: "[I]f we rid our minds of the idea that our language is the translation or cipher of an original text, we shall see that the idea of complete expression is nonsensical, and that all language is indirect or allusive—that it is, if you wish, silence."[36] Merleau-Ponty further observes: "[I]f we want to understand language as an originating operation, we must pretend to have never spoken, submit language to a reduction without which it would once more escape us by referring us to what it signifies for us, look at it as deaf people look at those who are speaking, compare the art of language to other arts of expression, and try to see it as one of these mute arts."[37]

Merleau-Ponty is one of those few Western thinkers who recognizes the power of silence in both linguistic and nonlinguistic communication. Silence is anything but a lack of communication; it is the overflow and excess that both Merleau-Ponty and Kristeva understand as the fundamental structure of language. This excess is not an issue that is exclusively related to the function of linguistic system. As Kristeva tells us, the control of the excess in language and communication is directly related to the power structure of a capitalist and patriarchal society. For Merleau-Ponty, it is most closely related to the ontological reality of beings, which makes enunciation an act of ambiguity. Merleau-Ponty's speaking language is the language that embodies the flesh of the world.

As perception is one's dialogue with things, speech (or speaking language) is one's dialogue with language. In either case, however, the speaking subject is not established with the power of the center; it has no priority. The indirect language—like the "semiotic" in Kristeva—might locate itself at the margins of sedimented language, but, again, like the semiotic, its existence cannot be nullified. The indirect language always "effects the mediation between my as yet unspeaking intention and words, and in such a way that my spoken words surprise me myself and teach me my thought."[38]

The speaking language that resists confinement in the sedimented language, however, is not the monster of the Lacanian language. Sartre seems assured that, later, Merleau-Ponty must have agreed with the Lacanian formula that our unconscious is structured like a language.[39] However, there exists a fundamental difference between Merleau-Ponty's approach to language, which is reciprocal with the speaking subject, and the Lacanian model in which language is already inscribed in one's unconscious. Merleau-Ponty's language is obviously not the traditional concept of language, in which "I speak." It is not exactly the Lacanian (or semiological) language, in which "I am spoken." The speaking subject in Merleau-Ponty is already displaced, but is yet to be totally disseminated, as in the latter. In Merleau-Ponty, as the subject is always already intersubjectivity, the subject and language are in communication with each other. They are in the relationship of interrogation; in the chiasmic space of interrogation, meaning emerges: ambiguous, transitory, and charged with traces of past, present, and the future.

In the concluding section of *Huatou Meditation*, Chinul presents two types of *huatou* language, relying on the work of Chinese thinker Dahui Zonggao (1089–1163). Chinul writes: "The practitioner of *huatou* must involve himself with live words, do not get involved with dead words. If one attains enlightenment by a direct confrontation with live words, one won't forget it ever; if one works with dead words, one won't even be able to save oneself" (HPC 737a).[40] Like Merleau-Ponty's "sedimented language," Chinul's "dead words" (K. *sagu*) are subjugated to a sign-system and produce conventional meaning. As opposed to dead words, "live words" (K. *hwalgu*) become the mediator between the subject and her original state of mind, by generating rapport between the subject and the world. Like Merleau-Ponty's "speech," "live words" realize the philosopher's attempt to communicate the muteness of existence that is hidden in the normative linguistic expressions. Chinul enhances his concept of "live words" and "dead words" with another pairing of two aspects of *huatou* meditation—"involvement with words" (K. *chamgu*) and "involvement with meaning" (K. *chamŭi*). Dead words can be paralleled by involvement with meaning, and live words, the involvement with word. Chinul criticizes the involvement with meaning as Huayan Buddhism's (and other doctrinal schools') approach to Buddhist teaching. In the involvement with meaning (dead words), the signification takes place according to the "stock of accepted relations between signs and familiar signification," as in the case of Merleau-Ponty's sedimented language. The subject in this case is situated outside of this signification, since the dualism of subject and object is sustained, and the gap between the linguistic rendering and the subject who tries to understand the doctrine still remains. Direct involvement with live words is characterized by the subject's engagement with the articulated linguistic expression, the signification of which cannot be institutionalized, but is singular to the situation at hand.

In both Merleau-Ponty and Chinul, the reality of nonexistence of the independent thinking subject does not annul the thinking. As Merleau-Ponty writes:

> There would be nothing if there were not that abyss of self. But an abyss is not nothing; it has its environs and edges. One always thinks of something; about, according to, in the light of something; with regard to, in contact with something. . . . I cannot

think of identically the same thing for more than an instant. The opening is in principle immediately filled, as if lived only in a nascent state.[41]

That one's thought changes from moment to moment and is neither the same
nor consistent in two consecutive seconds does not suggest the impossibility of
thinking. It does, however, indicate the necessity of rethinking the activity of
thinking itself. According to Zen Buddhism, commonsense logic often becomes a
barrier, instead of a facilitator, that prevents the subject from embodying linguistic
expression. This is because the familiarity of commonsense logic, in which Chinul
includes the logical articulation of Buddhism as represented by Huayan Buddhism,
disables the subject's capacity to see the cacophony of existence. The coherence and
harmony that are commonly considered the goals of thought systems or religious
ideas represent an arranged situation of existence. If a being is understood through
its "openness to the world," the world itself cannot but be incoherent by virtue of
its changeability. The seeming nonsense or lack of signification in Zen Buddhist
gong'an stories disarms the subject from the logicality of logic.

In the space where the traditional meaning structure fails to sustain itself, the
subject, who encounters a *gong'an* episode, questions the meaning of meaning,
as Merleau-Ponty's interrogator dialogues with that which is being interrogated.
Meaning emerges in the chiasmic space—the third space, like Plato's *khōra*—which
is neither the space of Idea nor that of the changeable. Questioning, or interrogation, in this sense, is not just one method for Merleau-Ponty and Chinul's *huatou*
meditation. It is the way one engages with the world. Understanding questioning
and interrogation in this manner also changes our way of understanding thinking.
Thinking is no longer the subject's privileged activity, exercised on the object. It
is a communal activity in which the subject is engaged with others through his
openness. The world revealed through this communal activity of thinking is the
world in which the subject's efforts to create a unified vision are constantly being challenged; it is a world in which seeming oppositions coexist, without being
regulated in the name of harmony or unity. Merleau-Ponty's phenomenology
and Chinul's Zen Buddhism tell us that the opposite of harmony and unity is not
chaos and disorder, but the coexistence of different voices; these voices reflect the
diversity of existence itself, undomesticated by human desire.

The world, for the Buddhist, is a constantly changing reality. The Buddhist
theory of dependent co-arising that explains the structure of change is based
on the idea of multilayered causation. The irony of this postulation as the basic
structure of the world is that the structure is actually unknowable. The world of
dependent co-arising is not like a bank account at all, despite its frequent presentation in this manner in the popular Western version of Buddhist karma. The fact
that each and every action one takes with intentionality has an influence on one's
future indicates, instead of a clear cause-and-effect theory, or a punishment-and-
reward paradigm, the absolute absurdity of human efforts to have a clear vision
of the world.

Jin Y. Park

Reality is unknowable in the ultimate sense, and, in this case, the unknowability is not just a version of agnosticism. This is because the Buddhist unknowability of the reality of the world does not underscore the limits of human faculties; rather, it is based on the "nonsubstantial" reality of the world. This nonsubstantiality, for Merleau-Ponty, is a chiasm of the subject and the world, which he calls the flesh of the world. Merleau-Ponty writes: "[W]e situate ourselves in ourselves *and* in the things, in ourselves *and* in the other, at the point where, by a sort of chiasm, we become the others *and* we become world" (italics in original).[42] In this constant interaction between self and the world, between a being and others, self or a being loses and, at the same time, earns its identity of nonidentity, only to realize the lack of very identity. This is the world of the double, in which both phenomena and noumenon annul themselves in their encounter of each: the noumenon effaces its seeming position of the "beyond," and phenomena lose their surface reality as independent entities. The Buddhist theories of dependent co-arising and emptiness are theories that efface their own possibilities of being theories. Merleau-Ponty's concept of chiasm, or the flesh of the world, is another such theory. Philosophy, for Merleau-Ponty, becomes itself by going against its already institutionalized meaning structure; so does Buddhism, for Chinul, become itself only when the practitioner overcomes its already institutionalized doctrine.

6

The Notion of the "Words that Speak the Truth" in Merleau-Ponty and Shinran

Toru Funaki

In order to facilitate a comparison between the philosophy of Maurice Merleau-Ponty and Japanese thought, I would like to focus on his philosophy of language. Among the thinkers of Japan, there are many who have developed their own ideas by consistently exploring the question of what language is. Even though this tendency is most prevalent in the Confucian studies of the seventeenth and eighteenth centuries, it can, in fact, be traced back to an earlier tradition of thought that suggested idiosyncratic sensibilities to and perceptions of language as it is the case with, for example, the notion of *kotodama* (literally, "the spiritual nature of words and language") that is found in the eighth-century *Manyōshū*.[1]

The thinkers of the new Buddhist movements that emerged in the twelfth century and are referred to as Kamakura Buddhism recaptured Buddhist thought, which had been transmitted to Japan from China (and Korea) since the sixth century, by being extremely sensitive to the historical conditions of each respective time period. Each of these movements, which culminated in a unique Japanese Buddhist philosophy that is exemplified by (the thought of) Zen and Pure Land Buddhism, reveals its own idiosyncratic sensibility toward language. In Zen Buddhism, for example, the practitioner aims at reaching an absolute stage where language is of no import as that stage lies beyond linguistic understanding. On the other hand, in Pure Land Buddhism, adherents are encouraged to examine the meaning of the chant *namu amida butsu* ("I entrust myself to the name of Amida Buddha") as the sole linguistic expression of the truth. Among the thinkers belonging to the Pure Land school, it is Shinran (1173–1262) in particular who has provided his own original interpretation of what it means to transcend human wisdom by evoking the name of the absolute. Shinran refers to this activity as "the mystery of evoking the name" (J. *myōgō fushigi*). I would like to compare Shinran's thought to Merleau-Ponty's philosophy with a particular emphasis on his conception "speaking words" (*parole parlante*).

From the beginning to the end, Merleau-Ponty's philosophy consistently revolves around the central question of what language is. He discusses the relationship between language and thought and presents his own theory of language in the *Phenomenology of Perception*. According to Merleau-Ponty, the traditional theory of language since Descartes has focused largely on "spoken words" (*parole parlée*). This conception implies that, in communication, words are circulated over an over again not unlike worn out hard currency. Such a theory of language fails to respond to questions such as "What is the actual meaning of words in the first place?" and "How can we conceptualize the new meaning of words that have already been used in a specific sense?" In this context, Merleau-Ponty introduces the concept of "speaking words" and thus investigates the formation of meaning in language.

Merleau-Ponty replaces the rhetoric of "spoken words" and "speaking words" that he introduced in his *Phenomenology of Perception* with the conceptual pair of "spoken language" and "speaking language" or, alternatively, with "constituted language" (*langage constitué*) and "constitutive language" (*langage constituant*) in *The Prose of the World*, and with the juxtaposition of the "experimental use" and the "creative use" of language in his essay "On the Phenomenology of Language." These various juxtapositions point to the same binary structure of language. Thus we can assume from their frequent repetition that the topic addressed by these juxtapositions was of great concern to Merleau-Ponty.

Having said this, I have to admit that it may not be particularly original within the context of modern Western philosophy to postulate such a contradiction with regards to language. Since the days of Descartes and Locke, it has been widely accepted that language possesses a dual function. Language functions as a tool of communication and, at the same time, as a means to congeal thought.[2] Philosophers disagree as to which of the two viewpoints constitutes the more fundamental function of language. These differences in approach generate discrepancies that effect even epistemology. In this chapter, I will not discuss the genealogy of these discrepancies but only indicate in what way the juxtaposition of the two terms by Merleau-Ponty differs from the dual nature of language suggested by Descartes and Locke. In other words, modern philosophical language theory since Descartes involves the assumption that language is a mere attire of thoughts. Merleau-Ponty's notion of "speaking words," on the contrary, implies that language not only mediates and congeals a thought but also generates the thought itself.

Since Parmenides, the concept of thought has been understood to possess the connotation that truth is acquired by distinguishing it from *doxa*. Only then may it be called "thought." Human beings encounter transcendent truth by means of thought. And this is where Shinran and Merleau-Ponty fit in. While they may disagree in what they consider to be truth, it is possible to discuss Merleau-Ponty's philosophy and the thought of Shinran under the same horizon insofar as both of them assume that language possesses the important function of connecting us with the transcendent. This is the objective the present chapter is trying to achieve.

"THE MYSTERY OF CHANTING THE NAME" (J. *MYŌGŌ FUSHIGI*)

Let us begin with an introduction to Shinran's thought. The idea of salvation by chanting the name of the transcendent—that is, Amida Buddha—emerged in the Indian Mahāyāna movement of the first century B.C.E. and is mentioned for the first time in texts such as the *(Larger) Sūtra of Immeasurable Life* (J. *Muryōjukyō*) and the *Amitābha-sūtra* (J. *Amidakyō*). In his chapter on "The Easy Practice" (J. *igyōhin*), which is included in the *Commentary on the Sūtra of the Ten Stages* (J. *Jūjū bibasharon*), the third-century Buddhist philosopher Nāgārjuna already states that "if one desires to attain immediately the stage of nonretrogression [J. *futaitenji*], one should evoke persistently the name of Amida Buddha with wholehearted respect." This idea of "chanting the name of Amida Buddha" (J. *shōmyō nembutsu*) was introduced to China as one aspect of Buddhist thought, which was referred to as the "teaching about the Pure Land" (J. *Jōdōkyō*). It was systematized in the sixth and seventh centuries by Tanluan (c. 476–572), Daochuo (562–645), and Shandao (613–681).

In the tenth century, the monk Genshin (942–1017) introduced the fundamental idea of the pure land to Japan when he wrote his *Essentials for Attaining Birth* (J. *Ōjōyōshū*) (985). However, Genshin emphasized, for some reason, the contemplation on the name of the Buddha (J. *kansō nembutsu*) over the practice of chanting it and encouraged the practitioners to envision the image of Amida Buddha in their mind. At the beginning, the practice of chanting the name of Amida Buddha was but one element of the Buddhist thought that had been transmitted to Japan. Eventually, Hōnen (1133–1212) diverged from the Tendai (C. Tiantai) school insofar as he believed that chanting the name of the Buddha fulfills the religious demand outlined in Buddhist thought entirely. Subsequently, he became the founder of the Pure Land school when he authored the *Selected Passages on the Nembutsu and the Primordial Vow* (J. *Senchaku hongan nembutsu shū*) (1198). Shinran was a disciple of Hōnen.

After he had been trained in Tendai Buddhism on Mount Hiei, the gateway to monastic life in Japan during that time period, Shinran became Hōnen's disciple upon receiving a divine revelation. It is recorded that, at that time, Shinran remarked the following: "For [myself] Shinran, outside of accepting and entrusting myself to what a good person declared—'just say the nembutsu and be saved by Amida'—there is no special consideration. . . . Suppose that I have been deceived by Hōnen Shōnin and saying the nembutsu fall utterly into hell—even then I should not regret at all . . . that one had been deceived; [but]

since I am one for whom any practice is difficult to accomplish, at all events hell is decidedly my home!"[3]

Although "the idea of becoming a Buddha upon birth in the pure land" (J. *ōjōshite jōbutsu suru*)—that is, becoming a Buddha who is born in the Western Paradise (J. *saihōgokuraku*) upon one's death—constitutes the ideal of the Pure Land teaching, Shinran declares that "at all events hell is decidedly my home!" From its inception, Buddhist thought has taught that the true meaning of salvation lies in the "detachment of the practitioner from the realm of birth and death," that is, in reaching a stage where one abandons a life that is spent in fear of death and in the pursuit of extending one's life span. Since this ideal and the attainment of salvation in the Buddhist sense was not easily understood by the common people, Mahāyāna Buddhism introduced the concept of the "skillful means" (*upāya*). This idea implies that since commoners are saved through the use of certain and more familiar images (of heaven and hell, so to speak), what is conveyed by the spoken word is, ultimately, not a matter of the truth. The Western paradise where Amida Buddha saves the believers is one of those images. Similarly, hell is another such image. Shinran's claim "[e]ven if I have been deceived by this good person (Hōnen Shōnin) and fall into hell, I should not have any regrets at all" constitutes such a skillful means. Does this exclamation of Shinran not imply that the true meaning of salvation does not lie in one's avoidance of hell and the concomitant birth in the paradise? There is no doubt that there must have been a more important issue that occupied Shinran's mind.

The most important key to understanding the teaching of Pure Land Buddhism is not to be found in the images of paradise and hell as the essence of the Pure Land thought is often explained but in the significance of chanting the *nembutsu*. Why does chanting the name of Amida make salvation possible? It is said that Dōgen, who established the sect of Japanese Sōtō Zen Buddhism, once ridiculed the Pure Land teaching by saying "[s]ince Shakamuni Buddha was an Indian, chanting 'namu Amida butsu' in Japanese will not be too different from the sounds the frogs on the footpaths through rice paddies make." This statement may sound rational to some degree. Nonetheless, it is important to examine the transcendent being that is called "Amida" by both Shinran and the *Sukhāvativyūha Sūtra*. The Sanskrit word for "Amida" ["Amitābha"], possesses the meaning of "infinite life, infinite light." But when we interpret "infinite" as "transcendent"—that is, as that which goes beyond human wisdom—and translate "light" into "the origin of truth" in the same way in which the phrase "light in nature" is used in Western Europe, we must come to the conclusion that Amida Buddha signifies "the origin of truth that transcends time." Here, "truth" designates the Buddhist concept of dharma and, more concretely, the fact that nothing possesses a substance. In other words, does not the phrase "the origin of truth" imply that one has to learn to retrace the non-being of all substances to oneself and thereby changes one's own life?

Then, can we say that such an origin and substance of the truth possesses "Being"? If there is no origin of the truth, then truth itself does not exist. But does this not imply that there is no salvation since salvation presupposes the existence of truth? On the contrary, the notion that there is an origin of truth implies a contradiction since it would falsify the above statement that "there are no substances." It may sound contradictory, but it is the paradox of this dilemma through which Amida Buddha appears. For example, it is said that Amida Buddha, who supposedly transcends time, was a practitioner (J. *biku*) called Dharmakāra Bodhisattva (J. *Hōzō bosatsu*) who endeavored to become Amida Buddha. Dharmakāra, then, made forty-eight vows, the eighteenth of which states as follows: "If, when I become a Buddha, all sentient beings in the ten directions, who entrust themselves to me joyously, aspire to be born in the Pure Land, or chant the *nembutsu* even ten times, are not born therein, I shall not attain complete Awakening."[4] In short, this vow suggests that unless he saves all sentient beings who chant the name of Amida Buddha, Dharmakāra will not transcend time and space or this empirical world wherein these people reside. We have to assume that, until this vow is fulfilled, Dharmakāra is not Amida Buddha, who constitutes the transtemporal truth. It is well known that there was a debate on the nature of Jesus Christ who became flesh in the spatio-temporal world.[5] Similarly, even Amida Buddha's existence possesses a translogical character. Amida Buddha exists within the spatio-temporal world and, at the same time, transcends it insofar as he enters the pure land together with those who call upon him as the one who has already transcended their world. Such a translogical thinking implies that Amida Buddha exists and, simultaneously, does not exist—that Amida transcends space and time and yet does not do so.

The mystery of the name that facilitates the salvation of the practitioner insofar as one chants the name denoting the origin of truth without recognizing the truth as such is an example of the "skillful means" that I discussed above. Insofar as it constitutes the characteristic nature and essence of Amida Buddha, the vow provides the possibility of a "skillful means." This means that, if Amida Buddha exists, those who chant the name have already been saved by the "power of the vow" (J. *ganryōku*). On the other hand, if Amida Buddha does not exist, chanting prayers would amount to nothing but the sound that frogs make. Since the existence of Amida Buddha cannot be proven by means of definitions in this empirical world, no kind of deduction or meditation in Zen practice will be able to either affirm or negate the existence of Amida Buddha. This is why Shinran emphasizes the importance of "faith" (J. *shinjin*)[6] in the following sense: "True and real shinjin is unfailingly accompanied by [saying] the Name. [Saying] the Name, however, is not necessarily accompanied by shinjin that is the power of the Vow."[7]

That is to say, Shinran asserts that chanting the name constitutes the necessary but not the sufficient condition of faith. While the act of chanting the name does not always indicate that the practitioner possesses faith, faith is always expressed by the invocation of Amida's name. The term "faith" here denotes the belief in the salvation of the self through Amida Buddha. The prerequisite of such an attitude toward salvation is the belief in the existence of Amida Buddha. By chanting the name with such a pious heart, the practitioner has already attained salvation by the same translogical principle that underlies the existence of Amida Buddha. This is so because the practitioner believes in the existence of Amida Buddha that supposedly manifests itself only after salvation is attained. In contrast, let us examine those whose practice of chanting the name is devoid of faith. The practice of chanting the name does not presuppose knowledge in the form of a hypothetical imperative that "those who chant the name of Amida Buddha will be saved." Much less does essence of that which is expressed in these words comprise a spell that possesses the magical power to manipulate reality. Those who chant Amida's name only to be saved presumably have not been saved yet. Therefore, they will not be saved even if they practice chanting the name of Amida.

Then why does Shinran contend that faith is always accompanied by chanting the *nembutsu*? Can we not assume that those who have faith are saved without the invocation of Amida? In order to respond to this question, we must first examine what Shinran means when he uses the term "faith." Let us thus examine the most famous phrases in his writings: "Even the good person realizes birth—what need is there to speak of the evil person!"[8]; "the person who performs good acts in self-power, because he lacks the heart that entrusts totally to Other Power, is not [in accord with] Amida's Primal Vow. However, when a person overturns his heart of self-power and entrusts himself to Other Power, he will realize birth in the true fulfilled land."[9]

The idea that the evil person will be saved in spite of being evil rather than the good person is, according to common sense, paradoxical. Shinran, however, argues that this is more understandable when one takes into consideration the *raison d'être* of Amida Buddha. A person who entrusts him/herself to the Other Power and who abandons the confidence in his/her own will and intelligence—that is, a person who may be considered to be an evil person—meets the actual criteria of Amida's Vow more so than "the person who performs good acts in self-power"—that is, a person who attempts to attain salvation based on his/her own intelligence and will.

This statement has evoked various interpretations. My own interpretation is as follows: The meaning of Amida Buddha's Vow lies in the salvation of all who desire salvation by chanting the name of Amida Buddha. The question of whether a practitioner performs good acts or bad acts in this world does not matter with regards to salvation. According to *Sukhāvativyūha Sūtra*, even bad acts do not impede one's salvation. The only stipulation for salvation the eighteenth vow identifies is that "[e]xcluded are only those who commit the five grave offenses (S. *pañcānantarya*, J. *gogyaku*) and abuse the true Dharma (S. *saddharma*, J. *shōbō*)."[10] The five grave offenses include matricide, patricide, killing a saint, injuring the body of Buddha (violating a corpse), and destroying the Buddhist *sangha*. "Abuse of the right Dharma" consists in slandering the Buddhist Truth (S. *dharma*, J. *hō*). As long as one avoids these evils and calls on the name of Amida Buddha, salvation is guaranteed.

A person, who assumes an attitude of self-power and possesses such intelligence and will as to never to perform these extreme evils, shall certainly be saved upon chanting Amida's name. Yet again, is it not hard for such a person, who possesses such an intellect, to simply believe in the efficacy of incantations? Such a person may question whether or not Amida Buddha exists and, moreover, whether Dharmakāra Bodhisattva existed prior to that. Even if Dharmakāra Bodhisattva existed, how does his vow bring about salvation? Does Amida Buddha hear the chants evoking his name? Why do incantations suffice to facilitate salvation? Is universal salvation really plausible? Or are there not any criteria for acts that increase the possibility of salvation? These questions call the practice of chanting into question as if it was a false teaching not worth believing in. Kamo no Chōmei, the author of the *Hōjōki*, was indeed very intelligent and wrote concerning this dilemma that "even while my tongue chants *Namu Amida butsu* for a few times, my mind does not stop." In this case, chanting is possible only as some kind of lip service since the more dominant one's intellect is, the harder it becomes for the practitioner to maintain his/her faith.

On the other hand, insofar as one assumes the attitude referred to as "Other Power" and abandons one's intellect and will, one may be carried away by desire and possibly perform evil deeds without understanding the circumstances others are in. Such a person constitutes a truly evil person who actually commits evil deeds. To his disciples who found it improper that evil persons should be saved, Shinran ordered "to go and kill one thousand people." When they hesitated, Shinran said, "because you lack the karmic cause enabling you to fulfill [what I said], even with a single person, you do not inflict harm. It is not that you do not kill because your own heart is good."[11] People ponder what is right and what is wrong in order to perform acts of goodness and to avoid evil. However, even an evil person exhibits the same tendency to do good for him/herself to at least some degree. It is because of this desire to do good that people also commit evil. This is the "self-power" that inevitably accompanies human consciousness. Therefore, Shinran asserts that human beings are incapable of performing good or evil actions. Good and evil are caused by "past karma" (J. *shukugō*), that is, by fate. When the evil person realizes the wrongness of his/her actions, he/she can fully understand the bottomless powerlessness of human intellect and will. As a result, only at the time when a practitioner abandons the desire for good conduct as something unattainable all together, he/she becomes aware that human existence necessitates salvation by entrusting oneself to the Other Power, and reaches the state where the belief in Amida Buddha has become possible.

Amida Buddha constitutes the infinite being that transcends finite human wisdom. Because there is a being that transcends the finite intellect of human beings, salvation based on the efficacy of the vows made by this transcendent being is possible. However, this differs from Pascal's wager. While the mind that relies on self-power to perform good deeds, at the same time, attempts to prove the essence of its own existence, a person who has abandoned intellect and will is uncertain of his/her own essence. Such a person has no other choice but to rely on Amida Buddha. In addition, when one realizes that the self is devoid of an essence, one already understands the truth of the Buddhist teaching. That is to say, when one entrusts oneself entirely to the Other Power and, consequently, chants the name of Amida Buddha, the effective power of the vow has already become manifest in one's existence. This is what is referred to as "possessing faith" in the first place.

This is the principle underlying Shinran's idiosyncratic interpretation. He consequently believed that the efficacy of chanting Amida's name even overcomes the extraordinary evil deeds that were identified by the *Sukhāvatīvyūha Sūtra*:

> The ocean of the inconceivable Name does not hold unchanged
> The corpses of the five grave offenses and slander of the dharma;
> The myriad rivers of evil acts, on entering it,
> Become one in taste with the ocean water of virtues.[12]

Why is this the case though? If there are extraordinary evil deeds that prevent salvation and cannot be annulled even by the invocation of Amida by a faithful heart, we will have to conclude that while chanting the name erases some evils, it in fact remains ineffective for certain evil actions. If this is the case, the efficacy of chanting the name is offset by one's actions, regardless of whether they are good or bad. Such reasoning, however, would contradict the intent of Amida's Vow, which does not punish or reward bad and good deeds performed in this world, respectively. In that case, chanting the name would be reduced to a mere appeal for salvation and be indicative of a belief wherein salvation is granted to people whose attitude is in accord with the criteria preordained by the transcendent. In fact, the practice of chanting the name itself is the criterion for good actions assigned by Amida Buddha. Repeating this chant faithfully many times was also considered a path toward salvation. If the activity of chanting the name accompanies some kind of power that engenders salvation, it must be a type of self-cultivation (J. *shugyō*). If this was so, the number of good deeds that one accumulates increases in proportion to the frequency with which one performs this practice. Such an understanding of chanting, however, suggests that the act of chanting the name itself is nothing but a mere speech act that constitutes one condition to guarantee the efficacy of the incantation. The fact that Shinran disregards the extraordinary evil identified by the sūtra, however, indicates his belief that the practice of chanting the name does not constitute a form of self-cultivation and that its efficacy works regardless of whether one's deeds are good or bad at all.

> The nembutsu, for the practitioner, is not-practice and not-good. Since it is not practiced out of one's own calculation (*hakarai*), it is called "not-practice." Since it is also not a good act performed out of one's calculation, it is called "not-good." Because it is totally Other Power and apart from self-power, for the practicer [*sic*], it is not-practice, [it is] not-good. Thus were his words.[13]

To Shinran, the practice of chanting the name not only does not constitute a form of self-cultivation but, moreover, does not even count as one's own action. Then, who is the subject that chants the name?

> [T]o begin with: Our coming to say the nembutsu, entrusting ourselves [without any doubt] that, saved by the inconceivable [working] of Amida's great Vow of great compassion, we will go out from birth-and-death, is itself the Tathāgata's working (*hakarai*); when we realize this, then our own efforts and designs (*hakarai*) are not in the least involved; hence we are in accord with the Primal Vow and will be born in the true and real fulfilled land. That is, when we entrust ourselves above all to the inconceivable [working] of the Primal Vow, the inconceivable [working] of the Name is also fully included; the inconceivable [working] of the Vow and that of the Name are one, without any difference whatever.[14]

It is, thus, Amida Buddha himself who calls upon his name. In sum, when one strives to eliminate the essential nature of one's own self to the extent that only the absolute Other Power exists, one reaches a point where Amida Buddha himself calls his own name through one's voice. At this time, it is confirmed that one has attained salvation. Such transcendent events occur in the body of a believer who has pure faith without any reliance on self-power. Put differently, the fact that these transcendent events take place indicates that one has, at last, acquired faith. Shinran states that even faith is bestowed by Amida Buddha. The very surprise one feels upon finding oneself chanting the name of Amida Buddha proves that faith was brought about by Amida's vow and that one's own salvation was predestined by him. Therefore, we have to assert that one's faith necessarily accompanies the invocation of Amida's name and that faith and this invocation are inseparable.

This distinct development of consciousness Shinran calls "lateral transcendence" (J. *ōchō*).[15] Human consciousness usually attempts to perform good deeds in order to strive for the truth. Subsequently, it is rooted in this life and cannot escape from the constraint of this very life. However, when the modality of consciousness is transformed the way Shinran described, the believer transcends "life and death" with the help of the absolute Other Power. This interpretation implies that the practice of chanting the name in such a way comprises neither a form of self-cultivation nor a spell. Even the notion of the "skillful means" does not appropriately capture it. It rather constitutes the pure cry from non-being of a person who seeks for salvation from non-being. At the same time, it is the voice of the transcendent that reveals itself in the invocation of its own name. Finally, it consists in the divine nature of the voice of the transcendent that becomes audible only when human beings become the medium in which the absolute is reflected.

THE TACIT *COGITO*

No thinker within the tradition of Pure Land Buddhism in Japan has investigated the unique principle underlying the invocation of Amida's name as a specific speech act more profoundly than Shinran. He explains that insofar as the practitioner chants the name once, salvation is guaranteed. If the practitioner continues to chant the name of Amida Buddha thereafter, it is only to express gratitude for his/her salvation. We can say that the speech act of chanting Amida's name is necessarily accompanied by a progression toward the transcendent origin of truth. This progression presupposes a fundamental transformation of the experience during which one realizes that the subject of the act is not the self but Amida Buddha, that is, the origin of truth. How can we recognize such a distinct speech act in experience? In other words, how can we understand the distinction of these fundamentally different two kinds of speech acts, a regular speech act whose subject is the self and a distinct one whose subject is the origin of truth?

When one wants to discuss the relationship between truth and reality in modern European philosophy, Descartes' *cogito* is particularly helpful. I would like to introduce Descartes' philosophy, which became the subject of Merleau-Ponty's phenomenology, before I commence my investigation of Merleau-Ponty's philosophy of language. While, according to Descartes, truth must eliminate all form of doubt, there is nothing in this world that cannot be doubted. He suggests in his *Meditations on First Philosophy* that the only thing beyond doubt is the existence of the self that contemplates that "there is nothing that cannot be doubted." If the existence of the self is in doubt, the idea of that "there is nothing that cannot be doubted" itself becomes an object of doubt. Even if we were to assume that there is an evil spirit who deceives the self into thinking that "there is nothing that cannot be doubted," we would have to postulate that the existence of the self is assumed as the object of deception. Consequently, it is impossible to deny the existence of the self as a "thinking substance" (L. *res cogitans*).

However, if the existence of the self is evidenced only by means of its ability to doubt, why should we accept the truth of what this self recognizes as "clear and distinct"? Descartes argues in the third meditation as follows: Since the subject that doubts also doubts its own trajectory of thought, it is a given that the subject knows its own finitude and imperfection. Finitude and imperfection imply the lack of infinity and perfection. If this is given, the fact that there exist the concepts of infinity and perfection in the thoughts of the self must indicate that the idea of God precedes anything else. Then, we must conclude that God's existence alone guarantees the existence of the self. It follows, furthermore, that what the self recognizes as "clear and distinct" is, in fact, nothing but the idea that God has already provided. Consequently, these concepts must be true.

Here, Descartes presents his response to the paradox characteristic of the relationship between truth and subject. This paradox can be summarized as follows: If the subject can discover truth by its own will, such truth does not transcend the subject. From this it follows that the subject is incapable of distinguishing truth from falsity, that is, from its own delusion. On the contrary, if truth manifests itself to the subject as that which is transcendent, whatever appears is necessarily true. If this is so, the question arises as to how we can explain why the subject makes mistakes. Therefore, as long as the statement "the subject can be deceived" is true in some sense, the subject, paradoxically, cannot discover the truth.

How, then, does the subject make mistakes? Descartes explains in his fourth meditation that the subject makes errors when its will goes beyond the limit of its understanding, and mistakes objects it cannot recognize and things it cannot identify unambiguously as the truth. In addition, in his *Passions of the Soul*, he contends that the will constitutes the mental activity that directs thought toward a specific object.[16] It is this will that may follow false opinions.[17] Since thinking is based upon the activity of the will, as long as cognition depends on the will, the subject is prone to be deceived. Furthermore, a question arises as to how false opinions are generated. Indeed, Descartes does not explicitly answer this question, but implies that false opinions may be the residue of past judgments that was brought about when passion assaulted or seduced the will. However, the question is how do past judgments remain in the mind of the subject? In the second meditation, we find Descartes' observation that "[a]lthough *I am thinking within myself silently and without speaking*, I always stumble over words and, more generally speaking, am completely deceived by everyday language"[18] (emphasis by the author). Even though the subject can already recognize the truth insofar as it judges what appears in perception by employing the concepts that are provided by thought, one tends to make an error by applying fallacious concepts because the words used in everyday language express a judgment that is based on past passions. Truth manifests itself to the subject in the transcendent form of an idea, yet it appears in one's thought as that which is given directly. In short, the subject that is restricted by particular passions fails to grasp the truth insofar as it is mediated by language. Although Descartes explains that language is a symbol produced by reason as a tool to express thought, in his *Discourse on the Method*, he also asserts that one must be cautious not to be deceived by this tool when we attempt to recognize truth in our thoughts.

Without developing this theme in any major way, Descartes presupposes that the speech act plays an ambivalent role in the pursuit of truth. The subject of unspoken thought (that is, the *cogito*) faces the truth, and is able to express this truth through language, because of "the habit of associating meaning"[19] with what simply consists of syllables and words. Once the subject begins to speak, however, it always runs the risk of being trapped by false judgments that are supported by past passions because it follows the habit of language. Therefore, Descartes believes that, while language is able to express the truth, it is not necessary for and sometimes even harmful to the discovery of truth. For Descartes, "the subject that thinks silently" alone is the subject that reaches the truth.

Now let us examine how Merleau-Ponty interprets and utilizes Descartes' reasoning. First, Merleau-Ponty critiques the idea of the *cogito* as follows: The certainty of perception confirms the object of perception. Similarly, the certainty of passion confirms the fact that we act. Therefore, as Descartes asserts, perception and passion do not require that they are confirmed by the thought about themselves. Perception and action are not finite and imperfect themselves, but illustrate the human attempt to transcend the imperfect objects that are given in the finite realm in order to move them into the realm of infinity and perfection. While Descartes rejects the idea that one's desire for perfection evidences one's own imperfection, Merleau-Ponty contends that "we are restoring to the *cogito* a temporal thickness."[20] The *cogito* recognizes truth, when it transcends itself within time rather than when it intuitively grasps a concept that transcends history, which, in turn, is formed by time.

Thus, it seems that Merleau-Ponty's position contradicts that of Descartes. Merleau-Ponty, however, soon concedes that what Descartes discovered as the *cogito* and as "the subject that thinks silently" in fact designates existence itself when he examines the historical significance of Descartes' *cogito*: "The tacit *cogito*, the presence of oneself to oneself, being no less than existence, is anterior to any philosophy, and knows itself only in those extreme situations in which it is under threat: for example, in the dread of death or of another's gaze upon me."[21]

Suppose that one proceeds from one perception to another or from one action to another. In this case, one simply denies the previous perception or action and, thus, does not pursue the truth. Thought constitutes the pursuit of truth. It may not constitute the universal truth beyond history, but it provides the conviction that the existing world is rational. According to Merleau-Ponty, the fact that human beings are born and lead lives gives rise to this idea that the world, in which human beings emerge and live, is inherently rational. Life is inclined to examine the question about what kind of entity the world is and never fails to aim at the truth while leaving falsity behind. This we call "existence." It also constitutes the fundamental condition for a consciousness that thinks.

It is understandable that anxiety in the face of death, or under the gaze of the other, may cast doubt on the rationality of the world and the meaning of one's own existence. However, this does not change the fact that this experience is more authentic and fundamental than the experiences of an other. Fear of death and the anxiety caused by the gaze of the other are merely engendered by the intersubjective world, which one already inhabits. If we were to apprehend a form of self-consciousness that is not confined to the world but that constitutes the direct manifestation of the self to itself, then we would have to admit the existence of a subjectivity that does not reside in the world. Is this position not akin to the presupposition underlying Descartes' proposal that there exists a second truth that transcends history? In response to this issue, Merleau-Ponty states in a rather conciliatory tone that "such a formula can be enigmatic" and adds as follows:

> Any particular seizure, even the recovery of this generalized project by philosophy, demands that the subject bring into action powers which are a closed book to him and, in particular, that he should become a speaking subject. The tacit *cogito* is a *cogito* only when it has found expression for itself.[22]

Contrary to Descartes, who maintains that the *cogito* must contemplate silently, Merleau-Ponty thus contends that the *cogito* must become the subject that truly speaks. In the chapter on language in his *Phenomenology of Perception*,[23] Merleau-Ponty argues that the phrase "the speaking subject" signifies our body. This subject must understand the vocabulary as well as the general syntax that are already formed by history generate mannerisms and, in the same sense, meaning in order to convey them to others. The pure subjectivity that thinks in silence is truly embodied and strives to verbalize by assuming that thought constitutes truth.

Now, what does this position have to do with Shinran's contention that only what is uttered by Amida Buddha constitutes truth? In Shinran's thought, "absolute Other Power"—that is, the negation of one's intellectual faculty and one's own will—emerges only when the subject exhaustively investigates the emptiness of the actions motivated by self-power. On the other hand, Merleau-Ponty's tacit *cogito* appears within the limits of the empirical world Buddhism refers to as "birth-and-death" only when the subject examines its own activity of thinking in its depth. Shinran contends that while chanting the *nembutsu* the subject becomes the mouth piece of Amida Buddha and thereby is led to the truth of "emptiness" that transcends birth-and-death. On the contrary, the tacit *cogito*, in Merleau-Ponty's theory, takes on the form of the embodied subject and approaches the truth of existence insofar as it manifests intelligence and will in the act of speaking. The truth of existence is a truth that, in experiencing various existents—in Buddhist terminology, forms (J. *shiki*)—corrects misconceptions insofar as the cognition of particular objects transcends itself. By the same token, it constitutes the truth that confirms passions insofar as each action transcends itself. The origin of such a truth lies in the contingency and the facticity of the world that is given as the commonality that one existent shares with others. It is only then that truth becomes possible.

Unless we consider the notion "form is no other than emptiness," the views on truth of these two thinkers contradict each other. Nonetheless, both Shinran and Merleau-Ponty share the insight that the other—that is, something other than oneself—constitutes the source of truth insofar as in the other the self encounters and experiences the border region of the realm of birth-and-death. In other words, the phrase "the self faces the words of the other" illustrates that this insight shared by Shinran and Merleau-Ponty constitutes the moment necessary for the transcendent truth to manifest itself.

Why is such a moment necessary for the truth? Shinran believes that, since the speech act of chanting the name of Amida Buddha establishes the content of Amida's original vow, it is fruitless to demand any additional response from the practitioner. Similarly, it is not clear why Merleau-Ponty suggests that a subject must express the truth when it becomes a speaking subject even though he acknowledges, at the same time, the existence of a subjectivity that can recognize truth. While he compares the moment when the tacit *cogito* begins to talk to the moment when a happy person begins to sing, the inevitability of such an event remains unclear. Why does Merleau-Ponty avoid the Cartesian—or should we say Zen-like—understanding that assumes a silent unification of the self with the truth?

SPEAKING WORDS

Let us not jump to any rash conclusions. In notes written in his later years, Merleau-Ponty contends that "the tacit *cogito* cannot exist" and "the chapter on the *cogito* is not related to that on language."[24] In his later years, Merleau-Ponty seemed to indicate that his discussions in the chapters on the *cogito* and on language in his *Phenomenology of Perception* differed and that the chapter on language was correct. However, how does the chapter on language explain what the *cogito* is? The following quote certainly disagrees with his discussion of "the tacit *cogito*": "A thought limited to existing for itself, independently of the constraints of speech and communication, would no sooner appear than it would sink into the unconscious, which means that it would not exist even for itself."[25]

What Merleau-Ponty means is that thinking as an action must always also be an activity of speaking words. Of course, we cannot say that the activity of speaking is identical to the act of thinking itself. For example, one can convey a certain meaning to others when vocalizing written language without thinking by oneself. By the same token, a person who is silent and does not use any words may suddenly be struck by an idea and may even feel impatient when attempting to put this idea into words. Nonetheless, this does not indicate that a thought exists independent from language. Merleau-Ponty explains that "this supposed silence is alive with words, this inner life is an inner language."[26] Never does a silent thought exist. A thought is not expressed by speech after it has been thought, but it exists as speech: "Speech, in the speaker, does not translate ready-made thought, but accomplishes it."[27] He further uses the phrase "thought in speech."[28] As is seen in the chapter on the *cogito*, we must say that the speaking subject occasionally thinks in speech rather than assuming that "the silent *cogito* is necessary for the speaking subject to exist."

What is at stake here is the distinction between two kinds of "words," which I introduced at the beginning of this chapter: the rather conventional speech act of "spoken words" (J. *katarareta kotoba*), on the one hand, and the speech act that completes a thought, which is referred to as "speaking words" (J. *kataru kotoba*), on the other. The phrase "speaking words" signifies neither the event when one utters words without vocalizing them as if to remain silent nor the instant when no words whatever are being uttered; rather, this phrase identifies the case when words are already at work in the physical disposition necessary for them to be uttered and to become speech in the next moment. We tend to think that the activity of thinking exists separately from the activity of speaking. However, the reason for this is that, when we analyze the speech act after the fact, we distinguish between "spoken words" and "speaking words." Thus we retrospectively commit the fallacy of identifying the former with speech and the latter with thought. One usually discovers meaning at the moment of thinking. Then, when we continue to think, we forget the words that have given shape to a thought, and assume that, in contrast to the words that remember this very thought at a later moment, there must be silent thought prior to speech. Thinking, however, constitutes the activity of verbalizing thought and is thus indistinguishable from the act of using words.

Depending on the situation, it could be possible that a speaker may not realize this distinction even in his or her own case since both kinds of words are involved in the same activity of speaking. It is possible that one may use words, believing that one is thinking, yet these words may merely constitute a memory of what one has already thought about in the past or a recollection of other people's opinions one has come across in a newspaper and or on television. Similarly, it could be that an amalgamation of memories may produce a seemingly unfamiliar expression. In this case, one may be endlessly contemplating and repeating the same idea in different words without specifically examining it. Therefore, there must be an inherent difference between these two kinds of words. The expressions we refer to as "spoken words," however, only facilitate communication with others and functions to entertain and distract, while the expressions identified as "speaking words" aim at that which is true. In the case of the former, the subject who speaks is merely engaged in a speech act similar to the act of perception, while, in the case of the latter, the subject transcends itself toward the truth through an extraordinary achievement.

Truth comprises a central concept in Cartesian philosophy. It is established when judgments are used to apply concepts to the phenomena of experience. Such judgments are not limited to the realm of thought, but progresses infinitely toward perfection. In Merleau-Ponty's philosophy, however, truth lies in perception as well as in action and proceeds toward the correction of misconceptions as well as the validation of action. Descartes would argue that in order for phenomenal objects to be considered true it is necessary that they are first transformed into thought. On the other hand, Merleau-Ponty contends that truth has to be explicated as ultimate truth in language.[29] Reflection on perception and action is always linguistic. It is only through language that we can find expressions of what is true. People usually call the activity by means of which these kinds of words move toward what is true "thought." But then, the question arises as to in what way this activity differs from that of the *cogito*. Merleau-Ponty explains the phenomenon of "speaking words" as follows:

> Here existence is polarized into a certain "significance" which cannot be defined in terms of any natural object. It is somewhere at a point beyond being that it aims to catch up with itself again, and that is why it creates speech as an empirical support for its own not-being. Speech is the surplus of our existence over natural being.[30]

I would like to explain what Merleau-Ponty means by this. Let us first look at the meaning that arises at the beginning of this process. We can distinguish between two aspects of cognition at that time, one that assigns to existence the quality of being and one that of non-being. We can say that when newly acquired words are assigned to the realm of non-being, existence can restore itself. This means that it is the "speaking words" that constitute existence belonging to the realm of non-being. While the subject that utters the "spoken words" is the human body, the subject who speaks the "speaking words" is, if we follow a literal interpretation, language itself. In fact, there is no word that itself speaks. But there exists the human body as the being, on the one hand, and, on the other hand, the "speaking words" possess the meaning of non-being at the very moment when they come into existence. At a subsequent moment, the human body transforms into the subject that speaks these words insofar as the form of existence that resides in the realm of being comprehends the "spoken words." It is at such an instant, when the universe of words expands, that, in this universe of words, a new meaning that is about to be thought arises. Is this not what Merleau-Ponty suggests? Therefore, the phrase "speaking" suggests a temporal gap between the corporeal existence on the one side, and the embodied subject that speaks words on the other. This does not mean that the self-identical subject thinks the truth, but it rather implies that the concrete qualities of the transcendent movement are discovered by means of this temporal gap. It goes without saying that it is this transcendence that facilitates the possibility of truth.

Yet does this observation differ from the assertion that "a tacit *cogito* becomes the speaking subject"? Merleau-Ponty explains in an essay on language titled *Prose of the World*, written soon after the publication of *Phenomenology of Perception*, as follows: "The meaning of the phrase, 'I think,' is: there is a place called 'I,' in which there is no differences between doing and knowing, or in which the being is united with the manifested being. In such a place, not a single impediment can be conceivable. Such an 'I' is incapable of speaking."[31]

In this paragraph, Merleau-Ponty strives to identify the confusion about the empirical subject that speaks—such a subject is usually explained by means of psychology—as his reason to criticize the idea of language defined in purely grammatical terms in analogy to an algorithm or, in other words, the position that understands language as the tool by means of which consciousness expresses its thought. For example, there are cases when people think they speak to others when, in fact, they speak to themselves or when people think they speak to themselves when, in fact, they hear other people talk. Furthermore, some people feel that other people already know what they are about to say. These pathological experiences illustrate the disorder referred to as "depersonalization" (*dépersonnalisation*)[32] in its extreme form, when it, in fact, constitutes the essence of a speech act. When it comes to language, we cannot distinguish between acting and perceiving. Similarly, we cannot always separate clearly what I say and what I hear, but it is rather that "the discourse speaks itself in me."[33] Consciousness does not first think and then express this very thought: "The acts of speaking and hearing do not only presuppose thought, but also, as its essential character, an ability that enables a real person and, possibly, several others, or presumably everyone, to dismantle and restore oneself as the foundation of thought."[34] Subsequently, the speaking subject that speaks is not a subject that speaks the truth when it emerges from the tacit *cogito*. It exists as "being-for-the-other" (*être-pour-autrui*) insofar as it necessitates the other outside of oneself as the condition of its existence and as the schizophrenic subject that always and continuously loses and recovers its own personality. The subject does not happen to think only when its existence is in a state of dissociation, but always speaks while it continuously disintegrates, in short, when it employs "spoken words."

Thus, the question arises as to how Merleau-Ponty explains the way in which "spoken words" are spoken. The phrase "spoken words" implies that words are already known, not unlike natural objects, and are ready to be used and to be perceived as objects that possess meaning. In linguistics, one traditionally finds two theories about the formation of language: the first is that such a system has been formed as a result of tacit conventions and habits; the second is that it has been formed by the act of signification that relies on natural symbols. Merleau-Ponty rejects both alternatives. He explains that there are several important phrases in any given language. After phrases have been obtained that express the essence of emotions such as, for example, surprise when seeing hailstones, then other phrases, complicated and diversified, develop based on the principle of correspondence. Using this theory, Merleau-Ponty can maintain that language has its root in the experience of nature on the one hand, while, on the other, it has been formed culturally in the intersubjective space as if it was a currency passed on from one person to another throughout the course of history. In this way, a complete system of vocabulary and syntax not unlike a universe has been constructed. In such a world, it is possible for people to perceive objects and to behave as if they were in the natural world.

Assuming that there is such a linguistic universe, Merleau-Ponty distinguishes between "words to be spoken" (J. *katarareru kotoba*)[35] and "speaking words," assigning some value to the latter. Merleau-Ponty suggests not only that the latter gives the former its structure and introduces the essences of emotions observed in nature into the vocabulary, but also that it changes the meaning of already existing words. However, with regard to these two kinds of words, Merleau-Ponty does not recommend abandoning false speech acts and turning toward the true ones; instead, he maintains that these two kinds of words mutually presuppose each other. Even if we were to assume that thought belongs to the realm of "speaking words," the juxtaposition of thought and language or that of the "tacit *cogito*" and the "speaking subject," which emerge when we assign thought to either one of two actions or one of two subjects, would simply be replaced by the juxtaposition of "spoken words" and "speaking words." However, does not Merleau-Ponty reduce the appearance of the transcendent entity that we call truth to the subject's conduct and deportment, as Shinran did? To answer this question, it is necessary to understand the juxtaposition of "spoken words" and "speaking words" within history.

If this were so, what are we supposed to think about the case in which the subject of the "words to be spoken" is able to use words by its own volition and to intentionally change their meaning? This is a matter, I would argue, not of truth, but of political power. The control of vocabulary and syntax by political powers can restrain the people's freedom and result in flattery of authority, while it will not permit the people to speak the truth. On the other hand, as Merleau-Ponty already mentions in his chapter on freedom,[36] under the general use of, for example, Lenin's expression "we are workers," the meaning of the word "worker" was changed and it came to denote "human beings, who are forced by the class system to engage in alienating labor and, as oppressed workers, are placed under a common destiny." Today, however, there is room to doubt whether this phrase is true. Here, Merleau-Ponty attempts to show that what people call "truth" is nothing but the words that capture the situation of a particular historical period, however brief, wherein they reside. Does this not imply that there is a thought of truth that is based on the historical circumstances as well as on life in its totality? Truth is neither something that subjectivity freely captures nor something that manifests itself in the field of consciousness. Similarly, words comprise neither false judgment that are merely based on confused thought nor ambiguous expressions that arise from the misuse of language. Such an understanding of words is nothing but a classification developed by political authority with the goal to suppress specific thought. Usually, authorities attempt to justify such an ideology by reverting to the assumption that "language precedes thought." However, while the thought of truth that appears in history may be politically construed as a false judgment or an ambiguous expression, it is able to resonate among people as the truth of a particular moment, which no expression surpasses in clarity. Is this not the phenomenon that Merleau-Ponty refers to as "speaking words"?

In the chapters on language and freedom, Merleau-Ponty suggests that truth exists within history. That, thus, raises the question of how each perception and each action relates to the totality of history, how perception and action can be expressed to others, and how they can resonate the words of others. He states the following:

> Phenomenology of truth is theoretically impossible, yet can be recognized by those who act out on truth. Acknowledging that there is truth indicates that our presence, being judged by all the events, becomes the truth. This occurs when I revisit and encounter all the projects by myself and others, when I succeed in expressing my thought and thereby release what was captured and confined within a being, and when I see the internal communication being established in the thickness of personal and interpersonal time.[37]

I believe that this paragraph concisely expresses Merleau-Ponty's notion of truth. However, from this paragraph we can deduce the significance that his theory of "the tacit *cogito*" has for his conception of truth. In short, the tacit *cogito* comprises one aspect of the self through which the speaking subject thinks. It further constitutes the self that has become the subject of existentialism, that contemplates its own birth and death, and that reflects upon the existence of others. In his chapter on the *cogito*, Merleau-Ponty poses the question of whether we can consider such "self" as "the origin of truth," that is, the foundation on which the speaking subject releases itself by means of "speaking words" at once into the realm of non-being. This question carries with itself an already negative connotation, yet Merleau-Ponty did not present any alternative to it. However, since his study was abruptly interrupted by his premature death, resolving this dilemma remains a task for those who follow in his philosophical footsteps.

CONCLUSION

It seems that Merleau-Ponty's own investigation into the question of how it is possible for "speaking words" to speak the truth remains without a conclusion. How did he, in the end, think of the "praxis that performs the truth"? Furthermore, the question arises as to who was Amida Buddha in the eyes of Shinran who incessantly pursued the question of how it is possible to commit oneself to the transcendent? He calls the state in which one awakens to the insight that it is absolutely impossible for the self to form or to know the truth and, thus, enters the realm of the other power the "natural suchness" (J. *jinen hōni*). Is not devotion to Amida Buddha nothing but the practice of leading a life in which the practitioner only sustains his or her own non-being? If this worldview is correct, the question arises as to the purpose of chanting the name of Amida Buddha as the "words that speak the truth."

   Both Merleau-Ponty and Shinran explore the question of how to understand the self on the basis of the "origin of truth." However, while the former investigates the being of the self that is trapped in the realm of birth and death, the latter focuses on the non-being of the self that transcends birth and death. These two philosophers were engaged in the same pursuit of the "origin of the truth" and share common interests even though they were separated by space and time. In short, both argue for the transcendence of that which speaks the truth and thus constitutes its origin as well as for the non-being of the subject, which such a transcendence presupposes. Merleau-Ponty, in particular, teaches us that that which speaks words constitutes, from the perspective of the subject, not simply a transparent activity, but it must enter the inevitable speculation that arises when we call into question thought and scholarship. It is the particularity of truth that truth itself is not only to be found in that which is simple and clear or that which is unconditionally affirmed. Truth cannot be expressed by merely placing words that are already known and used in everyday communication in an order according to logic. To the contrary, truth must appear in the consciousness of the self as something other than the self. We must not fall into the trap of turning language into a mystery. By the same token, we must not be oblivious to the particular character that language possesses, and reduce words to a mere system of symbols. I believe that, in this sense, both thinkers discussed in the present chapter continue to speak to us today.

Translated by Gereon Kopf and Yuki Miyamoto

7

Self in Space

Nishida Philosophy and Phenomenology of Maurice Merleau-Ponty

Bernard Stevens

The philosophy of Nishida Kitarō (1870–1945) may appear enigmatic to the reader trained in the philosophical traditions of Europe and America because his style of writing seems so idiosyncratic, and the expressions and phrases he uses lack clarity. However, the correlations of Nishida's thought to some themes central to French phenomenology may make his philosophy more accessible. In this chapter, I evoke affinities between Nishida and Maurice Merleau-Ponty (1908–1961). Indeed, one can find in the Merleau-Pontian reflections on the notion of "flesh" (*la chair*) true similarities to Nishida's notion of "active intuition" (J. *kōiteki chokkan* 行為的直觀).[1]

An exploration of Nishida's research, especially in reference to the notion of non-ego, places him within the philosophical movement that Paul Ricoeur calls "reflexive philosophy." Ricoeur uses this term to identify the post-Cartesian tradition, which, through its reflexive investigation of the self, defines the criteria for reflection as such. Reflexivity is the medium of reflection, and self-reflection the medium of the reflection on things.

Nishida relentlessly questions the apodicticity of the Cartesian *cogito* as well as the idealistic and phenomenological subjectivity that has stemmed from it. The reason for this concern lies in his conceptual proximity to their philosophical approach and in his attempt to define the (possibly imperceptible) particularity of his own standpoint in relationship to the Cartesian project. By establishing nothingness as the foundation of the ego—and thus making himself the heir of the Buddhist non-ego—he endeavors to find a new standpoint, which is an unheard-of position for the philosophy of subjectivity. It is precisely because his is a philosophy of the non-ego that Nishida's viewpoint constitutes one of subjectivity. This feature of Nishida's thought is reminiscent of the philosophical projects of, for example, Heidegger, who tried to overcome the metaphysics of subjectivity through a complete reworking of it with the notion of *Dasein*, Merleau-Ponty, who endeavored to give back to the *cogito* its primordial incarnation in the lived body (*corps vécu*), or Michel Henry, who is concerned with rooting the constituting *cogito* again within the living origin of its activity.

SELF-AWAKENING THAT IS IMMANENT IN LIFE

The self, which has been untiringly explored by Nishida using terms ranging from "pure experience" (J. *junsui keiken* 純粋経験) to "locus" (J. *basho*場所) or "active intuition," represents the idea of, not knowing oneself, but experiencing oneself and feeling oneself. It comprises subjectivity, not as the constitutive *cogito*, but as the interiority that grounds the *cogito*. Within the experience of the self, subjectivity appears to itself as the field of appearance as such. Self-experience is the background against which the appearance of the world and of things can come to be.

In his essay "The Intelligible World," Nishida introduces a threefold topological model of being.[2] Using this model, he locates the appearance of the world and of natural beings on the level of what he calls the "locus of beings" (J. *yū no basho* 有の場所). This comprises the level of reflection that is best illustrated by the Aristotelian type of thought—that is, logic that conceives of objects as substances. These objects are apprehended by the subsumptive judgment by means of the predicative proposition. This locus signifies the modality of being in which the self experiences the world. However, such an experience of the world, when limited to this dimension, happens at the expense of self-awareness of the self; such a "locus" is constituted at the price of bracketing the self in the form of an inverse phenomenological reduction.

In contrast, the place where the self experiences itself as the condition of its encounters with the world constitutes the second locus; this is the place where reflection becomes self-reflection, while subjectivity performs a return to itself and arouses self-awakening. This comprises the standpoint that is inaugurated by transcendental philosophy, opening the field of consciousness that is capable of predicating reality. Nishida calls this locus "oppositional nothingness" (J. *tairitsuteki mu no basho* 対立的無の場所) because, if it is indeed the source of signification, within its very immediacy it is nothingness (J. *mu* 無) or non-being; as such it is "opposed to" (J. *tairitsuteki* 対立的) or relative to the being that it is going to signify.

This locus is at first conquered by Cartesian doubt, which reveals subjectivity and identifies it as the locus of non-being where the world emerges. However, the Cartesian position immediately loses the very fact that it brought to light, insofar as it begins to reify this subjectivity as the modality of a soul or "thinking thing" (*res cogitans*). Rather than asserting the self as the source of reality, the Cartesian position reduces the former to a mere portion of the latter in the sense that it objectifies the ego. The Kantian position further thematizes subjectivity as meaning bestowing agency, but the Kantian transcendental ego tires itself out in the endeavor to signify the transcendent object. Within its unfolding of the formal transcendental, the more it does not include any intuition of subjectivity as such, only the presupposition of an *Ich denke* accompanies all representation. This is why the locus of oppositional nothingness cannot satisfy itself with the transcendentalism indicative of the *a priori* conditions of possibility. It has to deepen itself through a self-intuition that tries to explore, in the Husserlian mode, the very life of *noetic* activity.

Nishida is indeed parallel to Husserl in the manner in which he theorizes about subjectivity in action. In phenomenological reduction, reflection turns away from the world (the world of the natural or Aristotelian attitude as well as the world of Galilean science) and the locus of being in order to turn itself toward the condition of its appearance within the *noetico-noematic* correlation, which is equivalent to Nishida's locus of oppositional nothingness. In this way, phenomenology begins the exploration of *noetic* activity as the life of consciousness, that is, as the field of the "life-world" (*Lebenswelt*). This is the life of the mind as much as the everyday life within its irreducibility and its ever-new singularity. For Nishida, as much as for the later Husserl, actual reality is not identical to the notion of nature by positive sciences and abstract idealities, but constitutes life from wherein consciousness arises as that which gives perspective to the world. Bestowing meaning to ideality and science, life is itself a subjective givenness that exists within the intuition and the experience of self-affection. Phenomenology rescues consciousness from its preoccupation with the beings of the world and with a naïve conception of a world existing as such; it thus calls the world back to the web of subjective performances and to the universality of subjective operations that are synthetically connected. In other words, the world is in the process of constantly being constituted as the correlation between these two operations.

The movement that returns from the naïve scientific world to its foundation in the life-world is not complete unless this living-within is properly thematized in its very givenness. This shift in focus from the sphere of the world to the sphere of meaning, bestowing subjectivity in its very givenness, which was precipitated by transcendental philosophy and confirmed by the phenomenological reduction, opens a methodological space in which Western thought intersects with Eastern thought (essentially Buddhist), investigating the life of consciousness. It is this very space that Nishida has tried to map out with his "logic of locus" (J. *basho no ronri* 場所の論理), for it is here that the hidden depth of being is offered to us as an object of reflection.

Husserl believed that he could grasp subjectivity in its proper vein in the lived intuition of its evidence. Did he succeed? The intuition of the world, which opens up an endless succession of new horizons, is always subject to reshaping; it tends to follow new perspectives, which are always fragmentary and partial in nature and which reveal it. Self-intuition, on the contrary, claims to be apodictic and absolute. Yet the flux of consciousness, of which the constituting subjectivity is constructed, is always moving, wavering, indiscernible, infinite, and disappearing within its concrete mode. The only way of grasping it in its evidence is to reduce it to its typical structure, which is always identical to the same type of reality and every consciousness. In this way, the emergence of consciousness is itself eideticized in the same mode as the beings of the world, to which it is brought down, even though it had first tried to free itself from this world through transcendental reduction. The irreducible concreteness of conscious reality is itself reduced to an eidetic dimension. In the process of thematic grasping of subjectivity by means of the eidetic reduction, concrete reality is lost in favor of its ideatic representation and its ideal essence. In this way, the transcendental experience, immanent and indubitable, is paradoxically reduced to an experience that is intentional and thus transcendent. This is all the more so since the grasping of this intentionality takes place, as do the objects of the world, by means of fulfilling that which is always partial and provisional. Thus the subjectivity that makes one see remains itself unseen in its very reality. It becomes obvious that, in the end, even Husserlian phenomenology cannot grasp the primordial source of the flux of consciousness in its ultimate origin, which cannot be grasped within the sphere of Husserlian phenomenology since it is prior to time itself.

It appears that even the philosophy of Husserl did not escape the objectification of subjectivity to which the Cartesian *cogito* and the Kantian transcendental successively succumbed. Any self-reflection of subjectivity, including thinking and representing consciousness, inescapably ends up in its own decay to the ontic rank of an object of investigation, thereby obliterating its own origin. Any representational self-reflection rejects subjectivity in the exteriority of the world, using this external objectivity as the criterion of its own intimate constitution. The subject, when reduced to being the condition of the object, becomes itself an object, so to speak, and cannot be grasped in its pure subjectivity.

In order to escape from such a destiny of reflexive subjectivity, Nishida postulates a third sphere, namely, the most intimate locus of absolute nothingness (J. *zettai mu no basho* 絶対無の場所). From this place, self-awakening emerges as the locus of oppositional nothingness. This is the locus from which the constituting subjectivity and the world it constitutes can be mutually understood because this third sphere transcends both. What is located in this place does not comprise the act of seeing and representing but rather the source of the one and of the other while remaining unseen and unrepresented itself. The self, here, is no more understood as the condition of the object, but emptied of all objective content; it is radical nothingness. Reduced to its pure activity, the self is nothing but this activity beyond the limits of the individual self. The self is the field of the experience that precedes the experiencing subject, and the field is the locus of seeing, while itself invisible; it is the locus of seeing without a seeing subject. In sum, life as such precedes individual consciousness and gives birth to consciousness. This ultimate locus is accessed through a process of regression from cognitive activity to affective, aesthetic, and volitional activities. The self, taken in its ultimate origin, comprises affectivity, self-affection, pure (self) experience, and primordial pathos. It constitutes the locus where the most unshareable singularity of the self takes its roots in a dimension that comes before it, and from which it emerges; this is life. Thus, the Nishidian reflection ends up in a philosophy of immanence and of life, whose affinities with Husserlian phenomenology are less striking than with that of Michel Henry. The best introduction to Nishida's philosophy may be the ideas of Michel Henry as represented in his *L'essence de la manifestation*.

While Nishida's philosophy shares deep similarities not only with Henryan phenomenology, but also with the Freudian unconscious and the Schopenhauerian will, it nevertheless does not relinquish the subject to the blindness of primordial drives. On the contrary, Nishida calls this final sphere, which is the source of consciousness, the "intelligible world" (J. *eichiteki sekai* 叡智的世界). It comprises intelligibility that is put into light. For the horizon of absolute nothingness, which constitutes the root of the self, is not just the source of the self's vital singularity and primordial will, but also of its spiritual attitude, which includes the religious, the volitional, the aesthetic, and, thereafter, the cognitive. Intelligibility indeed is always founded in affectivity before it becomes cognitive or categorical; that is, it exists in the aesthetic contemplation of beauty, in the religious union with the sacred, and in the volitional action toward the good.

Rooted in its most intimate nature in the innermost depth of reality, the no-self, which is also nonsubstantial, can then embark upon its dialectic relationship with the world by becoming "active intuition"; it is thus engaged in society, culture, and in the various modes of being-in-the-world. The movement of the continuous deepening of self-awakening, which is suggested by Nishida's threefold topology, is followed, in the philosopher's itinerary, by the movement of the dialectic interaction of the self with the world. This interaction discloses the rhythm of the infinite variations of the "self-identity of absolute contradictories" (J. *zettai mujunteki jiko dōitsu* 絶対矛盾的自己同一). It seems clear that Nishida's thought reveals a close proximity to Merleau-Ponty's philosophy of the lived body (*corps vécu*), even though it is anchored in a position close to that of Michel Henry.

ACTIVE INTUITION—ACTION INSCRIBED IN THE FLESH

Merleau-Ponty developed a phenomenology that, while in agreement with the Husserlian criticism of objectivism and psychologism, refuses to withdraw to a transcendental egology that is forgetful of its origins. For Merleau-Ponty, the phenomenologist is not an "impartial spectator" who is capable of a pure eidetic glance. Instead, he finds himself bound to an irreducible facticity, which is not just that of a being-in-the-world, structured by "care" (*Sorge*), but that of a body carnally situated in the world. Existence enters reality through sensitivity and feeling, both of which are not merely transcendent of the world but rather constitute passivity to the world. Through the flesh the fact of seeing also makes me visible. There is a reciprocity between the body and the environment. It is on this level of the phenomenology of the lived body, which, simultaneously, sees and is seen, touches and is touched, feels and is felt in its interactions with its environment, that we find an affinity with Nishida's notion of active intuition.[3]

Nishida develops his concept of "active intuition" in the context of his reflection on the body and on the historical world (J. *rekishiteki sekai* 歴史的世界). Nishida tackled the question of the body during his "turn" in the mid-1930s; thus it is possible to call him a true forerunner of Merleau-Ponty. Nishida questions the status of the acting body on the level of active intuition—that is, on the horizon of the world—as historical reality. Nishida strives to overcome the notion of consciousness as reflection delimited by intentionality in order to include the praxis of our historical self. Nishida's philosophy thus overcomes the standpoint of representation in order to attain a concept that can theorize the self-determination of the world from the standpoint of self-awareness. The self-determination of the world on the level of active intuition signifies that the world constitutes dialectically what is formed as well as what is formative. Moreover, such a philosophy of active intuition overcomes the position of pure experience since the latter remains on the level of intellectual cognition, whereas the former evokes the practical and poetical dimension characteristic of an acting and producing body. The body precedes consciousness and is itself historically formed. Nishida's emphasis on the historicity of the body suggests that the latter is not limited to its biological dimension but includes the factuality of conscious life. The life of consciousness finds its origin in the factuality of bodily existence. It does not exist apart from bodily activity. Every intuition is active; intelligibility roots itself in sensibility. Nishida, like Merleau-Ponty, brings to the fore the ambiguity of the body, which is reducible neither to interiority nor to exteriority and possesses both objectivity and subjectivity; it is constituted by means of the dialectical relations between the poles of donation and reception, vision and action, and so forth. Vision belongs to intuitive apperception and receives a form of a perceived object as well as that of one's own body. This way, the body sees itself among the objects of the world wherein it can act. In addition, action that belongs to praxis is itself formative. Acting, the body develops a configuration of things and opens a perspective within which it can appear to itself. It is simultaneously formed and forming, seeing and seen; the acting body thus finds its origin "in the relationship between that which creates and that which is created in the form of a continuity of discontinuity (J. *hirenzoku no renzoku* 非連続の連続)."[4] Insofar as he proposes a notion of the body as that which is seeing as well as seen, Nishida joins Merleau-Ponty, who says in *L'oeil et l'esprit* that "the enigma of the body holds in the fact that it is both seeing and visible."[5]

For Nishida, the body is the instrument of the self-formation and self-expression of historical life. Beyond the perceptive and cognitive relation to things on the spatial axis of simultaneity, there is a poetic relation to them on the dynamic axis of time. The bodily insertion of the mind in a poetic rather than theoretic modality is, for the body, a way of inhabiting a world that is "made of the same material" (*fait de la même étoffe*), to use Merleau-Ponty's expression. Being an expression of the world, it is also a speaking body. In addition, if one considers the fact that ours is a historical and not just a biological body, it is safe to say that speech is a bodily gesture. Since it discloses sensibility and intelligibility, speech can be called the body of the mind. By the same token, language is the incarnation of reason. Language is a tool for man, as are his body and the worldly instruments around him. Through language, the body is not solely the expression of a meaning-bestowing subject; it constitutes a self-formative and self-expressive act of the world.

The fact that the body evolves on the level of active intuition suggests that the two moments of intuition and action are inseparable: one realizes itself as the other. Active intuition comprises the fundamental mode of the being of human beings in the world; it constitutes the very structure of our being-in-the-world. In *Logic and Life* (J. *Ronri to semei* 論理と生命),[6] Nishida develops his notion of the body as the ambiguous reality of active intuition. He underlines the ambiguity of the body in its dual function as seer (subject) and seen (object). One's body comprises the locus and the condition of such an ambiguity. What distinguishes Nishida's notion of the body as active intuition from Merleau-Ponty's notion of the lived body is that the latter essentially observes the way the body appears to itself in the sense that my body is visible to me. Because the body is mine, I grasp myself both as interior and exterior. The world appears here as the horizon of such a phenomenality. Nishida, on the other hand, underscores the exteriority of the visibility of the lived body. This means that the fact of seeing is what gives the body its exteriority. This fact is grasped independently of any consideration of the inner sense. The importance given to seeing diverts the attention from the inner feeling of bodily extension. It also signifies that the objectivity of the lived body implicitly suggests the existence of another seer. The visibility of the body is there for all. Nishida does not stress that the vision is mine, as Merleau-Ponty does, but rather emphasizes its neutral thingness: I see my body as others can see it, that is, as an object of the exteriority of worldly space. I see myself as an object of the world. This is Nishida's way of performing an inversion of the modern transparent and self-identical transcendental subject.

Nishida's inversion of the self goes still further. To Nishida, the body becomes the site of the self-appearance of the world itself to itself. The act of seeing what happens in the process of the self-appearing of the world is not just that of one individual subject. The corporal self is a transitory modality of the self-revelation of the world. In reflexive consciousness, the world constitutes that which sees itself. The self-awakening of the world takes place in human consciousness, and consciousness marks the advent of the world. In it, the world sees itself from inside. The appearance of the world does not merely indicate a single moment of intentional consciousness but nothing less than the topological turning of the world. When consciousness experiences itself, the world experiences itself at the same time. The historical body constitutes the self-expression of the world itself. This self-expression or self-determination of the historical world is located in a particular human body; it individualizes itself and thereby becomes its own ir-reducible source of autonomy.

The phenomenological interest of Nishida obviously does not limit itself to a prefiguration of the philosophy of Merleau-Ponty. The two complementary move-ments that animate Nishida's reflection—the deepening of self-awakening in the direction of the absolute nothingness of the intelligible world and the active intu-ition, which constitute the locus of the self-determination of the world—indicate a philosophical approach that locates consciousness in a source that is not simply preconscious but of a greater dimension than individual consciousness. This source can be understood as something that is superconscious and yet worldly. This immersion must not be understood as an eclipse of the individual in a dimension that precedes and dominates him, but rather—and this is more than once asserted by Nishida—as the condition necessary to establish more vividly its individuality through a better and truer way of grasping its very source.

8

Merleau-Ponty, Cézanne, and the *Basho* of the Visible

Gerald Cipriani

I

If there is a philosopher in the Western world who understood the nature of artistic experience with particular reference to the visible, it is Maurice Merleau-Ponty. Even more, many commentators agree that he was one of the first theorists to succeed in understanding such an experience. What he argued in his theoretical studies, he found embodied in the making of the artist and in the contemplation of the work of art. Of course, Merleau-Ponty's philosophy mutated during the course of his life, and if he was primarily concerned with the nature of perception and sensory experience in general in the 1930s or at the time of his *Phénoménologie de la perception* (1945), he subsequently became increasingly focused on visuality. In his last texts such as *L'Oeil et l'esprit* (1964), or *Le Visible et l'invisible* (1964), the painting was ascribed one of the privileged roles to celebrate, or even reveal, such a visuality. As a matter of fact, it is with Paul Cézanne in *Sens et Non-sens* (1948) that Merleau-Ponty started to bring to light the extent to which the experience of the artist and that of the spectator went beyond, or rather prior to, mere concerns with objective, representational accounts of reality. For Merleau-Ponty, the paintings of Cézanne were testimonies about one's way of relating to the world through sensory perception, and, by extension, about one's embodied way of being-in-the-world. As a matter of fact, if Merleau-Ponty's well-known text "Le Doute de Cézanne" from *Sens et Non-sens* must be understood in the light of his *Phénoménologie de la perception*; the same applies to *L'Oeil et l'esprit* and *Le Visible et l'invisible*. In this last phase, Merleau-Ponty increasingly directed his reflections toward building a universal ontology of art. Art had the power to make the visible emerge against the invisible background of the objective world—that is, the metaphysical world of preconceived or already established representations. In a way, art's authentic nature was to disclose the relationship between the visible and the invisible background of its occurrence.

One can only be struck by the similarities between Merleau-Ponty's understanding of the emergence of the visible against an invisible background and the Japanese Buddhist philosopher Nishida Kitarō's (1870–1945) conception of *basho*, which can be the "place" of form, consciousness, reality, creativity, and culture or religiosity, among others. *From the Acting to the Seeing* (*Hataraku mono kara miru mono e* 働くものから見るものへ, 1927) is the starting point of Nishida's complex reflection explicitly articulated around the idea of *basho*,[1] which culminated toward the end of his life in "The Logic of *Basho* and the Religious Worldview" (*Bashoteki ronri to shūkyōteki sekai kan* 場所的論理と宗教的世界観, 1945). In the philosophy of Nishida, *basho* corresponds more to a paradigm than to something that would have a single precise equivalence in Western languages. It has indeed equally been translated in English as "place," "topos," "location," or "field," among others. For this reason, the Japanese word *basho* will be kept throughout this chapter.

There is, in fact, much common ground between the philosophies of Merleau-Ponty and Nishida, such as dialectics, ethics, the body, the creative, and historicity, to mention a few, all of which bear the mark of Zen Buddhism to varying degrees. The present chapter will obviously have to limit itself to describing the extent to which Merleau-Ponty's conception of the invisible as background can be understood in terms of the Nishidian conception of *basho*, with particular reference to the paintings of Cézanne. What is the extent to which the *basho* of the visible world of artistic experience can be interpreted as the invisible objective world of representations?[2] It should be stressed that, more than a comparative analysis, this chapter should be understood as a dialogical reflection that brings together some aspects of the philosophies of Merleau-Ponty and Nishida. It is, however, necessary to recall how the Buddhist notions of reciprocity (dialectics), pure experience (the perception of things as such), and *soku* (something "is" in that it "is not") are pivotal to Nishida's fundamental axis of *basho*.

For Nishida, every self-determined thing is bound to be situated within a *basho*, which in the process discloses itself in a mutually inclusive relationship with this very thing. The purposive and nonhierarchical nature of this dynamic process unfolds ad infinitum. To put it differently, as there will always be a *basho* that relates to a particular thing in a mutually self-determining way, what Nishida calls "the logic of *basho*" (*bashoteki ronri* 場所的論理) is infinite and therefore groundless. As such the very conception of an all-encompassing *basho* leads to nothingness itself, the *basho* of absolute nothingness (*zettai mu no basho* 絶対無の場), which is undefinable and invisible, and within which all other *basho* are reciprocally self-determined through self-negation. More precisely, the place of absolute nothingness is the very movement of self-negation that makes these reciprocal relationships possible.[3] The self-determination of a particular thing, such as the appearing of Mont Sainte-Victoire, would take place through the self-negation of Cézanne's preconceived knowledge. That is, the perceptual "pure experience" of the suchness of Mont Sainte-Victoire is undistorted by conceptual finalities as Zen Buddhism has it. For Nishida, the relationships between all self-determinations and their *basho* are reciprocal, or rather dialectical, whether these relationships are those between the artist and the world, between the spectator and the artwork, or, more generally, between self-determined individuals, or even between individuals and the social or historical worlds. The self-determinations of individuals and worlds are therefore made possible through unmediated concrete experiences, including perceptual ones, whereby the dichotomy between subject and object is overcome, and where the separation between subjective and objective worlds is put aside. This was indeed realized in what Nishida called "pure experience" (*junsui keiken*純粋経験), whose nature was inspired by Zen Buddhism and at the same time conceptually justified under the influence of William James's radical empiricism.[4] What made Nishida's project akin to the undertaking of Western phenomenologists was his attempt to provide an understanding of our consciousness of "reality" (*jitsuzai* 実在) by means of "pure experience" through the perception of the suchness of things which Zen Buddhism considers ineffable.

Just as Merleau-Ponty advocated a phenomenological description of the perceptual experience of the visible, Nishida sought to articulate conceptually what occurs in the "pure experience" of things-as-such. During his life Merleau-Ponty remained not only suspicious, but critical of cognitive approaches that establish and preserve a separation between the human subject and its object of inquiry. If such a criticism is articulated in a systematic fashion in his first works, it appears fully developed in the last part of his life and his reflections on artistic experience. In his *Phénoménologie de la perception*, arguably the most important philosophical reflection ever undertaken on the topic, he criticizes any mode of thought that presents the human subject in a way that presupposes the world. The idealism found in Edmund Husserl's *Cartesianische Meditationen* (1950) and Immanuel Kant's *Kritik der reinen Vernunft* are, among others, his targets, but so is any method of research that reduces human beings to objects of study, for example, the kind of realism that one finds in empirical psychology.[5] The problem at the heart of this fundamental misunderstanding about human beings' embodiment in the world, which can only result in overlooking the true nature of artistic experience, is that the dominant subject does not open any world but presupposes it. For instance, if we were to follow Kant's method of understanding the formation of meaning in artistic experience, we would end up with a subject-centered set of rules for meaning experienced in its phenomenal nature to be possible. The nonsense of such an approach that preconstructs what has to be experienced in its immediate, unexpected, and lived dimension is self-evident. The human subject cannot precede the world it pretends to grasp, because it cannot be disengaged from the world in which it lives—it always belongs to such a world. Neither should it use its cognitive capacities to determine what the world is like in a realist fashion, as if human beings were pure disembodied consciousnesses. The subject should not be treated as "beyond" its embodied, finite life if one is to avoid this type of transcendence that gives shape and structure to meaningful experience. The ideal of a preconstructed world goes against any notion of human involvement in what is experienced. To define in a Kantian manner a set of a priori (universal and necessary) rules which makes phenomenal life possible is not conceivable. The idealist subject is disembodied as it presents itself, just like the realist one, in clear opposition to what it seeks to know, that is to say, the "object." Both idealism and realism belong to the category of what Merleau-Ponty calls "objective thought." Of course such a criticism of the pure subject was not at the time restricted to Merleau-Ponty. Jean-Paul Sartre in *La Transcendance de l'ego* questioned Husserl's notion of the pure ego when it came to working out cognitive experiences. The problem of the primacy of the subject's consciousness was also a feature of the first part of Sartre's *L'Etre et le néant* (1943), where the notion of *être* (being) was introduced to replace any idealistic conception of the significance of objects. In his *Phénoménologie de l'expérience esthétique* (1953), Mikel Dufrenne pledged in his own applied way against the same thing: intellectualist approaches lead to disembodiment. At the same time the "being" of Dufrenne's "aesthetic object" is potentially already there although waiting for the "subject" to actualize it in a sensory manner in perception itself. For him the potential "aesthetic object" is what he calls the "work of art" in its objective dimension; for Merleau-Ponty, "objective reality" is the potential "perceived world," or, to put it differently, the *invisible* world is the potential for the *visible* world to be. These are just examples of criticisms against, or challenges to, objective thoughts that have developed in the Western world. In some cases they have even been systematized in the form of the deconstruction of metaphysics. What is fundamental to bear in mind, however, is that Merleau-Ponty, following Edmund Husserl, was striving to retrieve a ground that Western metaphysics had lost. On the contrary, the pretheoretical ground before the separation between subject and object was, for Nishida, a point of departure that belonged to the tradition of Zen Buddhism.

Strikingly, both Nishida and Merleau-Ponty realized in the course of their life the dangers of falling into a mysticism of "pure experience" and a foundational theory of the preobjective world, respectively. Both stressed in different ways and at different stages the dialectical and therefore reciprocally complementary character of the relationship between entities and their *basho*, or between the *visible* and the *invisible*. For Nishida, beside Hegel's dialectics, the most profound influences regarding this aspect came from Buddhism, and more precisely from Rinzai Zen and Pure Land. The constitution of entities "in themselves" was only possible by means of their dialectical relationships with other persons or other worlds, whether social or historical, which thus became their *basho*. However, unlike with Hegelian and Marxist dialectics, under no circumstances should the self-determination of entities be understood as part of a hierarchical dynamics. The Buddhist conception of "reality" (in Nishida's philosophy, *jitsuzai* 実在) made of contradictory relationships between entities is, in essence, nonhierarchical.[6] Its Japanese version is that of *soku* (即), according to which something "is" in that it "is not." In Nishida's world, entities in formation are like complementary differentials that are always both located within and related to their *basho* in a mutually creative manner, with all the specific temporal and ethical dimensions they entail.

Importantly, Nishida's logic of *basho* should therefore not be understood as a theory that would explain the ways entities as various as judgment, meaning, or simply our consciousness are determined by their context. As the relationship between the *basho* and a particular entity is in such a logic nonhierarchical, the latter cannot be instrumental for the former to be determinant and vice versa. For Nishida, the person who perceives, interprets, or creates, just like what is perceived, interpreted, or created, is affirmed as "self-determination" (*jiko gentei* 自己限定) through the dialectical relationship that is established with what becomes a *basho*. Nishida calls such a self-determination, with some degrees of variation, a "contradictory self-identity" (*mujunteki jiko dōitsu* 矛盾的自己同一, or *mujun no jiko dōitsu* 矛盾の自己同一); this self-identity becomes almost *absolute* (*zettai* 絶対) in the case of religious experience.

At first glance, Nishida's interpretations of Buddhist notions of *soku* (something "is" in that it "is not") and of the perception of the suchness of things ("pure experience") seem to find echoes in Merleau-Ponty's conceptions of the dialectical relationship between the visible and the invisible and of the perception of the phenomenon of the visible. In a similar vein, the way Nishida conceptualizes the relationship between the individual and the universal comes close to how Merleau-Ponty ends up challenging Western metaphysics, with particular reference, once again, to the visible phenomenal world and the invisible objective world.

Nishida challenges Aristotle's "logic of the subject,"[7] which presents the universal predicate as an almighty determinant, and Merleau-Ponty does the same with the world of "objective thoughts."[8] For Nishida, the individual subject can be equally known as a *basho* that enables the universal predicate to determine itself. The relationship between the individual and the universal is not anymore unidirectional and hierarchical, as both are seen to be mutually determinant, following the creative reciprocal movement of the "logic of *basho*." The predicative plane is obviously only one type of universal, which can be that of any entity, such as "action," "judgment," or "being."[9]

II

Merleau-Ponty's conception of the invisible objective world that is set against the visible perceived world could then be interpreted as a particular instance of a universal, which is neither completely self-determined nor completely determinant. And just as the world is for Merleau-Ponty *stylized* each time it is perceived, universals are not static and are thought to be expressive.[10] This means that the expression of a universal depends on how it relates to the individual as its *basho* and, needless to say, vice versa. This is why Nishida thinks of the constitution of what he calls "reality" in terms of mutually creative relationships between persons, between society and individuals, and between history and particular events. For Merleau-Ponty the "reality" of Mont Sainte-Victoire is not in fact its objective permanence, but its stylized expression by means of its dialectical creative relationship with the artist. Each time and from whatever angle Cézanne paints Mont Sainte-Victoire, the universal of the mountain determines itself and mutates. Cézanne is then the *basho* of the universal of what is perceived. And, vice versa, the universal of the Mont Sainte-Victoire can be the *basho* of the expression of the individual artist. This is what, for Nishida, artistic experience teaches us, when the artist depicts the world as such, before, beside, or beyond the separation between the subjective individual and objective universal. Nishida's philosophy of *basho* is multilayered in the sense that what can be seen as being the *basho* of an idea, entity, or phenomenon at one level can itself be conceived in the light of another *basho* at another level. The metaphysical worlds of representations, objective knowledge, or abstractions previously mentioned in the context of Merleau-Ponty's phenomenology becomes then a particular instance of a *basho* within which artistic experience happens, but which the French philosopher would rather define in terms of invisible background.

Let us now turn more specifically to Merleau-Ponty's interpretation of Cézanne, and we will hopefully see the extent to which his conception of the objective world of knowledge and representation as invisible background both echoes and differs from Nishida's idea of *basho*. As is well known, Merleau-Ponty was critical of the almighty determinant power of what he called "objective thoughts." This criticism was in the Western world of course not restricted to Merleau-Ponty, as it has characterized much of the phenomenological movement and relatively recent systematic tendencies to deconstruct metaphysics. The very idea of a merely constituting subjective consciousness and autonomous objective reality is, for Merleau-Ponty, inconceivable. We are always already in the world prior to the split between subject and object with our body and our sensory perception. In perceptual experiences, the dichotomy between subject and object is overcome. The one who perceives is bound to "be-in-the-world" (*être-au-monde*) and "destined to the world" (*voué au monde*). As Merleau-Ponty puts it, "[t]he theory of the body is already a theory of perception."[11] In other words there is an inescapable practical embodiment that characterizes human nature.[12] There is, therefore, a primacy of embodied sensory perception, set against the objective world as an invisible background; this is comparable to Nishida's initial primacy of "pure experience," which developed subsequently into a nonhierarchical conception of the logic of *basho*. The primacy of embodied sensory perception is nonetheless what Merleau-Ponty believed the artist had the privilege to reveal in a unique way; this is best illustrated in the case of Cézanne. The awareness of such a practical involvement of the body in the world prior to any theorization (i.e., realism or idealism), was thought not only to be experienced by the artist himself, but also to be communicated, or, even more, celebrated.

As a matter of fact, it could be argued that, here, Merleau-Ponty is facing a paradox, if not a difficulty, that Nishida's multilayered philosophy of *basho*, as previously suggested, overcomes: The intentional evocation by an artist of a pretheoretical way of relating to the world may well end up being portrayed as a representation of this very embodied experience. If, as the French philosopher suggests, particular artistic practices are in a privileged position to communicate our bodily condition as being-in-the-world, then are not these practices "representing" precisely what happens prior to the split between subject and object, prior to theorization—in other words, prior to "representation" itself? We, then, end up with the genuine impossibility according to which artistic experience "represents" a state prior to "representation." The key to this loop may well be found in considering that we are in fact dealing with various levels of representation and their corresponding prerepresentational dimensions. To use Nishida's concepts, we have, in other words, several levels of mutually negating relationships between various self-determinations and their *basho*. At one level, Cézanne expresses his prerepresentational being in front of Mont Sainte-Victoire by painting lines and patches of colors as they appear from the mountain and before they become explicitly figurative. At another level (that of the spectator in front of the paintings), such a pictorial expression is a representation of what was Cézanne's perceptual experience prior to being realized in explicitly figurative representations.

We face the same difficulty when, in *L'Oeil et l'esprit*, Merleau-Ponty sees in this pretheoretical involvement in the world a "metaphysical significance" that is thought to be the essential characteristic of Modernism and of the cubists. There is indeed a metaphysical significance when modernism attempts to escape representation, and by so doing to recapture that moment prior to representation and recognition. If the experience of art is about a visual event that happens prior to representational frame of mind, prior to objectification, analysis and explanation, realism and idealism, then it has the ability to show the nature of our human condition and existence, that is to say the fact that before knowledge there is experience. The result is once again that of a seeming paradox: the "metaphysical significance" of particular artistic practices is precisely about their stance against metaphysics, objective thought, and representation.

Thus in "Le Doute de Cézanne" Merleau-Ponty suggests that the French artist attempts to recapture that moment of experience when perception and thought are not yet separated,[13] when there is no duality between the mind and the world, that is, when these two poles are still inseparable. Cézanne is thought to express the moment of experience when we retrieve that spontaneous embodied perception of things prior to objectification, prior to analysis and explanation, and prior to idealism and realism. This is exactly what Merleau-Ponty explains at a conceptual level in his study on perception, and this is exactly what he himself attempts to express in *L'Oeil et l'esprit* through a phenomenological description of, for example, the tiles of his swimming pool that he sees through the water. He gives an account of his perceptual sensory experience of the tiles as they appear prior to, or against the invisible world of preconceived knowledge—for instance, our knowledge of the fact that objects seen through water are always further away than what they look like.

I would say that on such an occasion Merleau-Ponty became like Cézanne himself, in the sense that he strove to render that moment of perception prior to representational frames of mind. The only difference is that the philosopher used words instead of paint. Both managed to find the means to express this primordial relationship with the world. For Cézanne, it was like telling the truth in painting, as he once famously said to his colleague Emile Bernard; for Merleau-Ponty it was like returning to the soil of the sensible, as he put it in *L'Oeil et l'esprit* when evoking objective thought: "[S]cientific thinking, a thinking that looks from above and thinks of the object-in-general, must return to the 'there is' that lies prior to it; it must return to the site, the soil of the sensible and wrought worlds as they are in our life and for our body."[14]

At the same time, we are bound to understand the reasons why French post-structuralist thinkers in particular, such as Jacques Derrida and Jean-François Lyotard, parodied, deconstructed, and challenged foundation-oriented thoughts, for example, in *La Vérité en peinture*[15] and *Discours, figure*, respectively.[16] The former derided foundational claims to "render the truth in painting" (*rendre la vérité en peinture*), whether they came from an art historian (Meyer Schapiro), a philosopher (Martin Heidegger), or the artist himself (Cézanne). Lyotard, for his part, described critically the privilege textual language had enjoyed over the visual for centuries in Western art when it came to establishing the foundations of truth (and how such a privilege had been used as a powerful tool in the hands of institutions). However, any such systematic criticism can also lead to overlooking the fact that Merleau-Ponty's "foundationalism" or Heidegger's "language of authenticity," in their time and place, were attempts to redeem an aspect of the human condition that Western metaphysics had obliterated, which is to say, embodiment and our belonging to the world. The foundational nature of these thoughts and cultural practices may well be justified on the basis of their historicity, which must indeed be taken as a *basho*. This, of course, equally applies to the foundational tendency of the Nishida of the first period that focused on the concept of "pure experience."

Merleau-Ponty presents Cézanne's work as a proper "gestural thought" (*pensée gestuelle*), an authentic visual thought that emerges against an invisible background, which is the objective world. It ensues that the gesture of the artist is not something that reflection should purify into concepts in order to see thought in it. Merleau-Ponty's pretheoretical "philosophy of the flesh" (*philosophie de la chair*),[17] as it is called, is what Cézanne expresses visually and whose thought must be seen as being embodied (*pensée incarnée*). We are therefore far from Hegel's understanding of art, which is constructed in relation to its ability to convey "spirit" (*Geist*), and which inexorably reduces the former to the function of medium. Merleau-Ponty says about Cézanne that "he thinks through painting" (*il pense en*

peinture). It is a "mute way of thinking" (*une pensée silencieuse*). Merleau-Ponty
was certainly one of the first, if not the first, in Western culture to acknowledge
this dimension of artistic experience, and once again such an experience should
not be confined to that of the artist. There is a degree of gesture, or even texture,
in the perceptual experience of the spectator, the listener, or the reader of the work
of art, or in any kind of aesthetic experience. What Merleau-Ponty tended, initially, to overlook is the nonhierarchical complementary nature of the relationship
between the embodied gestural thought of the artist and the invisible objective
world, which, at one level, can be that of abstractions, concepts, and representations—that is, the world of "universals."

To use an expression that Nishida would have probably held dear with his idea
of "absolutely contradictory self-identity" (*zettai mujunteki jiko dōitsu* 絶対矛盾
的自己同一),[18] the self-identity of the gesture of the artist can only be conceived
in its absolutely contradictory relationship with the objective world.[19] The latter
is then seen as the *basho*, the place, the location, or the field of the former, and
vice versa. As the objective world would then relate to the gesture of the artist in
a nonhierarchical way (in the sense that their relationship is both complementary
and differential), such a world should be thought of as a *basho* and not as a determinant background anymore. In the case of Cézanne, what shall, this time, be
called the invisible *basho* and the visible gesture of the artist are self-determined
by relating to each other in a contradictory way, and therefore in terms of complementary differences. This is, ultimately, one of the core themes of Merleau-Ponty's
unfinished *Le Visible et l'invisible*.

Cézanne's experience, or we could say that of the artist in general, is bound to
take place in relation to the world of abstractions, concepts, and representations,
all of which belonging to a paradigm that itself constitutes an invisible *basho*.
However, just as idealism and realism are presented by Merleau-Ponty as different forms of objective thoughts, we could think of reality as an invisible *basho* on
the same plane as the world of ideations (i.e., abstractions, concepts, representations, and so on). Once again, artists and Cézanne in particular, by expressing and
therefore revealing to us their perceptual, embodied sensory experience make us
confront the relationship between reality and the appearing of things. This has
always been one of the central issues investigated by and debated among phenomenologists. If I may recall the Greek etymology of the word "appearing," it is
the passive form of φαίνειν (phaínein: to show). The phenomenal dimension of
things has indeed to do with their "showing," or their "appearing." It takes place
here and now, unlike what is usually meant by the reality of things to which we
ascribe stable properties that make them recognisable and therefore universal. In
Cartesian philosophy the reality of things are characterized by their height, width,
and contours, all of which are held to be objective values. They are what Descartes
would call primary qualities. They are believed not to change; they remain the
same regardless of the angle of perspective, or to the distance from which we look
at the object. At the same time, it is acknowledged that the perceived thing also

has a color, a weight, and a texture. Descartes considers them secondary qualities. They are thought not to be fundamental, only secondary as they are relative. However, for a phenomenologist like Merleau-Ponty, who is interested in the constitution of things in the very process of appearing, color should be thought to play a role as important as other qualities when it comes to identify something as an entity.

Nishida seemed to have concerns of the same order, but there is at the same time a fundamental difference. Nishida's logic of *basho* is not based on the grasp of the affirmation of being through its "showing" or "appearing," but through its negation. The epicenter of the logic of the place is "nothingness" (*mu* 無) instead of being, with all the ensuing ethical consequences. The affirmation of any identity depends on its negation with regard to its *basho*. For Nishida, the point is to understand, in his own words, "the form of the formless" and not the affirmation of the form of being.[20] As a result, there cannot be any primacy of the sensory perception of the appearing of things, and the relationship between whatever self-identity and its *basho* is nonhierarchical.

Merleau-Ponty stresses that there cannot be separate sensory properties that must be purified and analyzed by the intellect in order to constitute a meaningful universal, or in order to constitute the idea of the object. Correspondingly, the perceived thing is never offered to one single sense; a color is never perceived when isolated from the other colors, or from the configuration to which it belongs. There is a unity and a correspondence of the senses that constitute what we feel is the reality of things. This is what Cézanne implies when he asserts that we see the velvety, the hardness, the smoothness, and even the smell of things. The way the senses cooperate contributes to giving us the feeling of the reality of things. In Merleau-Ponty's words from *L'Oeil et l'esprit*: "Because depth, color, form, line, movement, contour, physiognomy are branches of Being and because each of them can bring back the whole tuft, there aren't in painting any separated 'problems,' nor really opposed paths, nor partial 'solutions,' nor cumulative progress, nor irretrievable options."[21]

There is therefore a certain unity from which one cannot escape. The transparency of a glass is a mental abstraction, so is its fragility, its rigidity, or its crystalline sound. They all belong at the same time to the same reality. Such a unity is what Cézanne teaches us: it is about the unity of colors, forms, structure, and meaning. In an interview he gave to Joachim Gasquet,[22] he says that drawing and color cannot be distinguished. The more you paint colors, the more you draw. The more colors come together, the more drawing becomes evocative. Moreover, every single time a patch of color appears, it discloses its unity with the rest of the configuration, the drawing, the style, the theme, or even the physical space where the painting is displayed, as well as its historical, social, and cultural context.

This is also what triggered Cézanne's "doubt" as his undertaking privileges the visual. How is it possible to evoke the unity of things, the unity of senses, or the unity of the world, when one does so by privileging one single quality? The answer can arguably be provided by Nishida's logic of *basho*. We are here talking about a relationship between an invisible *basho*, whether concrete or abstract, and the appearing of such or such a quality. The appearing of a color shows, by negation, its unity with what is withdrawing at the time of its taking place, be it the drawing, the style, the theme, the physical surrounding space, or the historical, social, and cultural location of the painting. A particular quality or an entity shows its unity with its *basho* precisely by negating it, or emptying it, in order to appear. The *basho* of the visible is therefore an emptied invisibility within which the visible appears. Such an invisibility corresponds to Nishida's idea of "*basho* of nothingness" (*mu no basho* 無の場所). Viewed from this angle, Cézanne had no reason to doubt. His paintings, just like Merleau-Ponty's conception of the visible, are simply particular instances of self-identities that unite with their *basho* in an emptying, or contradictory mutual relationship. To put it differently, the unity between complementary differentials is disclosed each time a quality or an entity is perceived. Of course, unlike other entities, art has the power to highlight such a matter of fact. In Merleau-Ponty's philosophy, art celebrates perception.

III

In his *Phénoménologie de la perception* color is presented as a crucial element that contributes to a recognizable set of features as in a painting.[23] Color, then, becomes a quality as important as the primary qualities previously mentioned such as height, width, and contours, when it comes to perceiving things as entities. And like any other quality it is perceived as such partly because of its place, location, and field; in other words, because of the way it relates to its *basho*, which remains invisible at the time of perception. In the case of Cézanne's work, we identify a color as it is appearing to us because of its relation to the whole, because of the set of relations there are between the different elements in the painting as a whole. This has a particular impact on what we feel is the reality of things, whether they are colors, paintings, houses, nature, or more abstract entities such as the mind, history, or existence. Each time the appearing of a quality or an aspect of something is perceived, it contributes to building the feeling of its permanence, or, to put it differently, the sense of its reality. Each time I see the color blue, it reinforces my feeling of the permanence of blue. Each time I see a painting, I know more about the reality of the painting. From this follows that the reality of things, or, as paradoxical as it may sound, their permanence mutates in time. Such a reality is a felt permanence that we are bound to perceive through the particular. In a way the sense of reality actualizes itself in the very process of appearing here and now. This is what Cézanne was thought to have experienced in front of Mont Sainte-Victoire. Even more, this is what he attempted to communicate through his paintings. The permanence of the mountain is rendered through every single moment of his perceptual experiences, in a way that can therefore be seen as diametrically opposed to the impressionists' attempt to render the changing appearance of objects by, paradoxically, fixing them in time.

Overall the mutual nature of the relationship between reality, as a particular instance of what has been called in the context of this chapter the invisible *basho*, and the appearing of such or such a quality as a particular instance of what is perceived is paramount. Each quality appears as it is because of its location within the invisible *basho* of reality, which in turn becomes renewed each time one perceives such or such a quality. If we once again turn to Nishida's multilayered logic of *basho*, we may distinguish at least two dimensions of our sense of reality as an invisible *basho*. One tends to relate to space and the other to time. When we look at Mount Fuji near Tokyo, like the eighteenth-century Japanese artist Utagawa Hiroshige did, the mountain appears as such because of its being surrounded by the blue sky, trees, hills, and, further away, water, as well as because of the particular angle of perception. This environment can be understood as a spatial *basho*. In addition Mount Fuji also appears as such because of the past perceptual experiences of it, to which one unconsciously relates. This is a temporal *basho*. One's relationship to these two different and complementary *basho* is precisely what Cézanne was thought to express or to communicate in painting. In this sense, Cézanne was indeed rendering a truth in painting.

Painting, as it is typified by Cézanne, is not like what the Italitan thinker Leon Battista Alberti (1404–1472) suggested, that is, a window opened onto the world. Painting expresses a visible world in relation to, or rather within an invisible *basho*, which is equally fundamental. Nishida's nonhierarchical dialectics would present the visible as being as important as the invisible. The visible world given to perception and the invisible objective world relate to each other as absolute contradictory self-identities. A painting creates and opens its own visible world by expressing one particular angle of the objective world, whose possibilities for doing so are infinite and that is thereby equally renewed. To be more accurate and to refer to Nishida's vocabulary, one could say that the invisible *basho* of the visible world is like a background of infinite possibilities for particular and unique perceptions to be expressed. This infinite invisible *basho*, which becomes ultimately the very movement of self-negation that makes all creative reciprocal relationships possible, is indeed what Nishida calls the "*basho* of absolute nothingness." It is not a simple "background" but a place of equal ethical value to that of the appearing of the visible. This must be what Cézanne tried to teach us.

It goes without saying that the uniqueness of these perceptual experiences makes painting unable to reproduce or imitate any universal, or to use whatever *basho* as a model of representation. The mimetic project, in whatever form, of Western metaphysics becomes nonsensical. Merleau-Ponty himself says in *L'Oeil et l'esprit* that "[i]t is the work of art itself that has opened the field from which it appears in another light."[24] Cézanne, the artist, becomes the one who fixes on a canvass what would not be seen otherwise. It is, to use a phenomenological term, a visual "bracketing" of one aspect of the world. Painting therefore does not imitate the objective real world as if it were an already visible world that painting strived to look like. Painting, or art in general, is rather a form of "expression" in the sense that it expresses what could not have been seen without it. The artist makes us discover a world to which we belong without seeing it. Artists, for Merleau-Ponty and Cézanne, do not provide an illustration of the world, but make the world appear *as such* from an invisible *basho* that becomes slightly different with each perceptual experience.

Merleau-Ponty's entire philosophical undertaking is centered around finding ways to articulate this fundamental recovering of the "chiasm" (*chiasme*),[25] or this moment prior to the split between the mind and the world, or between representation and its object. This is also what Cézanne's artistic experience shows us: how to recapture that moment when the meaning of things emerges from the ways colors are arranged to configure something. Art was for Merleau-Ponty the privileged means by which such a way of relating to the world could be expressed. Within the category of art, particular practices seemed to equally occupy a privileged position. It could be argued that Cézanne was, to a certain degree, a phenomenologist who used paint as a medium. What interested him was not the question of the appearance of things (what), but of their appearing (how). It was for him a question that could be addressed only by *placing* himself within the preobjective world. Perhaps what Cézanne failed to see is that the appearance of things can only be thought as a *basho* of their appearing, and vice versa.

If there are common grounds between Nishida's Buddhism and Merleau-Ponty when it comes to understanding the chiasmic relationship between the visible and the invisible, the artist's experience and the world, self-identities and their *basho*, there are also fundamental differences. These, no doubt, have their origins in the different cultural traditions of the two philosophers; they concern the contextual *basho* of their philosophies. Both started with emphases on *pure experience* and *the primacy of perception*, respectively, and both moved toward a more dialectical conception of how these relate to their *basho*. However, Merleau-Ponty, who belonged to the philosophical tradition of being and affirmation, was naturally drawn to ascribing a particular status to the appearing of the visible against the invisible objective world as background. Nishida's philosophy, on the other hand, was grounded in the Zen Buddhist tradition of nothingness, where a "being" does not constitute a standpoint, as well as in the nonhierarchical conception of reality made of contradictory relationships between entities; these are expressed by the notion of *soku* according to which something "is" in that it "is not." For Nishida, nothingness was at least as important as being. And the invisible *basho* would have been that within which the *visible* could be seen.

* Generous grants from the British Academy, the Japan Society for the Promotion of Science, and the Great Britain Sasakawa Foundation enabled this chapter to be written as part of a research project conducted at Kyoto University.

9

"Place of Nothingness" and the Dimension of Visibility

Nishida, Merleau-Ponty, and Huineng

David Brubaker

How should we regard the search for philosophical languages capable of account-ing for such terms as "nothingness" and "self-nature" mentioned in the texts of Mahāyāna Buddhism? The idea of awakening to an intersection of self and nature is a heartening alternative to modern philosophies that affirm agency, spiritual life, and morality by distancing the self from nature and body, or else affirm real and objective existence in nature by treating the notion of self as an illusion. Today, as many of us search for such an awakening, it is helpful to review Nishida Kitarō's earlier attempt to develop a modern philosophy of the awareness of life mentioned in some accounts of Zen Buddhism. In what becomes a lifelong project, Nishida tests a series of technical terms. He experiments with the term "pure experience" in *An Inquiry into the Good* (*Zen no kenkyū*, 1911), his first major work, and finally settles on "place of nothingness" (J. *mu no basho* 無の場所) in *Funda-mental Problems of Philosophy* (*Tetsugaku no kompon mondai*, 1934). Although these two texts rarely refer to Buddhism or Zen, Nishida wrote about beauty and Buddhism before he authored them, and afterward he took the lead in applying his philosophy of the "place of nothingness" to such topics as religious faith, the sayings of Linji, the celebration of the Zen standpoint of the absolute present, and D. T. Suzuki's notion of spirituality.[1] Nobuo Kazashi has recently added an intriguing hypothesis as an option: he asserts that Nishida's notion of "place" (J. *basho* 場所) converges with Maurice Merleau-Ponty's use of the term "flesh" in *The Visible and the Invisible*. If Kazashi is correct, then *both* Nishida and Merleau-Ponty would provide us with a way to avoid Descartes' "body-mind dualism," to affirm "the body as the ground for our prediscursive and yet active communion with the world," and to discard "the usual, facile dichotomy of East and West in philosophy."[2] The idea that world cultures intertwine at their philosophical roots is a live and momentous option for us now, for the confirmation of this idea takes us one step closer to fruitful and creative exchanges of mutual benefit, and one step back from the "clash of civilizations" hypothesis and the faulty moral relativism on which it depends. In short, the study of Nishida's terms "pure experience" and "place of nothingness," together with Merleau-Ponty's philosophy of "flesh," may lead us to new ideas concerning Zen, spiritual awakening, self-nature, D. T. Suzuki's reading of *The Platform Sūtra* of Huineng (638–713), and roots of value shared on the many paths of spiritual practice.

However, scholars still debate the value and propriety of using philosophy, augmented with such terms as "pure experience," "nothingness," or "suchness," to describe the wisdom that emerges with Zen meditation. Bernard Faure objects strongly to Nishida's effort to find a philosophical system for describing Zen and its spiritual workings. He charges both Nishida and D. T. Suzuki with advancing a dualistic, utopian, and abstract "ideology of nothingness" that co-opts the spiritual practice of Zen and positions traditional Western philosophies as inferior.[3] He suggests that Nishida's project is not suitable for philosophy and that it belongs instead to religion and expressions of faith. It is legitimate to inquire whether Nishida uses "place of nothingness" in an ideological, metaphysical, or speculative way. But Faure's critique imposes a puzzling dilemma with two intolerable outcomes: either we stay with philosophy and *give up* the attempt to describe a preobjective place of intersection that may heal the split between spiritual life and existence in nature, or else we give up philosophy and *turn to faith* for a healing language and face charges of illusory belief, flight to metaphysics, cultural exclusivism, and the arbitrary favoring of one culture over another. How shall we resolve the many disagreements here, when they lead us to such difficult questions as the proper use of terms (e.g., "pure experience" and "place of nothingness") and the boundaries proper to philosophy itself?

With this text, I affirm that philosophers may use "nothingness" or "suchness" or "constitutive emptiness" to describe the body and a dimension of the senses that can lead individual selves to the wisdom and compassion that some practitioners of Zen Buddhism describe. In the first section below, I note Nishida's progress from writing on the topic of beauty and Buddhism to his selection of William James's term "pure experience." Nishida takes up "pure experience," as James does, in an effort to dissolve the dichotomy that troubles modern European philosophies—we are determined by natural conditions or else free thinkers with no roots in nature. Nishida seems to go beyond James; the individual seer is conscious that sensations offer something that precedes the conjunctive flow of experiences. The second section is an evaluation of Faure's arguments against philosophical use of the terms "pure experience" and "nothingness."[4] Faure claims that perceptions and experiences of objects by means of the senses never occur without concepts. I am inclined to agree. But it does *not necessarily* follow that philosophical thinking of one's own bodily senses must always consist solely of thinking about *objects* of experience for which cognition is essential; therefore, in principle, philosophy need *not* betray the Zen idea that there is an awakening to a unifying place in actual life that cannot be grasped by means of intellect. With the third section, I consider Nishida's term "place of nothingness." His concept of "place" introduces three new ideas: consciousness of self-existence through awareness of an opposing place of nothingness, the individual person acting within the objective place of the sociohistorical world, and the self regarded as the body of physical qualities. However, he claims that the self is unable to determine its own existence from within itself; it is the objective social and historical environment that confers meaning and self-identities upon the individual. The fourth section outlines Merleau-Ponty's philosophy of the flesh of the body, so that a comparison may be conducted with Nishida's philosophy of the place of nothingness. The point to remember is this: Merleau-Ponty's late writings describe the body in terms of secret and innate contexts of flesh that mingle but never blend with cognitive consciousness. His account of the self's body does seem to differ from the one advanced by Nishida. Merleau-Ponty *does* provide the idea that each individual may choose to notice an innate sensible context of flesh—such as the "constitutive emptiness" of the place of visibility—that provides a basis for self-consciousness, meaning, and value. Finally, I conclude that Nishida's idea of self-consciousness—intellect resisted by an unchanging place outside mind—can be combined with Merleau-Ponty's idea that the secret ground of visibility is a stable corporeal place that is a nothingness in comparison to the changing and determinate *objects* of visual experience that it displays. I apply this philosophical idea of visibility as a unique place of nothingness to some of the topics raised in Nishida's final writings: Zen, religious faith, and the existential awakening of the self that comes from acting in the everyday world. After weighing the readings that D. T. Suzuki and Youru Wang give for Huineng's *Platform Sūtra*, I use the idea of visibility as a place of nothingness to interpret Huineng's remarks on "self-nature."

NO-SELF AND PURE EXPERIENCE

What difficulties arise in the search for a philosophy that is able to accommodate the ideas expressed within traditional Buddhist texts? We may learn from Nishida's movement from writing about beauty and Buddhism to experimenting with the term "pure experience." James uses this term to describe an "instant field of the present," a "plain, unqualified actuality," which is talked of twice—once in the context of things and again in connection with our mental states.[5] Nishida reads James's articles concerning this field of actuality and mentions in a letter from 1910 that there is a resemblance to the expressions of Zen Buddhism (BL 108). Nishida proceeds to use the term "pure experience" in *An Inquiry into the Good*, his first major philosophical work. The challenges confronting Nishida become evident as he tries to combine modern European philosophies to express a consciousness that precedes the coming into existence of experiences.

Nishida's essay "An Explanation of Beauty" does indicate his early interest in the Zen notion of "no-self" (J. *muga* 無我). This essay of 1900 reformulates Immanuel Kant's aesthetics of disinterested satisfaction in an original way, by explaining the sense of beauty as a stable pleasure that arises from egolessness and an entry into "the Great Way of *muga*" (EB 215–217). According to Nishida, "you must confront things in the state of pure *muga*" in order to acquire an "authentic sense of beauty"; as a result, beauty becomes "a kind of truth that comes as a sudden stimulus from the depths of the heart," a truth that is attained "when we have separated from the self and become one with things" (EB 217). Since they "touch our heart strings," works of art promote a sense of beauty and selflessness that cannot be expressed in words; they express a truth comparable to the "open secret" mentioned by Goethe (EB 217). Nishida ends his essay by claiming that beauty, religion, and morality all stem from the "Great Way of *muga*": the differences are that beauty is linked with the *muga* of the moment, the selflessness of religion is eternal *muga*, and morality still belongs, in some small part, to intellectual discrimination, since it requires "the distinction between self and other, good and evil" (EB 217). Steve Odin states that Nishida's emphasis here upon "the state of pure *muga*"—or upon becoming one with things and not remaining detached from them as a separate consciousness or discriminating intellect—"clearly anticipates his Jamesian notion of an egoless 'pure experience' (*junsui keiken*)."[6]

With *An Inquiry into the Good*, Nishida shifts to the modern term "pure experience." In an essay of 1904, "Does 'Consciousness' Exist?" William James uses "pure experience" to refer to an undivided and instant field that may be experienced once as the knower (or as "mine") and again as a real object known. Nishida uses "pure experience" with the aim of dissolving the split between subject and object, or mind and body, that has troubled modern philosophy since Descartes. The opening paragraph of *An Inquiry into the Good* is quoted here:

> To experience means to know facts just as they are, to know in accordance with facts by completely relinquishing one's own fabrications. What we usually refer to as experience is adulterated with some sort of thought, so by *pure* I am referring to the state of experience just as it is without the least addition of deliberative discrimination. The moment of seeing a color or hearing a sound, for example, is prior not only to the thought that the color or sound is the activity of an external object or that one is sensing it, but also to the judgment of what color or sound might be. In this regard, pure experience is identical with direct experience. When one directly experiences one's own state of consciousness, there is not yet a subject or an object, and knowing and its object are completely unified. This is the most refined type of experience.[7]

This passage implies that there is a prior awareness of a color or sound before these are experienced as belonging to some external material object or as the perceptions in an observer. Nishida's stated aim is to avoid "the view that the whole world is simply our ideas" and the solipsism that arises for Descartes and Berkeley (IG 44). Later on in the book, Nishida returns to the example of sound, in order to argue against the materialist belief that the universe is given only as objects known to the scientist: "Nature conceived of as an objective reality totally independent of our subjectivity is an abstract concept, not true reality" (IG 68). To reinforce this critique, Nishida asks us to consider the example of the sound associated with music. Each of us experiences the universe directly as one melodious sound and unifying reality—or as pure experience and pure activity—*before* any experience of the sound as a measurable physical vibration. Even the body, considered as a physical object, is an abstraction or fabrication of thinking that is not independent of intellectual discrimination (IG 43, 47–48). Since experience of a color or sound as an external object cannot be divided from the same color or sound experienced as belonging to our own conscious thought, Nishida infers that the actuality of our contact with the world may be found by going *within the self* and taking notice of what it is that makes the content of ideas, feelings, and experiences concrete (IG 62, 76).

Does Nishida depart from James's way of using "pure experience"? According to David Dilworth, there is a noticeable difference. Nishida tries to advance the idea of an "emptiness" or "nothingness" that is a "richer unity" *behind* the thinner conjunctive unity of experiences that James describes. Nishida tends to reduce "all kinds of mental phenomena to experiential immediacy itself"; consequently, he "lacks James's empirical sense of the *flow* of experience" where intellectual contents are a conjunctive transitive relation.[8] In some sentences at least, Nishida does seem to suggest that an original color contains some element that is independent of perceptual thinking: "[O]ne looks at a color and judges it to be blue, but this judgment does not make the original color sensation any clearer. . . . Meanings or judgments are an abstracted part of the original experience, and compared with the original experience they are meager in content" (IG 8–9). But James regards consciousness of self and natural objects as a long conjunction consisting purely of *experiences* that are in *relations of knowing* to one another; the material stuff that a person directly lives as "the immediate flux of life" is purely a mosaic of many bits of experience. There is "no bedding," no "*general* stuff," which enables an observer to hold different pieces of experience together (ERE 26–27, 93). Since it is "just what appears, of space, of intensity, of flatness, brownness, heaviness, or what not," there is "no universal element of which all things are made" and "no aboriginal stuff or quality of being, contrasted with that of which material objects are made" (ERE 3, 27). To the extent that Nishida's descriptions of color and sound point to a plain field of the present that precedes particular experiences and knowledge, his account does have "a Zen nuance," as Dilworth notes.[9]

Those in sympathy with Nishida's project do find problems in *An Inquiry into the Good*. What problems arise? The self-critique that Nishida expresses in 1936 for the third edition of *An Inquiry into the Good* still seems apt today: "As I look at it now, the standpoint of this book is that of consciousness, which might be thought of as a kind of psychologism. I do think, however, that what lay deep in my thought when I wrote it was not something that is merely psychological" (IG xxxi–xxxii).

Nishida's use of the term "psychologism" implies that his early philosophy has a difficulty describing experiences as they originate from within because it refers to personal experiences as they are known objectively from without by the science of psychology.[10] Yet *An Inquiry into the Good* does show early signs of an effort to avoid reducing the life of a person merely to a string of experiences certified from the outside by psychology, for Nishida continues to use the term "consciousness" in order to imply the inwardness unique to an individual, whereas James would prefer to let the use of the term "consciousness" evaporate. However, this leads to a second problem. In trying to hang on to the idea that there is a consciousness of "richer" unity *within the self* that is more basic than experiences of objects, Nishida revives the very same European language of idealism (e.g., Hegel's idea of universal reason and the term "concrete universal") that James rejects.[11] Although they are in sympathy with Nishida's project, Dilworth and Masao Abe find that *An Inquiry into the Good* shows signs of an intellectualism that mars Nishida's attempt to describe the immediacy of concrete life, here and now.[12]

PROBLEMS WITH PHILOSOPHY
AND THE EXISTENCE OF NOTHINGNESS

Bernard Faure raises a formidable set of objections both to Nishida's use of "pure experience" and to the overall project of seeking a philosophy that describes the awakening referred to in Zen texts. He offers several arguments with the aim of persuading us to reject *all* attempts by philosophers, including Nishida, to describe some unity within the self that precedes the discriminations imposed by intellect. First, there is his argument from *epistemology*: no experience is ever pure, since all experiences are objects of understanding, intellect, and cognitive activity. Second, there is the argument from *concreteness*: terms such as "pure experience" and "absolute nothingness" contradict the Mahāyāna aim of nonduality and fail to describe actual life as it is actually lived, since they refer to what is abstract, utopian, and beyond ordinary experience and sociohistorical realities. Third, there is an argument from *philosophy*: philosophical language will always betray whatever "nothingness" may happen to denote, even if the term *does* refer to a genuine experience or authentic awareness, since philosophy will inevitably abstract such an experience or awareness into forms of understanding and concepts. Philosophy always abstracts its subject matter into forms of understanding, since it must express rational knowledge. The challenge posed here is not merely to Nishida's choice of words; the entire idea of seeking a philosophy for the spiritual notion of "nothingness" is in question. How good are these arguments? I accept the first argument provisionally. But I reject the other two because each presupposes the conclusion that it expresses.

Since Nishida does indeed use the term "pure experience" in his early writings, let us consider Faure's first objection that "pure experience" is a self-contradictory expression. This objection charges Nishida and any other philosopher who speaks of some precognitive object of experience with perpetuating "the myth of the given." This so-called myth is the belief that there is some category of *experience* supplied by the senses that is raw and independent of culturally supplied forms of understanding needed for cognition. To find support, Faure refers us to an essay by Steven Katz, who analyzes how "pure experience," "nothingness," and "ineffability" are used in many different religious and spiritual traditions, including those of Mahāyāna Buddhism and Zen.[13] As he begins to address what he calls "the epistemological aspects of the so-called Nishida philosophy," Faure states his argument succinctly by presenting a quote from Katz: "According to Steven Katz, 'there are *no* pure (i.e. unmediated) experiences. . . . That is, *all* experience is produced through, organized by, and makes itself available to us in extremely complex epistemological ways'" (KS 249). Thus, Faure shifts the discussion away from the existential question: What element is present during the actual having of an original sensation, such that each of us, on our own and for our self, is able to ascribe existence to the sensation as something actual and more than a mere idea? He substitutes an epistemological question: What conditions are necessary for having the kind of empirical (or sensory) object of knowledge that we call "an experience"? Faure's premise is that experiences are thoughts about objects that perform the function of *knowing*. His conclusion is that no experience or perception of a *determinate object of knowledge* is ever innocent (i.e., conceptless). Katz goes further than Faure—he extends the argument to all uses of "the given," "nothingness," and "suchness": "[E]xperience of *x*—be *x* God or *nirvana*—is conditioned both linguistically and cognitively by a variety of factors *including the expectation of what will be experienced*" (LEM 59).

How well does this first argument work? Faure's argument from epistemology may perhaps succeed against the notion that an *experience* occurs without participation by intellect. This point has its origin with Immanuel Kant: "[E]xperience is itself a species of knowing for which I need understanding."[14] Those who would use such terms as "pure experience" or "nonconceptual perception" need to give serious consideration to Faure's objection. *If* experience through the senses is always of objects, then it would seem that there is no experience purified of our thoughts of objects. But this leads us to a background question of greater importance: Must "nothingness," "the given," and "suchness" always refer only to sensible objects of experience that belong to knowledge? No. To rule out *all* possible uses of "the given" or "nothingness," Faure would have to *presuppose* or demonstrate here that these terms *must always* refer only to particular objects of experience. But is it not possible for you to observe from your own life, as I do for myself, that living contact with the natural world through the senses does *not* begin immediately with distinct experiences of *objects* understood consciously and cognitively? Even Kant himself seems to imply that any given *appearance*—considered as an object of sensory intuition or empirical knowledge—contains something *more* than forms of understanding: "That in the appearance which corresponds to sensation I term its *matter* . . . the matter of all appearance is given to us *a posteriori* only."[15] What does Kant mean? Surely Kant *must* mean—implicitly at the very least—that a visual appearance depends on having a sensation that includes some additional sensible context that is outside cognition. For if the senses deliver experiences that are composed of sensations, and if sensations are composed *exclusively* by the forms of mind that make them into objects of knowledge, then none of us could ever go outside our concepts to ascribe existence to a possible object represented in our own thinking. As Merleau-Ponty reminds us, philosophies of reflection, such as Kant's, begin with a tacit appeal to such a mainspring within sensation that is used as a ladder in a climb to the world of intellect; they proceed to pull the ladder up, analyze sensation only in terms of perceptual experience, and maintain the illusion that reflection is inspired by some prior presence of the world that is more than thought (VI 34–35). Therefore, the hypothesis suggested in *An Inquiry into the Good*—that a color presents something that precedes intellectual discriminations of particular objects of experience—remains a live option for us even today.

Faure's second objection is that all attempts to use such terms as "nothingness" to name an unchanging sensible ground that precedes transient experiences will name only a metaphysical abstraction outside the actual reality that we need to understand and act upon. His argument is that terms such as "pure experience" or "absolute nothingness" perpetuate a dualistic philosophy that favors the metaphysical over the natural, because they refer to what is abstract and utopian (i.e., to what has "no place"[16]). This objection relies on the following background premise: If the individual person is in an actual place of contact with natural life, then this contact must be defined by experiences of a "sociocultural reality" that produce a "return to the 'real thing'" (KS 255). The perhaps "ideologically uncritical" idea is this: the living individual person's place in nature is defined by what is known about the person as a materially existing and factually understood object of empirical knowledge. In short, Faure seems to subscribe uncritically to the modern doctrine of nature, which defines "nature" by the subject matter expressed in the experimental results of the natural sciences and psychology. He neglects to consider that each unique self-determining agent of history may need an undivided field of actuality that is prior to experience in order to personally ascribe existence to the feelings, experiences, documents, locations, and places mentioned in sociohistorical narratives. Thus, the question is still open: Can one use the terms "nothingness" and "suchness" effectively to denote some context of actuality—a place evident to oneself—that precedes experiences of visual objects? However, if we pursue this question and plan to remain allied with the idea that beliefs must be supported by the testimony of the five senses, then the remaining task is to describe how the senses give the individual person direct acquaintance with a sensible dimension, a concrete place, that cannot be perceived as an object of experience and knowledge.

The third objection articulated by Faure is of great difficulty and interest, since it concerns the limits of philosophy itself. He argues that no philosophical language will ever be able to convey the origins of enlightenment that arises through the practices of Zen Buddhism. Faure makes his case as follows. Suppose there *is* some precognitive ground or field, noticed by the self, that is independent of intellectual discrimination. Suppose also that this *is* indeed what Nishida and others are trying to describe by experimenting with "pure experience," "nothingness," "suchness," or any other term. Even assuming all this, Faure concludes that no *philosophy* will ever be able to express the ground designated by such terms:

> Assuming that such an experience can be found, any attempt to characterize it, even the least reifying one, will betray it. Thus, as a philosophical category used by the early Nishida and his disciples in various discursive contexts, "pure experience" came to function performatively and to produce specific effects outside the field of philosophy. (KS 250)

Once again there is an unexamined assumption at work here. This is it: the direct object of philosophy is *knowledge of objects*. Both Faure (KS 249) and Katz (LEM 26, 59, 65) emphatically insist that philosophy is essentially an epistemological project. As a result, Faure relies on the premise that the subject matter of philosophy is restricted to knowledge of objects; hence, his argument from philosophy is implicitly an *ontological argument*, in that it depends on the idea that philosophy itself is necessarily defined as a discourse that expresses knowledge or understanding of the being of objects. In short, even if there is some context outside intellectual determination, Faure will conclude that it has no being as an object of sensory experience; hence, it will forever remain nothing for us (i.e., a nonentity or a non-being) or something that cannot be ascribed existence as a real object in natural life. Thus, if philosophy is essentially a discipline that functions for the purpose of producing and expressing knowledge, then it will describe only cognizable objects of experience or relations of knowing between them. Since Faure would restrict us to a philosophy that defines "evidence of the senses" objectively—that is, in terms of objects of experience known to exist in the world of sense—and since the term "nothingness" refers to something that is not an object of empirical knowledge, it follows that philosophers will never be able to articulate evidence for the existence of the ground or context denoted by "nothingness," even if we agree at the outset that each individual person is already aware of such a ground. Faure goes on to suggest that even if there is some "pure experience" or precognitive awareness, this would be more typical of religious faith and not of philosophical thinking. To emphasize this conclusion, Faure quotes the writings of Hajime Tanabe, who states that Nishida reaches conclusions illegitimately "from premises taken from the field of religion and transferred to the field of philosophy, thereby transgressing the bounds of philosophy." Tanabe adds that "absolute nothingness cannot become the principle of a philosophical system," so any attempt to combine remarks about an awakening acquired through Zen practice with European languages of philosophy is guaranteed to fail (KS 251).

What about this third argument? Must the use of "nothingness" or *any* such term take us outside the domain of philosophy and into the realm of faith and religion? This third argument may be directed toward the "early Nishida," but it goes much further. It also challenges any philosopher who tries to name some inward and preobjective place within the self that precedes the ongoing flux of flow of different experiences. But my point is that Faure's conclusion—that Nishida must stray into the domain of mere faith—follows necessarily here, only if Faure presupposes as a premise the inferential claim that his argument as a whole is supposed to demonstrate: if a belief is held without any supporting evidence represented *in our empirical knowledge of existing things*, then the belief is held merely on faith. With this objective definition of "evidence" in operation, the result is a suppression of all attempts to explore and articulate the idea that each of the five senses provides the individual person with a dimension that precedes experience and perception of particular objects. By what right do modern philosophers dictate that philosophical thinking about a visible appearance must always be limited to thinking about the *kind of cognizable object* that is experienced by the mind? Is it not possible for you to perceive a visible *object* and then, in the next moment, to take notice and think of the *visible context* that precedes and persists through your perception of that object? Thinking is essential to philosophy; however, it does not necessarily follow that each of us must think of the world of sense exclusively in terms of existing objects of experience, once we agree to ascribe existence only to those objects that are evident to each of us through our own senses. Therefore, Faure has not demonstrated that we must take a metaphysical turn, away from the senses and Zen Buddhist commitments to nonduality, when we try to use philosophy to describe a sensible context that precedes the coming-to-be of an object of sense experience.

What *does* finally follow from Faure's three arguments? First, we do have a strong motive to find some *other* term such as "awareness"—instead of "experience" and "perception"—in order to differentiate thoughts about a sensible context that precedes experiences from thoughts about objects of experience that such a context may display. Second, Faure states that it is appropriate to interrogate any "*amerikajinron* (or *furansujinron*) ideology" that may distort the critical process of deconstructing movements like that of the Kyoto school (KS 272). So, we may indeed ask whether his interrogation of the relation between philosophy and Zen is distorted, because he assumes, without critical analysis, that philosophy must use "nature" and "evidence" exclusively in reference to objects of experience and empirical knowledge. In his recent writings, Faure is more accepting of the idea that philosophical thinking may intertwine with Zen insights. Speaking on behalf of Western thinkers, he grants that the discourse of Buddhism may be approached and followed in ways that make Western thought aware of its own driftings: "[W]e realize that it soon leads us into a terrain that is unknown to us (or that we have left fallow) and that at the same time it obliges us to rediscover certain truths that have been forgotten."[17] Thus, there is sufficient cause to turn once again to

Nishida and to study the way "place of nothingness" is used in his late writings. Does he help us rediscover some ground or place that unifies the self with the world of everyday life?

PLACE OF NOTHINGNESS: LOSS OF SELF
AND ACTING IN THE SOCIOHISTORICAL WORLD

How does Nishida Kitarō use the term "place of nothingness" in *Fundamental Problems of Philosophy*? He indicates a new direction: "We realize our self by living and acting in this world. That which resists our action, which conflicts with us, is the truly objective. It is something about which we can do nothing at all, for it truly transcends us."[18] In elaborating this new path, Nishida distinguishes at least five ideas of interest. First, there is the idea that self-consciousness arises from a relation of opposition between consciousness and what is unchanging and entirely other to it, that is, in relation to an *absolute nothingness* (J. *zettai mu* 絶対 無). Second, there is the idea of *place*, a self-determining point that permits self-consciousness by enabling the self to see itself in itself; the mere unity of knower and known within the self (e.g., the union of subject with object within the flux and flow of experiences) is not sufficient for self-consciousness. The third idea is that of the *sociohistorical world*, where the self-determining individual person acts in relation to another (e.g., an "I" in relation to a "Thou") and acquires meaning, self-identity, and moral standing. Fourth, the self that acts in the objective world may be regarded as *the body*. Nishida's philosophical term *place of nothingness* combines these four ideas in a particular way. One begins to exist as something entirely other or opposed to the "I" of intellect only after one acts as an individual person with a body in the place of the sociohistorical environment. It is necessary to consider these four ideas and the notion of "place of nothingness," so that we may go on to test the degree of convergence with Merleau-Ponty's philosophy of flesh. To prepare for this comparison, I raise the following question in this section: Does Nishida hold in his late philosophy that each of the senses presents some element that is resistant enough to the "I" of intellect so that it may serve as a place that permits self-consciousness and an idea of self-existence? I conclude that he does not. In Nishida's late philosophy, "true self" refers to the self-less individual who acts personally, with a physical body, in the objective place of social and historical interactions.

Nishida makes an important contribution by clarifying the relations *within* the self that are essential for self-consciousness and for one's own awareness of one's own existence. What must be the case within self-consciousness in order for the self to exist for itself? According to Nishida, "for the individual to determine itself there must first be what I have called the determination of 'place' [*basho*], i.e., a unity of absolute contradictories" (FP 6–7). The self remains for itself merely solitary and perhaps just a mere dream, until it is aware of its own relation or dialogue with something that is absolute (i.e., unchanging), persistent, and outside the world of intellect and its objects. Nishida helps by selecting the term "place" to refer to this absolute other, which is unchanging, beyond any opposition, beyond any coming-to-be or passing-away, that could render it relative.

> Self-consciousness cannot be merely the unity of subject and object; self-consciousness exists at the point where the self sees itself in itself. It exists at the point where the place [*basho*] is self-determining. But to see the self in the self would seem impossible. In contrast to that which exists in the self, the seer must be regarded as nothingness. (FP 44)

Self-consciousness begins where the self notices "itself in itself." One becomes aware of one's existence as something more than mere world of consciousness and intellect, because it is possible to notice, for oneself, that the flux of experiences that constitute mind are opposed and resisted by some *place* that is absolute and unchanging. If we are to say that the individual is self-determining, then there must be a self-determining place (FP 67).

The question of interest is this: How does Nishida choose to describe the *place* that is essential for each of us to acquire an awareness of our own existence as something other than mere mind? Before we turn to Nishida's answer, it is useful to think of the following hypothesis as a possible alternative: One arrives at the awareness that one exists for oneself as something more than mere consciousness, after noticing that some immediate dimension or element *within sensation* serves as a place that resists intellect and forms of thinking. On this hypothesis, it would be possible to speak of an original awareness that each *sensation* is accompanied by a self-evident place, a place of absolute nothingness in comparison to thinking, that gives one a way to externalize oneself, *for oneself.* Does Nishida hold that the "true self" is revealed through noticing that each of the five senses presents some containing context that is an unchanging nothingness, at least in comparison with intellect and thoughts about objects? No. For he states clearly that "the individual does not become an individual by returning within itself, and objectifying itself within itself, but in relation to other individuals, i.e., by relation to the absolute other" (FP 7). What stops Nishida from claiming that the place of self-existence is provided by the senses themselves? He leaves a trail of justifications. The terms "sensation" and "pure experience" still connote the "mere world of intellectual objects, which may only be a dream"; the idea of pure experience "does not avoid connoting a world of intellectual objects" (FP 2). He asserts: "Mere sensory objects are not true reality. They are rather objects of thought" (FP 65). Sensation does not avoid being an object of the intellectual self (FP 91). In short, Nishida regards sensations as objects of experience that are already entwined with mind. Thus it becomes clear that Nishida uses his own version of the argument from epistemology to reach a conclusion similar to Faure's; there is nothing in sensory experience that is not already conceptualized and therefore within the self's own world of intellect. He holds that it is impossible to find a place within a sensation or a visual perception that is absolutely other—or an absolute nothingness—to the "I" and its world of intellectual objects.

Moreover, Nishida also uses a version of the argument from philosophy to justify his belief that it is impossible for the senses to present the sort of opposing place that is needed for the rise of self-consciousness and a sense of one's own existence. He begins with the same hypothetical question posed by Faure: What if there *were* something sensible that is actually noticed by the self, a context noticed before—or between—each mingling with cognitive consciousness and the coming-to-be of an experience? Nishida responds in a similar way:

> From the standpoint of the mere intellectual self, the self may be thought to exist outside this world [i.e., the objective world of action], to be little more than an "eye" which sees. Moreover, such a thing would not be anything positive. It would be a mere non-entity for which knowing would cease to be. (FP 93)

According to Nishida, if one considers oneself as a mere eye that is able to look at some dimension of sensation that precedes focusing upon a particular object, then such an "eye," disconnected from cognitive understanding, would be a nonentity, not a positive object of knowledge, and without knowledge of itself or anything else. The echo of Kant seems unmistakable: "What is first given to us is appearance. When combined with consciousness, it is called perception. (Save through its relationship to consciousness that is at least possible, appearance could never be for us an object of knowledge, and so would be nothing for us; and since it has itself no objective reality, but exists only in being known, it would be nothing at all.)"[19] In short, what cannot be perceived as an object is nothing at all; for an entity to be something, it must be perceived. Nishida makes explicit what is merely implied by Kant: It *is* possible to think of oneself as exercising or looking with the eyes without seeing or focusing on any particular object of experience. Nevertheless, Nishida agrees with Kant's conclusion: If one were a mere "eye," one would be a nonentity, nonexistent, nothing at all, even for oneself. Thus both Nishida and Faure seem to use the argument from philosophy, which originates with Kant's modern claim that whatever is given to us through our own senses is nothing or of no value, until our own active minds form it into objects of experience and empirical knowledge.

So, what meaning *does* Nishida propose to give the term "place of the nothingness"? For him, the place of the sociohistorical world gives the selfless individual a sense of self-existence. Nishida argues that this does not turn individual persons into mere effects of material conditions; he insists that the self continues to act personally in a way that gives expression to social interactions. How does losing one's own "I" of intellect and acquiring a sense of self as an absolute nothingness lead to an awareness of self-existence? It seems that the self becomes aware of itself as existing as more than mere mind, precisely when it is acting in the place of the social environment.

> The environment which truly determines life must exist as the self-determination of individuals, i.e., as the determination of personal selves. In such as sense, true life must be social and historical. . . . The person is determined only in relation to other persons. Therefore, there must be the mutual determination of persons. Hence, that which stands against the I as the environment has the function of directly determining the I itself in the sense of what I call the determination of "nothingness." For we can be thought to find the self by losing the self in action. (FP 68)

To put this another way, the place of nothingness that enables the self to determine its existence is the same place of social interaction that enables each individual to acquire a self-identity. The true life of the individual person is determined by the objective social and historical environment (FP 68). The self determines that it is more than mere intellect (which could still be only a dream), because the self acts in the objective world in relation to the absolute otherness of another individual person who must be regarded as a "Thou" (FP 46). True life means to see the self objectively; the personal self is determined in the objective world by opposing another personal self (FP 66).

David Dilworth is correct that Nishida's late writings achieve a concrete fusion of individual and environment, or subject and object, by defining "the acting, personal self, and its real ontological dimensions, in essentially social and historical terms"; in short, self-determination presupposes the sociohistorical world in which action takes place.[20] Dilworth also seems quite right to conclude that Nishida's late philosophy presents "an interestingly 'modern' development of Mahāyāna Buddhist tradition," because it situates the immediate present of the creative and self-determining individual within "a radical socio-historical field."[21] The individual person acquires meaning from the interaction with others in the *objective* place of the social and historical world: "It is the precise function of 'true Nothingness' to be the ground, not of mere negation, but of the *absolute affirmation of individuals in the plural.* From this position which absolutely affirms individuals in the plural Nishida went on to elaborate a concept of creative, sociohistorical world."[22] Nobuo Kazashi arrives at a similar interpretation for Nishida's *Fundamental Problems of Philosophy*: Personal acts of the self-determining individual express the sociohistorical horizon of being, and this "expression is not so much the product of a particular individual as that of the field of sociohistorical being itself" (BL 116–17).

Nishida also describes how the acting self may be regarded as the body. He derives the idea that the self is the body from his claim that the self exists for itself by acting in relation to others in the concrete place of the sociohistorical world. Nishida offers an explicit argument:

> [The self] must determine itself. It can also be conceived of as a pure activity. Activity can produce further activity. But the self does not gain significance merely because of that. The self must also realize itself externally, i.e., it must determine objectivity. It must act. The self can therefore be regarded as the body. In the depths of the world

common to I and Thou, it can be conceived as the self-determining individual, while at the same time it expresses itself in the world which it shares with the Thou. The self does not exist in the depths of the mere consciousness of the I. (FP 65)

In short, since the self determines its own existence by acting in the objective place of the sociohistorical world, it can be regarded as the body. What does Nishida mean by "body"? He seems to define the self's body in physical terms. This reading is confirmed in passages where Nishida describes the relation between individuals in society: "There is no action in the strict sense when an individual simply determines itself. Therefore, we determine and oppose one another by being separated by our bodies and through absolute negation, i.e., physical qualities" (FP 29). It seems that only "physical qualities" oppose mind enough to give the individual person a sense of self-existence. So Nishida defines the self's body by physical actions in the objective world.

Nishida's decision to regard the sociohistorical world as the place of nothingness has two troubling side-effects. The first problem is that it becomes difficult to explain how the idea of freedom arises *from within* oneself as a unique individual. Nishida seems right to anchor self-existence at a place that resists the "I" of intellect and cognition; for this opens the possibility that the self may act freely or at least without constraint by its own preconceptions. But as soon as he makes self-consciousness dependent on a loss of self and on the awareness of an objective place that opposes the self, his account produces disadvantages: it is the sociohistorical world itself that is self-determining and purposeful. Since the individual person is determined only in relation to other individuals, "[t]he idea of a unique self-determining individual has no meaning" (FP 6). According to his philosophy, the self acquires meaning, value, and purpose only after acting with others in ways that express the place of the self-determining sociohistorical world. There is "no individual person without society"; and "there can be no unique person" (FP 43, 51). But then how do I decide, in advance and from my own unique life, that one type of action is better than another? In short, the problem is action without apparent motivation.[23] To avoid this problem, one may be inclined to try out the idea that one's own *senses* provide a unique place of value and a motive for acting in the sociohistorical world. As noted, Nishida rejects this option. But why? His reason is of interest. Nishida favors the objective social and historical world over the world of the self's own senses as the place of nothingness, because he wishes to *preserve* the idea the individual person is able to act freely. Nishida reasons as follows: If we select the self's own world of sensation and the senses as the place that gives a consciousness of self-existence and purpose in actual life, then the place of value and purpose becomes an objective world of mere sensation that contradicts the idea that each of us is free. Nishida writes: "Personal action loses its personal significance and becomes purely passive" (FP 73). Why does Nishida believe that awareness of one's own senses will contradict the idea that individual persons are free, self-determining, and autonomous? Again, his writings of 1934 indicate an

intertwining with assumptions about the world of sense contained in the modern
European philosophy of Kant. For Kant, the individual person cannot acquire an
idea of freedom from observing the world of sense: Insofar as a person belongs to
the world of sense—or takes itself as appearance and "in the appearance, that is,
in its visible acts"—it is not free but instead subject to the laws of nature expressed
by the natural sciences.[24] Kant offers this solution: It is possible to think of oneself
as free, by thinking of oneself as belonging to some dimension outside the visible
realm of sense. Kant proposes membership in the unknowable and invisible world
of things in themselves, while Nishida proposes membership in the sociohistorical world of acting individuals.

There is a second problem with Nishida's decision to treat the place of nothingness as the sociohistorical world. It becomes difficult to explain how the
idea of absolute moral value arises *from* one's own life as a unique individual.
Nishida rejects the senses as the site or place of absolute value: it is necessary to
disregard the senses, in order to preserve the idea of morality. *If* each self's own
world of sense is selected as the domain of purpose and value, then a categorical
principle of morality valid for all persons would become impossible: "the world
of the moral *ought*, i.e., Kant's kingdom of purpose, would come into opposition with free will" (FP 73). In effect, Nishida holds that freedom is necessary
for moral actions, and he agrees with Kant's statement that there is nothing of
absolute, unchanging worth within the realm of experiences that can provide
a moral principle valid for all persons. It is Kant who claims that what "holds
only for this or that person's senses" cannot hold as a moral principle valid for
everyone,[25] and that the world of sense "can vary considerably according to the
difference of sensibility [and sense impressions] in various observers."[26] Nishida
selects the sociohistorical world as the place that expresses and self-determines
its own value, purpose, and meaning; the value is expressed through acting individuals. What then is the origin of the meaning and value that the objective
place of the sociohistorical confers upon the acting individuals who express it?
Nishida's answer seems to be this: It is the self-determination of the absolute
place of nothingness that becomes the Good (FP 71), and personal action gains
significance and "exists as the Platonic realm of the Good," to the extent that
it occurs within the present of the self-determining sociohistorical world (FP
72–73). Does Nishida ultimately rely on speculative reason in order to believe in
some realm of value, a realm that is merely *possible* from the standpoint of the
senses, within which, Kant tells us, we must remain in order to ascribe existence
to objects? Either way, Nishida offers no account of how each of us acquires the
ideas of freedom, self-existence, and absolute worth from some place within
our own self. Like Kant, Nishida provides no explanation for how one finds a
motive from within one's own actual life to act in a morally purposeful way. His
promising talk of how the self becomes aware of its own existence is quickly
submerged into a talk of how meaning arises from objective sociohistorical relations between an "I" and a "Thou."

To summarize, Nishida's own use of "place of nothingness" is accompanied by four ideas. First, the self is aware that it is more than consciousness due to resistance by an absolute nothingness within the depths of the self. Second, the five senses do not oppose intellect enough to provide a place for ideas of self-consciousness, self-existence, freedom, and absolute moral value. Third, the self-less place of personal existence is the sociohistorical world. Fourth, the self's body consists of physical qualities. With these results, we are ready to turn to Merleau-Ponty's philosophy, in order to assess the degree of convergence.

LAKE OF NON-BEING: VISIBILITY AS PLACE AND NOTHINGNESS

What ideas about self and body are contained in Merleau-Ponty's *The Visible and the Invisible?* We must find answers to two immediate questions. Does his philosophy of the flesh of the body imply that the senses *can* resist consciousness enough to provide a "place of nothingness"? How does Merleau-Ponty regard the self's body? I argue that he points to the dimension of the self's own senses as a place of unchanging nothingness that resists thinking, because he describes the body in terms of innate and sensible contexts of flesh that precede experience and perceptions. Merleau-Ponty's aim is to rediscover in the exercise of seeing some enigmatic living referent that will explain how the self is aware of its own openness upon the natural world. He tries to install philosophy at the place of seeing and "in experiences that have not yet been 'worked over,' that offer us all at once, pell-mell, both 'subject' and 'object'"(VI 130). He asserts that each of us, as seers, can observe for our self how vision and perception are resisted by "the visible" that seems to rest in itself (VI 130). Visual perception includes at its heart a sensible element—the visible—that mingles but never blends with thinking. The red object that I experience is not merely given as a knowable object, a quale, a message, or bit of information determined by mind, about which there is nothing more to say. Instead, a visual perception of the color red is a temporary focusing of the gaze within a more general atmospheric existence; the perception is "bound up with a certain wooly, metallic, or porous [?] configuration or texture" (VI 131–32). My experience of the color red is a variant within the place of yet another dimension: "It is a concretion of visibility" (VI 132).

This leads us to the most radical and unconventional aspect of Merleau-Ponty's account: this thickness of the flesh called "visibility" may be regarded as a sensible place of one's own body. The term "visible" refers to the medium of flesh that is *between* the seer and the thing seen; it is "a thickness of the body" that enables the seer to enter into the heart of things (VI 135). In other words, perceptual thinking inhabits and is caught up in the porous texture or tissue of visibility provided by the body. The incorporation of vision within this connective medium of visibility—this tissue that mediates connection between thoughts and things—is the "natal secret" or origin of vision (VI 135–36). Since the term "visibility" refers to a texture of the self's own interior flesh, it is not "here" and "now" as physical objects are said to be (VI 139, 147). The sensible and corporeal sample of visibility is not publicly available; it is a secret opening upon the world of nature that is never directly accessible to others, who can possess and directly observe only their own samples. It follows that each individual person is a *sensible for itself* (i.e., a vision or gaze inhabiting the *exemplar sensible* offered by the dimension of visibility). To put this another way, the term "visibility" refers to a secret, self-determining, and unchanging place within the self that is an absolute nothingness in comparison to cognitive thinking.

What evidence does Merleau-Ponty offer for this idea that there is an innate visibility within the self that is prior to perceptions and experiences? By looking at his own original cases of visual perception, he finds a sample of the innate element of flesh. In his working notes of September 1959, Merleau-Ponty describes how changing *Gestalts* come-to-be and pass-away within the pivot of flesh that is lent by one's own body. He poses the question: what is the context that enables one to experience a *Gestalt, for oneself*? What is the X for whom a *Gestalt* is an object of experience? The passage merits a rereading:

> Who experiences it? A mind that would grasp it as an idea or a signification? No. It is a body—in what sense? My body *is* a *Gestalt.* It is a *Gestalt*; it is co-present in every *Gestalt*; it also, and eminently, is a heavy signification, it is flesh; the system it constitutes is ordered about a central hinge or pivot which is openness to . . . a bound and not a free possibility—And at the same time it is a component of every *Gestalt.* The flesh of the *Gestalt* (the grain of the color, the indefinable something that animates the contour or which, in Michotte's experiments, animates the rectangle that "creeps") is what responds to its inertia, to its insertion in a "world," to its field biases. (VI 205)

The point is clear: the body is co-present as the animating context that enables the seer to experience a *Gestalt* firsthand or in the flesh. "Flesh" refers here to what one, as a unique individual, is able to notice about one's own body: it is an inert ground—an absolute (i.e., unchanging) other—compared to the temporary experience of the form of the *Gestalt*. For Merleau-Ponty, the body provides a pre-cognitive context that cannot itself be grasped in the act of perceiving (VI 9). He eventually goes on to describe the "indefinable something that animates" the form of the *Gestalt* as "the visible": "my visible is confirmed as an exemplar" (VI 145). (He invites us to take an original look for ourselves. *I* find a similar visibility in my own case. And you?) Merleau-Ponty refers to a neglected dimension and adds a new philosophical grammar: As a *sensible for itself* with eyes, I can begin to speak of the dimension of visibility as an innate *"exemplar sensible"* and as a place that is "a thickness of my body" (VI 135). The tables have turned: I have my own sample that is the seed for the idea, an *intuitus mentis*, that "the visible" is a subject term for an unchanging dimension that is modified by changing objects of experience. This enables me to speak of "a second or figurative meaning of vision": I have the idea of an innate clairvoyance due to the animating presence of the secret visible context that always precedes my (second-order) visual experiences of particular objects or *Gestalts* (VI 145). Indeed, it is this self-consciousness arising from the way vision is *resisted by the visible* that gives meaning to Merleau-Ponty's phrase "the dimension of the composite of soul and body" (EM 136). He has a way to describe each *sensible for itself* and to make sense of a familiar conviction: "We *are* the compound of the soul and body" (EM 138).

Nobuo Kazashi provides a somewhat different reading for the passage just quoted. I take Kazashi to be suggesting in the passage below that Merleau-Ponty affirms two points: there is a field of visual experience that exhibits visible forms, and that the objective conditions of the body necessary for the visibility of that field are not visible. In a way this seems correct; my retinas, which are necessary for the dimension of visibility that I notice myself, are not directly visible for me as objects. But on Kazashi's reading of Merleau-Ponty's passage on experiencing a *Gestalt* for oneself, the body is "distinct and separate" from the visible field of perceptual experience:

> In sum, the *Gestalts* or forms that are visible in the field of perceptual experience emerge only by virtue of the matrix-Gestalt of our bodily ek-sistence, which is, in principle, invisible to us because we *are* the body. The forms or significations of visible objects and the forms of our bodily existence are empirically distinct and separate, but ontologically they form inseparable whole, which *is* a field of experience. (BL 115)

But I take Merleau-Ponty to be making a different point: perceptual experiences emerge for me, as an individual seer, by virtue of my own body, which *is actually visible* for me, by the principle of the flesh of the body. My own bodily life is not invisible and separate from the shapes, appearances, and patterns that I see, since each *Gestalt* that I see ("duck" or "rabbit") is inseparable from the secret dimension of visibility through which changing shapes and patterns are intimately presented to *me*. The element of innate flesh is an *observable* tissue or texture that enables me to be an individual eye witness to the intersection of thinking and body. If all this is correct, then Merleau-Ponty's late writings on the flesh of the body may diverge from Kazashi's interpretation. They would also diverge from Nishida's account of the self's objective body in *Fundamental Problems of Philosophy*.

However, Yasuo Yuasa cites Merleau-Ponty's *Phenomenology of Perception* as evidence for believing that Merleau-Ponty has an idea of the lived body that is very similar to Nishida's idea of the body of the acting individual in the sociohistorical world. According to Yuasa, both Merleau-Ponty and Nishida describe the body as a thing that sees and a thing that is seen.[27] For both, the self's body has a reflexive character: it is both subject and object. The body is the place of the self that sees for itself; it is something physical that is seen by others. Steve Odin finds that Yuasa "clarifies Merleau-Ponty's phenomenological description of how the human subject is physically incarnated in the network of interconnections."[28] What of this? Do Nishida and Merleau-Ponty have accounts of the body that converge after all? My reply is this: Merleau-Ponty changes his own account of self-embodiment. Scholars might perhaps find a convergence between Nishida's claim that the self may be regarded as the body and Merleau-Ponty's remarks in *Phenomenology of Perception*, but Merleau-Ponty himself notes that his late writings differ from his earlier ones: "The problems posed in *Ph.P.* are insoluble because I start there from the 'consciousness'—'object' distinction" (VI 200). Thus it is one thing for Yuasa to interpret Merleau-Ponty as stating, *in 1945*, that the body *which is seen* is the physical body that is seen by self and others. But this is not the body as interior flesh described later in *The Visible and the Invisible*. By 1960–1961, the sensible sentient is aware of its own secret interior of flesh that is not here and now as physical objects are. It is this radical change that enables Merleau-Ponty to claim that each seer exists for itself as a compound of thinking and visibility.

Merleau-Ponty's account is compatible with references to a place of absolute nothingness, since he refers to the context of visibility lent by one's own body with such terms as a "lake of non-being," "nothingness," and "constitutive emptiness." For example, in his working notes from September 1959, he uses the term "nothingness" in relation to the corporal pivot of visibility that persists beneath and between the changing *Gestalts* of perception. According to Merleau-Ponty, "[e]very Psychology that places the *Gestalt* back into the framework of 'cognition' or 'consciousness' misses the meaning of the *Gestalt*; it fails to express how consciousness is bound to the world through the visibility that is one's own flesh." Thus, *philosophy* has a special purpose—namely, to describe the place in which a *Gestalt* comes into being for the self: "It is being for X, not a pure agile nothingness, but an inscription in an open register, in a lake of non-being, in an *Eröffnung* [insertion], in an *offene* [opening]" (VI 206). What does Merleau-Ponty mean by an open register of non-being? The statement here—that a *Gestalt* occurs within a "lake of non-being"—suggests a *Gestalt* is not experienced in a context of total nothingness or complete annihilation; it is a temporary being inscribed within an observable register that itself has no being as an object of experience. Merleau-Ponty also uses the phrase "a certain constitutive emptiness" (*un certain vide constituant*), when he refers to the way Matisse's drawings and Moore's sculptures show a dimension of visibility that "sustains the supposed positivity of things."[29]

The idea of visibility fills a gap left in William James's radical empiricism. It meets the requirements James himself sets for any philosophy that would qualify as *more radical* than James's radical empiricism. James requires that any such philosophy introduces a principle of "*dis*union" that is able to make "experienced disjunctions," in the quasi-chaotic flux of different experiences, more actual. The principle of flesh—the idea of a sensible whole of visibility that is the corporeal context for the continuous conjunction of different visual experiences—does exactly that. The body, as it is immediately lived by a person, provides the directly witnessed element of visibility as an undividable whole, and this aboriginal corporeality becomes a self-evident and unifying hinge by which one visual experience passes into another. If philosophers agree to regard the sensible ground of visibility as something that is as actual for the individual seer as any experience (e.g., of space, intensity, flatness, brownness, heaviness), then they will break through the mosaic of James's radical empiricism and find a sensible ground that is more radical than the flow of particular experiences that are cognitive to each other. The principle of the flesh of the body does imply that it is possible for the individual to choose to create a hole, gap, *disunion*, or chasm in the continuity of experiences. The idea of visibility implies a stability that precedes a disjunction of possible objects of experience. The gap between experiences is filled neither by mere feeling, nor by an element of absolute idealism, such as F. H. Bradley's rational Absolute, which might threaten to pour metaphysical fictions into philosophy.

So, does Nishida's notion of "place" converge with Merleau-Ponty's philosophy of flesh that emerges in the early 1960s? It seems that they both refer favorably to a bodily place that is both outside the self or "I" of intellect and also essential for an awareness of self-existence. *But they diverge on how they interpret "body."* Merleau–Ponty's philosophy implies that the senses *can* provide a "place of nothingness" that resists consciousness, such that the self is able to acquire an idea of itself as a unique existential that is not a mere mind. Thus he can describe how each of us possesses a sensible uniqueness that enables us to personally determine the existence of our own self and each other. Moreover, if one is able to notice for oneself that one's thinking is resisted by the unchanging otherness of the place of one's sample of visibility, then each of us may be able to say that our own "I" of intellect is in relation to a "Thou" of our own existence. There may be an "I" in relation to a "Thou," even *within* the self of the individual. Merleau-Ponty does refer to the self's body, but he switches registers to describe the self's body as interior flesh. By contrast, Nishida refers to the self's body as belonging to physically acting individuals.

MEDITATION AND WISDOM: AWAKENING
TO THE IDEA OF VISIBILITY

What conclusions can we reach by comparing the writings of Nishida and Merleau-Ponty? Nishida gives a meaning in his late writings to "place of nothingness" that differs in some important ways from Merleau-Ponty's philosophy of flesh. Nishida's notion of "place of nothingness" leaves the self in a place of nothingness that is only resolved by the idea of acting in the objective world. Merleau-Ponty manages to describe a corporeal place that is outside the mind but still inside a world of sense unique to the individual. Given Merleau-Ponty's idea of a secret but preobjective whole of visibility, it is proper to reject Faure's claim that philosophy must betray even an authentic awareness of what is intellectually indeterminate. I proceed here to apply the idea of visibility as a place of nothingness to some questions concerning Buddhism, religious faith, and self-nature to which Nishida applies his notion of the place of nothingness.

There is a fresh option for philosophy at this historical moment. Given the option of interpreting the context of visibility as a sample of interior flesh, it follows that there are two ways to interpret one and the same body. Each body has two sides: "the body as sensible and the body as sentient" (VI 136), and "the body sensed and the body sentient" (VI 138). The body unites two leaves or surfaces that are the obverse and reverse of one another; and this creates a circular course of interpretation that has two phases. First, the individual seer may choose to take the context of visibility for granted and to focus upon the display of perceptible objects and phenomenal relations of cause and effect. Second, the seer may choose instead to take an interest in the context of visibility that is an otherness resistant to forms of thinking. Modern thinking undergoes a scrambling: the individual person acquires the idea of self-existence from a dimension that has heretofore been lumped with outer sense and the world of visible physical actions. For Merleau-Ponty, beyond one's own constitution as an ongoing conjunction of experiences, there *is* something. The Kantian transcendental ego? No. The self as an invisible thing in itself? No. The remainder beyond visual experiences is the sensible context of visibility as such. Each seer may be presumed to possess a similar secret context that precedes the experiences and sense impressions that differ over time or from one person to another.

When visibility is suddenly noticed as constitutive of one's own body—when I think of it as "mine" and sort it with the "me"—then we may say, to use James's language, that there is a local change that passes as a spiritual happening (ERE 153). By choosing to notice the sensible context of visibility as *mine*, I participate in a spiritual happening that occurs without transcending the body. Thus, there may be a spiritual feeling, when one regards the visible whole of one's own interior embodiment as a corporeal sample of what may be called one's own "inner nature." So, it seems that James is not entirely correct when he asserts that nature exhibits only *changes* (ERE 148). The principle of the flesh of the body helps to explain how I—as a sensible-for-itself—have a place from which to speak authoritatively, when I claim that the context of visibility is a place of nothingness that resists my intellectual ideas. Feelings of union with nature are no longer mysterious for any person who chooses to go beyond mere thinking about objects of knowledge and to notice the intersection of self and nature that is the gift of each whole of visibility. There is a way to describe how each of us may find value in actual life and reach an awareness of the sacred in our own innate corporeality that is the place for the here and now. Nishida's notion that the self of intellect is resisted by a place of nothingness can be combined with Merleau-Ponty's notion that visibility is a place of nothingness compared to our knowledge of objects. The result is a philosophy for a dimension within the self that is necessary for even mundane visual perception of the physical world. We may anticipate a new and unprecedented era of more global, cross-cultural, and inclusive philosophies that will combine a key value of modernism (i.e., the principle that beliefs must be based on the senses) with elements of indigenous spiritual traditions.[30]

The idea of visibility as a corporeal place of nothingness that is an absolute other compared to intellect may be of help to those who seek spiritual awakening. This idea may help us arbitrate between different interpretations for Huineng's *Platform Sūtra*, which includes a discussion about "self-nature." In his final writings, Nishida does refer explicitly to Zen and its roots in the sayings of Linji, and the writings of D. T. Suzuki (LW 87). Indeed, D. T. Suzuki develops a close reading of Huineng's *Platfrom Sūtra* that relies on an account of acting with the body that is remarkably similar to Nishida's. According to Suzuki, the practice of Zen is a way to notice "self-nature" and to be released from the passions and error; he asserts that Huineng uses "self-nature" to refer to a principle of bodily vitality that is present in all beings.[31] For Suzuki, awareness of "self-nature" emerges from the *use* of the body: "The body is no-body without its Use, and the Body is the Use. . . . By using itself, its being is demonstrated, and the using is, in Huineng's terminology, 'Seeing into one's own Nature.' Hands are no hands, have no existence, until they pick up flowers and offer them to the Buddha."[32] Suzuki's decision to link an awareness of self-nature to the use of one's body is remarkably similar to Nishida's claim that the self exists by acting with a physical body in the objective sociohistorical world. One possible objection is that both Nishida and Suzuki offer no account of how the senses enable one to acquire wisdom of one's own self-nature.

Buddhist scholar Youru Wang suggests a second interpretation for what Huineng may mean by "self-nature": "Huineng's 'self nature' emphasizes more plainly the possibility of existential awakening *within* the living body and mind of every sentient being. It underlines that every human being can actualize this possibility through the practice of nonattachment in all everyday circumstances."[33] On this reading, awakening to one's own self-nature seems to occur within the self. But Wang asserts that this existential awakening to one's self-nature has "the consequence of excluding any substances, essence or foundation outside the function of the human mind . . . the goal of this transformation is to flow together with all things through an empty mind, the mind devoid of self-attachment."[34] As a result, awakening to one's own self-nature seems to stop short at an awareness of mind.

Fortunately, with the idea of visibility, we may pass between these two interpretations. Awakening to one's own self-nature is to have one moment of thought for the sensible ground of visibility that may be noticed within the self, after cessation of all perception of objects of experience (i.e., cessation of perception of the ten thousand cognitive *thoughts of objects* that are of merely relative worth). Meditation becomes a technique for purifying one's mind of thoughts of objects of experience, so that thinking, "in passing *through the six gates* [sense organs], will neither be defiled nor attached to the six sense *objects*."[35] By practicing thoughtlessness with regard to objects of experience and desire, one does not stop with the thought that within the depths of the self there is nothing, vacuity, or annihilation;

instead, we acquire the idea that each of the five senses has its own sensible place (e.g., visibility as such) and that the senses "need not be defiled in all circumstances, and our true nature may be self-manifested all the time."[36] Visibility is a sample of the self's own nature, as it appears within the composite individual of thinking and flesh. Meditation (*dyāna*) and wisdom (*prajñā*) are one; for meditation frees the self from ten thousand experiences and makes it possible to notice the innate visibility that is the seed for the idea of one's own corporeal nature and that of each member of the community of sentient beings or sensible sentients. With two ways to think of the body, we may also be able to ask new questions, as Faure does, about how and whether accounts of the mind and body in this "passage called 'awakening'" are gendered.[37] Moreover, the way of interpreting Huineng's *Platform Sūtra* may prove Merleau-Ponty correct: we can learn from Chinese philosophies "to rediscover the relationship to being and the initial option which gave it birth, and to estimate the possibilities we have shut ourselves off from in becoming 'Westerners' and perhaps reopen them."[38]

The philosophy of flesh may enable us to link the spiritual notion of no-self with a corporeal exemplar of actuality that is noticed in an egoless way. Nishida's early idea of an indeterminate "true self," beneath the self of egoistic thinking, does seem to converge with the composite self which Merleau-Ponty describes in *Eye and Mind*: the "autonomous order of the composite of the soul and body" (EM 140). There may be a new way to interpret Nishida's claim that we value artworks because they "touch our heart strings" and supply an awareness of our unity with nature "from the depths of the heart." Perhaps art touches "our heart strings" and gives an awareness of our unity with nature "from the depths of the heart," because it exemplifies self-evident zones of flesh, such as the medium of visibility—a context unanalyzable as knowledge—that connect the individual person in a unique way with natural life.

Given the idea of the visible as a sensible exemplar within the self, it may also be possible to find a meaning for the term "faith" that is compatible with the Enlightenment idea that beliefs must be based on the evidence of the senses. My own self-evident dimension of visibility appears for me as an unchanging other (an absolute nothingness) in relation to my cognitive thinking, yet it enables me to keep watch and to determine, for myself, when and whether a possible object that I have in mind is finally *visible* and therefore actually existing for me. If I claim to observe this unchanging pivot of visibility that precedes my changing perceptions, my conviction concerning its presence is likely to be dismissed as a belief based on "faith" by those outside of me who require that the term "existence" be reserved for objects that are experienced and are empirically known. Thus, the practicing scientist may be tempted to regard my own belief in "my visible," in the secret exemplar of my existence as something other than mere mind, as faith without evidence. But for me this belief is inseparable from the dimension of my senses; it is not wish fulfillment. Merleau-Ponty initiates the use of the term "perceptual faith" (VI 11, 18–19), so it is possible to ask whether a personal "faith" in perception based on an innate sample of visibility may be helpful in explaining how a unique self acquires a faith in its own union with nature.

Modern philosophical doctrines for the terms "nature" and "philosophy" result in a blind spot that makes it difficult to voice the awakening to one's own self-nature that is mentioned in Buddhist texts. According to the first doctrine, "nature" is to be defined in terms of the subject matter of such disciplines as the biological or cognitive sciences. "Philosophy" is defined in modern terms as an epistemological project that always has knowledge as its product or direct object. It is time to reopen the question of what sort of descriptions qualify as "professional" and "philosophical." Perhaps the particular term "pure experience" is self-contradictory; but we must guard against the argument that "nothingness" and "suchness" cannot be used for philosophical investigation, because they refer to what is rarely given, exceptional, or characteristic of a pathological psychology. Merleau-Ponty's account of flesh and of "the coiling over of the visible upon the seeing body" has no name in philosophy (traditional or modern): "What we are calling flesh, this interiorly worked-over mass, has no name in any philosophy" (VI 146–47). Resistance to talk about such a cognitively ineffable place of intersection between self and nature is historically and culturally relative. One wonders whether resistance is due to a willful Orientalism, in Edward Said's sense, when philosophers affirm the idea that philosophy is exclusively an epistemological discipline and regard obvious exceptions from cultures across the globe as exotic, other, or mysterious.[39] Do "postmodern" philosophers escape from a willful denial of the sensible and preobjective exemplars of self-embodiment?

III

THE WORLD:
ETHICS OF EMPTINESS,
ETHICS OF THE FLESH

10

The Flesh of the World Is Emptiness and Emptiness Is the Flesh of the World, and Their Ethical Implications

Glen A. Mazis

INTRODUCTION

Both the import of Merleau-Ponty's articulation of embodiment culminating in his later notion of the "flesh of the world" and the central tenet of "emptiness" or *śūnyatā* articulated by many schools of so-called Middle Way Buddhism are misunderstood frequently. Merleau-Ponty is mistakenly interpreted to have articulated a sense of "self" whose locus is in the body and to have restored to being either a foundation or a positivity in embodiment by shifting the grounding of self from the traditional Western focus on consciousness (or reason) to embodiment. The Middle Way Buddhist sects and schools that concentrate on emptiness are often misunderstood to be advocating a devaluation and subsequent detachment from embodiment and from the perceptual world and its enmeshment of the senses with emotion, memory, and imagination. These latter phenomena are mistakenly taken to be categorically identified by the Buddhist doctrine of emptiness as delusions of desire, egoistic concern with a past history, and fantasies of grasping that Buddhism strives to leave behind as unnecessary fetters and distortions of human life. However, both these understandings of Merleau-Ponty and Buddhist doctrine are wrong and miss the central contributions to the epistemological and ontological understanding of human existence that have been accomplished by both Merleau-Ponty and Buddhism.

The power of comparative philosophy becomes evident in examining Merleau-Ponty's notion of embodiment (and the flesh of the world) in light of the Buddhist understanding of emptiness or *śūnyatā*. It is through this comparison that one can see aspects implicit in both philosophies that become visible and meaningful through the comparison. Although Merleau-Ponty is at pains to decenter the notion of self, to deconstruct the kind of abstractions upon which traditional notions of self in Western thought have been based, and to replace any notions of being with a radical notion of becoming or process, this emphasis is seen more clearly through the lens of emptiness. Although the Buddhist doctrine of emptiness asserts that once the distorting rationalizing constructions and categorizations of the ego have been wiped away, it is feeling and emotion that penetrate to the heart of each situation through compassion and the felt interconnection with all living beings, that the perceptual flux and flow that surrounds us is the true reality in which we must swim without anchor or foundation, and that this flow is one which moves spontaneously through our bodies as interwoven with the bodies of all living beings, Merleau-Ponty's ideas of embodiment and the flesh of the world make this dimension stand out more clearly. How the flesh of the world and *śūnyatā* are mutually enlightening is a fecund topic for a comparative philosophy to show its power in clarifying questions vital to human liberation.

THE FLESH OF THE WORLD IS ABOUT EMPTINESS

Merleau-Ponty's notion of the "lived body," the body-subject, and his later formulations of the flesh might seem to offer an ontological foundation *in the body*, or with a more sophisticated reading, perhaps an ontological foundation *in the complex* of the body and its *Gestalt* within the perceptual field, or within its intertwining with the world taken as matter of a different sort than the tradition had known—matter laced with affective, memorial, and imaginative dimensions. The body as described in Merleau-Ponty's work is often misunderstood as a self-collecting subjectivity capable of grasping itself in its corporeality, and then opening to a dimension of perceptual significance that is prima facie revelatory. One could take as a prime example of this interpretation a sentence like the one in the introduction to *Phenomenology of Perception* that reads "We are in the realm of the truth and it is 'the experience of truth' which is self-evident. To seek the essence of perception is to declare that perception is, not presumed true, but defined as access to the truth."[1] Yet to make this interpretation is to miss that Merleau-Ponty has radically redefined what he means by truth, by the sense of perception, the sense of self, and the kind of evidence that counts as positive for him. If one looks further in the paragraph, the original thought is completed by these sentences: "[T]he self-evidence of perception is not adequate thought or apodictic self-evidence. The world is not what I think, but what I live through. I am open to the world, I have no doubt that I am in communication with it, but I do not possess it; it is inexhaustible" (PhP xvi–xvii). For Merleau-Ponty, I cannot think the self or the world and grasp them, since they are richer than any ability of mind or understanding. As he says at the end of the introduction, their mystery is not a problem, "but their mystery defines them" (PhP xx).

For Merleau-Ponty, taking the embodiment seriously means philosophical insight must be transformed to achieve an apprehension akin to the heightened perception of artists like Balzac, Proust, Valery, or Cézanne, whom he mentions as having faced the world with a "kind of attentiveness and wonder" and a "demand for awareness" (PhP xxi)—similar to the heart of Buddhist practice. When almost five hundred pages later at the concluding passage of the *Phenomenology of Perception*, Merleau-Ponty asks how we can ever come to the answer to any of life's pressing questions, such as whether I should make this promise or risk my life for so little or give up freedom to fight for freedom, his answer on the basis of his exhaustive study of perception and embodiment is that there will never be any clear intellectual answers to even these questions, but rather only a sense that "your freedom cannot be willed . . . without willing freedom for all" and that "what is here required is silence" (PhP 456)—certainly responses resonant to the Buddhist attention to silence and the interconnection of all. Merleau-Ponty concludes that our existence lies in the act into which we throw ourselves without foundation but, for example, in answering the call of love and compassion when a person's son is caught in a fire (as described by Saint-Exupery) and there is no self and no body and no grasp of existence other than "your abode is your act itself. Your act is you. . . . You give yourself in exchange . . . . Your significance shows itself, effulgent. . . . Man is but a network of relationships, and these alone matter to him" (PhP 456). The kind of embodiment Merleau-Ponty shows us is the ability to leave behind the notion of a contained body—a corpse-body, as he calls the notion of body as object—and to see embodiment as the way we are inextricably caught up in relations with all that is, and we, our embodiment, are nothing more and nothing less.

To spontaneously do the right thing happens when we actualize our freedom as embodied beings where "freedom is always the meeting of the inside and outside" (PhP 454). This means we must clear away what obstructs our release into the flow of the world, what gives us the illusion of self-containment, and affirm what he states at the start of the work: "[T]here is no inner man, man is in the world, and only in the world does he know himself" (PhP x). Again, this sense of embodiment echoes how emptiness surpasses the obstacles constructed to achieving the meeting of the inside and the outside, for there is no inside as psychic interior, nor outside as objective other. At the beginning of his thought in the *Phenomenology of Perception*, Merleau-Ponty says: "We must therefore avoid saying that our body is *in* space or *in* time . . . I am not in space and time, nor do I conceive space and time; I belong to them, my body combines with them" (PhP 139–40). He ends this chapter by articulating how our body is the medium for the world as it sounds itself through us and in that sense "the body is essentially an expressive space" (PhP 146). There are no good words in Western thought and the traditional philosophical vocabulary to express this desubstantialized body taken up into the flow of the world, so Merleau-Ponty already in this book calls embodiment in relation to the world "but a hollow, a fold, which has been made and can be unmade" (PhP 215)—the kind of language he will start using exclusively at the end of his life, but already sprinkled in these early pages. Merleau-Ponty has just been struggling to explain how when "my consciousness is saturated with this limitless blue," the blue of the sky somehow "thinks itself in me" (PhP 214). This, too, is a precursor to his later central idea of "reversibility," that in perceiving the body joins up with a perception achieved cojointly by all the beings of the world.

The failure to realize how much subjectivity has been desubstantialized and decentered in Merleau-Ponty's work is continued when commentators on the later work take "the flesh of the world" or "the chiasm" of body/world in a positivistic sense that sees a becoming one of subject and object, of body and world, a sense of coincidence between the two, even though Merleau-Ponty is very clear that this is not what he intends to articulate: "The world seen is not 'in' my body, and my body is not 'in' the visible world ultimately: as flesh applied to flesh, the world neither surrounds it nor is surrounded by it. A participation in and kinship with the visible, the vision neither envelops it nor is enveloped by it definitively."[2] The relation of the body and world is one of participation, of kinship, that there are two, yet they intertwine as one—just as his repeated image of the chiasm portrays—two separate optic nerves intertwined and working as one or two strands of DNA that are one gene while they are two also. As Merleau-Ponty continues to articulate this logic, he continues: "[M]y body as a visible thing is contained within the full spectacle. But my seeing body subtends this visible body, and all the visibles with it. There is a reciprocal insertion and intertwining of one in the other. Or rather, if as once again we must, we eschew the thinking by planes and perspectives, there are two circles, or two vortexes, or two spheres, concentric when I live naively, and as soon as I question myself, the one slightly decentered with respect to the other" (VI 138). This is the relationship Merleau-Ponty will continually try to elaborate, how there can be both oneness and two-ness, intertwining yet the uniqueness of every living being. It is that same logic of emptiness at the heart of Buddhism. It is also the same insistence that this sense will not emerge if we reify phenomena, but must be able to see them as vortical, unfolding, emerging, inseparable from all that is around them, evanescent, in flux, change, transition.

Similarly to the relationship among all that is the flesh of the world, the notion of "reversibility" that is at the heart of his later ontology is never simply a reciprocity of body and world, that the two terms just swing back and forth between each other in some sort of seamless unity—that, for example, as I see the tree, the tree now sees me. Besides being an absurd anthropomorphism, this would not capture the ambiguity of perception and the way of intertwining Merleau-Ponty is expressing in a sense parallel to emptiness: "To begin with, we spoke summarily of a reversibility of the seeing and the visible, of the touching and the touched. It is time to emphasize that it is a reversibility that is always immanent and never realized in fact. My left hand is always on the verge of touching my right hand touching the things, but I never reach coincidence; the coincidence eclipses at the moment of realization" (VI 147). For Merleau-Ponty, there can be no coincidence, because there is neither a subject, nor an object to come together in order to coincide. This would posit a kind of substantiality, a kind of being, that the notion of "flesh of the world" is meant to undermine. As Merleau-Ponty phrases it: "There is for example no absolute flux of singular *Erlebnisse* [experiences]; there are fields and a field of fields" (VI 171). There can be no absolute flux, no absolute things, but rather there are fields, in which things, people, creatures intertwine, interweave, yet do not lose the wonder that each is each and yet not without the others—an order of a differing logic than that which can be put into substantialist language and dualistic thought. What connects or make one the things of a field? Nothing, yet everything, because in their unsubstantiality, all beings are open and caught up with all others. This is the same point that Keiji Nishitani, a Kyoto School thinker, tries to make about Buddhist concept of emptiness (*śūnyatā*):

> [T]his does refer to a "unity" of subject and object such as we find it variously ex-plained in the history of philosophic thought East and West. That is to say, we do not presuppose a separation of subject and object and then work toward their unifica-tion. The unity of the absolute near side is not the result of a process, but rather the original unity of absolute openness and absolute emptiness. Its standpoint is neither a monism or a dualism of any sort. It is the absolute one, the absolute self-identity of the absolutely two: the home-ground on which we are what *we* are in our self-nature and the home ground on which *things* are what they are in themselves.[3]

No escape into a unity, or a monism of rationality, is possible; rather, a responsive-ness to all beings.

Merleau-Ponty's reversibility is not about unity, not about subjects and objects, but about how one is two and how each act of perception and expression is both mine and not-mine. Reversibility, even as asymmetrical and inexhaustible in such a way that it is not about closure and coincidence, does bring about this inter-weavement, as he explains later in the same passage:

> I am always on the same side of my body; it presents itself to me in one invariant perspective. But this incessant escaping, this impotency to superpose exactly one upon the other, the touching of the things by my right hand and the touching of this same right hand by my left hand, or to superpose, in the extraordinary movements of the hand, the tactile experience of a point and the "same" point a moment later, or the auditory experience of my own voice and that of others—this is not failure. For if these experiences never exactly overlap, if they slip away at the very moment they are about to rejoin, if there is always a "shift," a "spread," between them, that is precisely because my hands are part of the same body, because it moves itself in the world, because I hear myself both from within and from without. I experience—and as often as I wish—the transition and metamorphosis of the one experience into the other. (VI 148)

Merleau-Ponty continues by saying this gap between these things and people, or between people, that nevertheless are one in vision, in touch, or in speech, is not an "ontological void" but rather is a "spannedness" among all beings as of a flesh of the world.

A deeper reading of Merleau-Ponty reveals that there is no "the body" in his writings. The body as a noun, let alone as anything like substance does not exist for Merleau-Ponty. The body is "bodying." As bodying, the self that emerges as embodiment is foundationless too, always emergent among all the being of the world. Merleau-Ponty states: "He who thinks, perceives, etc. is this negativity as openness, by the body, of the world" (VI 246). Embodiment is an ongoing emergence, an upsurge, an interweavement, a kind of bringing forth that has no foundation and yet is everywhere. The flesh of the world is a denial of body or mind as substance and also of matter as substance. Merleau-Ponty states: "The flesh is not matter, is not mind, is not substance" (VI 139). Merleau-Ponty is denying that there is any foundational essence for substantiality as a source of the upsurge of perception. He is also denying that there is anything in the world that is the object of perception as some substance standing over and against it. These vortices that are body or bodying and the perceived of the world are spirals of transformation that find themselves within moments of meaning together, but are nothing outside of these effulgences, these emergences of sense. Another allied notion is the "depth" of the world: "Either what I call depth is nothing, or else it is my participation in a Being without restriction, a participation primarily in the being of space beyond every (particular) point of view. Things encroach upon one another because each is outside of the others."[4] Things are not primarily located in a Cartesian space of discrete locations and boundaries; they are caught up with one another, encroaching upon one another, enmeshed with one another through their transformations in a "movement by vibration." Further in this last published essay, "Eye and Mind," Merleau-Ponty names embodiment as the site of "the deflagration of being": "There is a human body when, between seeing and the seen, between touching and the touched, between one eye and the other, between hand and hand, a blending of some sort takes place—when the spark is lit between the sensing and the sensible, lighting the fire that will not stop burning" (PR 163). The perceiver, through embodiment and through the senses, enters into "a fission" that is the process of embodiment as a losing of a collected experience of self to a never-ending encroachment of all things upon all things that is the primary depth of existence. So Merleau-Ponty says of vision: "Now perhaps we have a better sense of what is meant by the little verb 'to see.' Vision is not a certain mode of thought or presence to self; it is the means given me for being absent to myself, for being present at the fission of Being from the inside—the fission at whose termination, and not before, I come back to myself" (PR 186). Perceiving is not a grasping, not a capturing, but rather the body's way of losing itself in the ever-streaming blaze or fission of beings that are the field of existence and give us back ourselves as a way to be who we are with them.

Merleau-Ponty's articulation of embodiment takes us into a logic of not-one-not-two, and undermines any notion of the substantiality of body or self; it uncovers embodiment as a relation to all other beings, finds its locus in something which is neither mind nor matter, and takes ambiguity, mystery, and indetermi-

nacy as hallmarks of apprehending what is; it further takes perception and all human apprehension and expression as a cojoint achievement with all other beings,
and finds embodiment to be the entryway into a fire or fission among all beings
that journeys us throughout the world as our distinct way of coming to ourselves.
These ideas can be seen to make much more sense, not against the backdrop of
Western thought and philosophy, but as ideas that presuppose the Buddhist concept of emptiness.

EMPTINESS (*ŚŪNYATĀ*) IS ABOUT
EMBODIMENT IN MERLEAU-PONTY'S SENSE

There may be no greater articulation of emptiness in the Buddhist tradition than
the widely circulated and chanted *Heart Sūtra*. For Buddhists, especially those
of the Middle Way, the *Heart Sūtra* famously points toward the state of spiritual
liberation achieved in emptiness as that of "No eye, ear, nose, tongue, body, mind:
No form, sound, smell, taste, touch . . . no act of sensing."[5] This might seem at
odds with the path of Merleau-Ponty's thought. It could, if taken out of its proper
context and understanding, be taken to be enunciating a doctrine that leaves behind the body—as does much of Western metaphysical and theological thought
that relegates the body to ontological inferiority, and takes embodiment as the
aspect of the human condition that must be transcended in order to achieve
epistemological and spiritual clarity. Similarly, the Buddha declares in his famous
"fire sermon":

> All things, O monks, are on fire. And what are these things which are on fire?
> The eye is on fire. Things seen are on fire. Eye vision is on fire. Impressions received
> by the eye are on fire. Whatever sensation is connected with the eye, is on fire.
> With what are these on fire?
> With the fire of desire, with the fire of hate and delusion; with birth, old age, death,
> sorrow, lamentation, misery, grief, and despair.
> All things are burning.
> The ear is on fire; sounds are on fire . . . The nose is on fire; odors are on fire . . . The
> tongue is on fire; tastes are on fire. . . . The mind is on fire; ideas are on fire. . . . Whatever
> sensation, pleasant or unpleasant, is connected with the mind is also on fire. . . .
> All things are burning. . . . Cultivate aversion, O monks, and be free of the fire of
> desire.[6]

These declarations might also seem to many to cast the body's sense perception and its concomitant emotional significance as epistemologically, as well as
spiritually, delusional. They do. However, they do so by pointing to a perversion
of embodiment and the perceptual life. Rather than ruling out a body-centered
approach to emptiness, the *Heart Sūtra* and the Buddha's sermon are deconstructing a habitual misuse of perception and bodily experience by the mind of ego and

desire in order to clear away a truer sense of perception and embodiment that can only emerge in emptiness.

The *Heart Sūtra*'s classic formulation of emptiness is "Here, O Sariputa, form is emptiness, and the very emptiness is form; emptiness does not differ from form, form does not differ from emptiness; whatever is form, that is emptiness, whatever is emptiness, that is form. The same is true of feelings, perceptions, impulses and consciousness" (BS 162–63). Falling under the realm of form are supposed things as diverse as self, body, the good, the evil, the One, God, substance, soul, the other, truth, certainty, reason, happiness, self-identity, mind, life, death, and so on indefinitely, including, too, the most mundane. There will not be any way to grasp firmly any aspect of reality by any particular category and even this denial itself is foundationless, empty. These insights follow from the same interdependence we have already been exploring in Merleau-Ponty's notion of the body. A very clear and modest statement of emptiness is contained in Stephen Batchelor's commentary on Nāgārjuna's writings and his formulation of emptiness: "[H]e announces that 'contingency' is the key to understanding what it means for them [life and language] to be empty. A self, a plant, a body or a time is empty because it is incapable of being neatly circumscribed as a thing cut off from other things. Selves, plants, bodies and times are utterly contingent on the complex interplay of conditions, attributes and language with which they are not identical and from which they are not different. To know emptiness is not to negate these things but to be dumbfounded by the sheer fecundity of life."[7] There are no circumscribing forms as there are no self-contained boundaries in the way in which all beings are only found in the midst of all other beings—as embodied or material all beings are of a time and a place interwoven within a context, situated. This is emptiness, not as a loss of being, but as a gain in the intertwining or interdependence of all. Only the insecure individual's desire and the West's philosophical need for self-identity is lost as an impossible goal.

Descartes was almost driven to despair when he saw that after burning, the wax of a candle contained nothing that remained fixed until he could "see" with his mind the idea of substance, the underlying being that was not visible to his senses but that must be the stable ground underlying the perception of passing away and interdependence. In interpreting the *Heart Sūtra*, Kosho Uchiyama has the opposite feeling and realization when considering a flame burning from a candle (a famous image already used by the Buddha to articulate the insubstantiality of the self to King Melinda):

> In this respect, we are as selves quite like the flame of a candle. As wax melts near a lit wick and burns, it emits light near the tip of the candle. For the most part, this place from which the light is emitted remains the same and appears as a fixed shape; it is this seemingly unchanging shape that we refer to as flame. That which I call I is similar to the flame. Although both body and mind are an unceasing flow, since they preserve what seems to be a constant form, we refer to them as I. Therefore, actually there is no existing I as some substantial thing; there is only ceaseless flow. This is true not only of the sentient being I, it is true of all things.[8]

There is no existing I as empty, nor a candle nor flame, but that is because as a flow phenomenon, as an intertwining or enlacing, to use Merleau-Ponty's words, what they are is only caught up among other beings and their continual emergence or unfolding. Western philosophy and culture has only hearkened to the negative moment of emptiness and not its wondrous side: "To be empty of a fixed identity allows one to enter fully into the shifting, poignant, beautiful and tragic contingencies of the world. It makes possible an acute awareness of life as a creative process, in which each person is inextricably involved. Yet, despite the subjective intensity of such a vision, when attention is turned to the subject itself, no isolated observer is to be found" (VC 44–45). Although as Dōgen says, "forgetting oneself is to be awakened by all things," in the Western tradition, it is the loss of center, of foundation in a stable self, which has been striking about emptiness and not the gain of an openness to all things and a cooperation in all aspects of perception, apprehension, and expression with innumerable cojoint partners.

Buddha's fire sermon is an apt phenomenology, because the body allows itself to be used as the vehicle of ego, as the guarantor of the mind's construction of a ground, and provides seemingly a singularity needed for the illusion of self-subsistent individuality and identity. It makes embodiment into an isolated condition, cut off from a world that it then desperately craves. In *Being Bodies: Buddhist Women on the Paradox of Embodiment*, Michele Martin writes: "[T]he first way we apprehend a self is the most obvious: no distinction is made between what we think of our self and our body. . . . We also treat our body as an object that our self possesses: 'my hair,' 'my face.' And further, we also assume that a self exists because it has the body as a support: it feels like some solid basis for who we are. So, here the body plays object to our self as subject. Or the reverse could be true."[9] Put in Merleau-Ponty's terminology, this distortion of perception is the "experience error" and indicates a "second-order" or "high-altitude" approach to embodiment—a putting into perception our rational constructions such that we experience them as there in the first place. The objective, the substantive, is constructed on the basis of a more primary experience. It is this construction of a stable self that gives rise to the destructive aspects of perception, emotion, feeling, desire, and other aspects of embodiment as leading to torment and violation of others: "Fixations about self and things sustain the largely unconscious holding pattern in which we hover above the world of immediate experience. Although fixation appears to freeze the self into an undisturbed, isolated cell, the tightness of the grip spawns chaotic torrents of thoughts, images and emotions. Like squeezing the trigger of a gun or pressing a button to set off an alarm, fixations such as egoism, craving, conceit and opinionatedness erupt as proliferating streams of longings and worries" (VC 63). The clinging to a stable self and constructing the world to allow this in a subject-object dichotomy paradoxically plunges us into a helter-skelter of sensations, passions, feelings, and so on. We will return to this dimension of distorted perception when we examine the ethical implication of the notion of flesh of the world and emptiness.

Emptiness, if embraced, leads us to another experience of the body. However, it is the experience of embodiment as empty that is key to realizing the emptiness of all existence. Martin expresses this: "To understand the body as a reflection of emptiness is to know that form is emptiness and emptiness is form. . . . The body, experienced as empty form, appears though it is empty and it is empty though it appears. Its emptiness and appearance are inseparable. Since it is empty, it is not solid or real, and since it appears, it is not mere nothingness."[10] As she aptly puts it, the body in the world is like the reflection of the moon in the water. Nāgārjuna, perhaps the most articulate thinker and poet of emptiness in any Buddhist tradition, explores embodiment and emptiness in this verse:

> If my eyes cannot see themselves,
> How can they see something else?
> Were there no trace of something seen,
> How could I see at all?
>
> Neither seeing nor unseeing see.
>
> Seeing reveals a seer,
> Who is neither detached
> Nor undetached from seeing.
> How could you see,
> And what would you see
> In the absence of a seer?
>
> Just as a child is born
> From father and mother,
> So consciousness springs
> From eyes and colorful shapes.
>
> Without these eyes,
> How could I know
> Consciousness, impact,
> Feeling and thirst?
> Clinging, evolving,
> Birth, aging and death?
>
> Seers seeing sights explain
> Hearers hearing sounds
> Smellers smelling smells,
> Tasters tasting tastes,
> Touchers touching textures
> Thinkers thinking thoughts. (VC 86–87)

Nāgārjuna here articulates that only a visible can see and its vision is not *its* vision but must also be of the visible and originate in the things seen as much as in the seeing. The seer is not behind vision, apart from it, in a consciousness or self, for example, but only emerges from the seeing. Our so-called consciousness is not ours, but arises from colors and shapes and the world of things and qualities, yet it is we who see and hear and touch and think. Yet there is only this fire lit between the seer and the seen, and between the seer himself or herself and the seen and also with all the seeing among all the visibles, and so forth for all the senses and so forth for thinking which arises from this bodily enfolding within the world. This description matches Merleau-Ponty's notion of the flesh of the world as articulated in *The Visible and the Invisible* in a myriad of statements similar to "he who sees cannot possess the visible unless he is possessed by it, unless he *is* of *it*" (VI 134–35).

This lack of distinction between subject and object is also key to formlessness or emptiness insofar as seeing is not categorizable as seeing nor hearing as hearing; there is merely an enlacement of beings on all levels emerging through each other. This is expressed by Thich Nhat Hahn, when he states:

> This is the first flash of lightening. The Buddha goes directly to the heart of the prajnaparamita, presenting the principle of formlessness. He tells us that a true practitioner helps all living beings in a natural and spontaneous way, without distinguishing between the one who is helping and the one who is being helped. When our left hand is injured, our right hand takes care of it right away. It doesn't stop to say, "I am taking care of you. You are benefiting from my compassion." The right hand knows very well that the left hand is also the right hand. There is no distinction between them. This is the principle of interbeing—co-existence, or mutual interdependence. "This is because that is." With this understanding—the right hand helping the left hand in a formless way—there is no need to distinguish between the right hand and the left hand. (RM 203–4)

There is no such thing as "helping" or even the "right hand" as "helper." It is the same way that there is no "perceiving" or "thinking" or self or thinker. To embrace the formlessness of the *Heart Sūtra* and "to go beyond, way beyond"—to see that there are no eyes, ears, nose, tongue, and so on—is to liberate the body from metaphysical desperation (in the sense of Sartre's analysis of the isolated ego trying through its body to capture from the world a metaphysical foundation of the "in-itself"). The desperate body, the body of rationalizing perception *has* eyes, ears, nose, tongue, and consciousness with which to localize the so-called determinate properties of the world projected as set against it in order to grasp them both epistemologically and egoistically, as instantiating the values which would allow the ego's project of incorporation of them to defy the insecurity of groundlessness. To go beyond into emptiness is to refind a body within a neverending dialogue among all things that has no set basis, meaning, or goal.

The body is a primary site of the Buddha's Noble Truths that life is suffering, that suffering comes from grasping, and that suffering can be overcome. Essential to grasping is the categorization of the world into self-subsistent entities of stable properties that begin the process of "conditioned coproduction" that transforms perception from an open contact into a labyrinth of distorted constructions that is the cause of insatiable desire and suffering. Embodiment allows itself to become a primary source of suffering, because it is also the way to transform suffering into another state of awareness and existence which ends this delusion and grasping. As Joan Tollifson states:

> Apparent embodiment in a particular perishable form, with a complex brain, is un-doubtedly at the root of our illusory sense of separation from the totality. . . . Paradox-ically, the body also offers the way home, for it is in fully meeting whatever appears as pure sensation that we discover the emptiness of form—the undivided wholeness of being that has no solidity, no boundaries, no limits—that which no word or image can capture, in which everything is included.[11]

Embodiment, if attended to and articulated from within the jostling depths of its enfolding-unfolding, its deflagration, or, as Merleau-Ponty calls it, its unwind-ing, its *serpentement*, articulates the world and perceptual experience as *śūnyatā*. This is what the Buddhist practitioner achieves through meditative practice of varying types—all of which focus on the heart of embodiment, its breathing, and its ways of resonating with the larger world, then embodiment is the way to cut through delusions and become empty: "[W]e find this body [the dharma body] in its coming to be and passing away compared to a diamond for its hardness, its brilliancy, and the sharpness that enables it to cut through all things."[12] The empty body opens us to the emptiness of the world, sometimes also calling "dropping off body-and-mind."

In the working notes to *The Visible and the Invisible*, Merleau-Ponty decon-structs the apparent "transcendence of the thing" when he states: "The transcen-dence of the thing compels us to say that it is a plenitude only by being inexhaust-ible, that is, by not being all actual under the look—but it promises this total actuality, since it *is there*" (VI 191). Merleau-Ponty recognizes the perceptual, the world around us does not have the actuality we seek of it, the closure we would have rather than its inexhaustibility. He continues:

> When we say that—on the contrary—the phantasm is not observable, that it is empty, non-being, the contrast with the sensible is not absolute. The senses are apparatus to form concretions of the inexhaustible, to form existent significations—But the thing is not really observable: there is always a skipping over in every observation, one is never at the thing itself. What we call the *sensible* is only the fact that the indefinite [succession] of *Abschattungen [showings, perspectives]* precipitates. (VI 192)

For Merleau-Ponty, there are not sensible objects, as much as we tend to intel-lectualize our experience to meet this demand, but rather series of showings, ap-pearances, and emergences of meaning that retains its vitality and truthfulness in keeping open the promiscuity among all things and perceivers. This is also what

Avalokiteśvara Bodhisattva in the *Heart Sūtra* means when he says there are "no touchables or objects of the mind, no sight-organ-elements . . . no mind-conscious elements" (BS 163). There are no foundational entities outside of the process of this perceiving which is a deflagration, a consuming of all "outsides," of all sense of substance or true being. There is only *śūnyatā*, which is the ongoing transformation and relational intertwining of all beings such that they do not truly exist on their own and they do not exist as having substance or fixed form. They are the vitality and effulgence of meaning as well as its mystery and ongoing hiding in being brought fourth ceaselessly. Batchelor puts this more simply as "[e]mptiness includes the sun, moon, stars, and planets, the great earth, mountains and rivers, all trees and grasses, bad men and good men, bad things and good things, heaven and hell; they are all in the midst of emptiness" (VC 28). This insight is also expressed briefly in the Chinese Zen Master Sengcan's (d. 606) seventh-century verses: "When we return to the root, we gain the meaning/ When we pursue external objects we lose the reason/ . . . Transformations going on in an empty world which confronts us/ appear real because of ignorance" (BS 172). Yet, like Merleau-Ponty, Master Sengcan cautions "be not prejudiced against the six sense objects," for it is in the wealth of perception of "the ten thousand things" that we return to meaning's "origin and remain where we ever have been" (BS 174). Like the perceiving body, what is perceived is distorted when constructed as substantial or objectified, but is equally the "home-field," as Nishitani calls the world perceived in emptiness, of the salient meaning of body/mind and all beings.

The logic that Sengcan invokes to explain the relationship that "the object is an object for the subject, the subject is a subject for the object" is the same that Merleau-Ponty seeks to articulate in avoiding either a dualism or a monism, when he uses the image of chiasm, in which there is both one and two, or rather neither one nor two, but something else. Sengcan, in denying of suchness that "there is neither 'self' nor 'other'" but also that there is not "direct identification," declares "We can only say 'not two'" (BS 174). For him, this is the origin of the sense of emptiness and its realization. Similarly Merleau-Ponty declares: "[S]tart from this, there is not identity, nor non-identity, or non-coincidence, there is inside and outside turning about one another" (VI 264). The process of embodying does not have a centered subject, nor confronts an actual world, but rather opens unceasingly onto this "not two" deflagration of being that consumes such metaphysical or personally psychological presumptions in the way the increasing realization of *śūnyatā* clears the field of such obstructing constructs. In the next sentence Merleau-Ponty identifies the sense of self and embodiment that results from seeing this "not identity, nor non-identity": "My 'central' nothingness is like the point of the stroboscopic spiral, which is who knows where, which is 'nobody'" (VI 264). Merleau-Ponty embraces the *śūnyatā* of embodiment as leading to the "no-self" of experience's root which is also the experience of a world of emptiness.

Perceptions, as they have been taken by traditional Western philosophical perspectives as either comprised by intelligible phenomena, in the sense of rationally determinable instantiations of categories of judgment (intellectualism), or insular inputs that can be grasped in their own terms as quantifiable or as corresponding to discrete facets of brute reality (empiricism), are notions of body-within-the-world to be surpassed by either Buddhist or Merleau-Pontean analysis. Both perspectives return to a more profound, experientially open, and expressive sense of embodiment as the experiencing of the world as moving through us in returning to itself, rather than the operation and achievement of an "ego-dominated" or constructed sense of perception as the product of an abstracted rationality. The Western epistemological stances of intellectualism and empiricism are not just theories about the body and perception: they describe ways that the ego imposes obscuring dimensions onto perception. Here, Buddhism is more explicit in demonstrating that theories are embedded in ways of life that are not only destructive to the emergence of truth as uncovering, but also are the central source of needless pain and frustration in human life. However, implicit in Merleau-Ponty's philosophy is a sense of the liberating capacity of embodiment to not only articulate the truth of the world, but add to the meaningfulness of human existence.

THE FLESH AND EMPTINESS AS AN ETHICS OF THE HEART, PERSONAL TRANSFORMATION, AND SPONTANEOUS RIGHT ACTION

Merleau-Ponty is often said to have no articulated ethics within his ontological and epistemological analyses of the lived body or the "flesh of the world." There seem to be no norms of conduct, standards for moral action, nor uniform decision-making procedures when faced with moral dilemmas. Similarly, from a Western perspective, Buddhism (and especially Zen, Mādhyamikan, and other Middle Way Buddhist schools) can be criticized as lacking ethical discourse, not by lacking well-articulated precepts for ethical conduct, since they are more exhaustively delineated and extended in Buddhist scriptures than in many Western ethical systems, but rather because of its sense of "spontaneous right action," which would seem to mitigate against the higher authority of moral judgment, reason, and adjudication by universal principles. Kant tells us that the moral worth of an action originates from its being an act dictated by reason, judgment, and in opposition to the pull of inclinations.

Merleau-Ponty does articulate an ethics and it is similar to Buddhism's "spontaneous right action." That is why many readers of Merleau-Ponty do not see it. This approach to ethics is not recognizable as such from a traditional Western philosophical perspective, because it denies that rational decision-making, cleaving to universalizable standards of judgment, and fighting the body and its emotional vectors of immediate responsiveness to the world and other living beings are the heart of an ethical life or the source of its acts. Both Merleau-Ponty's philosophy and Buddhist thought suggest that rather than being the epitome of the ethical life, such achievements are an inferior approach, perhaps fitting as a first step toward the ethical life, perhaps a stop-gap measure for those alienated from embodiment and its surer responsiveness to the dignity and value of all living and non-living beings, and sometimes an obstacle to the needed sensitivity and sense of one's place in the environment that is called for by the deepest ethical commitment. Both Merleau-Ponty's and Buddhist thought rely on reclaiming embodiment's access to the heart—the heart of compassion—which is the deepest source of the sense of the ethical and entails breaking the claim of the intellect to master the world according to its categories and dictates.

If this is true then, both Merleau-Ponty's and Buddhist ethics are at odds with the Kantian sense that ethical action proceeds from a sense of duty and is the result of a judgment of reason. The Kantian perspective tends to set the norm in thinking about what constitutes an ethics within traditional Western thinking. This assessment is not only Eurocentric, but besides being incorrect, it is ethically dangerous. The centrality given to reflective judgment in the ethical life is the result of a dualism that overvalues the rational and the powers of the mind, and also demonizes embodiment and its powers of emotional response. Rather than the overarching sense that should guide the ethical life, such normative ethics are an "ethics of despair." This despair stems from a pessimism about the possibilities for human transformation and community. The driving force of this misjudgment is a misunderstanding of the body. The ethics of duty owed to the self-legislation of reason can be, however, a necessary and powerful limit of aberrant behavior in an alienated society that misunderstands embodiment. It is also, in this sense, an "ethics of the last resort" without which we would be lost. Despite this cultural and historical necessity for rational, normative ethics, the more salient understanding of embodiment and emptiness in Merleau-Ponty's thought and in Buddhist thought allow for a greater augmentation of the ethical life.

If we return to the passage examined earlier in this essay in the concluding passage to Merleau-Ponty's *Phenomenology of Perception*, we cannot but notice that he ends the book posing ethical questions—the key ethical questions in a person's life—and saying the notion of embodiment that has emerged from the world is the key to responding to those questions. The first part of his statement is a recognition that reason and reflection—although they might reason out our duties in a social contract, like to pay taxes or stop at the red light or honor our employment contract—cannot give adequate ethical responses to questions that (outside of any set rationalized agreement) are at the heart of life's purpose and meaning: "[F]reedom flounders in the contradictions of commitment, and fails to realize that without the roots which it thrusts into the world, it would not be freedom at all. Shall I make this promise? Shall I risk my life for so little? Shall I give up my liberty in order to save liberty? There is no theoretical reply to these questions" (PhP 456). The question of why reason is insufficient here has been answered by the preceding parts of this essay. To see the world through categories is to see a distorted reconstruction of the world, mistakenly taken as its source and foundation. Both Merleau-Ponty and Middle Way Buddhism have allowed us to see that emptiness does not go anywhere else, there is no other realm to aspire toward for answers, meaning, or virtues, and that although indeterminate and shifting, intertwined and ungraspable, things and other people call out to us through our embodiment or body/minds to join with the significance emerging for us with others and to act to further achieve this blossoming together.

We are not separable beings and I cannot be free, or happy, or achieve well-being without all others doing so. This is why Merleau-Ponty ends the book with these lines, which follow the questions just cited:

> But there are the *things* which stand, irrefutable, there is before you this person whom you love, there are these men whose existence around you is that of slaves, and your freedom cannot be willed without leaving behind its singular relevance, and without willing freedom for all. Whether it is a question of things or of historical situations, philosophy has no function other than to teach us to see them once again more clearly, and it is true to say that it comes into being by destroying itself as a separate philosophy. But what is required here is silence, for the hero lives out his relation to men and the world. "Your son is caught in the fire, you are the one who will save him. . . . If there is an obstacle, you would be ready to give your shoulder provided only that you can charge down that obstacle. Your abode is your act itself. . . . Your significance shows itself, effulgent. It is your duty, your hatred, your love, your steadfastness, your ingenuity. . . . Man is but a network of relationships, and these alone matter to him." (PhP 456)

Merleau-Ponty makes the claim that only silence can yield an appropriate ethical response to questions of life and death and action. This is because ethical action does not depend on ideas, ideals, or aspiring toward modeled virtues, but is the way that the world reaches me through embodiment in the overwhelming compassion and empathy for others that is not a maxim, but rather is embodied in my shoulder banging into the door of the burning building. It is spontaneous right action, foundationless, yet suspended among all the beings of the world—a network of lives and beings.

It is the silence of emptiness that draws us away from the self-perception of insular interest and indifference to others into an empathy and compassion. The failure to return to the body's silence, to experience the emptiness of existence, is the heart of why some people cannot feel compassion, while those who can dwell in the silence of emptiness are open to the significance of life emerging in helping others, standing effulgent before them, intrinsically worthwhile, ultimately meaningful, even if one cannot give any rational proofs why this should be the case. Batchelor discusses the journey to realization of the eighth-century Indian monk, Śāntideva, who continued Nāgārjuna's verse articulation of emptiness, but with a greater emphasis on compassion—the Bodhisattva way. He poses this question to himself why some people are not spontaneously drawn to respond to the suffering of others. Batchelor writes: "Shantideva realizes that this is due to a deep, visceral clinging to the idea of being a separate self. As long as one is in thrall to this fixation, spontaneous concern for others will tend to be felt only for those who fall within the range of what is 'mine.' The pain of those outside this range can then be treated with indifference and even satisfaction" (VC 32). The cognitive problem that we have already seen is a cause of alienation for those who are clinging to a sense of self is also an ethical problem, since it blocks the compassion and the need to help others that underlies any set of rules of conduct and gives them their basic meaning and sense. Śantideva realizes the affective import of emptiness: "[E]mptiness not only eases the cognitive constriction of self-centeredness, it generates feelings of empathy" (VC 32).

At the core of the ethical life is facing the fear of losing the security of the sense of self that one vainly tries to achieve through clinging to an ego or stable self-subsistent identity. This may be the most important transformation—an ongoing one—that is necessary to be ethical, and yet it is unaddressed in traditional Western ethical systems. It is through the breaking through of the need for self-subsistent identity that reveals what was true all along—namely, that we are only humans as intertwined inseparably with others. The Western emphasis on agency in ethics, self-legislation, and autonomy may themselves be an ethical problem. Emptiness allows us to experience that in order for me to be good, the clinging to the sense of me is hurtful to this moral aim: "'Emptiness' is counterintuitive because it contradicts the deepest sense a person has of being 'me.' Yet, as Shantideva makes clear, emptiness does not eliminate 'me,' but transforms it. Contrary to expectation, an empty self turns out to be a relational self" (VC 33). This brings us to the heart of another approach to ethics than that of following rules through judgments: Who one is becomes *transformed* in such a way that right action, moral action, is no longer an issue, a dilemma, but is like breathing. Or another way to say this would be to say that in emptiness we are open to life itself and become more alive. This feeling of vitality and interconnection invariably is also a sense of love—that affective well-spring which the West has sought as a source of ethics, but often from which its ideas have distanced itself. Tollifson writes: "This awakening is about coming alive to what is actually happening right now. In this aliveness, the body and the whole world of form is more vibrant and present than ever before, but isn't solid anymore. The stories (and the people we apply them to) are no longer fixed. In this openness that no longer knows what everything is, there is freedom. This not knowing is love. In this open being, every moment is devotion." In opening to the capacities of embodiment, perception, and feeling as empty, we are led toward others and ethical action in a spontaneous manner inseparable from the cleared nature of perception itself.

Yet the West has often distrusted that the world shows its true face and therefore distrusted whether we can immediately respond to it in compassion. If the world is just our construction, then it may be constructed in self-centered or evil ways that must be rationally interrogated and revealed before we are fooled by

them. So, here at the heart of ethics, epistemology and morality cannot be separated. In this way, the differing epistemologies and ontology of Merleau-Ponty
and Middle Way Buddhism can be appreciated in their ethical significance.
Merleau-Ponty begins the *Phenomenology of Perception* with the criticism of
empiricism and intellectualism that they fail to acknowledge the "physiog-
nomic character of the data" with which they deal (PhP 19). He contends that
"the shape of the world" is to be recognized as "the source which stares us in
the face" (PhP 23). For Merleau-Ponty, it is the weave of things, others, nature,
and cultures that assume a primordial face-to-face relation with us. Traditional
Western philosophy has missed this face of the world because it has failed to see
"an object or a body" as they "look 'gay' or 'sad,' or 'lively' or 'dreary,' or 'elegant'
or 'coarse'" (PhP 23). They have missed those lines of attunement, of emotional
orientation and expression of how it stands with that object or person in relation to their surrounding world by excluding "from perception the anger or the
pain which I nevertheless read in a face, the religion whose essence I seize in
some hesitation or reticence, the city whose temper I recognize in the attitude
of a policeman or the style of a public building" (PhP 23–24). This means that
in some way Western culture itself is like Schneider, the patient used as a case
study of the damaged embodiment in the *Phenomenology of Perception*, who
cannot recognize spontaneously the felt meaning of those who confront him,
the embedded significance revealed through the lived body or the flesh of the
world. For him, this is the result of the shrapnel lodged in part of his brain,
but we can achieve this perceptual lack through philosophy and by our stance
toward the world. The tradition from Plato through Descartes to Kant that tells
us to mistrust this immediate sense of our situatedness and of others and instead to figure it out through rational judgment is asking us to proceed to live
like the brain-damaged Schneider. Furthermore, the reliance of rational reas-
sessment fosters a sedimented disbelief in perception and feeling. This, in turn,
transforms embodiment from an intertwined apprehension of the whole to a
manipulative disjunct with the world, so that indeed embodiment's access to the
flesh of the world is restricted. We set up a vicious cycle of enclosure.

Like Merleau-Ponty, Middle Way Buddhism demonstrates how evil actions,
actions that violate one's own truer being and the being of others, is really a
matter of misperception, a matter of not-knowing the world as it stands before
one, covered by distortion and driving one to moral violation. The Buddha's
"fire sermon" is an analysis of how the body's perceptions become unperceiv-
ing by being ripped out of interconnectedness by the powers of the ego that has
followed the rational, categorical mind in making discriminations to the world
revealed by feeling and thereby created the craving for what is set apart and seen
as desirable. What is especially telling in the Buddhist articulation of conditioned
coproduction is the link between seeming ethically neutral rational categories in
knowing the world that are detailed in their causal link to the arising of egoistic
desires that turn embodiment's spontaneous feelings into cravings prone to self-

violation and violence toward others. From mere consciousness of the object, a process is detailed wherein positing name and form gives rise to properties and then to valuations of these properties to desires to possess them (BS 186). As Rosen Takashina has written: "Whether this heart is the Buddha heart or not is the cause which determines good or evil for us. And if we stress our ego and do not cut off the thoughts, the Buddha heart does not appear." The problem is "the knowing" that informs the heart, which skews our perceptual experience of the world and others: "The thoughts of the impure heart are topsy-turvy, for it sees reality upside down. . . . Of course the mischievous operation of the senses is not natural: their true working is not wrong. But the impure heart misuses them and only lets them work in wrong directions" (BS 139). It is the thought categories that make reality into a set of objects which are self-subsistent and also construct my being as self-subsistent that gives rise to these cravings and simultaneously blocks a truer embodied interrelatedness to other beings. Merleau-Ponty would call such a reconstitution of the open depth of embodiment, the "experience error" of high-altitude thinking.

However, in the Buddhist perspective, "the heart is not in itself two; it is only classified in these two ways according to its workings. The pure heart is the pure heart of our own nature, our natural heart which is not a whit different from the Buddha heart" (BS 141). The ethical breakthrough is not in learning the precepts and in following them as obligations from on high that dictate conduct, for this is seen as the beginner's stage that one refrains from ethical misconduct because "one feels obliged to abstain." Rather, one is to become transformed in such a way that at the level of highest ethical conduct, one follows all the precepts because "one has lost all temptation not to do so," as explained in one of the Pali commentaries (BS 72). It is then that the pure Buddha heart shows itself in spontaneous right action. This transformation of the person can only occur, however, as Takashina says, when the intellect abandons "the understanding of the discriminating impure heart, which thinks 'I' and 'my' and 'I do it'" (BS 143). It is by realizing that we are not isolated rational agencies, self-subsistent subjects confronting a world of objects, by experiencing this through Buddhist practice as bodies that we come to clear the embodied perceptual insertion in the world from misperception and violent and unethical inclination to one that is compassionate and responsive to our intertwinings with other beings. As Dainin Katagiri phrased it: "The Buddhist precepts are not moral or ethical imperatives given by someone that people must follow. They are the ground of Buddha's world . . . in the light of the teaching of impermanence . . . a kind of energy, moving, functioning, working dynamically, appearing, disappearing, always supporting our life" (RM 106–8). It is in clearing the intellect of the categories that block our experience of our insertion in this dynamic, interwoven becoming, we become ethical.

Similarly, for Merleau-Ponty, this enveloping perceptual insertion in the world is not a more superficial sense of the world or solely an absorption in the simple tasks of solidifying egoistic identity. This perceptual insertion in the world contains layers, juxtapositions, and dimensions, which are mythic, oneiric, emotional, imaginary, and so on, in ways that riddle the nexus of tasks with other meanings, directions, and orientations, which he calls the incompossible or enjambed sense of phenomena in having depth (PhP 264–65). For example, he relates how our practical world of the sense flashes away before the power of musical space to uplift us. In the later, incomplete *Visible and the Invisible*, Merleau-Ponty calls this the "verticality" of the flesh. Each percept vibrates or encroaches upon dimensions of meaning within the thickness of the perceptual as "wild being" (*l'être sauvage*), and as a Buddhist might well say, Merleau-Ponty shows how a universe of meaning dances right there in any simple percept (VI 132). What is most important for ethical considerations is to note that the "verticality" of the flesh is present *in its lateral relations*, in the plane of this perceptual world, without recourse to a vertical ascent beyond the world, to some higher source.

Even in the *Phenomenology of Perception*, Merleau-Ponty had defined the power of embodiment's perceptual life as "this subject-object dialogue, this drawing together, by the subject, of the meaning diffused through the object, and, by the object, of the subject's intentions" (PhP 132). There is an unfolding of "the taking up of external by internal and of internal by external" (PhP 132). The reciprocity occurs, however, through the drawing together of what is different. The perception of the world is already entering a dialogue, a give and take, but one in which the perceiver is "a power which is born into, and simultaneously with, a certain existential environment, or is synchronized with it" (PhP 211). So that, even though Merleau-Ponty says that "to see a face . . . is to take a certain hold on it" (PhP 253), this hold is not to be understood as an appropriative grasping. Rather, this seeing is a gesture like reaching for the other hand *to be taken hold of, in taking hold of it* or like taking the optimal distance of dialogue with the landscape I am about to paint in order to "join the aimless hands of nature" (PhP 262), as Cézanne put it (quoted by Merleau-Ponty).

This sense of dialogical insertion within the world will be expressed more radically in *The Visible and the Invisible* where he says of the body: "[I]f it touches and sees, this is not because it would have visible before itself as objects: they are about it, they even enter into its enclosure, they are within it, they line its looks and its hands inside and outside. If it touches and sees them, this is only because, being of their family, itself visible and tangible, it uses its own being as a means to participate in theirs, because each of the two beings is an archetype for the other, because the body belongs to the order of things as the world is universal flesh" (VI 137). Although asymmetrical and incomplete, there is a mutual enfolding into each other of the perceiver and perceived. When Merleau-Ponty does give a rare and brief mention to how human gazes encounter each other in the world, at the end of the first section of *The Visible and Invisible*, he speaks of the *intermonde*—the "interworld"—"where our gazes cross and our perceptions overlap" (VI 48), which again is a reference to a lateral relation, an encroachment or enfolding among persons and with things and events where there is "an intertwining of my life with other lives, of my body with the visible things, by the intersection of my perceptual with that of others, by the blending of my duration with the other durations" (VI 49). This is the kind of coming together that can give rise to a sensitivity to others that is the deeper ethos of the moral life.

The resonating bodies of living beings are part of an enveloping sense that I can enter, not as confronting "pure individuals, individual glaciers of beings, nor essences without place and without date," but rather as an expressive site, who "have about themselves a time and a space that exist by piling up, by proliferation, by encroachment, by promiscuity." This flesh of meaning into which persons are intertwined is "of the same ontological vibration" and even with individuals of different cultures, communication is possible "through the wild region wherein they have all originated" (VI 115). This is very much parallel to what the editors of *Tricycle*, the Buddhist journal, are trying to articulate in making their readers see the sense of the five Buddhist precepts. They explain that it is problem of our minds as they have constructed reality, given our philosophical sense of the world which has informed our thinking, that there are permanent selves existing in isolation from other permanent selves, to whom we then have the burden and obligation to reach out to in care. Rather than this picture, they explain: "The 'sword of compassion' in Mahayana teachings is used to cut through the illusion of separation, of self and other, of this or that. Compassion may be understood to be the functioning of an interconnected, interdependent reality."[13] The revelations of embodiment in perception and feeling are distorted by what Merleau-Ponty would call the sedimentation of a dualistic worldview. We have failed to see in the West how this transforms us and alters our experienced reality away from an initial kind of "transitivism," as Merleau-Ponty calls it, of corporeality and feeling among young children before the age of three, for whom "there is simply no radical distinction in the child between his own hand and that of another" (PR 149). These feelings of inseparability with the embodiment, affective life, and experience of the other resurface in love, but are largely covered over by our cultural life. Yet Merleau-Ponty believes these childhood experiences remain as a source of possible reintegration with others for "childhood is never radically liquidated" (PR 138). As he says of an important moral feeling, akin to compassion: "Sympathy would emerge from this. Sympathy does not presuppose a genuine distinction between self-consciousness and consciousness of the other but rather the absence of a distinction between the self and the other" (PR 146). It is not only that Merleau-Ponty's sense of the body, and also that of the Middle Way Buddhism moves ethics from norms, reason, and judgment to the affective life of the body as compassionate, but also the nature of the body as mine and the direction of authority as coming from above are also altered, as we will explore in the next and final section.

FLESH AND EMPTINESS OPEN A HORIZONTAL
ETHICAL COMMUNITY OF ALL LIVING BEINGS

The contrasting "high-altitude" approach of finding rational, universal ethical norms, the source of which is beyond the immediate perceptual realm rips us from our interwovenness in the world and not only denies us access to the world of immediately experienced compassion, but it also makes us look above ourselves for guidance in ethics, and as part of autonomy leads to not only a substantialized sense of self and embodiment, but also an atomized one. Merleau-Ponty said of such an approach that it takes persons and "transforms them into puppets which move only by springs" (VI 77). It is to be in a state that fails to experience that within embodiment the immediate sense of ethical responsibility lies in our immediate responsiveness to others as emerging from an empty being who is "but a network of relationships and these alone matter." Given his stark characterization of an ethics dictated by a higher authority as reducing humans to puppets, it could be said that for Merleau-Ponty traditional Western dualistic ethics is dangerous. This attitude is echoed in Buddhist concerns, as revealed in this discussion of the meaning of the first Buddhist precept to abstain from killing:

> In Zen and in other Mahayana traditions in East Asia, there is the tendency to translate this precept into the more unfamiliar concept of non-killing. This view emphasizes a nondualistic reality in which there is no killer and no killed. From the Mahayana perspective, all apparent separations are illusions. The meaning of life in these traditions extends beyond biological definition; maintaining a non-dual consciousness supports life, and not maintaining such awareness is considered a form of killing. (RM 113)

Such an ethical notion makes the most serious ethical transgression out of thinking of ourselves or other persons as atomized beings. This is a serious implication to consider: Is the basic framework of thinking of much Western philosophy and ethics, as well as the subject-object way people tend to live their lives, and increasingly so within consumerist culture, a kind of violence itself?

Philosophically, the move to nondualism flies in the face of the long Western tradition since Plato. He inaugurated the assessment that becoming open to the spontaneity of embodiment relegates humans to the realm of non-being, as he put it in *The Republic*. Only aspiring toward the rule of reason and its imposition upon the chaos of embodied, affective life could carry humans toward being—a state they could never achieve while embodied.[14] Yet emptiness is not an embrace of non-being, nor is Merleau-Ponty's sense of intertwining of vortices or ongoing, foundationless emergence. Rather than an opposition of being and non-being, Merleau-Ponty asserts: "A negativist thought is identical to a positivist thought, and in this reversal remains the same in that whether considering the void of nothingness or the absolute fullness of being, it in every case ignores density, depth, the plurality of planes, the background worlds" (VI 68). Merleau-Ponty acknowledges that the other person's body does present me with an absence, "but not just any absence, a certain absence and a certain difference in terms of dimensions which are from the first common to us and which predestine the other to be a mirror of me as I am of him, which are responsible for the fact that we do not have two images side by side of someone and ourselves, but one sole image in which we are both involved" (VI 83). It is an encounter which presents me with as yet unknown depths, but ones that in my own incompleteness are inseparable from others. It is very much akin to the central doctrine of Madhyamikan thought summed up as "a relationship whereby that which does exist derives its being not from itself, but from 'another.'" However, this relatedness "must transcend the polarity of self and other, without negating my deliberations and discriminations. Dependent co-arising signifies both the negation of essence and the validation of such deliberations and discriminations."[15] This identity of being and non-being, articulated by Merleau-Ponty in his descriptions of the flesh of the world and by Buddhist thinkers in articulating emptiness, is also part of how we must think of persons as each being responsible, yet each being woven into a larger fabric, as Merleau-Ponty phrases it. Embodiment is not an atomizing local phenomenon—we are of a shared body with others.

Embodiment for Merleau-Ponty is "the involvement of men in the world, and of men with one another, even if it can only be brought about by means of perceptions and acts, is transversal with respect to the spatial and temporal multiplicity of the actual" (VI 85). No person is an inviolable one, but is a many, entering into promiscuities with others. This is sacrilege to a schema which demands a metaphysically unitary essence as reflection of a Higher One. For Merleau-Ponty, the resort to a being of a higher power is to take on false evidence and to empty signification by cutting off our experience of being that is lateral and transversal, not hierarchical. To claim to have evidence from a God or higher power "is a spell cast over the world that turns our expectations into derision" and "is not only a risk of non-sense, but much worse: the assurance that things have another sense than that which we are in a position to recognize in them" (VI 94). The only metaphysics that Merleau-Ponty could make sense of was an interpretation of this embodied, engaged, perceptual life: "Metaphysical consciousness has no other objects than those of experience: this world, other people, human history, truth, culture."[16] Again, this is parallel to Buddhist nonmetaphysical stance intended by emptiness: "The term dependent co-arising as 'arising only in dependence'— without essence—allows one to inquire into the mutual relationships of all beings. In this sense, the realm of mutual relatedness, of absolute relativity, constitutes an 'absolute' otherness against selfhood and essence. Such an absolute is not a separate world apart from me, but an absolute in which my interrelated activity has absolute meaning."[17] Ethically, it is to our immediate commitments in our shared embodiment that we are called by our interdependence.

In *La Nature*, Merleau-Ponty further articulates how the intertwining of the flesh, of the visible and the invisible, and of the *Ineinander* of the sensible is a *chiasmatic relatedness to animality*. There is a "lateral union of humanity and animality,"[18] and the human corporeal schema is seen as an incorporation of relations with the world such that "I see through the eyes of the others . . . the world."[19] However, it is not only through the eyes of other humans that I see, but as flesh there is a "circuit of the visible and with the world" that Merleau-Ponty says is an "*Einfuhlung* with the world, with things, with animals, with other bodies that is comprehensible with this theory of the flesh."[20] As entering an unfolding of the world which has depths and dimensionalities wherein perception is the lining of the dream or the dreamlike sense of the waking (the oneiric) and where the dream is the other side of perception, Merleau-Ponty is able to show where both animals and humans are situated within the world in the unfolding of sense that intertwines between both and with the verticality of matter itself, not as an inert substance, but as part of a circulation of sense. As Merleau-Ponty is able to articulate that life on this planet is not built up from the inert to the mechanical to the spiritual, but rather begins with the decentering swirl on all levels of animate and inanimate life in a denser, more plural sense, the sense of transcendence as standing beyond one's own limits of understanding is not to a higher realm, but rather within a circulation of planetary sense. As Merleau-Ponty concludes toward the end of *La Nature*, "the relation between humans and animals is not a hierarchical relation but a lateral one" and the outcome of seeing the human body as insertion into flesh is to "see a relationship of intercorporeity with the biosphere and all animality."[21] This is not only an epistemological and ontological insight, but is also a new sense of the human in relation to the planet as an ethical community. This is the kind of insight that has long been embodied in the spirit of the ethical Buddhist life, when the Buddha in his "great going forth" from the palace stopped in the fields and came to his first great insights into the compassion for all living beings:

> There he saw the soil being ploughed, and its surface, broken with the tracks of the furrows, looked like rippling water. The ploughs had torn up the sprouting grass, scattering tufts of grass here and there, and the land was littered with tiny creatures who had been killed and injured, worms and insects, and the like. The sight of all this grieved the prince as deeply as if he had witnessed the slaughter of his kinsmen. He observed the ploughmen, saw how they suffered from the wind, sun and dust, and how the oxen were worn down by the labor of the drawing. And in the supreme nobility of his mind, he performed an act of supreme pity. He then alighted from his horse and walked gently and slowly over the ground, over come with grief. (BS 42)

This passage is unparalleled in the scriptures of the world for the depth of grief of its spiritual leader for even worms and insects, oxen, and all living beings. It is the sense of our interrelatedness with all living beings that informs the first Buddhist vow when members of the Sangha—the community that is seen as much a treasure as the Buddha and the truth of Buddhist insight, the Three Refuges—vow to become enlightened, not for the sake of their own souls or integrity, not for the good of Buddhists or even humanity, but "for the sake of all living beings."

Merleau-Ponty's articulation of language and of community as found within the "flesh of the world" leads him away from an anthropocentrism that has long dominated the so-called Western tradition of philosophy and, even more destructively, of ethics. The relationship of the face-to-face is first of all with the world, an enveloping world of the body, of flesh, as a dynamic unfolding within the sensible. It is not that the particularly human excellence of the reflective, the abstract, and the categorical cannot enlarge the scope of our homeland, but if Merleau-Ponty's new ontology, informed by a new ontology of nature, is to be taken seriously, then they are not its primordial ground. If we are part of a circulation of sense of which we are not the author, the arbiter, or the highest expression, but one very fascinating and powerful expression in certain distinct avenues, it is not warranted to center decisions of right and wrongful action on our specific rational dicta. To appeal to a judge of "higher authority" of immaterial origin who returns us to this earth from a vantage above it, where we are its central focus and application within this material realm, flies in the face of the world presented to us as flesh, and we as of it. It is a metaphysical belief in some other realm that gives certain of our thoughts foundational status as reflective of this nonevidential revelation.

Given the current historical context of massive alienation from the earth, from embodiment, from the sense of emptiness that reveals the interdependence of all beings, the ethics of appeal to a higher authority has a moral efficacy in prohibiting the continued alienated manipulation of others as alien objects in a setting of indifference. Our faulty traditional dualistic ontology of subject versus object, matter versus spirit, and self versus others has brought us to this dire situation that the reality of other humans is not always accessible to people. The experience of embodied subjects laterally related to other humans, animals, and objects within a world, given an alienated construction of experience, may seem far-fetched. Against this background, the voice of authority may speak against the voices of consumerism, crass materialism, and individualism to which a certain misunderstanding of the body, mind, and self have transported us. To be brought up short in the sort of commonplace exploitation of others, which can lead to violence, is laudatory.

The insertion in the flesh of the world, a prolongation of perception seen as having vertical depths of feeling, imagining, memory, and so on, leads to a different sense of kinship, one akin to the long-ago articulated Buddhist sense of compassion and one that speaks to us in our animality as embodied creatures capable of spontaneous acts of graceful connection. In this ethos, there is a transformation of the relationship between people and within the person that wells up from the world and overruns multiple levels of expression and action. On November 23, 1946, shortly after the ravages of World War II, with its incomprehensible violence toward all others, Merleau-Ponty addressed the *Société francaise de philosophie* to present the main idea of his work and ended with a reflection on the possibility of ethics (PR 12–27). He stated that "nothing guarantees us that morality is possible . . . but even less is there any fatal assurance that morality is impossible" (PR

26). For himself, Merleau-Ponty stated, he found the remedy to skepticism and pessimism was "here as everywhere else the primacy of perception." He did not think that a rationality separated from experience was the answer. He said the Christian God, which of course would also be true of the Hebrew God, offered believers "another side of things," but for him, it was necessary that "the other side of things be visible in the environment in which we live" (PR 27). The primacy of perception is not an ethically neutral phenomenon. As Merleau-Ponty eloquently phrased it: "If, on the contrary, as the primacy of perception requires, we call what we perceive 'the world,' and what we love 'the person,' there is a type of doubt concerning man, and a type of spite, which becomes impossible" (PR 26–27). In other words, the kinship felt within the depths of the perceptual, within the movements of the flesh, brings us to a sense of community for which radical hate and violence toward others becomes undermined and impossible in our transformation from within this sensibility.

The call to authority is with us to stay for the foreseeable future, and with the current dominant ontologies embedded in cultures based on consumption and domination, it is a necessary restraint on violation and also a prod to more relational openness. However, many of us believe that in the longer run, it is necessary for the planet's welfare and greater thriving to cultivate an appreciation of the sense of the flesh that Merleau-Ponty articulated, for only then can we enter into nonhierarchical and dialogical relations with all living and even non-living beings on this planet. There is something wrong with an ethics that bases itself on the sense that we have a unique calling above the destiny of the rest of the planet, and a falsity about its underlying ontology. Reason is an undeniable excellence, but it does not endow us with an exclusive status of spiritual worth represented by notions of soul or personhood or intrinsic value. The Buddhists have long demonstrated all living and non-living beings can only be treated compassionately—together—or, as Merleau-Ponty rightly states, the flesh of the world is fragile.

11

Merleau-Ponty and Nāgārjuna

Enlightenment, Ethics, and Politics

Michael Berman

The twentieth-century French phenomenologist Maurice Merleau-Ponty's thought and the contemporary scholarship on his philosophy lend themselves to the projects of comparative philosophy. In this vein, the second-century Indian Buddhist monk Nāgārjuna's Mādhyamika Buddhism (Buddhism of the Middle Way) presents points of contact and divergence with Merleau-Ponty's thought that make such a comparison fruitful, deepening, and enlightening. Specifically, Merleau-Ponty and Nāgārjuna's philosophical approaches to politics and ethics can be synthesized into a greater whole. The former can be given an ethical character via the use of virtue ethics as informed by Buddhist ethics; the latter can have his political thought deepened through an understanding of the historical and contextual nature of human existence.

Both Merleau-Ponty and Nāgārjuna use an existential analysis of experience in the development of their positions. Not surprisingly, the philosopher of ambiguity has much in common with the philosopher of emptiness (*śūnyatā*). Merleau-Ponty's indirect ontology[1] of the *flesh* explores the chiasmatic character of a philosophy that is generated by our interrogation of perceptual faith. One of the consequences of his new approach is the rejection of essentialist and substantialist claims. This is nearly identical to Nāgārjuna's concerns in his *Mūlamadhyamakakārikā* (Treatise on the Middle Way). Paralleling Merleau-Ponty's refutation of the philosophies of reflection (Descartes), negation (Sartre), and intuition (Husserl) in the opening chapters of *The Visible and the Invisible*, Nāgārjuna refutes, via the use of the Buddhist tetralemma or "four-tiered logic" (which he also employs in *The Precious Garland* to some extent), the positions of the Sarvāstivāda[2] and the Sautrāntika/Pudgalavāda (personalist schools).[3] Their respective refutations basically undermine positions that absolutize and reify terms and doctrines, for these schools of thought in both the Western and

Indian traditions rely on a "high-altitude thinking" (*pensée du survol*) and ascribe to (inherent) self-existence (*svabhāva*). Thus the ontological positions that both philosophers espouse bare remarkable similarities, especially in their emphases on the perceptual experiences of the lived body, the limitations and pernicious-ness of language, and the pitfalls of philosophical absolutes. Upon these dynamic foundations, this chapter will build an ethico-political approach that has implica-tions for comparative philosophy's larger projects.

The first section uses Merleau-Ponty's political thought to draw out certain im-plications embedded in Nāgārjuna's philosophy. For Nāgārjuna, the bodhisattva (an enlightened being) and the Buddha are moral and ethical ideals:

> As long as any sentient being
> Anywhere has not been liberated,
> May I remain [in the world] for his sake
> Even though I have attained enlightenment.[4]

Yet what roles can such enlightened beings play in the political realm, espe-cially when these ideals seem to demand that the Buddhist practitioner cut off his/her connections to the world of change (*saṃsāra*) and suffering (*duḥkha*[5])? By understanding these connections via Merleau-Ponty and a positive concep-tion of *freedom*,[6] this section shows that the attainment of *nirvāṇa* (enlighten-ment) is not necessarily an *apolitical* act. That this is so is illustrated by the all encompassing, unlimited nature of "the Great Compassion [that] is the root of the Way of the Buddha."[7] We are limited in this respect, for, as in accordance with the Tibetan tradition, Buddhist compassion is either only implied in Nāgārjuna's philosophical works (such as the *Mūlamadhyamakakārikā*) or not at all located in such works.[8] I hold that the former is the case as based on his references to the Eightfold Noble Path and the chapter devoted to the Fourfold Noble Truth in the *Mūlamadhyamakakārikā*.[9] This chapter will draw on Nāgārjuna's short piece *The Precious Garland* to illustrate the ethical and political views that are merely implied and alluded to in the *Mūlamadhyamakakārikā*.

A conspicuous absence in Merleau-Ponty's philosophy is an ethics and an account thereof. We have, however, an indication in which direction the later Merleau-Ponty may have wanted to proceed in terms of ethics. He explicitly states that the establishment of the wonder (*thaumazein*) that we experience in our encounters with the world would give us a metaphysics qua an existential analysis, "and would at the same time give us the principle of an ethics."[10] Yet this claim was never systematically developed.[11] Some have attempted to scour Merleau-Ponty's ample political writings in order to derive an ethics. Without debating the legitimacy of this procedure, we will use these writings as a guide in uncovering an ethics based on an understanding of his existential analysis, that is, his phenomenology. This skeletal frame is fleshed out by Nāgārjuna's ethical views.

This chapter also shows that Merleau-Ponty could accept certain aspects of the Eightfold Path, though this would then *force* his thought into accommodating the soteriological ends of Buddhism. In this regard, both Nāgārjuna's thought and Buddhism's fundamentally ethical stance function as (self-) corrective mechanisms that maintain firm connections to our relationally originated nature as social beings. There is a strong possibility for Merleau-Ponty's acceptance of these ends, but only if his ontology were to approach the *flesh* of the world from within the *abyss*, that is, from something akin to the nonperspective of *śūnyatā*. That is to say, given his existential phenomenology, Merleau-Ponty's brute Being *calls* for a two-level notion of truth, much like that held in Mādhyamika Buddhism. Thus, his principle of an ethics grounded in an indirect ontology (as developed in *The Visible and the Invisible*) evinces an understanding of the nature of enlightenment (*prajñā*) without explicitly ascribing to such an experiential state. Merleau-Ponty's understanding of *humanism* and *freedom* also support this claim. These two aspects of his ethics constitute the major themes of the conclusion part of this chapter.

I will then begin by addressing human virtues in light of the existentially grounded ethics of Merleau-Ponty and Nāgārjuna. This will illustrate the manners in which these two philosophers have had their thought broadened in application and depth through this analysis. The concluding section closes with some prescriptions for comparative philosophy. These prescriptions stem from Merleau-Ponty's and Nāgārjuna's existential analyses of human virtues. Comparative philosophy can provide ways for addressing how the influences of sociohistorical forces shape and prefigure our virtues and ethical relations to one another.

ETHICAL PHENOMENOLOGY

Nāgārjuna's recommendations for the political realm draw upon Buddhist ethics as based on compassion (*karunā*), pragmatic understanding (*vijñāna*), and the experiential nature of momentariness or impermanence (*anitya*). Essentially, Nāgārjuna wishes that governments and political institutions adopted as their own the soteriological ends of Buddhism. Salvation, in a political sense, becomes ideological for Nāgārjuna:

> If your kingdom exists for the doctrine [Dharma]
> And not for fame or desire,
> Then it will be extremely fruitful,
> If not its fruit will be misfortune. (PG 66)

As an ideology, this doctrine explicitly rejects any attempts to turn its contents into dogma. This ideology is thus nonrigid and open; it is meant to be an ideology without dogmatism. It is, as Nolan Pliny Jacobson says, reflexively self-correcting.[12]

There is, however, a pessimistic aspect to Nāgārjuna's views concerning government and salvation. There is a point where a ruler ought to give up his/her rule in
order to lead a strictly religious life:

> However, if through the unrighteousness
> Of the world it is hard to rule religiously,
> Then it is right for you [the king] to become a monk
> For the practice and grandeur [to which it leads]. (PG 77)

If one is prevented from governing along lines that would lead the people toward
salvation, then it is acceptable to withdraw from political life in order to concentrate on attaining salvation. This seems to advocate a selfish attitude toward
nirvāṇa, but perhaps Nāgārjuna is actually trying to warn rulers and weed out
incompetent governors by appointing compassionate ones (PG 65). In other
words, from a pragmatic perspective, not all rulers can be accomplished leaders.
Some ought to step aside for their own good and the good of the people, and allow
others to take their place, for the new rulers may be more capable of governing
compassionately. After all, he reminds kings,

> You did not bring your kingdom with you from your
> Former life nor will you take it to the next,
> Since it was won by virtues, to act
> For it without virtue is wrong. (PG 68)

The kinds of leaders, who could rule according to compassion and with a sense of
the impermanency of their own works, would have to be "sufficiently tough new
men"[13] or individuals who follow, what Merleau-Ponty calls, the *virtues* of a *new
humanism*.

Merleau-Ponty's new humanism arises out of his phenomenology. He addresses the question of intersubjectivity, within which relations are characterized by an (implicit) ethics, from an experiential perspective. The interrogation
of our perceptual faith grounds the possibility of proper philosophy, the recognition of the mutual world we all share, and the syncretic identification we have
with others via our lived bodies:[14] "Just as the perception of a thing opens me
up to being, by realizing the paradoxical synthesis of an infinity of perceptual
aspects, in the same way the *perception of the other founds morality* by realizing
the paradox of an *alter ego*, of a common situation, by placing my perspectives
and my incommunicable solitude in the visual field of another and of all others"
(emphasis added).[15]

Perception of the alterity of the other is the ground for morality. For Merleau-
Ponty, the other plays a significant role in the formation of the self.[16] The self and
other originate in a relational sphere that is both existential *and* ethico-moral.
These two aspects are contained in his doctrine of autochthonous organization,
wherein the experiential world is not only implicitly meaningful, but it is also

meaningfully and relationally structured.[17] The relational nature of existence alludes to the moral components of this existential analysis.

There are two general characteristics that inform the implicit morality of Merleau-Ponty's philosophy. These are his new humanism and his understanding of freedom. Merleau-Ponty is heavily indebted to Hegel, Marx, and Weber for these ideas. But to trace these connections would draw us too far afield from this present context. Suffice it to say that Merleau-Ponty's existential analysis of perception and the limitations of language (and by extension, the rigid philosophical systems based on [historical] principles) led to his rejection of the totalizing trends in Marxist and communist thought. Simply put, no single existentially grounded philosophy can totally account for the nature and structure of history or the world; thus Marxism, though a valuable paradigm in his eyes, cannot capture the complete meaningfulness of history, just as no one perspective can attain an absolute objective position of pure high-altitude thinking (*pensée du survol*). With this critical or "hyperdialectical"[18] acceptance of Marxist philosophy in mind, let us turn to his understanding of humanism and freedom.

HUMANISM

Merleau-Ponty's understanding, development, and advocacy of a new humanism took place upon his break with Marxism in the 1950s.[19] This version of humanism is ontologically grounded, but since his ontology was never fully completed, his new humanism remains in a perpetual state of *birthing*. An outline of its features only provides us with a sense of how it would have fit into his indirect ontology of the *flesh*. The ethical prescriptions of Buddhism are used here to aid in completing the delivery of this neonate ethics.

In the concluding paragraph of his essay on Machiavelli, Merleau-Ponty writes: "[B]y humanism we mean a philosophy which confronts the relationship of man to man and the constitution of a common situation and a common history between man as a problem."[20] These are some of the abstract conditions of what humanism would entail. These conditions are intersubjective, perspectival, and temporal. In a different essay, Merleau-Ponty distinguishes between two types of humanism:

> Western humanism is a *humanism in intension*: a few are the guardians of the treasure of Western culture; the others obey. It would be to admit that Western humanism subordinates factual humanity [that is, humanity of the *flesh*] to a certain idea of man and to the institutions which support this idea, just as the Hegelian state does, and that in the end it has nothing in common with *humanism in extension*, which admits that there is in each man—not in so far as he is an organism endowed with such and such distinctive characteristics but in so far as he is an existence capable of determining himself and situating himself in the world—a power more precious than his products. (Italics original)[21]

There are types of Western humanisms that are reductionistic; these are evidenced by the political manifestations of totalitarianism (e.g., fascism, communism, and even laissez-faire capitalism). These reductive political ideologies subordinate the masses to the control of an elite, such as the state, political party, or capitalist corporation. Each version treats human beings according to a specified idea or principle and obscures their essential alterity. This essential alterity inheres in each person as a quality more valuable than that which they can manufacture within the socioeconomic structures of the state.

Humanism in extension calls for the *respectful universal* treatment of each and every human being without delimiting the individual's worth or *value* according to some pregiven and historically contingent principle that neglects their individual alterity. As Rudi Visker claims:

> We need to reconceive our notion of universality and to understand how we can be grafted onto it by our own singularity. And because this grafting is a difficult operation, we need to come up with an ethics, in the sense of an *ethos* which tells us how to live our attachment since the mere fact that one is "in" philosophy (or "in" any other world) does not automatically mean that one's dwelling there is as it should be—the reverse, as we all know, is more often the case.[22]

Humanism in extension is not limited to parochial concerns of institutions and individuals; it has a broader applicability. Such applicability is universal in the sense of it being for all those who exist, but the fact that one exists does not mean that one automatically acts in an ethical manner. This is similar to Nāgārjuna's understanding of human temporality; it is both the source of and the means out of *duḥkha*. This draws on the "way of emptiness" of Nāgārjuna, for "ethically, [the] negation of cravings, especially of egoistic desire, will enable one to love all men equally. *Nirvāṇa* is for all people."[23] This does not indicate that humanism in extension is in any way equivalent to *nirvāṇa*, but that both are universally available and attainable. For further elucidation of this point, we can draw upon Nāgārjuna's call to extend our compassion beyond the mere confines of our egoistic or subjective needs: "Just as you love to think/ What could be done to help yourself,/ So should you love to think/ What could be done to help others" (PG 55). Continuing in this altruistic vein of the golden rule, he says: "Provide help to others/ Without hope of reward,/ Bear suffering alone and/ Share your pleasures with beggars" (PG 57). Nāgārjuna's compassionate and altruistic ethical standards can thus provide content for the humanism in extension of Merleau-Ponty. For both thinkers, ethics is a universal concern, though the concrete concerns addressed by Buddhism are not necessarily those that would be in Merleau-Ponty's philosophy; this is not the same as denying their compatibility with the latter's possible ethics, for philanthropy and altruism could very well be *virtues* contained by humanism in extension.

Merleau-Ponty and Nāgārjuna would reject attempts to capture the *sense* of ethics via the systematic utilization of principles. Merleau-Ponty once stated in an interview that we do not possess the grounds to support the belief that the human world is a cluster of rational wills, that it could, like a learned society, be governed by rules of order based on laws derived from timeless principles,[24] or make its decisions through academic debates in which the most rational end up convincing all the others.[25]

To be certain, within the continental philosophical tradition this claim undermines Kant's ethical schema of the categorical imperative and Habermas's theory of communicative action with its ideal speech conditions. For our purposes, however, it is important to understand why Merleau-Ponty holds that "[m]orality cannot consist in the private adherence to a system of values. [This is so because] principles are mystifications unless they are put into practice; it is necessary that they animate our relations with others. Thus we cannot remain indifferent to the aspects in which our acts appear to others."[26]

To subjectively hold on to ethical principles does not constitute a workable moral system of ethical behavior. They can mystify or reduce the other, and thereby violate the other's integrity through disrespecting the other's alterity. But even when they are put into practice, they *animate* our interactions with others; they *do not* determine what these actions are. Similarly, the bodhisattvas and Buddhas match their compassion to those who are still enthralled by desires and cravings; they do so in their enlightened attempts to alleviate the suffering of others. There is no single formula or set of formulae that determines which actions are ethical, though these principles can provide moral ideals that motivate such behaviors. Simply stated, it is the recognition that, first, supposedly noncontingent principles are indeed contingently originated, and second, their application must always contend with the contingencies of experience, that is, the essential ambiguities of existence. This does not deny the efficacy of moral principles; rather, it denies their absolute authority to dictate right and wrong.

The way others perceive us is indicative of the intersubjective world that we all share; however, why is it that we take an interest in the appearances of our actions to others? Perhaps Merleau-Ponty's enigmatic statements on the origin and extermination of evil can shed some light on this question:

> Evil is not *created* by us or by others; it is born in this web that we have spun about us—and that is suffocating us. What sufficiently tough new men will be patient enough to really re-weave it?
>   The remedy we seek does not lie in rebellion, but in unremitting *virtù*. [This is a] deception for whoever believed in salvation, and in a single means of salvation in all realms.[27]

On a surface reading of these statements, one could easily conclude that he rejects the idea of salvation, but this is not exactly what he intends here. Just like Nāgārjuna, Merleau-Ponty holds that evil arises in the interactive relations of societal conditions in both the public and private spheres, but just as Nāgārjuna holds that from the enlightened perspective there is no difference between *saṃsāra* and *nirvāṇa*,[28] Merleau-Ponty holds that as much as these interrelations can give rise to evil, they are also the resources by which we can attain salvation from them. Evil for Merleau-Ponty is composed of those relationally arisen conditions of our sociality that suffocate or stifle our lives. What is evil about them is that they control our lives and reduce (via principles or overt violence) our interactions to the desires for money, power, and/or property. These desires are given concrete form via language. Only through the use of what Merleau-Ponty calls the hyperdialectic *or* the self-corrective mechanisms,[29] exemplified in Nāgārjuna's philosophy, can we throw off their suffocating *grasp* on us. This is partly entailed in the realization of *nirvāṇa*, but it is also an essential characteristic of our perceptual openness to worldly experience: "Suddenly it will become obvious that 'national ambition,' 'counter-subversion,' and the financing of private schools do not make a nation live and breathe. This [is the] *abyss* of modern society."[30] Only through the reappropriation of this abyss (notice its pejorative use in this case) can we find relief from the evils that we have historically foisted upon ourselves.

Salvation or relief from evil is not the simple unwavering adherence to a set of ethical principles. Rather, unremitting *virtù*, if it is to be worthwhile, must be actively taken up and reappropriated by those sufficiently tough new individuals who can practice it. In this sense, Merleau-Ponty is alluding to a heroic or agonal model of political action, such as found in Arendt[31] or Confucius.[32] These models ought to be political leaders with *integrity* and *vision*.[33]

Another virtue that humanism in extension entails is the *courage* to do what is right for the greater good—though not necessarily in terms of a strict utilitarianism caught up with beneficial social consequences, such as the maximization of happiness and minimization of pain for the greatest number of people. Courage for Merleau-Ponty's neonate ethics would have to entail resoluteness and determination; such virtues were exemplified in a positive sense by the French Resistance during the Nazi occupation, and in a negative or ill-fated sense by Bukharin at his trial.[34] Buddhist thought would act as a corrective measure in this latter example and reject such standards of behavior, for one must realize the ultimately impermanent nature of all consequences. Damien Keown's critical appraisals of utilitarian and consequentialist thought in relation to notions like *karma* and *cetana* ("volition") dovetail with this assessment. Keown's take on *śīla* (moral conduct) in the Buddhist tradition emphasizes its mutual relation to *prajñā* (wisdom) and *samādhi* (meditation), analogous to the legs of a tripod, and he concludes that the best description of Buddhist ethics entails viewing it as a virtue ethics of character.[35] Nāgārjuna's *Precious Garland* certainly stands as strong evidence for this conclusion, especially the last chapter on "The Bodhisattva Deeds" (PG 78–93). Thus, "Briefly the virtues observed/ By Bodhisattvas are /Giving, ethics, patience, effort,/ Concentration, wisdom, compassion and so forth" (PG 83).[36]

Such virtues can be used to fill in those gaps only hinted at by Merleau-Ponty, thus providing the missing (nonmetaphysical) substance to his claim he has not forgotten the ethical other: "It was never my intention to posit the other except as an ethical subject, and I am sure I have not excluded the other as an ethical subject."[37] *Virtù* as principle, for Merleau-Ponty, is vacuous unless acted upon. For Nāgārjuna: "From the simultaneous perfection/ Of all those seven [virtues] is attained/ The sphere of inconceivable wisdom/ The protectorship of the world" (PG 83). This protectorship, from the mundane viewpoint, can only indicate political rule, which is exactly what Nāgārjuna has in mind with *The Precious Garland* since it was written explicitly as advice for a king. Merleau-Ponty, in addition, understands that principles animate political actions, but these actions must not be solely dictated by principles, for even in these principles' seeming timelessness, they are essentially limited and contingent. They can be employed to rationalize actions, and thus under the aegis of morality, they can become sources of violence. A case in point is the idea of "the white man's burden." This Anglo-American and European slogan was used to extend military and financial empires around the world during the nineteenth and twentieth centuries. But the socio-political colonialism and imperialism employed to "civilize" the world destroyed and forever altered non-European cultures. These actions are still affecting, both positively and negatively,[38] those who were (are?) subject to the major world powers/states. Merleau-Ponty's political writings show that he was acutely aware of how Cold War political camps (empires) justified their actions by appealing to moral and ethical principles. These in actuality only functioned to rationalize the brutalizing and violent practices of the superpowers upon those who were subject to foreign rule.[39] These states *rationalized* the *violence* that they spread across the world.

What, then, would a government look like with these ethico-political insights of Merleau-Ponty and Nāgārjuna that could avoid this violent imperialism? For Nāgārjuna, an enlightened king would head his ideal government (PG 62–77). His advocacy of a feudal monarchy makes his ideas sound anachronistic. Oppositionally, Merleau-Ponty's political outlook is thoroughly modern in this respect; he would rather have more democratic institutions that would allow for greater participation by the state's citizenry.[40]

Though this is an important (and nearly insurmountable) difference, let us turn to the kind of ideology along which the state ought to be organized. This ideology would be one grounded in the existential analyses of both philosophers. In this regard, the universal aspects of Buddhism's humanism resonate with Merleau-Ponty's humanism in extension; both advocate a kind of egalitarianism.

A government that adheres to this existential ideology employs compassion as the virtue of rulership. A compassionate king (PG 66) or government cares for his or its subjects *without* differentiating between the lowliest paupers and most honorific guests. Thus, compassion as a virtue would become a universal standard applicable to all within (and even without [PG 66]) the state. Such enlightened rulers even extend these actions, as based on Buddhist ethical principles, to criminals and murderers, though in slightly different fashions (PG 67). There is, however, the possible misapplication of such principles, for they could spark events such as religious *jihads.* This would be a violation of the nonviolent actions prescribed by Buddhism; the imposition of beliefs or principles on others is certainly a cause and perpetuation of *duḥkha* by the aggressor for not only the other, but also for the aggressor him-/herself. To this end, the soteriological goals of Buddhism must be realized—that is, enlightened rulers, sufficiently tough individuals or bodhisattvas, ought to govern according to an ideology of salvation as based on the experiential creativity of a relationally originated existence. This can only be realized in the attainment of freedom for the rulers and all others.

FREEDOM

Merleau-Ponty's understanding of freedom can provide, at least in an abstract manner, the means for those subject to violence by which they can liberate themselves via their own existential capacities. This illustrates the manner by which humanism in extension can be realized. The implications of this conception of freedom fit well into Nāgārjuna's (negative) ontology[41] and Buddhist precepts.

Following Merleau-Ponty, we, as existential entities who are *in* and *of* the world that is autochthonously organized, interrogate our perceptual faith. As such, experience presents itself as intrinsically meaningful. Merleau-Ponty, echoing Sartre, holds that our very existence means that we are *condemned* to meaning, and thereby condemned to *freedom* and *responsibility*.[42] Experience is always more or less significant; language is the articulation of experience's significances (or meaningfulness) via thematization. In what sense (*sens*), then, are meaning and freedom connected?

Meaning is always contextual. It originates in the dynamic interaction of the figure-ground relation that is perceptually (and cognitively) interrogated, that is, between what is thematized and the phenomenological horizon in which it is situated. Freedom exists, or better yet, *emerges* in a similar fashion. Merleau-Ponty's question regarding the nature of freedom describes the *style* of this emergence:

> What then is freedom? To be born is both to be born *of* the world and to be born *into* the world. The world is already constituted;[43] in the first case we are acted upon, in the second we are open to an infinite number of possibilities. But this analysis is still abstract, for we exist in both ways at once. There is, therefore, *never determinism and never absolute choice*, I am never a thing and never a bare consciousness. In fact, even our own pieces of initiative, even the situations which we have chosen, bear on us, once they have been entered upon by virtue of a state rather than an act. The generality of the "role" and of the situation comes to the aid of decision [judgment], and *in this exchange between situation and the person who takes it up*, it is *impossible to determine* precisely the "share contributed by the situation" and the "share contributed by freedom." (Italics added)[44]

Herein we have an implicit understanding of *karma*, that our own actions and choices "bear on us" like "a state rather than an act": "In Buddhist reasoning [*karma*] is no outside force, but the inherent activity of every process."[45] We are reminded here of Damien Keown's consistent admonishment that one should avoid reducing *karma* to sheer consequentialism or a law of moral retribution. Following his advice, we can note that Merleau-Ponty's description above is in line with Nyanaponika Thera's claim that the past, "though in a latent state, may become active at any moment when conditions are favorable."[46] Freedom's context is not simply situational, but also temporal. As Jay L. Garfield says: "At each moment we are the total consequence of what we have done and of what we have experienced."[47] Furthermore, the impossibility of determining the contributed share of the situation and the person in the exercise of (political or ethical) judgment is indicative of the inherent *ambiguity* of existence and freedom. From the Buddhist perspective: "All phenomena are indeed impermanent, but that entails both that they do not inherently cease [for they do not inherently exist] and that their effects are *indefinite* in scope" (italics added).[48] We are caught between two conceptually determined extremes wherein *neither* determinism *nor* absolute choice is adequate to the phenomena of freedom. Freedom is always somewhere between the exchanges or *reversible* relations of actor and situation. Freedom is thus perspectival on the part of the actor, and situated due to the existential context in which it emerges.

Freedom for Merleau-Ponty is always *situated freedom*. These are the reasons why we are condemned both to meaning and to freedom; they are coextensive, yet nonidentical. Situated freedom arises within the phenomenological horizon of our experiences. Merleau-Ponty writes: "If freedom is to have *room* in which to move, if it is to be describable as freedom, there must be something to hold it away from its objectives, it must have a *field*, which means that there must be for it special possibilities, or *realities which tend to cling to being*" (italics added).[49] He further states: "We therefore recognize, around our initiatives and around that strictly individual project which is oneself, a *zone* of generalized existence and projects already formed, significances which trail between ourselves and things and which confer upon us the quality of man, bourgeois or worker" (italics added).[50] This field or zone of meaning is composed (though not exhaustively) of various social, economic, political, and cultural elements that provide us with the metaphorical appendages with which to grasp and grapple the world. We experience the world with these various aspects of our individuality, and it is these very constituents of our subjectivities that *open* the possibilities of existence for interrogation and exploration. Each person is a psychological and historical structure, and has received, with existence, a manner of existing, a *style*.[51] This style of existence is individual freedom as found in human sociality, that is, intersubjectivity. Freedom is realized not only through the phenomena that we experience around and within us, but also through our relations with others: "Our relationship to the true passes through others. Either we go towards the true with them, or it is not towards the true that we are going."[52] The projects of freedom and the search for truth are intersubjective and situational. It is in this sense that Nāgārjuna's thought connects with Merleau-Ponty's understanding of freedom.

Freedom for Nāgārjuna is the attainment of *nirvāṇa*. This kind of freedom can be understood, following Walpola Rahula,[53] in both a positive and negative fashion. In the negative sense, *nirvāṇa* is the blowing out or destruction of desire for self and self-existents. In the positive sense, *nirvāṇa* is complete unfettered freedom to experience the totality of the world. However, this positive conception may still seem vacuous, for what does it actually prescribe one to do? In this context, to get caught up with particulars, to grasp after our attachments to principles, only leads one off the *path of the Middle Way*. The path is composed of various mental and physical practices that are curative (of suffering) and ethical (in intent). The path does not rely on rational or moral principles to justify the actions it advocates; rather, these actions are grounded in the very nature of our existential experiences. These actions stem from that which one *can do responsibly and virtuously*.

Merleau-Ponty's generalized field or zone of freedom applies in this manner to Nāgārjuna's nirvanic freedom in its positive sense. Freedom for both is *not* an attainment of a position *outside* of the world, liberated from bodily existence. Instead, it is the total emersion into the existence of the lived body within the context of its essential or originary sociality. It is the recognition and acceptance of the fundamental interconnectedness of oneself with not only the world environment, but also the people who coinhabit it. Our existence is ethical at an originary level. Levin's comments on the virtue of *justice* provide an example of this:

> Our sense of justice is deeply rooted, firmly grounded in the body of our experience. There is a preliminary sense of justice _already_ schematized in and by the flesh: this sense is an original ideality, a *logos*, which gives the flesh its ethical and political axis; this sense is an implicate *logos*, which already lays down, of our intercorporeality, a direction for further exertions, and gathers us into forms of communication by which we can extend its _enlightening rule_. (Underlining added)[54]

The freedom we exercise with regard to this aspect of our experiences is not directed from outside of existence back into it; it is directed from within the world as one is contextually situated within it. Thus, just as language infuses the world with thematized meaning, our freedom infuses our interrelations with others and the world with the power of *initiating action* and meaningfulness. Situated freedom, in accordance with Jacobson, is an aspect of worldly *creativity*.[55]

The ability to initiate, to begin an action, is an integral aspect to freedom. Language, particularly spoken language (*la parole originaire*), exemplifies how freedom functions. Originary language is the kind of speech "which institutes new meanings" (TPP 165). It is not restricted to the sedimented meanings of an ossified tradition. It seeks to open the constraints of *le langage*. Such expression creates new meanings out of the past, thereby opening the future to novelty while simultaneously changing the meaning that the past has for us. Just as the creation of meaning has repercussions across the tradition of the past, and that which will be, temporal existence (dehiscence) is the place wherein acting upon previous actions prefigures that which will be. It is through acting upon our reappropriations of traditions or past histories from which newness and novelty emerges. Freedom is phenomeno-logically bound to temporal becoming. As such, it is part and parcel of our exis-tence. The employment of our situated freedom grounded in our existences ought to support the virtues of humanism in extension. The creation of meaning and the origination of a relational social ontology, which realizes these virtues, would be the establishment of a *politics of ambiguity*[56] or *contingency* (TPP 165).

A politics of contingency holds that the significance of a situation cannot be completely accounted for by some theoretical model based on rational principles. A situation's significance is more understandable from the perspective of those who live it. That is not to say that those who are not subject to the situation's exigencies fail to understand the situation's significance: *relative distance* does not entitle an observer with a privileged position of complete objectivity from which to judge the significance of a situation. And this does not claim that those who live through the situation maintain an ultimately or absolutely privileged posi-tion with regard to the situation's significance. Both extremes must be avoided, for there are always ambiguities in the significances of any situation. Thus, the meanings that can be articulated with respect to the significance of a situation are inexhaustibly manifold and necessarily include various perspectives on the experience itself.

This theoretical (epistemic) modeling of a situation's significance underlies the political thought that can be derived from Merleau-Ponty's later phenomeno-logical explorations. The politics of contingency assumes the situatedness of a (political) experience. Once this is coupled with humanism in extension, politics becomes

[a] politics of and for the "people" rather than the Prince: a politics of and for those whose experience of contingency, ambiguity, and the flesh cannot be easily disavowed (denied, distorted or dissimulated from themselves) or mystified by the various rhetorics of transcendence, universality and necessity which maintain the power of Princes by masking the ambiguities of the particular flesh which is the specific and contingent condition of their privilege. (TPC 171)

This means taking up a position from the perspective of those who are oppressed, or *suffering* (that is, *duḥkha*), á là compassion (*karuṇā*), and making the same decisions and judgments which they would make, thereupon bearing the brunt of the consequences of said actions (*karma*): "It means giving up the illusion of political purity or control and always running the *risk* of being in the wrong, and assuming *responsibility* for this" (TPC 181; italics added). Political purity is as ephemeral as absolute, noncontingent principles that are supposedly universal and timeless. There are no ultimate answers in the political realm; *there are no final solutions* (TPC 174 and 180). In other words, the politics of contingency is essentially ambiguous, perspectival, and dynamic. It "takes both its point of de-parture and its always provisional 'ends' from the local and historical specificities of particular political experience . . . [and] it offers us a future and a world to be made, the resources for doing it, and the challenge" (TPC 183) of an originary politics that is grounded upon, but not determined by, history.

There are three implications for a politics of contingency that follow these (provisional) guidelines. Firstly, and this has implications for comparative philosophy as a whole, there are no rigid boundaries that demarcate the political, supposedly public realm from that of the private realm; nor do these boundaries apply rigidly to nationalistic claims:

> Provide all types of support
> For practitioners who do not seek it
> And even for those living
> In the realms of other kings. (PG 65)

"It cannot be restricted to the polis" or state, for it is "a profoundly radical politics that reaches to the very roots of our being" (TPC 177). This politics is not based upon material wealth, individual rights, or metaphysical ideals; the politics of contingency is grounded in the very nature of our existence as lived bodies subject to *duḥkha*. This is an existence that is decidedly ethical, as characterized by the autochthonous organization of Merleau-Ponty's relational social ontology and by Nāgārjuna's dharmic understanding of intersubjectivity. This understanding of human sociality reaches across the artificial establishment of political borders. It recognizes the essential interconnectedness of human beings with one another and the world they share.

Secondly, as a consequence of the first implication, the *reduction* of the other's alterity to the status of an *enemy* must be *judged* as an act of (metaphysical) violence whose outcome manifests itself physically in the advent of wars and genocide. To be sure, the final solution of the Nazis and the recent ethnic cleansing in Eastern Europe and Africa exemplify the dehumanizing and violent effects of such absolutist principles. In these cases, there was/is the lack of respect for the other and a shirking of responsibility for acting upon such judgments—in other words, these unethical actions that ignore our experiences as social entities, and exemplify the consequences of attachment and desire, are *duḥkha*. They illustrate the nature of state-imposed, or at least institutionally organized (via the military), violence.

The third implication is the dynamic nature of the politics of contingency. This politics is based upon our existential experiences, and as such, *temporal* considerations must play a role in its development and establishment. Under the auspices of temporality, the virtues of humanism in extension are realizable: respect, responsibility, philanthropy, altruism, tolerance, openness, courage, compassion, and so forth, all have temporal dimensions. The initiations of these ethical actions in both the political and social realms begins in the present, but are directed toward the future via an understanding of the past; this is the virtue of *vision* as mentioned above. Since there are no absolute final solutions, these actions always present us with some amount of peril or hazard. There is always the chance that such actions will turn out to be the wrong thing to do: "The possibility of a future may rest on our risking the whole present" (TPP 169), for there is "no way of protecting oneself from the exigencies of moral choice and 'political' responsibility within both the personal *and* public sphere" (TPC 181). Action and judgment are fundamentally temporal. There are no absolutes to which one can appeal in order to establish a legitimate, absolute foundation for our behaviors and decisions. Rather, contingency drops us into the *chiasm* of existence.

The world of the *flesh*, the samsaric realm, is dynamic and open. There are no static normative rules that dictate an ultimate set of actions. This is not to say that we should go as far as Kalupahana's Jamesion pragmatic interpretation of Nāgārjuna's understanding of societal norms.[57] Instead, this position ought to be modified to take into account the historical and cultural significance of the situation's particularities. Neither in ethics nor in politics can there be any guarantees. In this sense, we must, as Watson states, be unremittingly vigilant in our understanding of the philosophical tradition upon which we stand, and in this case, we must be ever vigilant about the political ideals that we accept from our leaders and theorists.[58] The future is open to us. It is a matter of our correct appropriation of the sociohistorical and physical resources at hand by which we can act according to humanism in extension or compassion. Merleau-Ponty's understanding of our situated freedom (qua politics of contingency) as coupled with Nāgārjuna's existential analysis of *duḥkha* provides us with the framework in which to realize an existentially based ethics.

VIRTÙ

We can characterize this existential ethics by expanding on Merleau-Ponty's notion of virtues. The study of this ethics cannot be strictly theoretical, for it must also be phenomenological. It is grounded in a relational social ontology that arises through the conditions of our intersubjective relations.

Our world is a human world, a human world that is fraught with meanings and freedom. The realization of freedom and meanings within our intersubjective context is what human virtues can express. This expression is found in the *virtùs* that manifest themselves in our existential experiences. Such virtues are not based on rational objective laws imported into the world via some transcendental faculty (qua shades of Kant), nor are they solely dictated by some thematized version of historical contingency (qua facets of Marx). These virtues are indicative of the experiential relation that occurs, in its most basic form, in the *meeting* between the self and the other. Levinas and Buber present this phenomenon in decidedly theological terms; however, under Merleau-Ponty and Nāgārjuna's eyes this meeting is outright existential. A strictly metaphysical account (what Levinas would call ontology) of this meeting, for the latter two, has detrimental effects in terms of the imposition of principles, and the subsequent reduction of freedom and perpetuation of *duḥkha*. The phenomenology of the encounter for Merleau-Ponty and Nāgārjuna is indeed ethical, but also psychological, physiological, creative, and metaphysical; in fact, it is all of these and more, *simultaneously*. Understanding and experiencing these intrinsic aspects of our sociality is what Buddhism's *momentariness* can provide to Merleau-Ponty. Within the interval of the specious present of Buddhist momentariness, the *virtùs*, such as compassion and *openness* (just to name a few), can all be realized.

The freedom needed for Merleau-Ponty's new humanism in extension emerges from the temporality of experience and the openness of the relational origination of *śūnyatā*. Nāgārjuna and Buddhism's *nirvāṇa* is nothing other than Merleau-Ponty's *chiasmatic abyss*. Merleau-Ponty's understanding of the *flesh* of the world is firmly situated in the dynamic flow of *saṃsāra*; existence is situational and perspectival in terms of the lived body's relational conditions (*pratītyas*). Herein we find the source of virtues. The interrelational, dynamic, and open world-matrix of interlocking phenomena is our home which we inhabit and which inhabits us. In this sense, the meaningfulness of the world is also constituted by the ethical aspects of our inherent sociality.[59]

Human virtues signify the ground from which we understand each other as essentially social creatures whose existences are interrelational. *Virtù* incorporates the recognition that oppositional ideas (e.g., universality and particularity, and identity and difference) are bound together, not merely at conceptual and cognitive levels, but in the existential and experiential modes of living. The recognition of these essential aspects in our lives demands of us ethical behaviors, but through violent means, both physical and metaphysical, these behaviors have been curbed and limited (as evidenced by the worldwide empires and wars of the last two centuries). It will be *imperative* for us to deal with the differences and similarities of individuals and cultures in the twenty-first century. This will be the task of comparative philosophy.

CONCLUSION

Merleau-Ponty and Nāgārjuna develop their notions of intersubjectivity within the context of their own versions of a relational social ontology. Their conceptions of what constitutes a subject have some striking resemblances. Neither one of these thinkers wishes to ascribe some kind of inherent self-existence (qua substance) to the subject. Each person is a composite of many different factors, conditions, and relations. In fact, without the contributions of all of these facets the development of personhood would not be possible. These two philosophers would interpret this last statement differently. Merleau-Ponty would hold that each of us indeed experiences our own self, which entails that these variables are actual; this is evidenced by the existential nature of the situated lived body. On the other hand, Nāgārjuna would understand that since all of these variables arise in relation to one another, none of them inherently self-exists; they are empty and non-self-existent. Therefore, the existence of the subject is indeed an impossibility, and Buddhism rejects its inherent self-existence. But, given these opposing existential judgments, Merleau-Ponty and Nāgārjuna both adhere to the fact that intersubjectivity is central to our experiences. This must be our point of departure for approaching ethics.

Ethics in the context of these relational social ontologies is eminently intersubjective. Merleau-Ponty's phenomenology begins with a discussion of the carnal perceptual experience of the other, yet to finish this, he makes an implicit appeal to ethics. Nāgārjuna's understanding of intersubjectivity is grounded in Buddhism's ethical and moral tenets. Thus, as based on the confluences of these relational social ontologies, the ethics that Merleau-Ponty's philosophy has lacked can be filled in by the tenets of Buddhism. This has given us some concrete prescriptions by which to realize what Merleau-Ponty called *virtù* and humanism in extension. Similarly, with Nāgārjuna's thought, we can supplement the doctrine of no-self with an understanding of Merleau-Ponty's phenomenology of the lived body.

In conclusion, what general recommendations can we make for comparative philosophy? Firstly, though there are significant differences between the questions, methods, and answers of various cultures and philosophies, we should not look upon these as deterrents. Rather, we should appropriate these in a creative manner, for they are not hindrances. They provide that rough ground which gives us enough traction to support our comparisons. Without differences there would be no need for comparison, let alone communication or interaction. Intersubjectivity is a prime example of the existential consequences of difference or *alterity*. Our sociality evidences alterity within the context of our relational origination as subjects. Subjectivity, the sameness of the ego, self, or *ātman*, arises within the dynamic flux of the interlocking phenomena that constitute intersubjectivity. We are in a community before we find our selves. The characteristics that make this community possible are the conditions that make subjectivity possible. These conditions are implicitly ethical. The comparative discussion of Merleau-Ponty and Nāgārjuna's philosophies has shown that the ethical relation is an originary (or preoriginary qua Levinas) existential aspect of human phenomena.

Secondly, these differences that are intrinsic to intersubjectivity demand of us an ethics that *supports* alterity. This ethics, however, must avoid the Kantian move that levels these differences via the rational application of categorical imperatives. Instead, this ethics must be one of respect and responsibility. Respect in the sense that these differences should not only be *appreciated*, but also *preserved* for their uniqueness. In addition, this preservative side must be performed responsibly, for we must represent alternative viewpoints to the best of our ability by *nurturing* that which is *other* to our lifestyles and cultures. We ought to avoid metaphysical violence or the colonization of consciousness (qua Tseney Serequeberhan);[60] in other words, we must be careful of imposing our ideas and categorical schemes onto others, for the consequences of this destroy our chances at communication by reducing alterity to the categorizations of identity and similitude. Without differences, the fusion of our experiential horizons would be neither necessary nor possible, for there would only be one horizon to which all would be assimilated. In such a case, one set of principles is reified and imposed upon all phenomena and peoples; everyone is reduced to the same conceptual paradigm, and no room is left for alternative viewpoints or the creation of different perspectives. The Hegelian-Marxist conception of history is a perfect example of this reductive cognitive and cultural imperialism; the world is *simplified* into the historical paradigm of modern Western industrialization. This covers, hides, levels, and glosses over the particularities of socio-culture identities and the individualities of persons. The same could be said of Nāgārjuna's critiques of the essentialist claims regarding the Abhidharmic elements of existence (dharmas) by the Sarvastivada. Though useful *tools* for understanding historical and economic forces for Merleau-Ponty or the constituents of experience for Nāgārjuna, neither would *dogmatically* adhere to the Hegelian-Marxist or Sarvastivadin tenets. Ambiguity and novelty as the consequence of the creativity inherent in the relational origination of phenomenal existence precludes the acceptance of absolutist structures like these cognitive methodologies.

This leads to the third recommendation. To avoid the violent metaphysical impositions of conceptual structures (like Hegelian-Marxist or Sarvastivadin essentialism), we must maintain an attitude of self-critical examination of our own ideas and motives. Merleau-Ponty calls this *style* of philosophizing hyperdialectical because of its *autocritical* nature. We need to make explicit the value-laden characteristics of our own categories and interrogate the motivations behind our own projects. Essentially, we must follow the Eleatic imperative "Know thyself!" in order to know the other, for that self is intimately, relationally, and ethically bound up with the other. Such self-understanding supplements the Indian aphorism *Tat tvam asi* ("you are that"), which indicates a person's existence within the world. Thus self-knowledge and understanding is intimately interwoven with comprehension of one's own relation to the world and others.

This comparative and synthetic dialogue has broadened these thinkers' ideas. Merleau-Ponty's philosophy has been shown to have soteriological and ethical possibilities that resemble certain Buddhistic tenets. Nāgārjuna's views on intersubjectivity are distinctly ethical in character; this has significant repercussions for his understanding and prescriptions for political institutions. The implications of this discussion for comparative philosophy have provided a number of prescriptions and developmental goals toward which to strive. These implications certainly impact on the methodological approaches that comparative philosophy uses, but, more important, they are based on existential grounds that provide the ground and framework for such methods. These grounds can draw on the existential analyses and relational social ontologies of Merleau-Ponty and Nāgārjuna. The essential characteristics of their ontologies are the ethical connections between persons in a community. Such connections, however, are not limited to a given individual community, for they extend beyond the boundaries of self-imposed and even other-imposed categories. We are all fundamentally interconnected as existential social creatures, for we are situated by the contexts of our lived bodies and sociohistorical conditions. Comparative philosophy can then arise through the autocritical reappropriation of these conditions via an acceptance of our ethical responsibility to and for others. This cuts across boundaries without destroying them in our efforts at interpretation and communication. This is the essence of a *proper* comparative philosophy.

* This chapter was originally a chapter in my dissertation, and was subsequently published as "Merleau-Ponty and Nagarjuna: Enlightenment, Ethics and Politics," *Journal of Indian Philosophy and Religion* 7 (October 2002): 99–129. The present chapter is a much-revised effort. I would like to thank Professor Chandana Chakrabarti, the editor of *Journal of Indian Philosophy and Religion*, for graciously granting permission to reprint this essay.

12

Ki-Energy

Underpinning Religion and Ethics

Shigenori Nagatomo

Do no evil, perform good, and purify the mind-complexes

Dōgen, Shōbōgenzō Shoakumakusa

Owing to the rapid development of communication devices as well as an increasing exchange among the peoples of different cultures and traditions, it appears that the contemporary world faces the issues of dealing effectively with the diversity of ethnic traditions.[1] This situation suggests that the contemporary world stands at the threshold of a new age, demanding a new and deeper understanding of human nature across the boundary of traditions, cultures, and philosophies. At the dawn of the new century, it is quite appropriate and timely then to call our being afresh into question focusing on the issue of "religion and ethics" in the new century.

But what does it mean to thematize "religion" and "ethics" on the same plane of discourse? And what is the philosophical meaning of the "and" connecting religion with ethics? In order for this conjunction to make sense, we must assume that there is somehow and somewhere the same source of human experience out of which both religion and ethics can meaningfully emerge. This calls for a search for a common denominator that links both religion and ethics together. Before identifying this common denominator and articulating it, I would like to note a few of the major problematics that modern Western philosophy has suffered in dealing with the issues of religion and ethics.

PROBLEMATICS

Modern Western philosophy has focused on the standpoint of *ego-cogito* as an epistemological foundation for all intellectual endeavors, and this standpoint has been criticized as falling into various "ego-predicaments."[2] I will single out one salient element and propose to characterize it as fissure (in two senses), which I believe will enable us to identify the issues to be resolved. The first is an internal fissure, which the *ego-cogito* suffers, because it is a divided self, a split between rationality and irrationality (emotion-instinct) with the emphasis on the former.[3] This was one of the problems in Kant's ethical theory.[4] More broadly, it is the fissure generated by the Cartesian mind-body dualism. One of the implications derived from this fissure is that the meaning of religious experience, which lies buried behind a-rationality, has been obscured, and even has become concealed in the contemporary world. The second is an external fissure between the plural *ego-cogitos*, that is, the problem of the other, or the problem of establishing an intersubjectivity between the two *ego-cogitos*, both of which have a serious implication for ethics insofar as a goal of ethics is to recognize and establish two homogeneous personalities. This is a consequence of the often-observed subject-object dichotomy, which the *ego-cogito* employs as a principle mode of knowing.

Keeping in mind these two senses of fissure we must ask: "What is the common denominator that makes a conjunction between religion and ethics possible?" Among the various avenues that exist in demonstrating the existence of a common denominator, I would like to single out and propose the concept of *ki*-energy and its corresponding lived experience. The concept of *ki*-energy may tentatively be understood as an invisible psycho-physical energy such that it goes beyond the mental and the physical, but is a source out of which both the mental and the physical spring forth as phenomena. The term "invisible" qualifying the psycho-physical energy is employed in this formulation to mean that it is inaccessible through external perception.

The order of my inquiry is as follows. I shall first articulate Merleau-Ponty's concept of the "intentional arc" (*l'arc intentionnel*) while establishing connections with *ki*-energy, and then advance a concept of what I call "the field of intercorporeality" by reinterpreting Merleau-Ponty's concept of the intentional arc as a preparatory ground for establishing an intersubjectivity. Based on this concept of the field of intercorporeality, I shall then attempt to analyze both the internal and external fissures vis-à-vis the theory of *ki*-energy as they pertain to the ethical issue. And lastly, I shall briefly demonstrate how the ethical issue is deeply related to the religious issue.

KI-ENERGY IN MERLEAU-PONTY'S "INTENTIONAL ARC"

The Unilaterality of the Intentional Arc

The phenomena of *ki*-energy have not been thematized explicitly as a philosophical concept in contemporary Western philosophical treatises. However, we can find a remarkable correlate to this concept and to its corresponding lived experience in Merleau-Ponty's *Phenomenolgy of Perception* when he articulates the body-scheme (*le schéma corporel*), particularly in reference to his concept of the intentional arc.[5]

His concept of the intentional arc is a hypothesis to describe the activity of lived body, and its active relation to an object, together forming a unilateral relationship. More specifically, it designates a function of what Merleau-Ponty calls the "habit-body" (*le corps habituel*), the body that is habituated through the process of sedimentation. The habit-body is demarcated from the physiological body (or object-body). Merleau-Ponty sees in the concept of "habit-body" an appropriation of various skills and gestures, or generally the manner of an individual's comportment toward an object in his/her environments. Moreover, he contends that every comportment of our object-body, when it engages an object, is prepared in advance, albeit preconsciously,[6] by the motor intentionality (*l'intentionnalité motrice*).[7] The motor intentionality is a preconscious way of our engaging an object. Merleau-Ponty writes: "In [the] action of the hand which is raised towards an object [there] is contained a reference to the object, not as an object represented, but as that highly specific thing towards which we project ourselves, near which we are, in anticipation, and which we haunt."[8]

Here is a description of our lived-world, our immediate environments, and how we relate ourselves to and engage things in the immediate lived-world. In this passage, we witness an initial characterization of motor intentionality where Merleau-Ponty speaks of us "project[ing] ourselves" to an object. He specifies this motor projection as the threads of the body's intentionality. He observes: "My flat is, for me, not a set of closely associated images. It remains a familiar domain round about me only as long as I still have 'in my hands' or 'in my legs' the main distances and directions involved, and as long as *from my body intentional threads run out towards it*" (emphasis added).[9]

The threads of the body's intentionality mentioned above are called the "intentional arc." It casts an *invisible* net to the object(s) prior to the intentionality of consciousness, and therefore, according to Merleau-Ponty, the body's intentionality is more primary than the intentionality of consciousness. This contention is made in the above quote as the denial of "a set of closely associated images," which is constituted by the intentional act of consciousness. Rather, the operation of the body's intentionality is to endow preconsciously a "primary meaning" to a "primary world" organized through the body's intentionality. Consequently, Merleau-Ponty maintains that the intentionally constituted object vis-à-vis consciousness is "secondary."[10]

The "primary world" designates in this context a "lived space"[11] that is organized and sedimented through the body's intentionality. The body's intentionality, which forms the "basis of the primary meaning" for the "primary world," is then an "original or basic intentionality" (*l'intentionnalité originale*).[12] It is "basic because it is the 'basis' which supports all the activities of human existence." Referring to almost all the activities of human existence as "the life of consciousness," Merleau-Ponty observes:

> [T]he life of consciousness—cognitive life, the life of desire or perceptual life—is sub-
> tended by an "intentional arc" which projects round about us our past, our future, our
> human setting, our physical, ideological and moral situation. . . . It is this intentional
> arc which brings about the unity of the senses, of intelligence, of sensibility and motil-
> ity. And it is this which "goes limp" in illness.[13]

The originality claimed for the "intentional arc" (i.e., the threads of the body's intentionality projected "round about us") is so recognized in virtue of the fact that it is the foundation for all the life-activities of human existence. The test for the working of this originality rests in the discovery that when the intentional arc malfunctions or becomes dysfunctional, the living body with its lived experience becomes "limp."

Merleau-Ponty's characterization of the "intentional arc" as that which supports a normal healthy condition of the body parallels, at a physiological level, the view of disease held by acupuncture medicine. According to acupuncture medicine, a pathological state is a consequence of an imbalance of *ki*-energy in the body or its stagnation in a particular meridian. Moreover, *ki*-energy is not detected in a corpse, but only in a living body.[14] Here we witness a remarkable physiological correspondence between Merleau-Ponty's concept of "intentional arc" and the *ki*-energy espoused in acupuncture medicine.

The main point, then, that I wish to observe in this brief account of Merleau-Ponty's concept of "intentional arc," is an association with the concept of *ki*-energy. In order for Merleau-Ponty's "intentional arc" to be formed and become functional, he must presuppose a certain kind of energy issued from the lived body; otherwise, no arc, however invisible, can be formed. I would like to identify the energy responsible for forming an "intentional arc" to be none other than *ki*-energy. This identification of the source for the formation of "intentional arc" may seem rather capricious. However, when Merleau-Ponty speaks of "one's own body" (*le corps proper*),[15] from which the intentional arc is projected, as "a third term" (*un troisieme terme*) that is neither in-itself nor for-itself, neither the physiological nor the psychical,[16] the above identification proves to be no longer accidental, for the notion of "a third term" coincides roughly with the tentative definition of *ki*-energy given at the outset, although admittedly there is no mention of energy in the concept of "a third term."

THE BILATERALITY OF INTENTIONAL ARC

When Merleau-Ponty characterizes his concept of "intentional arc" as that which is issued from the lived body to an object, what he has mainly in mind is a unilateral direction. That is, his analysis of "intentional arc" focuses only on the projection of *ki*-energy from one lived body toward an (inanimate) object. However, it could be inferred that another "intentional arc" is issued from another lived body, as when, for example, two persons engage themselves in conversation. That is, if the perspective is shifted from one lived body to another, the second lived body must equally form an "intentional arc." This perspectival shift is not a theoretical impossibility for the lived body, unlike the *ego-cogito*, which is extensionless and confined within itself, because the lived body, according to Merleau-Ponty, extends itself toward an object through the function of its "intentional arc." This suggests that unlike the unilateral concept of "intentional arc" there must be a lived experience that involves a bilateral "intentional arc" when, for example, two lived bodies interact in a given situation.[17]

There is no explicit treatment of bilateral intentional arc in Merleau-Ponty's writings, but he hints at such a possibility when he speaks of "subject-object dialogue" (*le dialogue du sujet avec l'objet*). Merleau-Ponty writes:

> [T]he normal subject penetrates into the object by perception, assimilating its structure into his substance, and through this body the object directly regulates his movement. This *subject-object dialogue*, this drawing together, by the subject, of the [primary] meaning diffused through the object, and, by the object, of the subject's [bodily] intentions—a process which is physiognomic perception—arranges round the subject a [primary] world which speaks to him of himself, and gives his own thoughts their place in the world.[18] (Emphasis added)

In characterizing the activity of this dialogue Merleau-Ponty speaks in reference to the subject's perception of "penetrating" into an object and "assimilating" its structure within itself. If we take "penetration" and "assimilation" in a physical sense, the point of Merleau-Ponty's observation is entirely missed, for he is concerned here with neither the sense of physical "penetration" nor physical "assimilation." If the terms "penetration" and "assimilation" were to have any meaning in the context of this "dialogue," they would have to refer to an *invisible* energy the working of which is more subtle than the physical. This same point seems to be observed when Merleau-Ponty speaks of the object as the "diffusion" of the primary meaning spreading from the object. As we recall, the tentative definition we gave *ki*-energy was an *invisible* energy of psycho-physical nature. This "diffusion" of invisible energy is the second point I wish to observe in Merleau-Ponty's concept of the "intentional arc."

The above point of *ki*-energy being the third term of psycho-physical nature leads us to take note of another point, namely that, given this invisible energy, there must be a mutual interfusion of this energy between the subject and the object as a condition for the "subject-object dialogue" to take place,[19] or, in case of the multiple lived bodies, a bilateral "intentional arc." This point of mutual interfusion of the invisible energies between the multiple lived bodies is the third connection that I wish to establish between Merleau-Ponty's analysis of "intentional arc" and *ki*-energy. In order for this mutual interfusion of *ki*-energies to occur, we must further note that there is an emanation or a projection of *ki*-energy issued respectively from the respective lived bodies.

Where there is a mutual interfusion of *ki*-energies emanated respectively from each of the multiple lived bodies, a field of what may be called an intercorporeality is formed "out in the open." The term "inter" in "intercorporeality" is used here first to designate a sense of "among" and so acknowledges the plurality of lived bodies in the formation of this field, while the term "corporeality" is used to acknowledge the source of emanating energies. The field of "intercorporeality" indicates a temporary interfusion of the *ki*-energies, confluenced together when plural lived bodies come together. We therefore recognize that the bilateral "intentional arc" is realized in this field of intercorporeality qua the *ki*-energies, which in turn is the precondition for the mutual interfusion of invisible *ki*-energies to occur. What this suggests to the issue of establishing a ground for intersubjectivity is that neither the self nor the other can exist independently from each other, because if our analysis of the field of intercorporeality is correct, it implies that the other and the self emerge concurrently along with the interfusion of the invisible *ki*-energy.

Another implication of recognizing the mutually emanative interfusion of *ki*-energies is that there is no one-sided view of taking the one as active and the other as passive in the dialogue. In fact, the fixed active-passive scheme does not arise in the bilateral "intentional arc" or in the field of intercorporeality. Rather, two entities entering into this relation of mutual interfusion must be characterized by an interchangeability; the concept of bilaterality presupposes that that which engages can turn into that which is being engaged, and vice versa. This position mitigates two philosophical positions: one that recognizes an active meaning-bestowing function[20] solely in the alleged transparency of "consciousness" and the other that regards the subject as a passive recipient of "meaning" (empiricism).

We must briefly touch here the preconscious status of the field of intercorporeality. In recognition of the ontogenesis of the preconscious operation of the field of intercorporeality, reflective consciousness associated with the allegedly transparent consciousness is not useful in bringing this preconscious operation into full awareness. It requires an awareness that occurs when the level of activity of the allegedly transparent consciousness is lowered, that is, when this consciousness is totally relaxed. This is because the preconscious occurrence of the field of intercorporeality has its ontogenesis in the depths of the lived body, the depths here denoting the regions of the coenesthesis (comprised of kinesthesis and somesthesis), emotion-instinct, and the unconscious.[21]

ATTUNEMENT

Attunement of *Ki*-Energy in Ethics

The questions we must raise now in view of the problematics outlined at the outset, as they are concerned with ethics, are how does the theory of *ki*-energy propose to answer the questions "Why is there a fissure within the *ego-cogito*?" and "Why is there a fissure between the plural *ego-cogitos*?" According to the theory of *ki*-energy, both of these senses of fissure occur because a discrepancy or disharmony of *ki*-energies is temporarily created. The internal fissure as it pertains to the interior of the *ego-cogito* is due to a disharmony or discrepancy of *ki*-energy within the *ego-cogito* (for example, between rationality and irrationality, or between the mind and body). Experientially, this will translate into a state of struggle, or alternatively an indecision of will, which is induced as a consequence of overemphasis or one-sided emphasis on one aspect of *ego-cogito*—namely, rationality or intellect—without tending to develop the other equally important aspect: a-rationality, or, more specifically emotion-instinct. The external fissure as it pertains to the relationship among the plural *ego-cogitos* arises because when the field of intercorporeality is established "out in the open," for example, between two individual *ego-cogitos*, there also occurs a dissonance of *ki*-energies in this field, or, to use a Sartrean example, a petrification of the other vis-à-vis the look (*un regard*). According to the theory of *ki*-energy, a practical solution for the problem in both cases lies in bringing the disharmonious, dissonant *ki*-energies into the state of harmony. Here we have a glimpse of treating both the internal and external fissures as they pertain to one of the major issues of ethics through the common denominator of the *ki*-energy.

Let us discuss this dissonance or disharmony of *ki*-energy in light of the field of intercorporeality, while also making references to the agent responsible for its formation. This agent we may call the "embodied *ego-cogito*." This phrase is introduced here to remind us that the *ego-cogito* is an incarnate thinking being always with its concrete living structure.

The field of intercorporeality, which is created temporarily through the confluence of the *ki*-energies and which is emanated from the embodied *ego-cogito*, is not free of qualitative flare. This suggests that the *ki*-energy responsible for the creation of the field of intercorporality is invested with various conflicting qualities as well. We may use the term "attunement" to characterize the state in which there are no conflicting qualities present in the embodied *ego-cogito* or in the field of intercorporeality. Contrasting this state of "attunement," we may use the term "out-of-attunement" to characterize the state in which there are conflicting qualities present in the embodied *ego-cogito* or in the field of intercorporeality. The concept of "attunement" is derived from our previous analysis concerning the notion of interchangeability observed in the bilateral "intentional arc" of interfusing *ki*-energies. This interfusion of *ki*-energies suggests that there is an interplay of these interfusing energies, which we designate by the term "attunement." When there is no conflict or struggle in the interplay of these interfusing energies, the term "attunement" may be used to describe a qualitative structural relationship obtaining in the field of intercorporeality created by the embodied *ego-cogitos*.

Traditionally, the theory of *ki*-energy has divided the various qualities of the *ki*-energy in two major categories: yin and yang (darker and brighter), or more or less negative, and more or less positive *ki*-energy. Yang, a brighter positive energy, is a creative, pro-life tendency, while yin, a darker negative energy, is a destructive and pro-death tendency. When seen in light of the yin/yang polar category, the disharmony or dissonance created within the embodied *ego-cogito* or in the field of intercorporeality translates into a *predominance* of the one equality over the other, or, more specifically, more yin quality than yang in the embodied *ego-cogito* or in the field of intercorporeality. According to the theory of *ki*-energy, the reason then that there is a fissure both in the interior of the embodied *ego-cogito* and in the field of intercorporeality is due to the imbalance between the yin and the yang qualities, bringing about the predominance of the one over the other. Both of these cases are in the state of "out-of-attunement," needing to bring the embodied *ego-cogito* or the field of intercorporeality into the state of "attunement," if we are to avoid a conflicting ethical situation or a struggle within the embodied *ego-cogito*.

What we must analyze here concerning the ethical aspect of *ki*-energy, insofar as it is concerned with the fissure, is the case in which there is more yin quality than yang quality. In the ethical sphere this predominance of the yin over the yang colors the field of intercorporeality in various gradations of failing to recognize the other as a personality, ranging from a state of conflict to the state of indifference. When this predominance is applied to the embodied *ego-cogito*, it experiences a struggle of various gradations ranging from a repressive state to a schizophrenic state.

Where and when there is a predominance of yin, the embodied *ego-cogito* is temporarily affected by such negative emotions as anger, hatred, inappropriate sexual desire, or, in ethical terms, an impulse for evil. The emotive state also clouds the deeper religious dimension of human being, because all that is religious—the sacred, the luminous, and the divine—is concealed behind the a-rationality qua the emotive-instinctive state.

We must now give an articulation of an experiential correlate to the concept of "attunement" and "out-of-attunement." What is an experiential correlate to the concepts of "attunement" and "out-of-attunement"? As we recall, these two concepts arose from our analysis of the field of intercorporeality and the embodied *ego-cogito*, where there are emanative interfusions of the subtle *ki*-energy. Where there are conflicting qualities in the flow of the *ki*-energy, we have designated the state as being "out-of-attunement," and where there are no such qualities, we have designated it as being in "attunement." These two states in the flow of the *ki*-energy are determined by the experience of what I call "felt inter-resonance." This phrase purports to describe how the fissure is discerned within the embodied *ego-cogito* or in the field of intercorporeality. The embodied *ego-cogito* feels a resonance in the predominant flare of *ki*-energy emanated either within itself or within the field of intercorporeality; the degree to which it perceives a resonance is correlative with the degree of the fissure that is created within itself or in the field of intercorporeality. The wider the fissure is, the weaker is the feeling of resonance; conversely, the narrower the fissure, the stronger the feeling of resonance. There is then a proportionality in the experience of "felt inter-resonance," ranging from a total unawareness to a clear discernment. What accompanies the experience of "felt inter-resonance," then, is also a proportionality of discernment of the predominance of the *ki*-energy. This experience is not, however, rooted in the intellectual judgment where there is a clear split between the subject as knower and the object as known. It is rather rooted in the *feeling judgment* where there is no such split. This feeling-judgment is performed in extending one's *ki*-energy toward the flow of the *ki*-energy in the interiority of the embodied *ego-cogito* or toward the flow of the *ki*-energy in the field of intercorporeality.

The preceding analysis gives a picture of what constitutes an ethically right person. A person who qualifies to be ethically right is the one (1) who can discern the predominance of the yin in the flow of the *ki*-energy present in the embodied *ego-cogito* as well as in the field of the intercorporeality, (2) who is endowed with the power of transforming this predominance into the state of "attunement," and (3) who can perform (1) and (2) with a caring heart.

We have briefly concentrated our analysis primarily on the ethical dimension in an attempt to give a theoretical plausibility of understanding in the ethics vis-à-vis the common denominator that is the *ki*-energy. This analysis has been confined, however, to our natural, everyday standpoint—that is, without dealing with the transformative process—which can be effected in the embodied *ego-cogito*. When we begin to examine this transformative process, we will plunge ourselves into the examination of religious aspects insofar as the theory of *ki*-energy is capable of charting it.

Attunement of the *Ki*-Energy in Religion

All that is religious is denied to the embodied *ego-cogito* so long as it remains in the natural, everyday standpoint. This is because *ki*-energy, which spreads from the individual *ego-cogito*, is delimited by its "natural" propensity. The *ego* of the embodied *ego-cogito* centers things around itself for its own sake and this is its "natural propensity." An ethical implication of this self-centering function is exemplified by the fact that there occurs, however infrequently, in the embodied *ego-cogito* an impulse for evil, or to use the broader characterization introduced in the previous section, there occurs a predominance of yin over yang. This propensity is a delimitation of the embodied *ego-cogito* only insofar as it remains being "natural" in the sense that no human contrivance is added to the lived body, to the way it came into existence at birth. This delimitation makes the religious experience impossible, for it prevents the embodied *ego-cogito* from having unions with all that is religious such as a union with the inner cosmos, a union with the physical nature and a union with the outer cosmos. An assumption here is that the religious experience is concealed in the greater domains of experience.

Accordingly, the function of self-centering, though it appears to be important in our everyday life, is a barrier to entering into the religious experience of union. The religious dimension for the embodied *ego-cogito* lies concealed behind its a-rationality, or alternatively behind the *ki*-energy manifested as the emotion-instinct. Admittedly, the *ki*-energy qua the emotion-instinct is in part the source for the impulse to evil as we have seen in the previous section in terms of the predominance of the *yin* over *yang* quality, but this *ki*-energy qua the emotion-instinct is also an indispensable energy for the maintenance and development of the embodied *ego-cogito*. To use the phrase employed in the previous section, the task of entering into the religious dimension is to transform the predominance of yin into the predominance of yang, and eventually to live in the state of pure yang. This transformation of the predominance of yin into the predominance of yang is an existential project. In this process of transforming the yin predominance to the yang predominance, each reconfiguration must be accompanied with the development of both mental and physical stability in a newly created combination, and one moves step by step toward the predominance of pure yang. In this manner, "attunement" is constantly at work.

The natural propensity mentioned above as a delimitation for entering into the religious experience, when it is translated into the terms of the *ki*-energy, means that the embodied *ego-cogito* is endowed with a "natural" combination of more or less yin and more or less yang qualities, although its *ratio* may differ from individual to individual. Given this natural combination, what is the modality of engagement, which the embodied *ego-cogito* assumes? When we note the fact that there occurs a predominance of yin over yang, the embodied *ego-cogito* must have a unique modality of engagement specific to the natural combination. This modality I should like to designate as "tensional" modality. "Tensional" modality, or its nominal form "tensionality," characterizes the manner through which a combination of both the yin and yang quality of *ki*-energy maintains, however implicitly, a *tension* in its "natural" balance. In terms of its experiential correlate, it suggests that the embodied *ego-cogito* encounters an eruption of the a-rational surge, mostly under the guise of various negative emotions and instincts. In other words, when the embodied *ego-cogito* experiences "without reason" the power surging from the depth of its being, such an *ego-cogito* is said to embrace in its living structure a tensional modality of engagement. Tensionality then conceals a real possibility that the emotion-instinct takes over the rational working of the embodied *ego-cogito*. This is a further specification of what we called in the previous section "predominance of yin over yang quality of *ki*-energy."

Nevertheless, this is simply a tendency. *Ki*-energy is characterized by its fluidity and, therefore, the theory of *ki*-energy does not consider such a tendency as an inherent limitation of the embodied *ego-cogito*. Rather, the theory maintains that this tendency can be restructured by transforming the way in which the emotion-instinct functions naturally. Let us designate this transformative process as the "de-tensional" modality of engagement, meaning that this modality is an existential process of "going out of" the tensional modality that characterizes the embodied *ego-cogito* in its natural combination of *ki*-energy. The "de-tensional" modality of engagement, when interpreted in light of the goal of entering into the religious dimension, is a practical process of transforming the predominance of yin into the predominance of yang. Or, to put it differently, the "de-tensional" modality of engagement is a restructuring of the "natural" combination of the yin and yang *ki*-energy in such a way that it starts assuming a new combination in which the yang proportionally predominates the yin.

In the "de-tensional" modality of engagement, it then becomes crucial to develop an ability to detect the way of how the negative emotion-instinct of the embodied *ego-cogito* functions. Here, the theory of *ki*-energy reinterprets the erupting emotion-instinct as a flow of *ki*-energy. This reinterpretation is supported by the fact that *ki*-energy is the source out of which both the physical and the psychical emerge as phenomena, the emotion-instinct being an aspect of the psychical.

Among the many specific *technes* for detecting the pattern of erupting emotion-instinct in the flow of *ki*-energy, breathing and meditation may be examined in the order mentioned. Breath is a sign of life, without which the embodied *ego-cogito* cannot sustain its life. In this sense, breath is closely related to *spiritus*, a form of *ki*-energy. How the embodied *ego-cogito* breathes reflects its mental/spiritual condition: there is a definite correlation between the state of mind, and the pattern and rhythm of breathing.

Breathing is ambiguous in the natural propensity of the embodied *ego-cogito* in that it can be performed either voluntarily or involuntarily, here interpreting the former to be the function of the *ego-cogito* while the latter the function of the unconscious. Since the embodied *ego-cogito* breathes involuntarily most of its waking moments, its breathing is governed by the unconscious. This in turn suggests that the *ego-cogito* is subtly controlled by the unconscious, the seat of emotion-instinct. Conscious breathing then brings this unconscious activity into a conscious awareness, and thereby attempts to establish a temporary connection with the unconscious.[22] Since the unconscious is the base out of which emotion-instinct emerges, this temporary connection, when repeated, serves to regulate how the emotion-instinct functions, because the unconscious activity of the emotion-instinct will be brought to a conscious awareness. Conscious breathing functions in the de-tensional modality of engagement as an indirect way of regulating the a-rational behavior of emotion and instinct. Seen in this light, the de-tensional modality of engagement is a way of consciously appropriating the behavior or pattern of the emotion-instinct.

Meditation, on the other hand, allows the *ki*-energy to appear in the form of various images as "wandering thoughts" like bubbles in a carbonated drink.[23] It is interesting to note that in the outer rim of the *Garbha-maṇḍala*, which depicts a deepening and ascending process of meditation according to Shingon tradition, are portrayed the various threatening images formed by negative *ki*-energy.[24]

This suggests that in the initial stage of meditation, the yin quality of *ki*-energy is released. As one deepens the transformative process of meditation, the images with clear and luminous powers are increasingly depicted as one moves toward the center of the *Garbha-maṇḍala*, suggesting that the predominance of yin is replaced with the predominance of yang.[25] This process roughly corresponds also to the Pure Land Buddhist's classification, given in *Kanmuryōjukyō*, according to the clarity and precision of images actively visualized, so as to determine how meditation has deepened.[26]

As one moves into the region of the religious, characterized by such words as the divine, the sacred, and the luminous, through the various images of higher beings, one starts appropriating a constellation of the inner cosmos, which has stood opposed to the embodied *ego-cogito*. When this appropriation takes place, the natural combination of the yin and the yang is reconfigured in such a way that the predominance of yang becomes characteristic of a religious person. In this process, the *ego* of the embodied *ego-cogito* drops and its lived body enters into a subtle dimension of the body. When this occurs, the *ki*-energy is no longer a manifestation qua the physical or qua the psychical. It is no different from the region of luminous light where there is no fissure, internal or external.

CONCLUDING REMARKS

By examining the breathing and meditation, we have come back to the initial definition of the *ki*-energy, which was an invisible psycho-physical energy that goes beyond the mental and the physical but is a source out of which both the mental and the physical spring forth as phenomena. *Ki*-energy as the invisible physical energy has been traced back to the breathing, while the *ki*-energy as the psychical energy was examined through meditation in reference to the images that appear in the course of meditation. Finally, the source out of which both the physical and psychical emerge is hinted at as the luminous light.

However, beyond this dimension of *ki*-energy, there still lies a greater depth of religious experience. This is where the theory of *ki*-energy must stop, because we have already reached the limit of its capacity insofar as the religious experience through the *ki*-energy is concerned.

* A version of this chapter appeared in *Zen Buddhism Today*, Annual Report of the Kyoto Zen Symposium, 8 (October 1990): 124–39.

13

Merleau-Ponty and Asian Philosophy

The Double Walk of Buddhism and Daoism

Jay Goulding

This chapter presents a unique perspective on Maurice Merleau-Ponty and Eastern philosophy. It illustrates the intersections of phenomenology with Buddhism and Daoism. In this process, Merleau-Ponty himself has a shadow: Kuang-ming Wu. Wu's deep insight has helped generations of thinkers grapple with complex relationships between and among Buddhism and Daoism in particular. What is little appreciated is Wu's knowledge of phenomenology. Influenced by John Wild at Yale—a pioneer of phenomenology in the United States—Wu incorporates Merleau-Ponty in his scholarship. Particularly inspired by Merleau-Ponty's body phenomenology, Wu argues that the West thinks too much with the mind and forgets about the body. The East lets the body do the thinking and the mind disappears into it.

Along these lines, this chapter utilizes a variation on the ancient Chinese method of "matching meanings" (C. *geyi*) throughout by comparing Eastern thought with Eastern thought, that is Buddhism with Daoism. One way of explaining this matching is through the works of Merleau-Ponty. His writing on the body has an uncanny similarity to both Buddhist and Daoist thought. As such, it helps to explain the heart of Eastern and Western philosophical intersections. Like Wu, Merleau-Ponty has an expanded understanding of the body (both corporeal and noncorporeal). Unlike Wu, Merleau-Ponty is only able to scratch the surface of these connections. Hence, Wu's work helps tease out Merleau-Ponty's unspoken contributions. In the explication of philosophy and society, phenomenology is concerned with the layering of experiences, which are stratified into a complex whole. This stratified layering is reminiscent of the blending of philosophical traditions in China. The concept "communicative" is not one that simply expresses reason through discourse. "Communicative" refers to a matrix of expressions both verbal and nonverbal, both visible and invisible. It is a "thickness of being" between people and events, as Merleau-Ponty might say. The concept "body" is not simply the physical body but a "chiasm" of experiences reaching between people and events. We see this in metaphors such as the "body of literature" or the "body of history." Hence, the "communicative body" refers to an intertwining of relationships, which balance our personal and communal understandings of both material and spiritual crossings of experience. In Buddhism, not all meaning is meaningful. Silence does away with words and meaning, yet is "full" of the experience of knowing. Chan/Zen meditation is an example of silence deconstructing meaning. Likewise, Zhuangzi demonstrates a parallel vocabulary for Daoism. Communications are not simply verbal. If you catch the fish, you no longer need the trap; if you have the words, you can do away with the images. "Words without words" (C. *yan wu yan*) is a Daoist principle of nonverbal communications. Not all meaning shows itself through words. In Chan/Zen, awakening or enlightenment (C. *wu*) is a parallel achievement beyond words and only arrived at through forms of meditation.

For Zhuangzi, clarity is not so easily achieved. Language takes an uncertain path. Hence, Zhuangzi makes fun of language: To use a horse to show that a horse is not a horse is not as good as using a non-horse to show that a horse is not a horse. Here he is responding to the ancient sophist Gongsun Long's "white horse is not a horse" (C. *bai ma fei ma*), which claims that "horse" is naming a shape, and "white" is naming a color. Thus a "white horse is not a horse."[1] He is not interested in logic. He is concerned with "the ontological consistency of self-so-ness."[2] As Wu argues: "[W]e can afford to affirm things in their differences (using a no-horse to show that a horse is no-horse), accepting everything as 'such'" (BC 196). Zhuangzi calls this "the double walk" (C. *liang xing*) (BC 195), taking both logical roads simultaneously in order to "tarry at the pivot" and "respond end-lessly and freely" (BC 196). Zhuangzi writes: "Where none of that or this obtains its counterpart—people call it the Tao [*Dao*] Pivot. Then the Pivot begins to obtain its middle point of the circle, and with it, it responds till there-is-no end" (BC 140–41). Ironically, Daoism and Buddhism also exhibit this double walk as they move in tandem.

In a phenomenological manner, Chinese philosophy explores communications through three interwoven views of the body or what I call the heavenly body, the earthly body, and the body of the Void. These can be aligned with three distinct philosophies in China: Confucianism's heavenly body, Daoism's earthly body, and Buddhism's body of the Void. Confucianism strives for the perfect body of heavenly peace, Daoism strives for the body of longevity, and Buddhism for the body of transformation.

For Laozi, humans are trapped in a net, a web of complex experiences, fragments of myths and dreams amongst and between these bodies. The Daoist communicative body is "heaven's net," which is vast and infinite. It is in between heaven and earth (C. *tiandi zhi jian*). With it, we engage in what Wu calls "net thinking" or "body thinking."[3] As such, Chinese philosophy manifests itself through the body (of history, of self, of civilization) as a communicative matrix. The Yellow Emperor Huangdi explains this as a "visceral manifestation" (*zangxiang*), a crisscross of energy meridians through which Chinese civilization passes and doubles back in its self-perpetuating renewals.

THREE CHINESE BODIES

The Merleau-Ponty translator and philosopher of the body John O'Neill provides a bridge between Western and Eastern views of the body. As a "communicative body"—a matrix of human experiences within language—the East Asian body fits O'Neill's "organic history" as a complement to Western philosophical positions. Inspired by Merleau-Ponty, O'Neill explains:

> We need to underwrite the official history of truth as philosophers have conceived it with an "organic history" that accounts for the real historicity of truth. To do so, we have to rediscover the spiritual interior of the lived body, to show that the human body is a psychophysical body whose aesthesiology makes it conformable to the world of things and persons in the same fashion as it is itself a *communis sensorum*. This is not discoverable outside language. All the same, language is preceded and always surrounded by those silent bodies of things and persons whose destiny of becoming speech we are trying to describe.[4]

The East Asian body helps in "rediscovering the spiritual interior of the lived body" that O'Neill addresses. Through its flux of linguistic, philosophical, medical, and cultural configurations, the East Asian body assists O'Neill's and Merleau-Ponty's project to "rearticulate seeing, speaking, and thinking before they are organized around the mind and body or subject-object dualism."[5] In both Buddhist and Daoist fashions respectively, ancient Asian thought tends to dissolve these Western dualisms before they take hold, thus winning the fight before it begins. Buddhism brings them into a void, thus negating their polarities while Daoism harmonizes their oppositions into a "way" of knowing and unknowing.

Merleau-Ponty's interest in East Asia was no doubt influenced by his close friend Jean Paul Sartre. Sartre's phenomenology was in turn influenced by Kuki Shūzō, a celebrated student of both Martin Heidegger and Edmund Husserl and expert on both Buddhism and Daoism. While Kuki dialogued with Sartre in the 1920s, Merleau-Ponty dialogued with the Japanese philosopher Awano Yasutaro in the 1930s.[6] Merleau-Ponty's 1956 essay on Eastern philosophy "Everywhere and Nowhere" is informed by these dialogues. Merleau-Ponty reminds us of the Daoist Laozi who is and who is not, who occupies the betweenness of time but is never far from himself or others, who renders obsolete the boundaries between city and country, between official and peasant, between human and animal, between Heaven and Earth, between East and West. In his radical doubt of the visible world, Merleau-Ponty himself becomes a kind of Buddhist monk. He explains:

But this possession of self and truth, which only the West has taken as its theme, nevertheless flits through the dreams of other cultures, and in the West itself it is not fulfilled. What we have learned about the historical relations of Greece and the Orient, and inversely, all the "Western" characteristics we have discovered in Oriental thought (Sophistry, Skepticism, elements of dialectics and logic), forbid us to draw a geographical frontier between philosophy and non-philosophy.[7]

Although Merleau-Ponty is merely skimming the surface of East Asian thought, he sees it dissipating the barriers between philosophy and popular culture and between Eastern and Western thought "in each culture's lateral relationships to the others, in the echoes one awakes in the other."[8]

From these detailed quotes, it is possible that Chinese thought makes an impression on Merleau-Ponty's views of the body as he formulates a chiasm between "flesh" and "idea" emerging from "a certain hollow, a certain interior, a certain absence, a negativity that is not nothing."[9] Such thinking prompts him to argue that "the split between vision and the visible, between thought and being do not, as they claim, establish us in the negative. . . . And what remains is not nothing, what remains are mutilated fragments . . . and they regenerate it under other names—appearance, dream, Psyche, representation" (VI 105–6). The "not nothing" connects him with the dreamscape which East Asia illuminates, especially in Buddhism and Daoism. As Merleau-Ponty continues: "It is in the name and for the profit of these floating realities that the solid reality is cast into doubt" (VI 106). Merleau-Ponty's intersection of being and nothingness transports us to the Floating Life (C. *fusheng*) of Qing China and the floating world (J. *ukiyo*) of Tokugawa Japan, both of which are dominated by Buddhist and Daoist thought. In assembling some fractal identities of the East Asian body, each fragmented mythology is a particularized representative of the whole in both its visibility and invisibility. Similar to Merleau-Ponty, Wu writes:

We can either believe in stories and myths for their own sake, or live in them as we live in language, using them to express the web of things. Here, we think of the vast corpus of Buddhist stories alongside Daoist folktales. Chuang Tzu (sic) *used* bits of myths, legends, and stories, freely quoting and misquoting from them, to reflect the "heaven's net" (Lao Tzu) [*sic*] that is vast and loose yet losing nothing. (BC 67)

China's history reveals intersections with the phenomenology that both O'Neill and Merleau-Ponty propose. Rather than be held to binary opposites struggling for the upper hand (mind/body, subject/object) or for redemptive overcoming, China neither subscribed to scientific rationality nor dialectical reversals. Chinese civilization invented written language along with an enormously elaborate web of scientific/religious/philosophical thought that bound the sky to earth with a cushion of Buddhist meditative emptiness—the Void. Yet this Void was not simply empty but full to the brim with the contradictions of lived experience. China's strength came from "the web that had no weaver."[10] The Void was a conduit for society to appear and disappear. China's greatest communicative accomplishments either stood outside of language or tried to resist its trap. Its unseen corporeality represented by the unseen meridians of energy in Chinese medicine stretched across the world long before the artificiality of national boundaries or borderlines.

DAOIST *DAO*, BUDDHIST *DAO*

In ancient China, Confucian philosophers witnessed the resignation and withdrawal of Laozi, a senior administrator who established "the way of the water," his response to the overly bureaucratic stagnation of life. Laozi was purported to have said: "The Tao that can be told is not the eternal Tao. The name that can be named is not the eternal name."[11] Centuries later, Confucianism encountered many forms of Buddhism coming into China from the Silk Roads. The rich interaction between Buddhist monks and Daoist priests in the Lu Mountains where there were thousands of temples generated a plethora of responses to Confucianism. From this era, a famous Buddhist *gong'an* ironically echoes Laozi's words:

> A student asks, "What is Dao?"
>
> The master answers, "The ordinary mind is Dao."
>
> "Is there any method by which I can obtain it?"
>
> "If you have the intention to obtain it, then you cannot obtain it."
>
> "But if I give up all intention to obtain it, how can I see Dao?"
>
> "The Dao is beyond knowing and unknowing. To 'know' something is merely to be fooled into perceiving that you understand it. 'Unknowing' means that one is ignorant about the subject. To obtain Dao is to experience the void. Here are no boundaries or limitations."[12]

The above dialogue is the undoing of dialogue. It echoes Merleau-Ponty's veto on "geographical frontiers" or barriers. The back and forth of discourse, question and answer, are silenced by the immediacy of the Void, which dissolves the duality and closure of dialogue in favor of the lived experience in its spontaneous practice. Although from different traditions, the *Dao* of Daoism is resonate in the emptiness of Buddhism, a hollow replete with meditative inscriptions.

Dao responded to bureaucracy by retreating, focusing on emptiness, breathing, and meditation, life-energy flow, and yin/yang polarities. Both Daoist and Buddhist adopted the posture of beggar or vagabond. Daoism promoted longevity; Buddhism offered attainable salvation within one lifetime. "Awakening" through knowledge of the Four Noble truths and the Eightfold Path could be achieved through meditation, breathing, right conduct, and correct eating. Buddha was very attractive because he offered this knowledge, not only in a single lifetime but immediately, through meditation, to achieve pure stillness and access to one's true self. On the one hand, Buddhism listed paths of right conduct, similar to Confucian ideals; on the other, it attempted to embrace nothingness, similar to Daoism. Both Buddhism and Daoism resisted highly disciplined systems of thought while utilizing breathing systems to open energy channels for good health. Martial arts were negotiated between the Buddhist Damo (Bodhidharma) and Daoist priests at Shaolin. After the sixth century, Buddha, *Dao*, and Confucius were so intertwined that a Chinese thinker could not easily split them up. Hence, we have the idea of the three teachings as one, *sanjiao heyi* (harmony of three teachings). In a sense, Daoism provided a cosmology for Buddhism through an elaborate system of energy flow and combined opposites based on yin/yang. Buddhism opened up the possibility of cleaning the mind's mirror through contemplating *gong'an* (irreconcilable paradoxes) in seated meditation. When Buddhist scholars tried to explain the meaning of Buddhism, they turned to Daoist texts of Laozi and Zhuangzi.[13] Some fanciful accounts saw Buddhism to be a strange form of Daoism with the disgruntled, expatriated Laozi teaching in India.[14]

As in-betweenness, China constitutes a phenomenal chiasm as a seamless connection in the Void. Self and other, inside and outside, individual and society meld into the flesh of civilization. Nonverbal communication through meditation, the renunciation of meaning, and the rejection of identity principles leave us with neither rational nor dialectical thought but with *dipolar* thought. Dipolarity holds two mutually dependent, oppositely charged entities together by forging an invisible whole. Roger Ames calls this "polarism." Ames observes: "By 'polarism,' I am referring to a symbiosis: the unity of two organismic processes which require each other as a necessary condition for being what they are. In this paradigm, each existent is autogenerative and self-determinate. Each participant in existence is 'so-of-itself.'"[15] Obviously, yin and yang are good examples of dipolarity or polarism, linked and oppositely valenced as woman-man or dark-light or absence-presence. As a synonym, Hwa Yol Jung employs the term "diatactics" as "the logic of ontological difference": "The term *diatactics* . . . [is] *the logic of correlating* two (or more) disparate phenomena as complementary. As it is spelled dia/*tactics,* moreover, it arouses literally the intimate sense of touch (tactility) and broadly the interplay of the senses including the incorporation of mind and body."[16] In describing the dipolarity of yin and yang, Jung likens diatactics to Merleau-Ponty's "hyperdialectic ambiguity," the twice going round that preserves the ontological difference rather than dissolve it in the name of identity.[17]

The Asian body is not strictly the body of the West. It is not an anatomical configuration of organs. The Chinese body is a matrix of energy lines, something like Merleau-Ponty's *chiasm* or *khora*—the crossings of experience between subject and object (see VI 130–55, 266).[18] The physical organ is a token that connects to energy meridians that link the stars to the body to society to writing. The Chinese character for meridian (C. *jing*) also means scroll or book, as in the Daoist *Yijing*.

The old Chinese character represents a skein of silk guided by the banks of a river. Writing is confluent with the way of the water.

Bringing Merleau-Ponty into a cosmological scheme, the body is a complex intersection of energy lines suspended between Heaven and Earth. Likewise with Chinese writing: "Characters are born from ink, ink is born from water; water is the blood of characters."[19] John Hay tells us that writing itself has a body, a bone, a sinew, and flesh, connecting us to the energy of the clouds. Chinese calligraphers often held their pens to the clouds to absorb the universal body of energy (C. *lingqi*) before beginning a day's work: "Brush strokes have 'bones' and 'arteries,' characters have 'skeletons' and 'sinews.'"[20] The entire cosmogony of Chinese life from Heaven to Earth, from city to country, from society to the individual is connected through meridians of vapor that "manifests" through writing. The ancient Chinese character *zang* means "viscera" or a "storehouse." In its Buddhist reading, it refers to holy books, scrolls, or scriptures. Together with the ancient Chinese character *xiang* as "manfestation" or "icon," it means "visceral manifestation" (C. *zangxiang*). Nathan Sivin calls this "orbisiconography":

> Anatomy is concerned with the organism as a structure of parts, and orbisiconography (tsang-hsiang [*zangxiang*]) with the dynamic interplay of what is best described as a number of functional systems. Any normal Chinese-English dictionary, for instance, will define *kan* simply as "liver." In medicine (as opposed to, say, cooking) this word seldom refers to the physical organ, but rather to the energetic sphere ("orb") which the organ serves as a material substratum.[21]

Recalling Merleau-Ponty, both Buddhism and Daoism live under the spell of the metaphor of the body that defines their life-worlds.

MERLEAU-PONTY'S IN-BETWEENNESS BODY

As I have discussed elsewhere,[22] the ancient Chinese body navigates between Buddhist and Daoist imagery. It includes three overlaps: (1) the complete body as process; (2) the in-betweenness body of yin/yang and Heaven/Earth; and (3) the crossing/intertwining body of propriety/righteousness. Heaven-Void-Earth as Nothing-Emptiness-Being is corporealized by the complete-in-betweenness-crossing/intertwining body. The complete body seems more or less to align with Confucianism in its perfection of virtuous rotations; the in-between body seems more or less to align with Buddhism in its ephemeral take on life; the crossing/intertwining body seems to align with Daoism in its struggle for corporeal longevity. Merleau-Ponty's idea of the body falls between the Buddhist and the Daoist bodies. The following chart summarizes these configurations:

Heaven (*tian*)	Nothing (*wu*)	complete body (*shen*)	Confucianism
Void (*kong*)	Emptiness (*kong*)	in-betweenness body (*xing*)	Buddhism
Earth (*di*)	Being (*you*)	crossings/intertwinings body (*ti*)	Daoism

These three bodies represent a threefold scenario of Heaven-Void-Earth.

The first idea of the body was *shen*, the "entire psychosomatic person," a "lived body" as found in *Daodejing*. Roger Ames explains that *shen* links up to homophones meaning "stretching out," "extending," or "spirit."[23] As a complete body, *shen* aligns with Heaven. To be in Heaven is to reside in a state of balanced harmony. The complete body connected to *xin*, the heart-mind. Hence, the Chinese self is an inextricable crossing of body-person (*shen*) and heart-mind (*xin*).[24] The second idea of body is *xing*, which is "the form or shape, the three-dimensional disposition or configuration of the human process."[25] This body-self stands between Heaven and Earth, between yin and yang. As a body of in-betweenness, it resides in the Buddhist Void. The Void of East Asian life parallels Merleau-Ponty's "intertwining" or "chiasm." The Chinese "betweenness" of self is not merely a physical body but a phenomenology of existential intertwinings, between Heaven and Earth, between one and another, between idea and thing. The third idea of body is *ti* or physical bones. *Ti* is closely connected, as Ames relates, with the Confucian virtue *li* (propriety, decorum). This body aligns with Earth. The body mediates the Confucian virtues of propriety (C. *li*) and righteousness (C. *yi*). Interestingly, the homophone for the three Chinese bodies *shen, xing, ti* (spirit, form, and body) also means "immortality" as *shen, xing, ti*. The Chinese character for the "immortality" (C. *xian*) consists of a person (C. *ren*) and a mountain (C. *shan*), that is, an immortal is a person being like a mountain.

In a proto-Merleau-Pontean description, R. H. Mathews explains *ti* as "The Body. The whole person. The trunk; the limbs. . . . The essentials of; the substance of . . . Thickness. Style."[26] *Ti* as the body of social responsibility brings shape to a person's character and generates a thickness of skin. Likewise, Merleau-Ponty writes: "[T]hickness of flesh between the seer and the thing is constitutive for the thing of its visibility as for the seer of his corporeity" (VI 135). Like the Buddhist view, Merleau-Ponty's body is neither "spiritual" nor "material" nor "mind" nor "substance" (VI 139); it rests in-between, as Merleau-Ponty writes: "There is a body of the mind, a mind of the body and a chiasm between them" (VI 259). Wu explains that the difference between Merleau-Ponty and Chinese body-thinking is the difference between "argumentative self-critical clarification" and "spontaneous praxis."[27] He insists that after Merleau-Ponty exposes the flesh of the world, he should "*forget* about it all . . . as in Chuang Tzu's cool self-loss and roaming nonchalance in the world."[28]

As a "middle kingdom" (C. *zhongguo*), China floats between Heaven and Earth. The Buddhist occupies the Void between Heaven (nothingness) and Earth (Being), the invisible and the visible, the unreal and the real. By sinking into the middle, the Buddhist would always be in the right position for moral rectitude. The above chart is encapsulated in the Tiantai Buddhist expression, *kong, jia, zhong*—unreality, reality, the mean doctrine.[29] Emptiness as the middle doctrine eliminates both extremes of unreality (noumenon) and reality (phenomenon).

The myopic Buddhist monk thinks he sees flies in his begging bowl. His illusion is real although the flies are not. All phenomena are the same. Why try to champion the real over the false when all existence is merely empty? While phenomenal concerns are ephemeral, emptiness alone remains. The person of emptiness is the person of moral stature. The equiprimordiality of these phenomenological crossings in Buddhist co-origination parallels Merleau-Ponty's idea of the gaze, the "thickness" between seer and thing. As he writes: "The flesh is . . . midway between the spatio-temporal individual and the idea, a sort of incarnate principle that brings a style of being wherever there is a fragment of being. The flesh is in this sense an 'element' of Being" (VI 135, 139).

MERLEAU-PONTY'S SPATIAL SYNCRETISM AND QING LITERATURE

As such, Merleau-Ponty facilitates an understanding of the phenomenological melding of Daoism and Buddhism in Qing China (1644–1912). While various types of religious and philosophical Daoisms flourished, four major forms of Mahāyāna Buddhism were prevalent: Chan (Meditation), Tiantai, Jingtu (Pure Land), and Huayan (Flowery Splendor). Although long traditions established their uniqueness, they were collectively known as "Buddhism." Richard Smith writes: "Indicative of both the syncretic capacity of traditional Chinese thought and the accommodating outlook of Mahayana Buddhism, the Chinese had a common saying: 'The Tiantai and Huayan Schools for [metaphysical] doctrine and the Jingtu and Chan schools for practice.'"[30] Merleau-Ponty's chiasm helps interpret the Chinese phenomenal body as layerings upon layerings of Confucian, Daoist, and Buddhist thought.

Not only did Buddhism harmonize the disputes between Confucianism and Daoism but it also was a "correlational diatactics"[31] in its transformational nature. Even the Ming Confucian Wang Yangming became "a Buddhist in disguise."[32] The Buddhist concept of *kong* (emptiness) was equated with the Daoist *wu* (nothingness). Qing was a period of Buddhist and Daoist rejuvenation; it was a floating life as Shen Fu elaborates in his *Six Records of the Floating Life*, where one spends life dreaming about meandering clouds and watching lotus blossoms float on ponds.

As an artistic recluse, the Manzhou Emperor Qian Long secretly supported scholars such as Cao Xueqin (c. 1715–1763/1764) or Shen Fu, who fictionally critiqued the society while resuscitating ancient Chinese philosophical cornerstones. As a Buddhist and Daoist story of metaphor and allegory, Cao's *Dream of the Red Chamber* expresses meaning by means of other meaning. Readers needed conceptual grids to pass over the text. Buddhism, Daoism, and Confucianism afforded ready-made bodies of analyses as they were inscribed into daily concerns, household matters, festivals, and marketplace activities.

Phenomenologically speaking, *Red Chamber* is a mother's womb, a choral birth chamber. Whereas the Greek concept of "metaphor" refers to bearing across ideas from one plane to another, the Chinese world metaphor (C. *yinyu*) relies on revelation of the concealed; whereas the Greek *allegoria* (allegory) "speaks otherwise" to a configuration of images, the Chinese *yuyan* or *fengyu* refer to the clarification of language and its intentions; whereas the Greek inspired "hermeneutics" recalls the messenger god (Hermes) bringing the news, the Chinese *jieshi* relies on the breaking down (analysis) of the message. Merleau-Ponty helps move from the Greek to the Chinese here. Whereas we see a speech/idea alignment in the Greek, we see a Merleau-Pontean corporeality of speech in the Chinese: "hidden" places, "residence" of language, and "analysis" as a somatic "solution."

Comparatively, the heavenly stone in *Red Chamber* and the stone monkey in *Journey to the West* recite a long list of the visible and the invisible within the Chinese body.[33] The stone of *Red Chamber* (also known as *The Story of The Stone*) is intriguing because it shifts symbolism from a fertility icon of "healing" "cosmic" energy into a stone of unknowing, "a new fictional persona" somewhere between "ignorance" and "divine intelligence."[34] This stone is a "liminal" entity, a question mark that leads to a conceptual threshold, reminiscent of Merleau-Ponty's phenomenology of perception. Wang Jing explains:

> The *Dream* and the *Journey* have long served as the two most celebrated showcases of a narrative mode that breaks down all the boundaries between the human and the animal, between the immortals' and monsters' domains, between mythical and mimetic discourse, and finally, between Confucianism, Buddhism, and Taoism. . . . I would include a final set of marginality—the stony mode of thinking—embodied in the ambivalent psychic makeup of Pao-yu [*sic*] and Wu-k'ung [*sic*]. Half heavenly creatures and half earthbound, half beastly or inanimate and half human, these two heroes manifest shifting phases of marginal existence. Caught in the precarious equilibrium between the conscious and the unconscious, Pao-yu [*sic*] and Wu-k'ung [*sic*] continue to talk in a double-voice ambiguity that is built on the paradox of knowing and unknowing.[35]

The "double-voice ambiguity" of the wise fool, echoing Merleau-Ponty's double-go-round of ambiguity,[36] finds its enunciation in the playful dialogues of *Red Chamber*'s Buddhist monk and Daoist priest who contemplate Bao Yu's journey to Heaven and the stone's journey to Earth. The thickness of self and other extends into the mythical realm of the invisible. The shared body is a twofold doubling: Buddhism strives for the next life while Daoism tries to prolong this one. Written in the late Ming Dynasty, *Journey to the West* was even the subject of the Tokugawa woodblock artist Hokusai.[37] It collects four personifications: Tripitaka the uncertain monk, Monkey the scheming trickster, Sandy the steadfast warrior, and Pigsy the unbridled glutton.[38] These four incarnations are layers of the Buddhist meditative body. Their diverse configurations make for exciting times during the search for the secret scrolls of wisdom in the West. Merleau-Ponty's "spatial syncretism" is a useful idea in explicating this fourfold body as "a presence of the same psychic being in several spatial points, a presence of me in the other and the other in me."[39] Consequently, the Buddhist and Daoist liminal world that Wang describes as "womb and tomb" melds with Merleau-Ponty's "the hollow in which time is formed,"[40] or even into Zhuangzi's "the multitudes of hollows . . . made empty" (BC 136).

IKI (ESSENTIAL SPIRIT) AND MERLEAU-PONTY'S GAZE

No one better anticipates the intersection of Merleau-Ponty's "hollow" and East Asian thought than the Japanese philosopher Kuki Shūzō, an expert on both phenomenology and Buddhism. Having studied in Germany with Heidegger and Edmund Husserl, Kuki returned to France where he gave Jean Paul Sartre a copy of Heidegger's 1927 book *Being and Time*. Kuki's 1928 Paris lectures greatly influenced the French intellectual scene. It is quite possible that Merleau-Ponty attended Kuki's lectures. The ideas of "thickness" of being, "double" ambiguity, and "retrograde" time as familiar terms for regular readers of Merleau-Ponty might have found their motivation in use by Kuki.[41] In *The Structure of Iki*, Kuki examines the term *iki*. In Tokugawa, it meant refinement, spirit, purity; today it refers to style or chicness.[42] When he speaks of the fleeting layerings of *iki*, he retains the Japanese characters (*hiragana*); otherwise he relies on other Chinese characters (J. *kanji*) for the representation of essential spirit (J. *iki*) or its running mate *sui* (purity), especially in relation to *bushido* (warrior spirit).[43] Resurrecting the Confucian era's idea of the scholar-knight, the Japanese empower the Chinese character for scholar to also mean warriors (J. *samurai*).

When the samurai moves forward, time moves with each step. As the Buddhist monk Dōgen relates, his body is a being-time (J. *uji*)[44] or, as Merleau-Ponty might say, a "time in being." He carries the four virtues with him: rectitude, valiance, honor, and charity. Yet his footsteps disappear in the snow behind him as he moves toward his own death.

Kuki concentrates on *iki* in the latter part of Tokugawa, the Bunka-Bunsei (early 1800s), where it applied mostly to the town merchants of Edo.[45] He creates a phenomenal body between the detached gallantry of *bushido* and the emotionless abandonment (*akirame*) of Zen Buddhism. That body displays its physical apparatus in the "floating world" of Yoshiwara, the "gay quarters" of Edo. The site for his corporeal discourse on moments of *iki* is that of *geisha*. The *geisha* were forbidden by Tokugawa law to take money for sexual favors. Kuki's site, then, is far removed from the present day. Given the thrust of his argument, we might take *iki* a little further back into the Genroku period (early 1700s), the time of "The Treasury of Loyal Retainers" (*Chushingura*) that challenged both samurai pride and Edo rituals. The floating world (J. *ukiyo*) of Genroku was a misty demi-monde, an escape from daily worries and probably the most creative period in Japanese culture. It was a phenomenal body where the walker walked the boundless boundary. Whereas Shen Fu and Bau Yu's "floating life" was a state of mind, the *ukiyo* was a physical place to make dreams. The courtesan's walk is a perfect example of the relationships engendered by Kuki's coquettishness (J. *bitai*). Anticipating Merleau-Ponty's gaze as "the thickness of the look and of the body" (VI 135), Ihara Saikaku (1642–1693) writes:

> A courtesan, also, has many special ways of walking. When she sallies forth, she usually wears no socks and adopts a floating walk; on reaching the house of assignation, she trips in nimbly; in the parlour she uses the soft-footed gait; this followed by a hasty gait as she goes up the stairs. When it comes to leaving, she lets the servant arrange her sandals for her and slips them on without even looking; in the street she walks with her head held high and does not step aside for anyone.[46]

The courtesan becomes the walk and the look; the look and the walk becomes the courtesan. As Merleau-Ponty might say, the "self" flows into the other of the onlookers' gaze. There is no boundary between the two. The invisible betweenness is *iki*. The object of her gaze is her flesh. She floats as she walks. This is her *bitai* as a moment of *iki*. In his early account, "Geisha," Kuki writes: "It is important to know that in order to become a *geisha*, a rigorous examination in music and dance must be undergone. The ideal of the *geisha* at once moral and aesthetic, that which is called *iki*, is a harmonious union of voluptuousness and nobility."[47] For Kuki, as for the floating world of Tokugawa, dreams are empirical, given that the "floating world" is real. This Buddhist inspired argument is a precursor of Merleau-Ponty's proclamation on "floating realities" that is worth stating again:

> The destruction of beliefs, the symbolic murder of the others and of the world, the split between vision and the visible, between thought and being do not, as they claim, establish us in the negative; when one has subtracted all that, one installs oneself in what remains, in sensations, opinions. And what remains is not nothing, nor of another sort than what has been struck off: what remains are mutilated fragments of the vague *omnitudo realitatis* against which the doubt was plied, and they regenerate it under other names—appearance, dream, Psyche, representation. It is in the name and for the profit of these floating realities that the solid reality is cast into doubt. (VI 105–6)

Saikaku's courtesan (*agejoro*) upholds Confucian virtues through the flattering art and urban refinement and elegance (*akanukeshita*).[48] Courtesanship is one of the pure realms of *iki*. As a scholar and calligrapher, the amorous woman creates a Buddhist body of decorum around her despite fate's cruel turn, similar to Merleau-Ponty's body phenomenology. Close yet so far, she grasps at *sabi* (loneliness of near awakening).

Like the Chinese scholars whom he so closely studied, Kuki intertwines Buddhism and Daoism, exploring their mutual interlocking and great divergences. His interaction with Heidegger anticipates a Merleau-Pontean phenomenology. His influence in France in the 1920s was sure to have rubbed off on Merleau-

Ponty in later years. For him, *bushido*, as Japan's great "ethic," holds fast to its code as described by the linguist Motoori Norinaga: "Its ideal consists only in living and dying the 'cherry blossom, exhaling its perfume in the morning light.'"[49] Motoori's phrase is reminiscent of Lord Asano's *Chushingura* death poem, "the cherry blossom is more beautiful when it falls than in full bloom." In Kuki's corporealization of Buddhist aesthetics, art releases the visible for the invisible; art disrupts its physical habits in order to grasp emptiness. For Kuki, Laozi captures the aesthetic of Japanese painting from *Daodejing*: "That which is incomplete will be entire, that which is empty will be filled."[50] The unifying gestures of yin/yang in Laozi's "breath of the void" is a gentle swish of the artist's brush: "The breath of the void, it is the brushstroke. Here wreathed in haze a mountain brings itself to life; there a river gleams; here is a dreaming moon; there a cloud hiding all. The taste for simplicity and for fluidity arises from nostalgia for the infinite and from the effort to efface differences in space."[51]

Doubling Tokugawa into the present day, Oida Yoshi, an internationally renowned *nōh* and *kabuki* theatre performer and movie star, offers a Merleau-Pontean view of *iki*. He proclaims the appearance and disappearance of the actor's body. When Oida was a child, he pretended to be a ninja. He tried to be "invisible" in front of people. As a performer, he "disappears" in front of viewers rather than "perform" for them. The best actor is the one who does not act. The awakened audience must "forget" that there is an actor.[52] Oida's Buddhist story could easily have been written by Merleau-Ponty. The monk-sage responds to the question "Who am I?" with the answer "You are a plate":

> The sage chose the symbols of "plate" and "offerings," to clarify the difference between *Yu* (existence) and *Mu* (nothing). *Yu* is like "phenomenon"; it is the visible effect of action. We see it, hear it, recognize it. It is like the precious objects offered to the gods. *Mu* is like "form"; it is difficult to detect, yet it gives rise to the diversity of phenomenon. In describing his student as a plate, the sage was reminding him of this deeper level of existence. In the same way, the invisible part of the actor is the plate that gives rise to and supports the visible action of the performance. You don't notice its presence. Only its absence.[53]

Once again, we think of Merleau-Ponty's "certain absence, a negativity that is not nothing" (VI 151). The plate disappears into the Void as it stands between nothingness and being. Oida continues: "Consider the Heart Sutra in Buddhism. It says: 'phenomenon is emptiness and emptiness is phenomenon.' In a sense, everything arises from 'emptiness' or 'nothingness.' You admire the beauty of blossoms on a tree. But if you slash open the tree to discover what creates this beauty, you will find 'nothing.'"[54] The Japanese for stage (*butai*) means the stage of dance. Stage or platform can also mean body (*tai*) as used for ancient Chinese pronouns. The stage as a platform for the body makes the human body "the blood of the dancing body."[55] The making and unmaking of the phenomenon is the "place" of the Void where "things" appear and disappear in the chiasm, as Merleau-Ponty might say.

CONCLUSION

The floating worlds of China in the Qing Dynasty and Japan in the Tokugawa Shogunate offer examples of literature and philosophy through the influence of Buddhism and Daoism, which constitute a "body-thinking," as Wu suggests. They connect the visible and invisible and the silent and the spoken as Merleau-Ponty theorizes. Heaven and Earth are connected through the Void that illuminates the concealed in a way allowing beings to be. Literature and poetry become "the thickness" of being that permits the move from dream to waking state to dream. East Asia resides not in what is spoken but in what is unspoken, an undefined, invisible body of phenomenal place, like the empty center of a Buddhist *gong'an* or a Daoist wheel, emanating vitality from an empty source. The spoken and the silent meld into a fleshy hollow of communication, which is not limited by words. Merleau-Ponty is crucial to understanding the "double walk" of intersections between Buddhism and Daoism through his chiasmic encounters. In his typically gentle and indirect way, Merleau-Ponty shows us that we have much to learn from Buddhist and Daoist modes of philosophizing:

> Indian and Chinese philosophies have tried not so much to dominate existence as to be the echo or sounding board of our relationship to being. Western philosophy can learn from them to rediscover the relationship to being and initial option which gave it birth, and to estimate the possibilities we have shut ourselves off from in becoming "Westerners" and perhaps reopen them.[56]

Notes

INTRODUCTION

1. Maurice Merleau-Ponty, "Avant-Porpos," *Les Philosophes célèbres* (Paris: Editions d'art Lucien Mazenod, 1956), 7. English translation of "Avant-Propos" and other section introductions from *Les Philosophes célèbres*, "Everywhere and Nowhere," *Signs* (1960), trans. Richard C. McCleary (Evanston, IL: Northwestern University Press, 1964), 126–58, 126.

2. Merleau-Ponty, "Everywhere and Nowhere," 135.

3. Merleau-Ponty, "Everywhere and Nowhere," 138.

4. Merleau-Ponty, "Everywhere and Nowhere," 138.

5. Maurice Merleau-Ponty, *The Phenomenology of Perception*, trans. Colin Smith (London: Routledge, 1962), vii.

6. Merleau-Ponty, *The Phenomenology of Perception*, vii.

7. Merleau-Ponty, *The Phenomenology of Perception*, xv.

8. Merleau-Ponty, *The Phenomenology of Perception*, 95.

9. Maurice Merleau-Ponty, *The Primacy of Perception, and Other Essays on Phenomenological Psychology, the Philosophy of Art, History, and Politics*, trans. James M. Edie (Evanston, IL: Northwestern University Press, 1964), 12.

10. This is also translated into "dependent origination" or "mutual interdependence."

11. Merleau-Ponty, *The Phenomenology of Perception*, 214.

12. Merleau-Ponty, *The Phenomenology of Perception*, 214.

13. Merleau-Ponty, *The Phenomenology of Perception*, 357.

14. Merleau-Ponty, *The Phenomenology of Perception*, 420.

15. David Shaner, *The Bodymind Experience in Japanese Buddhism: A Phenomenological Study of Kūkai and Dōgen* (Albany: State University of New York Press, 1985).

16. Dōgen, "Ikka myōju," *Shōbōgenzō 1*, ed. Kōshirō Tamaki, 105–20 (Tokyo: Daizōshuppan, 1993), 115.

17. Shigenori Nagatomo, *Attunement through the Body* (Albany: State University of New York Press, 1992), 113.

18. For a further discussion of "unilateral intentional arc," see chapter 11.

19. David Shaner calls the former "third-order bodymind awareness" and the latter "first-order bodymind awareness"; Shaner, *The Bodymind Experience in Japanese Buddhism*, 48.

20. Thomas Kasulis, *Zen Action/Zen Person* (Honolulu: University of Hawai'i Press, 1981), 73.

21. Kasulis, *Zen Action/Zen Person*, 73.

22. Shaner, *The Bodymind Experience in Japanese Buddhism*, 48.

23. Daisetz Teitaro Suzuki, trans., *The Laṅkāvatāra Sūtra: A Mahāyāna Text* (Delhi: Motilal Banarsidass Publishers, 2003), 123–24. The *Sūtra* states: "It is said by the Blessed One that from the night of the Enlightenment until the night of the Parinirvana, the Tathagata in the meantime has not uttered even a word, nor will he ever utter; for not speaking is the Buddha's speaking."

24. Scholars have contended that the passages, instead of being a creation of Bodhidharma, had developed into the current format in the process of Zen Buddhism's attempts to create its own identity. The passage consisting of sixteen Chinese characters was not put together until the time when Zen Buddhism was established as an independent school, as Peter Gregory states: "These different lines were not subsumed together into a unified vision of the tradition as a whole until the end of the period with the writings of Tsung-mi (780–841)—but even that remained only another contending claim when it was put forth" (Peter Gregory and Daniel Gets, ed., *Buddhism in the Sung* [Honolulu: University of Hawai'i Press, 1999], 4). According to Griffith T. Foulk, it was not until 1108 that all four lines appeared together (Griffith T. Foulk, "Myth, Ritual, and Monastic Practice in Sung Ch'an Buddhism," in *Religion and Society in T'ang and Sung China*, ed. Patricia Buckley Ebrey and Peter N. Gregory [Honolulu: University of Hawai'i Press, 1995], 155 and 199n16).

25. Maurice Merleau-Ponty, "On the Phenomenology of Language," in *Signs*, 84–97, 84.

26. Jacques Lacan, *The Four Fundamental Concepts of Psycho-Analysis* (1973), trans. Alan Sheridan (New York: W. W. Norton & Co., Ltd., 1981), 20.

27. Merleau-Ponty, "On the Phenomenology of Language," 88.

28. Merleau-Ponty, "On the Phenomenology of Language," 89.

29. Merleau-Ponty, "On the Phenomenology of Language," 91.

30. Nishida Kitarō, "Kōiteki chokkan" (Acting Intuition), *Nishida Kitarō zenshū* (Collected Works of Nishida Kitarō), volume 8 (Tokyo: Iwanami Shoten, 1988), 541–71.

31. James Hatley, "Introduction: Interrogating Ethics," in *Interrogating Ethics: Embodying the Good in Merleau-Ponty*, ed. James Hatley, Janice McLane, and Christian Diehm (Pittsburgh: Duquesne University Press, 2006), 1.

32. Maurice Merleau-Ponty, "Introduction," in *Signs*, 35.

33. Merleau-Ponty, "Introduction," in *Signs*, 35.

34. Hugh J. Silverman, "Introduction," in *Philosophy and Non-philosophy since Merleau-Ponty*, ed. Hugh J. Silverman (Evanston, IL: Northwestern University Press, 1997), 1–7, 4.

CHAPTER 1

1. (Trans.) Following Merleau-Ponty, Hyong-hyo Kim uses the expression *la pensée de survol* several times in this chapter. Alphonso Lingis, the English translator of *The Visible and the Invisible*, makes a note on this expression as follows: "Merleau-Ponty likes to

call the unsituated point of view of objectivist thought a *pensée de survol*—'a high-altitude thinking' as (Benita Eisler translates in John-Paul Sartre's *Situations* [New York, 1965], 229)" (Maurice Merleau-Ponty, *The Visible and the Invisible*, trans. Alphonso Lingis [Evanston, IL: Northwestern University Press, 1968], 13 ff 7). In this translation, I follow the precedent and translate *la pensée de survol* as "a high-altitude thinking." Throughout the notes, any notes for which the translator is responsible are preceded with "(Trans.)."

2. (Trans.) *L'exigence ontologique* is also translated into the "ontological need."

3. Maurice Merleau-Ponty, *Le Visible et l'invisible* [hereafter Vi] (Paris: Gallimard, 1964), 107. (Trans.) English translation by Alphonso Lingis, *The Visible and the Invisible* (Evanston, IL: Northwestern University Press, 1968), 76 [hereafter VI]. Citations from these texts will be marked in the text with the above abbreviations, followed by page numbers.

4. (Trans.) Fazang, 華嚴策林 T 45.1872.597a‑598a, 598a.

5. Maurice Merleau-Ponty, *Phénoménologie de la perception* [hereafter Pp] (Paris: Gallimard, 1945), 382–83. (Trans.) English translation by Colin Smith, *Phenomenology of Perception* [hereafter PhP] (London: Routledge, 1962), 331–32.

6. Maurice Merleau-Ponty, "L'homme et l'adversité," in *Signes* (Paris: Gallimard, 1960), 292. (Trans.) English translation by Richard C. McCleary, "Man and Adversity," in *Signs* (Evanston, IL: Northwestern University Press, 1964), 230.

7. (Trans.) In Korean, both *rien* and *néant* are translated into the same Korean expression *mu*. In the English translation used here, the former is translated as "nothing" and the latter as "nothingness."

CHAPTER 2

1. For an introduction to Yasuo Yuasa's life and work, see Manabu Watanabe, "In Memoriam: Yuasa Yasuo 1925–2005," *Nanzan Institute for Religions and Culture Bulletin* 30 (2006): 55–61; Erin McCarthy, "Yuasa Yasuo 1925–2005: A Retrospective of His Life and Work," *Religious Studies Review* 33, no. 3 (July 2007): 201–8.

2. For a discussion of Yuasa's approach to the relationship between religion and science, see David Shaner, Shigenori Nagatomo, and Yasuo Yuasa, *Science and Comparative Philosophy: Introducing Yuasa* (Leiden: E. J. Brill, 1989).

3. See especially Yasuo Yuasa, "Shūkyō tetsugaku" (Philosophy of Religion), in *Yuasa Yasuo zenshū* (The Collected Works of Yasuo Yuasa), volume 2 (Tokyo: Hakua Shobō, 2000), 6–267.

4. Yasuo Yuasa, *Shūkyōkeiken to shintai* (Religious Experience and the Body) (Tokyo: Iwanami Shoten, 1997), 60.

5. David Shaner, *The Bodymind Experience in Japanese Buddhism: A Phenomenological Study of Kūkai and Dōgen* (Albany: State University of New York Press, 1985).

6. Dōgen, *Shōbōgenzō 1*, ed. Kōshirō Tamaki (Tokyo: Daizōshuppan, 1993), 94; Yasuo Yuasa, *Shintairon: Tōyōteki shinjinron to gendai* (The Theory of the Body: East Asian Mind Body Theory and Contemporary World) (Tokyo: Kōdansha Gakujutsu Bunko, 1992), 147. See also Yasuo Yuasa, *The Body: Toward an Eastern Mind-Body Theory*, trans. Shigenori Nagatomo and T. Kasulis (Albany: State University of New York Press, 1987), 116.

7. Dōgen, *Shōbōgenzō 1*, 95. Yuasa, *Shintairon*, 147. See also Yuasa, *The Body*, 116.

8. Yasuo Yuasa, *Ki, shugyō, shintai* (Ki-energy, Self-Cultivation, and Body) (Tokyo: Hirakawa Shuppansha, 1986), 62. See also Yasuo Yuasa, *The Body, Self-Cultivation, and*

Ki, trans. Shigenori Nagatomo and Monte S. Hull (Albany: State University of New York Press, 1993), 37.

9. Yuasa, *Ki, shugyō, shintai*, 62. See also Yuasa, *The Body, Self-Cultivation, and Ki*, 37.

10. In his translation of the *Secret of the Golden Flower* (*Taiyi jinhua zongzhi* 太一金華宗旨), Richard Wilhelm renders *hun* as "animus" and *po* as "anima." He states that "[i]n any case, animus (*hun*) is the light, yang-soul, while anima (*po*) [*sic*] is the dark, yin-soul"; Richard Wilhelm, "A Discussion of the Text," in *Secret of the Golden Flower: A Chinese Book of Life*, trans. Richard Wilhelm (San Diego: Harcourt Brace Jovanovich Publishers, 1962), 15.

11. Yasuo Yuasa, *Shintai no uchūsei* (The Cosmology of Body) (Tokyo: Iwanami Shoten, 1994), 9.

12. Yuasa, "Shūkyō tetsugaku," 79.

13. Shaner, *The Bodymind Experience in Japanese Buddhism*, 111.

14. Kūkai as quoted in Yuasa, *Shintairon*, 209. See also Yuasa, *The Body*, 156.

15. Yuasa, *Shintairon*, 208. See also Yuasa, *The Body*, 155.

16. Shaner, *The Bodymind Experience in Japanese Buddhism*, 110.

17. Shaner, *The Bodymind Experience in Japanese Buddhism*, 110.

18. Yuasa, *Shintairon*, 181. See also Yuasa, *The Body*, 137.

19. Yuasa, *Shintairon*, 186. See also Yuasa, *The Body*, 141.

20. Yuasa, *Ki, shugyō, shintai*, 286.

21. He explains that "[i]ndividuation means precisely the better and more complete fulfillment of the collective qualities of the human being"; Carl Jung, *Two Essays in Analytical Psychology: The Collected Works of C. G. Jung*, volume 7, trans. R. F. C. Hull (Princeton, NJ: Princeton University Press, 1977), 173–74. The goal of this process he refers to alternatively as the "mana-personality" (ibid., 227) and the "self " (ibid., 177). In other places he also uses the expressions "the *coincidentia oppositorum*" and "the *unus munus*"; see Carl Jung, *Mysterium Conjunctionis: The Collected Works of C. G. Jung*, volume 14, trans. R. F. C. Hull (Princeton, NJ: Princeton University Press, 1977).

22. Shigenori Nagatomo, *Attunement through the Body* (Albany: State University of New York Press, 1992), 177–254.

23. For a more detailed elaboration of this bidirectional intentionality, see chapter 12.

24. Nagatomo, *Attunement through the Body*, 222–54.

25. Ibid., 113.

26. Nagatomo prefers "living body" over "lived body" (*le corps vécu*) since he believes that the latter term indicates that the tension between mind and body has not been resolved and thus implies a residual dualism; Nagatomo, *Attunement through the Body*, 16.

27. Yuasa, *Shūkyōkeiken to shintai*, 122.

28. Yuasa, *Shūkyōkeiken to shintai*, 121.

29. Yuasa, *Shūkyōkeiken to shintai*, 127.

30. Yuasa, *Shintairon*, 204.

31. Yuasa, *Ki, shugyō, shintai*, 70–85. See also Yuasa, *The Body*, 42–54.

32. Yuasa, *Ki, shugyō, shintai*, 168–75. See also Yuasa, *The Body*, 118–21.

33. One could push this comparative approach even further and look for commonalities between the four layers of the body and Jung's four psychological complexes. Not only can the first two layers be identified with the conscious dimension and layers 3 and 4 with the unconscious ones, it may be further possible to suggest that layers 1 and 4 are collective to some degree, not unlike Jung's *persona* and *anima/us*, while the middle two layers seem personal in nature such as the *ego* and the *shadow*.

34. I am using this term to articulate Merleau-Ponty's conviction that perception constitutes an activity and presupposes an intentional engagement with the environment; Gereon Kopf, *Beyond Personal Identity: Dōgen, Nishida, and a Phenomenology of No-Self* (Richmond: Curzon Press, 2001), 51.

35. Nishida Kitarō, "Kōiteki chokkan" (Acting Intuition), in *Nishida Kitarō zenshū* (Collected Works of Nishida Kitarō), volume 5 (Tokyo: Iwanami Shoten, 1988), 541–71.

36. Tetsurō Watsuji, "Genshi bukkyō to jissen tetsugaku" (Early Buddhism and a Philosophy of Practice), in *Watsuji Tetsurō zenshū dai go kan* (The Collected Works of Tetsurō Watsuji), volume 5 (Tokyo: Chikuma Shobō, 1995); Yasuo Yuasa, *Watsuji Tetsurō* (Tetsurō Watsuji), 123.

37. The term *vijñapti-mātra* identifies the central philosophy of one of the two basic Indian Mahāyāna Buddhist schools, Yogācāra Buddhism.

38. It is one of the basic tenets of Shingon Buddhism that the practice of *maṃḍala* meditation, the incantation of *dhāraṇī*, and the performance of specific hand positions (*mudrā*) are designed to purify the mind, the speech, and the body so that Great Sun Buddha (S. *Mahāvairocana*; J. *Dainichi Nyorai* 大日如来) will be manifested in the present body.

39. Maurice Merleau-Ponty, *Phénoménologie de la perception* (Paris: Gallimard, 1945), 114; Michel Henry, *Généalogie de la psychoanalyse* (Paris: Presses Universitaires de France, 1985).

40. See Yuasa's article on Descartes' *Meditations*: Yasuo Yuasa, "Wasureta dekaruto" (The Forgotten Descartes), in *Yuasa Yasuo zenshū daiyonkan* (The Collected Works of Yasuo Yuasa), volume 4 (Tokyo: Hakua Shobō, 2003), 231–69.

CHAPTER 3

1. Maurice Merleau-Ponty, *The Primacy of Perception*, trans. James M. Edie (Evanston, IL: Northwestern University Press, 1964), 16.

2. Maurice Merleau-Ponty, *Phenomenology of Perception*, trans. Colin Smith (London: Routledge, 1962), 85 [hereafter PhP].

3. PhP, 214–16.

4. T46.703c.

5. PhP, 216.

6. PhP, 254.

7. PhP, 428.

8. PhP, 430. Cf. 325: "In order to perceive things, we need to live them."

9. PhP, 430.

10. But one crucial adjustment must be made. From the Tiantai point of view, it is not quite adequate to simply say "there is *another* subject, an anonymous subject, a pre-subject, underneath my subjectivity, which already belongs to the world." The problem with this formulation is the *singularity* of the "other" subject which I am. This transposes the putative "oneness" that has just been displaced from my surface subjectivity, as if it resided elsewhere. But our point is that this "other subject" is precisely "the world" itself, and "the world" can never be a single synordinate world. The anonymous subject which acts, feels, perceives, wills, and thinks in my every single moment of experience is not any single unequivocal being with a particular unambiguous project of its own, e.g., some determinate orientation to the world. It is the "Three Thousand," all possible conflicting quiddities and expressions of quiddities, *each* of which can equally be read as the doer of my deeds, the seer of my sights,

the willer of my will. Merleau-Ponty, with his focus on the inseparability of ambiguity and being, is in a position to appreciate this, but his quasi-existentialist notion of a single "project," or consistent orientation to the world, coordinates all our relations into a single unambiguous narrative identity, or one way of "being-in-the-world" that corresponds to a particular unambiguous preunderstanding of the world, or mode of being-there.

11. PhP, 93.

12. Maurice Merleau-Ponty, *The Visible and the Invisible*, trans. Alphonso Lingis (Evanston, IL: Northwestern University Press, 1968), 147. Henceforth cited as VI.

13. VI, 148.

14. T46.783a.

15. T46.781a.

16. T46.784c.13–30.

17. Zhili makes this point about Avalokiteśvara:

> Avalokiteśvara has realized the dharma-nature of evil, and thus is free and at ease within evil. This is why he can freely and effortlessly respond to all difficulties experienced by sentient beings everywhere. The essential point is that all living beings and their environments are Avalokiteśvara's marvelous body and marvelous mind. All sentient beings create difficulties for themselves there within the sagely mind and matter; even the three types of karma which seek help are Avalokiteśvara himself. For this reason as soon as a stimulus appears, the response occurs immediately. If you constantly contemplate in this way, how could you fail to benefit all things together with Avalokiteśvara? (T34.956c)

This last rhetorical question points to the reversibility and performative twist to be discussed in a moment.

18. T46.782c.

19. It might be objected that this "inherence in each other," where the other is reducible to an element in the self and simultaneously the self is reducible to an element in the other, so that neither is ultimately reducible to the other, still undermines the most basic feature of our anxiety-ridden relations with others in a concrete intersubjective relation: that is, the sense of unknowability of the other, and especially of the way the other views and objectifies us, the unpredictability and uncontrollability of the other's attitude and treatment of us, so vividly and convincingly analyzed, for example, in the section on "Being for Others" in Sartre's *Being and Nothingness* (trans. Hazel Barnes [New York: Washington Square Books, 1966], 301–556). But it must be recalled that the general premise for the whole theory here is the "ungraspability" (C. *bukede* 不可得) of all dharmas whatsoever, which means, among other things, their ultimate unknowability and indeterminability. In Tiantai this means not that they are ultimately or really a blank, but that they are not ultimately even blank or not blank, and, in fact, that any determination made about them always falls out its own bottom into its opposite, and even the opposite of the dyad of it and its opposite, and so on. To be seen as a Buddha sees you is to be seen in every possible way at once, so that he always sees you also as the opposite of what you would like to be seen as, what you seem to yourself to really be, and so on. Indeed, this also implies that anytime you are misunderstood by other people, they are, to the extent that they are unknowing bodhisattvas viewing you, seeing something true about you, an aspect of yourself of which you were heretofore ignorant. Every idiotic misapprehension they have about you is the truth. The Buddha in your own mind is a concept of a viewer who views you thus (i.e., who from the standpoint of your own self-knowledge gets you all wrong, objectifies you not only as your body and your past as against your pure inner

uncertain subjectivity, as Sartre would have it, but even as every other possible form of objectivity). This, it seems to me, accounts for the eternal and constitutive element of anxiety and disparity, the split and alienation, in the relation that makes it still genuinely intersubjective.

20. Cf. Zhili's extensive treatment of this question in his subcommentary to Zhiyi's comment on the statement "This mind makes the Buddha, this mind is the Buddha" from the *Foshuoguanwuliangshoufojing* (佛說觀無量壽佛經 Visualization of Buddha Amitāyus Sūtra). Zhili takes this as indicating that the Buddha, like any other particular dharma, can be exclusively characterized neither as created by practice (*xiu* 修) or inherent in the nature of things (*xing* 性), and thus it is equally true to say that it is created by practice or that it is inherent in the nature of things, by the familiar Tiantai principle of "the nonduality of nature and practice." See T37.220b. Indeed, this self-verifying performativity of the concept of the Buddha, Tiantai's pragmatic equivalent of the ontological argument, can perhaps be viewed as a doctrinal basis for the Tiantai emphasis on Pure Land practices of reciting the name and visualizing the body and environment of Amitābha Buddha, for by thus thinking that there exists somewhere an all-seeing "Buddha" who sees us thinking that he exists, the Buddha we have always been is made to exist.

21. T46.452b.

22. T46.451c.

23. PhP, xiv.

24. T46.452a. In the *Jingangpi*, Zhanran asks rhetorically:

When the practitioner contemplates mind, is this mind an object? What are the samenesses and differences that allow them to be named seer and seen? When the practitioner contemplates mind, is this mind one or many? What are the samenesses and differences that pertain to oneness, manyness, mind and object in this case? When the practitioner contemplates mind, is he also contemplating the body? Is he also contemplating the environment? When the practitioner contemplates mind, he is enmeshed in delusion, karma and suffering. Are these within? Without? The same? Different? When the practitioner contemplates mind, is the Buddha-nature within this mind originally pure? Or does it become pure? When the practitioner contemplates mind, do the mind, Buddhas and sentient beings, all causes and effects, all bodies and environments, all dharmas and their marks intersubsume so that all are the same?

The point, obviously, is that to contemplate the mind is also to contemplate the body and the environment: seeing mind is seeing world.

25. Ibid., 314b; ibid., 214a.

26. Ibid., 214a.

27. T46.432a.

28. Maurice Merleau-Ponty, "Eye and Mind," in *The Primacy of Perception*, 167.

29. Merleau-Ponty, "Eye and Mind," 167.

30. VI, 135–36.

31. VI, 148.

32. VI, 136.

CHAPTER 4

1. Hee-Jin Kim, *Dōgen Kigen—Mystical Realist* (Tucson: University of Arizona Press, 1975), 128.

2. Maurice Merleau-Ponty, *Phenomenology of Perception*, trans. Colin Smith (London: Routledge, 1962), 236.

3. Francis Dojun Cook, trans., "Hotsu Mujō Shin," in *How to Raise an Ox* (Los Angeles: Center Publications, 1978), 120.

4. Cook, "Hotsu Mujō Shin," 121.

5. Merleau-Ponty, *Phenomenology of Perception*, 82.

6. Merleau-Ponty, *Phenomenology of Perception*, 130.

7. Norman Waddell and Abe Masao, trans., "One Bright Pearl: Dōgen's Shōbōgenzō Ikka Myōju," *The Eastern Buddhist* 4, no. 2 (October 1971): 113.

8. Merleau-Ponty, *Phenomenology of Perception*, 205.

9. Gary Brent Madison, *The Phenomenology of Merleau-Ponty* (Athens: Ohio University Press, 1981), 30.

10. Norman Waddell and Abe Masao, trans., "Dōgen's Shōbōgenzō Zenki 'Total Dynamic Working,' and Shōji, 'Birth and Death,'" *The Eastern Buddhist* 5, no. 1 (May 1972): 75.

11. Merleau-Ponty, *Phenomenology of Perception*, 167.

12. For a more complete discussion of the notion of element, see Madison, *The Phenomenology of Merleau-Ponty*, 176–77, and Remy C. Kwant, *From Phenomenology to Metaphysics: An Inquiry into the Last Period of Merleau-Ponty's Philosophical Life* (Pittsburg: Duquesne University Press, 1966), 62–63.

13. Maurice Merleau-Ponty, *The Visible and the Invisible*, trans. Alphonso Lingis (Evanston, IL: Northwestern University Press, 1968), 136. Three articles that discuss Merleau-Ponty's notion of flesh at length are Raymond J. Devettere, "The Human Body as Philosophical Paradigm in Whitehead and Merleau-Ponty," *Philosophy Today* 20 (Winter 1976): 317–26; Atherton C. Lowry, "The Invisible World of Merleau-Ponty," *Philosophy Today* 23 (Winter 1979): 294–303; and Francois H. Lapointe, "The Evolution of Merleau-Ponty's Concept of the Body," *Dialogos* (April 1974): 139–51.

14. Merleau-Ponty, *Phenomenology of Perception*, 403. James F. Sheridan Jr. notes the danger of this type of approach to the problem of consciousness in *Once More from the Middle: A Philosophical Anthropology* (Athens: Ohio University Press, 1973) when he writes: "[T]he temptation to found the conscious upon the pre-conscious, the deliberate upon the pre-predicative always leads us to run the risk of committing the error of making the indefinite fundamental and our formulation of the relation between indefiniteness and definiteness as the articulation of experience or as a development from the implicit to the explicit suffers from that temptation" (12).

15. Merleau-Ponty, *Phenomenology of Perception*, 297.

16. Madison, *The Phenomenology of Merleau-Ponty*, 55.

17. Norman Waddell and Abe Masao, trans., "Dōgen's Fukanzazengi and Shōbōgenzō zazengi," *The Eastern Buddhist* 6, no. 2 (October 1973): 123. For a comparison of Martin Heidegger and Dōgen on thinking, see my article titled "The Leap of Thinking: A Comparison of Heidegger and the Zen Master Dōgen," *Philosophy Today* 25 (Spring 1981): 55–62.

18. Merleau-Ponty, *Phenomenology of Perception*, 138–39.

19. See John D. Glenn Jr., "Merleau-Ponty and the Cogito," *Philosophy Today* 23 (Winter 1979): 310–20.

20. Norman Waddell and Abe Masao, trans., "Dōgen's Bendōwa," *The Eastern Buddhist* 4, no. 1 (May 1971): 146–47.

21. Merleau-Ponty, *Phenomenology of Perception*, 235

22. Norman Waddell and Abe Masao, trans., "Shōbōgenzō Genjōkōan," *The Eastern*

Buddhist 5, no. 2 (October 1972): 134.

23. Merleau-Ponty, *Phenomenology of Perception*, 203.

24. Norman Waddell and Abe Masao, trans., "Shōbōgenzō Buddha-Nature I," *The Eastern Buddhist* 8, no. 2 (October 1975): 103.

25. Merleau-Ponty, *Phenomenology of Perception*, 130.

26. Samuel B. Mallin, *Merleau-Ponty's Philosophy* (New Haven, CT: Yale University Press, 1979), 113.

27. Mallin, *Merleau-Ponty's Philosophy*, 20–21.

28. Merleau-Ponty, *The Visible and the Invisible*, 9.

29. Lapointe, "The Evolution of Merleau-Ponty's Concept of the Body," 148.

30. Norman Waddell and Abe Masao, trans., "The King of Samadhis Samadhi: Dōgen's Shōbōgenzō Sammai Ō Zammai," *The Eastern Buddhist* 7, no. 1 (May 1974): 121.

31. See T. Kasulis, *Zen Action/Zen Person* (Honolulu: University of Hawai'i Press, 1981), who notes that the term "molting" is to be preferred because it is a recurrent event (91).

32. Waddell and Abe, "Dōgen's Bendōwa," 134.

33. See Remy C. Kwant, *The Phenomenological Philosophy of Merleau-Ponty* (Pittsburgh: Duquesne University Pres, 1963), 96–111.

34. Norman Waddell and Abe Masao, trans., "Shōbōgenzō Buddha-nature II," *The Eastern Buddhist* 9, no. 1 (1976): 98. A fine article on Dōgen's understanding of the Buddha-nature is presented by Abe Masao, "Dōgen on Buddha Nature," *The Eastern Buddhist* 10, no. 1 (May 1971): 28–71. The key to understanding Dōgen's concept of the Buddha-nature lies in his notion of throughness, according to Masanobu Takahashi, in *The Essence of Dōgen*, trans. Yuzuru Nobuoka (London: Kegan Paul International, 1983).

35. Merleau-Ponty, *Phenomenology of Perception*, 153

36. Merleau-Ponty, *Phenomenology of Perception*, 240.

37. Richard M. Zaner, *The Problem of Embodiment: Some Contributions to a Phenomenology of the Body* (The Hague: Martinus Nijhoff, 1964), 181.

38. N. A. Waddell, trans., "Being Time: Dōgen's Shōbōgenzō Uji," *The Eastern Buddhist* 12, no. 1 (May 1979): 118.

39. Waddell, "Being Time," 121.

40. Waddell, "Being Time," 118.

41. Waddell, "Being Time," 123.

42. Kim, *Dōgen Kigen*, 117.

43. Merleau-Ponty, *Phenomenology of Perception*, 239–40.

44. Waddell and Abe, "Shōbōgenzō Genjōkōan," 136. See also Hee-Jin Kim, "Existence/Time as the Way of Ascesis: An Analysis of the Basic Structure of Dōgen's Thought," *The Eastern Buddhist* 11, no. 2 (October 1978): 43–73.

45. Waddell and Abe, "Shōbōgenzō Genjōkōan," 136.

46. Kim, "Existence/Time," 64.

47. Merleau-Ponty, *Phenomenology of Perception*, 354.

48. Kasulis, *Zen Action/Zen Person*, 91.

49. Waddell, "Being Time," 119.

50. Waddell, "Being Time," 116.

51. Abe, "Dōgen on Buddha Nature," 69.

52. Kim, "Existence/Time," 52.

53. Waddell, "Being Time," 120–26.

54. Merleau-Ponty, *Phenomenology of Perception*, ix.

55. Merleau-Ponty, *Phenomenology of Perception*, xi.

56. Merleau-Ponty, *Phenomenology of Perception*, xi.

57. Merleau-Ponty, *Phenomenology of Perception*, xv.

58. Merleau-Ponty, *Phenomenology of Perception*, xvii.

59. Waddell and Abe, "The King of Samadhis Samadhi," 118.

60. Waddell and Abe, "The King of Samadhis Samadhi," 121.

61. Waddell and Abe, "Dōgen's Bendōwa," 134.

62. Reihō Masunaga, trans., *A Primer of Sōtō Zen: A Translation of Dōgen's Shōbōgenzō Zuimonki* (Honolulu: East-West Center Press, 1971), 103.

63. Abe, "Dōgen on Buddha Nature," 45.

64. Waddell and Abe, "Dōgen's Fukanzazengi," 123 and 128.

65. Kim, *Dōgen Kigen*, 77.

66. Norman Addell and Abe Masao, trans., "Shōbōgenzō Buddha-nature III," *The Eastern Buddhist* 9, no. 2 (October 1976): 72.

67. Waddell and Abe, "Shōbōgenzō Buddha-nature I," 100.

68. Merleau-Ponty, *Phenomenology of Perception*, xx.

69. Richard Zaner, "The Alternating Reed: Embodiment as Problematic Unity," in *Theology and Body*, ed. John Y. Fenton (Philadelphia: Westminster Press, 1974), 61.

70. Zaner, "The Alternating Reed," 62.

71. Merleau-Ponty, *Phenomenology of Perception*, 164.

72. Madison, *The Phenomenology of Merleau-Ponty*, 70.

CHAPTER 5

1 Maurice Merleau-Ponty, "Philosophy and Non-philosophy since Hegel," trans. Hugh J. Silverman, *Philosophy and Non-philosophy since Merleau-Ponty*, ed. Hugh J. Silverman (Evanston, IL: Northwestern University Press, 1997), 9–83, 9.

2. Merleau-Ponty, "Philosophy and Non-philosophy since Hegel," 9.

3. Merleau-Ponty, "Philosophy and Non-philosophy since Hegel," 9.

4. Merleau-Ponty, "Philosophy and Non-philosophy since Hegel," 15.

5. Maurice Merleau-Ponty, *Phénoménologie de la perception* (Paris: Gallimard, 1945), v. English translation by Colin Smith, *Phenomenology of Perception* (London: Routledge, 1962), xx.

6. Maurice Merleau-Ponty, *Le Visible et l'invisible* (Paris: Gallimard, 1964), 62. English translation by Alphonso Lingis, *The Visible and the Invisible* (Evanston, IL: Northwestern University Press, 1968), 39.

7. Merleau-Ponty, *Le Visible et l'invisible*, 67; *The Visible and the Invisible*, 43.

8. Merleau-Ponty, *Le Visible et l'invisible*, 127; *The Visible and the Invisible*, 93.

9. Merleau-Ponty, *Le Visible et l'invisible*, 128; *The Visible and the Invisible*, 93.

10. Jacques Derrida, *Positions*, trans. by Alban Bass (Chicago: University of Chicago Press, 1981), 44.

11. Merleau-Ponty, *Le Visible et l'invisible*, 183; *The Visible and the Invisible*, 139.

12. See chapter 10 of Fazang's *Wujiao zhang* T 45.1866.499a–509a; English translation, Francis Harold Cook, "Fa-tsang's Treatise on the Five Doctrines: An Annotated Translation," Ph.D. dissertation, University of Wisconsin, 1970, 404–540.

13. Francis Cook states:

First of all, it is a universe in which phenomena have been not only restored to a measure of respectability, but indeed, have become important, valuable, and lovely. Second, to accept such a worldview would entail a radical overhauling of the understanding of traditional Buddhist concepts such as emptiness and dependent origination. Finally, it would have meant that many of the important dogmas of Indian Buddhism would have to be abandoned, such as the belief in gradual self-purification, the difference between the noumenal and phenomenal orders, and the distinctions of the stages of progress.

Cook, "Fa-tsang's Treatise on the Five Doctrines: An Annotated Translation," 2.

14. Dushun, *Huayan wujiao zhiguan*, T 45.1867.512 b.

15. Merleau-Ponty, *The Visible and the Invisible*, 4.

16. Chinul's relation to Huayan Buddhism is far more complex than what I explain here. For more detailed discussion, see chapter 9 of my book, *Buddhism and Postmodernity: Zen, Huayan, and the Possibility of Buddhist Postmodern Ethics* (Lanham, MD: Lexington Books, 2008).

17. Merleau-Ponty, "Philosophy and Non-philosophy since Hegel," 14.

18. Merleau-Ponty, "Philosophy and Non-philosophy since Hegel," 13, 14.

19. Chinul, *Susimgyŏl* (Secrets on Cultivating the Mind), *Han'guk Pulgyo Chŏnsŏ* (Collected Works of Korean Buddhism, hereafter HPC), 4, 706b–714c, 710b–c. English translation by Robert E. Buswell, *Tracing Back the Radiance: Chinul's Korean Way of Zen* (Honolulu: University of Hawai'i Press, 1991), 105.

20. Pojo Chinul, *Kanhwa kyŏrŭiron*, HPC, 4. 732 c–737c, 733c. English translation is mine unless noted otherwise.

21. Herbert Fingarette, *Confucius—The Secular as Sacred* (New York: Harper & Row, 1972), 40.

22. Merleau-Ponty, "Philosophy and Non-philosophy since Hegel," 15.

23. "The Oak Tree in the Garden," in *Wumen guan*, case 37, T 48.2005.297c:

"What is the meaning of Bodhidharma's coming to China?" a monk asked Zhaozhou.
"The oak tree in the garden," Zhaozhou replied.

For English translations of *Wumen guan* and *Biyan lu*, see Thomas Clearly, trans., *Unlocking the Zen Koan: A New Translation of the Zen Classic Wumenguan* (Berkeley, CA: North Atlantic Books, 1997); Thomas Cleary and J. C. Cleary, trans., *The Blue Cliff Record* (Boston: Shambhala Publications, Inc., 1992); Katsuki Sekida, trans., *Two Zen Classics: Mumonkan (The Gateless Gate), Hekiganroku (The Blue Cliff Records)* (New York: Weatherhill, Inc., 1977).

24. "Three Pounds of Flax," in *Wumen guan*, case 18, T 48.2005.295c; the same episode also appears in *Biyan lu*, case 12, T 48.2003.139c:

"What is Buddha?" a monk asked Dongshan.
"Three pounds of flax," Dongshan replied.

25. "A Dog Does Not Have the Buddha-Nature," in *Wumen guan*, case 1, T 48.2005.292c:

A student asked Zhaozhou, "Does a dog have the Buddha nature?"
"Wu," Zhaozhou replied.

26. As a dialogue between the Chan master and his student, the *gong'an* (or encounter dialogue) presents a paradox or illogical phrase to the practitioner as exemplified in end-

notes 23–25. The *huatou* tradition obviously did not begin with Chinul, who relied heavily on his predecessors in his account of *huatou* meditation in his work *Huatou Meditation*. The irony of Chinul's position in the text, however, is that he introduces *huatou* as an alternative to the theoretical rendering of Huayan Buddhism and the Sudden School. But how does one write a theoretical text which demonstrates the impossibility of theorization? In this sense, Chinul's *Huatou Meditation* faces greater difficulties than classical *gong'an* texts, such as *Biyan lu* (Blue Cliff Records) and *Wumen guan* (The Gateless Gate), in the Chinese tradition; or *Sŏnmun yŏmsong jip* (Compilation of Examinations of and Verses on Precedents in Sŏn School), edited by Chinul's successor Hyesim, in the Korea tradition.

27. Maurice Merleau-Ponty, "On the Phenomenology of Language," in *Signs* (1960), trans. Richard C. McCleary (Evanston, IL: Northwestern University Press, 1964), 86.

28. Merleau-Ponty, "On the Phenomenology of Language," 84.

29. Merleau-Ponty, "On the Phenomenology of Language," 84.

30. Merleau-Ponty, "On the Phenomenology of Language," 86.

31. Merleau-Ponty, "On the Phenomenology of Language," 90.

32. Maurice Merleau-Ponty, *The Prose of the World* (1969), trans. John O'Neill (Evanston, IL: Northwestern University Press, 1973/1981), 10.

33. Merleau-Ponty, *The Prose of the World*, 10.

34. Merleau-Ponty, *The Prose of the World*, 13.

35. Merleau-Ponty, *Le Visible et l'invisible*, 167; *The Visible and the Invisible*, 125.

36. Maurice Merleau-Ponty, "Indirect Language and the Voices of Silence," in *Signs*, 43.

37. Merleau-Ponty, "Indirect Language and the Voices of Silence," 46.

38. Merleau-Ponty, "On the Phenomenology of Language," 88.

39. Jean-Paul Sartre, "Merleau-Ponty," *Situations*, trans. Benita Eisler (London: Hamish Hamilton, 1965), 211.

40. Originally from *Dahui yulu* (The Records of Dahui) 14, T 47.1998.870b.

41. Maurice Merleau-Ponty, "Introduction," *Signs*, 14.

42. Merleau-Ponty, *The Visible and the Invisible*, 160.

CHAPTER 6

1. The *Manyōshū* comprises a collection of classical poetry and is usually considered to be one of the great literary achievements of Japanese culture (note of the translators).

2. Here, Funaki refers to Locke's distinction between the secondary signification of language that implies conventionalism and its primary signification that results in nominalism (note of the translators).

3. Shinran, "Tannishō" (A Record in Lament of Divergences), in *Shinran zenshū* (Complete Works of Shinran) *Bekkan* (*Addendum*), 3–40, ed. Mizumaro Ishida (Tokyo: Shunjūsha, 2001), 7–8; Shinran, *Tannishō: A Primer—A Record of the Words of Shinran Set Down in Lamentation over Departures from his Teaching*, trans. Dennis Hirota (Kyoto: Ryūkoku University Press, 1982), 54–57. While this piece was written by Shinran's student Yuien, it is usually attributed to Shinran himself.

4. *The Sūtra of Immeasurable Life*, T 12.360.265c–279a, 268a.

5. Funaki refers here to the council of Nicea (325 C.E.), where the divine nature of Jesus Christ was decided, and the council of Chalcedon (451 C.E.), which decreed that Jesus Christ constituted one person but possessed two natures, human and divine (note of the translators).

6. The Japanese original here, *shinjin* (literally, the "heart of faith"), denotes the attitude of faith a believer displays toward the object of his or her devotion (note of the translators).

7. Shinran, *Kenjōdo shinjitsu kyōgyōshō monrui* (Teaching, Practice, Faith, and Realization), in *Shinran zenshū* (Complete Works of Shinran), volume 1, ed. Mizumaro Ishida (Tokyo: Shunjūsha, 2001), 170; "The True Teaching, Practice, and Realization of the Pure Land Way," in *The Collected Works of Shinran: The Writing*, volume 1, trans. and ed. Dennis Hirota, Hisao Inagaki, Michio Tokunaga, and Ryūshin Uryūzu (Kyoto: Jōdo Shinshū Hongwanjiha, 1997), 107.

8. Shinran, "*Tannishō*," 8; Shinran, *Tannishō: A Primer*, 59.

9. Shinran, "*Tannishō*," 8–9; Shinran, *Tannishō: A Primer*, 61.

10. *Wuliangshoujing*, 268a.

11. Shinran, "*Tannishō*," 20–21; Shinran, *Tannishō: A Primer*, 93.

12. Shinran, "Jōdo kōsō wasan" (Hymns of the Pure Land Masters), in *Shinran zenshū* (*Complete Works of Shinran*) *Daiyonkan*, volume 4, 487–530, ed. Mizumaro Ishida (Tokyo: Shunjūsha, 2001), 502; Shinran, "Hymns of the Pure Land Masters," in *The Collected Works of Shinran: The Writing*, volume 1, trans. and ed. Dennis Hirota, Hisao Inagaki, Michio Tokunaga, and Ryūshin Uryūzu (Kyoto: Jōdo Shinshū Hongwanjiha, 1997), 371.

13. Shinran, "*Tannishō*," 12; Shinran, *Tannishō: A Primer*, 71.

14. Shinran, "*Tannishō*," 15–16; Shinran, *Tannishō: A Primer*, 79.

15. According to the glossary provided by the editors of *The Collected Works of Shinran*, volume 2, the word is translated as "to leap crosswise beyond birth-and-death" and as "crosswise transcending." Dennis Hirota et. al., "Glossary of Shin Buddhist Terms," in *The Collected Works of Shinran: The Writing*, volume 2, trans. and ed. Dennis Hirota, Hisao Inagaki, Michio Tokunaga, and Ryūshin Uryūzu (Kyoto: Jōdo Shinshū Hongwanjiha, 1997), 309.

16. René Descartes, *Les Passions de l'âme*, *Œuvres Philosophiques de Descartes*, volume 3, ed. Ferdinand Alquié (Paris: Édition Garnier Frères, 1963), 18.

17. Ibid., 49.

18. René Descartes, *Philosophical Writings*, trans. and ed. Elizabeth Anscombe and Peter Thomas Geach (London: Thomas Nelson and Sons Limited, 1971), 73.

19. René Descartes, *Les Passions de l'âme*, 50.

20. Maurice Merleau-Ponty, *Phénoménologie de la perception* (Paris: Gallimard, 1945), 456; Maurice Merleau-Ponty, *Phenomenology of Perception*, trans. Colin Smith (London: Routledge, 1962), 398.

21. Merleau-Ponty, *Phénoménologie*, 462; Merleau-Ponty, *Phenomenology*, 404.

22. Merleau-Ponty, *Phénoménologie*, 463; Merleau-Ponty, *Phenomenology*, 404.

23. Merleau-Ponty, *Phénoménologie*, 213–49; Merleau-Ponty, *Phenomenology*, 174–99.

24. Maurice Merleau-Ponty, *Le Visible et l'invisible* (Paris: Gallimard, 1964), 229. The chapter on *cogito* appears in Merleau-Ponty, *Phénoménologie*, 427–70; Merleau-Ponty, *Phenomenology*, 369–409.

25. Merleau-Ponty, *Phénoménologie*, 206; Merleau-Ponty, *Phenomenology*, 177.

26. Merleau-Ponty, *Phénoménologie*, 213; Merleau-Ponty, *Phenomenology*, 183.

27. Merleau-Ponty, *Phénoménologie*, 207; Merleau-Ponty, *Phenomenology*, 178.

28. Merleau-Ponty, *Phénoménologie*, 209; Merleau-Ponty, *Phenomenology*, 179.

29. Merleau-Ponty, *Phénoménologie*, 221.

30. Merleau-Ponty, *Phénoménologie*, 229; Merleau-Ponty, *Phenomenology*, 197.

31. Maurice Merleau-Ponty, *La Prose du Monde* (Paris: Gallimard, 1969), 26.

32. Merleau-Ponty, *La Prose du Monde*, 29.

33. Merleau-Ponty, *La Prose du Monde*, 28.

34. Merleau-Ponty, *La Prose du Monde*, 29–30.

35. "Words to be spoken" is Funaki's translation of the same French expression *parole parlée*, which was earlier translated as "spoken words." Funaki intentionally uses different translations in Japanese of this same French expression to add additional nuance by making a distinction between "spoken words" and "words to be spoken" (note of the translators).

36. Merleau-Ponty, *Phénoménologie*, 497–521; Merleau-Ponty, *Phenomenology*, 434–56.

37. Maurice Merleau-Ponty, *Éloge de la philosophie* (Paris: Gallimard, 1953), 150.

CHAPTER 7

1. Similarly, Michel Henry's (1922–2002) notions of immanence and life (*la vie*) reveal surprising affinities to Nishida's conception of the *locus* (J. *basho* 場所) of self-awareness, or, better, "self-awakening" (J. *jikaku* 自覚).

2. See Nishida Kitarō, "Eichiteki sekai" (The Intelligible World), in *Nishida Kitarō zenshū* [hereafter NKZ] (Collected Works of Nishida Kitarō), volume 5 (Tokyo: Iwanami Shoten, 1988), 123–85.

3. It is the unpublished thesis of Kuroda Akinobu, which we read for his *viva voce* examination at the University of Strasbourg (May 20, 2003), that first drew our attention to this issue: "Enjeux, possibilités, et limites d'une philosophie de la vie: Kitarō Nishida au miroir de quelques philosophes français."

4. NKZ 8: 547–48.

5. Maurice Merleau-Ponty, *L'Oeil et l'esprit* (Paris: Gallimard, 1964), 18.

6. NKZ 8.

CHAPTER 8

1. Nishida Kitarō, *Collected Works of Nishida Kitarō* (*Nishida Kitarō zenshū* 西田幾多郎全集, NKZ, nineteen volumes) (Tokyo: Iwanami Shoten, 1979). *From Acting to Seeing* (NKZ 4) is the work that starts a fundamental reflection on what will become Nishida's most celebrated concept, *basho*. Inspired not only by Plato's ideas of the *topos* from the *Phaedo* (NKZ 4, 159) and the "chōra" from the *Timaeus* (NKZ 4, 209), but also by Aristotle's conception of the soul as the location where forms take place (NKZ 4, 213) from *De anima*, the notion of *basho* is expounded in a section of *Hataraku mono kara miru mono e* simply titled "Basho." A translation of this text exists in German as "Ort" (1999) in *Logik des Ortes. Der Anfang der modernen Philosophie in Japan*, trans. Rolf Elberfeld (Darmstadt: Wissenschaftliche Buchgesellschaft), 72–139.

2. The "*basho* of the visible" is an expression specifically formulated for the purpose of this chapter.

3. See in particular Nishida's *Fundamental Problems of Philosophy* (*Tetsugaku no kompon mondai* 哲学の根本問題), NKZ 7, 201–453, in which 絶対無の場所 is presented as the absolute place of mediation, not only between self-determined individuals, but also between them and the social and historical worlds.

4. It is in the first period of his philosophical life that Nishida developed his concept of "pure experience," which is so central to the work that made him famous, *Zen no kenkyū* (An Inquiry into the Good 善の研究), NKZ 1, 3–200.

5. Merleau-Ponty's criticism of empirical psychology was originally undertaken in his *La structure du comportement* (Paris: Gallimard, 1942). Whether it is J. B. Watson's behaviorism or I. P. Pavlov's deductions based on the observation of reflexes, neither of them are able to give a faithful account of the nature of human experience, due to their mechanistic and analytic approaches.

6. The Buddhist theory of the *soku* is presented in Nāgārjuna, *Philosophy of the Middle Way*, trans. D. J. Kalupahana (Albany: State University of New York Press, 1986).

7. Nishida, NKZ 5. The system of universals according to self-awakening (*Ippansha no jikakuteki taikei* 一般者の自覚的体系).

8. Of course such a criticism against objective thoughts has in the Western world not been restricted to Merleau-Ponty, as it characterizes much of the phenomenological undertaking and recent systematic drives to deconstruct metaphysics. As far as art is concerned, Merleau-Ponty's is probably the first philosophy built from the standpoint of painting. He is the first to present the visual as an "ontology" in its own right, and in *L'Oeil et l'esprit* he suggests that painting has always had the power to interrogate vision itself. For instance, painting has always had the power to show that the eye cannot see itself seeing. This ontology of the visual is at work in self-portraits when the one who usually sees becomes the one who is seen, and therefore becomes the perceived object itself. Such an ontology, according to Merleau-Ponty, can also be found in paintings that depict artists experiencing the act of representation, if I may put it this way, such as in Velaquez's *Las Meninas*, Courbet's *L'Atelier*, or seventeenth-century Dutch paintings and their obsession with reflected images. One could almost talk about a visual *cogito* proper to painting—that is, the awareness that the eye cannot see itself seeing unless it becomes objectified or represents itself. In *L'Oeil et l'esprit*, Merleau-Ponty writes: "Ce n'est pas un hasard, par exemple, si souvent, dans la peinture hollandaise (et dans beaucoup d'autres), un intérieur désert est 'digéré' par 'l'oeil rond du miroir.' Ce regard préhumain est l'emblème de celui du peintre. Plus complètement que les lumières, les ombres, les reflets, l'image spéculaire ébauche dans les choses le travail de vision" (Paris: Folio/Essais, 1964, 32).

9. Nishida talks about, among others, the "concrete universal" (*gutaiteki ippansha* 具体的一般者), the "universal of action" (*kōiteki ippansha* 行為的一般者), the "universal of being" (*yū no ippansha* 有の一般), or the "universal of judgment" (*handanteki ippansha* 判断的一般者). There are other types of universals, such as the predicative plane or the concrete universal. They all constitute different facets of what he calls the "self-awakened universal," which is "the place of nothingness" (*mu no basho* 無の場所).

10. Nishida, NKZ 6, *The Self-Awakened Determination of Nothingness* (*Mu no jikakuteki gentei* 無の自覚的限定, 1932). Nishida argues that the "self-awakened universal" cannot be static. It must be thought as being active and expressive. There are particular instances of such creatively mutating *basho*, such as the Thou, or the historical and the social worlds. It is at this stage that Nishida thinks of the constitution of what he calls "reality" in terms of mutual relationships between persons, between society and individuals, and between history and particular events. These creative relationships are therefore what he describes in terms of "dialectical." Therefore, whether it is the formation of the self, society, or history, one always moves from what is already created to creative action.

11. "La théorie du corps est déjà une théorie de la perception" (Maurice Merleau-Ponty, *Phénoménologie de la perception* [Paris: Gallimard, 1945], 529).

12. Merleau-Ponty's fundamental philosophy of "body and world" (*corps et monde*) is to be found in the first two sections of his *Phénoménologie de la perception*. See "Le corps"

and "Le monde perçu," 81–232 and 233–419. The third and final section deals with themes such as *cogito*, "temporality," and "freedom." See "L'être-pour-soi et l'être-au-monde" in *Phénoménologie de la perception*, 421–520.

13. Maurice Merleau-Ponty, *Sens et non-sens* (Paris: Nagel, 1948), 15–44.

14. Merleau-Ponty, *L'Oeil et l'esprit*, 12–13.

15. Derrida in *La Vérité en peinture* (1978) deconstructs the very notion of "truth" in painting by confronting Cézanne's sayings on the subject to Martin Heidegger's conception of "origin" of the work of art in *Der Urpsrung des Kunstwerkes* (1967), as well as the art historian Meyer Schapiro's counterargument against the latter in *The Reach of Mind: Essays in Memory of Kurt Goldstein* (1968).

16. In *Discours, figure* (1985), Jean-François Lyotard shows his suspicion about any foundational tendency not only in Merleau-Ponty's phenomenology, but also in Ferdinand de Saussure's structuralism.

17. Merleau-Ponty declares in *Le Visible et l'invisible* that "[w]hat we call flesh, that internally worked through mass, does not have any name in any philosophy"—"Ce que nous appelons chair, cette masse intérieurement travaillée, n'a de nom dans aucune philosophie" (Paris: Gallimard, 1964, 193).

18. See, for example, Nishida, NKZ 9, "Absolutely Contradictory Self-Identity" (*Zettai mujunteki jiko dōitsu*, 絶対矛盾的自己同一, 1939), 147–222.

19. Although Nishida does not deal specifically with the relationship between the "gesture of the artist" and the "objective world" in those terms, his essays on art and aesthetics can be found in *Nishida Kitarō senshū (Selected Works of Nishida Kitarō)*, ed. Ken'ichi Iwaki, volume 6 (Kyoto: Tōeisha, 1998).

20. Nishida, NKZ 7, 445. In the text "a culture of feeling is that of the form of the formless and of the voice of the voiceless."

21. Merleau-Ponty, *L'Oeil et l'esprit*, 88.

22. See Joachim Gasquet, *Cézanne* (Paris: Editions Cynara, 1988).

23. See Merleau-Ponty, *Phénoménologie de la perception*, 345–77.

24. Merleau-Ponty, *L'Oeil et l'esprit*, 62.

25. See Merleau-Ponty, *Le Visible et l'invisible*, "L'entrelacs—Le Chiasme," 172–204.

CHAPTER 9

1. For a translation of Nishida's earlier essay on the beauty of art and Buddhism, see Steve Odin, trans., "An Explanation of Beauty: Nishida Kitarō's 'Bi no Setsumei,'" *Monumenta Nipponica* 42, no. 2 (Summer 1987): 211–18 [hereafter EB]. For the use of the idea of the *place of nothingness* in a discussion about religious faith, Zen, Linji, and D. T. Suzuki, see Nishida Kitarō, *Last Writings: Nothingness and the Religious Worldview*, trans. David A. Dilworth (Honolulu: University of Hawai'i Press, 1993), 85, 108 [hereafter LW].

2. Maurice Merleau-Ponty, *The Visible and the Invisible*, ed. Claude Lefort, trans. Alphonso Lingis (Evanston, IL: Northwestern University Press, 1968). See Nobuo Kazashi, "Bodily Logos, James, Merleau-Ponty, and Nishida," in *Merleau-Ponty: Interiority and Exteriority, Psychic Life and the World*, ed. Dorothea Olkowski and James Morley (Albany: State University of New York Press, 1999), 107–20, 117–18 [hereafter BL].

3. Bernard Faure, "The Kyoto School and Reverse Orientalism," in *Japan in Traditional and Postmodern Perspectives*, ed. Charles Wei-hsun Fu and Steven Heine (Albany: State

University of New York Press, 1995), 248–51, 255 [hereafter KS].

4. Faure is primarily concerned with arguing in objection to Nishida's notion of "pure experience" and D. T. Suzuki's notion of "wisdom" (*prajñā*). He also asks the following question: Was Nishida an active supporter of an ultranationalist ideology, or merely a defender of Japanese culture? For careful scholarship and documentation on this issue, see Michiko Yusa, *Zen & Philosophy: An Intellectual Biography of Nishida Kitarō* (Honolulu: University of Hawai'i Press, 2002), 271–77 and 314–18. Yusa describes the social-cultural-political environment in which Nishida lived and includes relevant lectures that he delivered in 1937 and 1941.

5. See William James, "Does 'Consciousness' Exist?" and "A World of Pure Experience," in *Essays in Radical Empiricism* (Lincoln: University of Nebraska Press, 1996), 4, 23, 74 [hereafter ERE].

6. Steve Odin, *Artistic Detachment in Japan and the West: Psychic Distance in Comparative Aesthetics* (Honolulu: University of Hawai'i Press, 2001), 129.

7. Nishida Kitarō, *An Inquiry into the Good*, trans. by Masao Abe and Christopher Ives (New Haven, CT: Yale University Press, 1990), 3–4 [hereafter IG].

8. David Dilworth, "The Initial Formations of 'Pure Experience' in Nishida Kitarō and William James," *Monumenta Nipponica* 24, nos. 1–2 (1969): 93–111, 96, 99.

9. Dilworth, "The Initial Formations of 'Pure Experience' in Nishida Kitarō and William James," 96.

10. Nishitani Keiji provides a helpful interpretation; he argues that James's use of "pure experience" results in an unsatisfying psychologism, since a philosophy such as radical empiricism rests on a method of science that simplifies and abstracts personal experiences into psychological elements (e.g., perception, feeling) and fails to describe experience as it is lived concretely from within. See Nishitani Keiji, *Nishida Kitarō*, trans. Yamamoto Seisaku and James Heisig (Berkeley: University of California Press, 1991), 78–82. According to Nishitani, Nishida mentioned a particular walk in which a bee buzzed near his ear and brought about a "moment of direct hearing"; Nishida was awakened to the standpoint of pure experience, "of nothingness or non-ego" (55).

11. Dilworth, "The Initial Formations of 'Pure Experience' in Nishida Kitarō and William James," 105, 109–10.

12. Masao Abe, "Nishida's Philosophy of Place," *International Philosophical Quarterly* 28 (Winter 1988): 355–71, 371. Abe argues that *An Inquiry into the Good* still suffers at times from a reliance on language of "objective consciousness," where the underlying unity of consciousness is explained merely in terms of reason and spirit.

13. Stephen T. Katz, "Language, Epistemology, and Mysticism," in *Mysticism and Philosophical Analysis*, ed. Stephen T. Katz (New York: Oxford University Press, 1978) [hereafter LEM].

14. Immanuel Kant, *Critique of Pure Reason*, trans. Norman Kemp Smith (New York: St. Martin's Press, 1965), 22–23.

15. Kant, *Critique of Pure Reason*, 65–66.

16. The English word "utopia" stems from the Greek words *ou* (no) and *topos* (place).

17. Bernard Faure, *Double Exposure: Cutting Across Buddhist and Western Discourses*, trans. Janet Lloyd (Stanford, CA: Stanford University Press, 2004), 174.

18. Nishida Kitarō, *Fundamental Problems of Philosophy: The World in Action*, trans. David Dilworth (Tokyo: Sophia University, 1970), 1 [hereafter FP].

19. Kant, *Critique of Pure Reason*, 144.

20. David A. Dilworth, "The Concrete World of Action in Nishida's Later Thought," in *Japanese Phenomenology: Phenomenology as the Trans-Cultural Philosophical Approach*, ed. Yoshihiro Nitta and Hirotaka Tatematsu (Dordrecht: Reidel Publishing Company, 1979), 250.

21. Dilworth, "Nishida's Later Thought," 253.

22. Dilworth, "Nishida's Later Thought," 261.

23. With regard to this problem, scholars may wish to investigate the degree of convergence between Nishida and the existentialism of Jean-Paul Sartre. Dilworth writes that "[t]he phrase *mu no basho* can literally be translated as the 'nihilic place' of consciousness, somewhat reminiscent of Sartre's notion of *le néant*" (Dilworth, "Nishida's Later Thought," 251). Sartre does make some similar claims: one is free to the extent that there is no preconception of a fixed or unchanging nature that impels action; one cannot seek from within oneself the true condition that will impel one to act; one is at first nothing and then defines oneself by the ensemble of one's acts. See Jean-Paul Sartre, "Existentialism," in *Existentialism and Human Emotions*, trans. Bernard Frechtman (New York: Citadel Press, 1990), 5, 27, 32.

24. Immanuel Kant, *Grounding for the Metaphysics of Morals*, trans. James Ellington (Indianapolis: Hackett, 1993), 53.

25. Kant, *Grounding for the Metaphysics of Morals*, 24.

26. Kant, *Grounding for the Metaphysics of Morals*, 52–53.

27. Yasuo Yuasa, *The Body: Toward an Eastern Mind-Body Theory*, ed. Thomas Kasulis, trans. Shigenori Nagatomo and Thomas Kasulis (Albany: State University of New York Press, 1987), 50–51.

28. Steve Odin, *The Social Self in Zen and American Pragmatism* (Albany: State University of New York Press, 1996), 370–71.

29. Maurice Merleau-Ponty, "Eye and Mind," in *The Merleau-Ponty Aesthetics Reader: Philosophy and Painting*, ed. Galen A. Johnson (Evanston, IL: Northwestern University Press, 1993), 144.

30. For a helpful affirmation of the hypothesis that religious traditions remain a resource today, see Henry Rosemont, *Rationality and Religious Experience: The Continuing Relevance of the World's Spiritual Traditions* (Chicago: Open Court, 2001), 3–4, 40. I agree with Rosemont that some traditions of religious practice may help philosophers to articulate a feeling of belonging in nature with others and to articulate a dimension of actual life that the West has ignored or forgotten. But I add this: philosophers must *not* let living scientists, as professional producers of knowledge, appropriate the term "body" in whatever way may suit them and to dictate how it may then be used in philosophical discourse (70).

31. D. T. Suzuki, *Zen Buddhism, Selected Writings of D. T. Suzuki*, ed. William Barrett (New York: Doubleday, 1996), 174.

32. Suzuki, *Zen Buddhism*, 174

33. Youru Wang, "The Chan Deconstruction of Buddha Nature," in *Buddhisms and Deconstructions*, ed. Jin Y. Park (Lanham, MD: Rowman & Littlefield Publishers, 2006), 133 [hereafter CD].

34. Wang, "The Chan Deconstruction of Buddha Nature," 133.

35. Huineng, *The Sūtra of Hui-neng*, trans. A. F. Price and Wong Mou-lam (Boston: Sambhalla, 1990), 85. Steve Odin also finds that the *Platform Sūtra* expresses the idea that thoughtlessness and detachment from experiences of things are a means for facilitating *prajñā* insight and engagement with the six senses (Odin, *Artistic Detachment in Japan and the West*, 146–47).

36. Huineng, *The Sūtra of Hui-neng*, 97.

37. Bernard Faure, *The Power of Denial: Buddhism, Purity and Gender* (Princeton, NJ: Princeton University Press, 2003), 328: "Perhaps our mindless emphasis on the mind to the detriment of the body is itself characteristic of a masculine vision of things." Faure also questions the tendency of some to judge spiritual progress by detachment from what is concrete, this-worldly, and immanent. He affirms and cites the comment by Carol Christ: "Who says that transcendent is 'better' than 'immanent'?" (329).

38. Maurice Merleau-Ponty, "Everywhere and Nowhere," in *Signs*, trans. Richard C. McCleary (Evanston, IL: Northwestern University Press, 1964), 139. For a companion piece that refers to Huineng and discusses the idea of visibility in relation to care and compassion, see my "Care for the Flesh: Gilligan, Merleau-Ponty, and Corporeal Styles," in *Feminist Interpretations of Maurice Merleau-Ponty*, ed. Dorothea Olkowski and Gail Weiss (University Park: Pennsylvania State University Press, 2006), 229–56.

39. Edward Said, *Orientalism* (New York: Vintage Books, 1994).

CHAPTER 10

1. Maurice Merleau-Ponty, *Phenomenology of Perception*, trans. Colin Smith (London: Routledge, 1962), xvi. Any further references within this chapter to this text will be indicated by PhP within parentheses followed by the page number.

2. Maurice Merleau-Ponty, *The Visible and the Invisible*, trans. by Alphonso Lingis (Evanston, IL: Northwestern University Press, 1968), 138 [hereafter VI].

3. Keiji Nishitani, *Religion and Nothingness*, trans. Jan Van Bragt (Berkeley: University of California Press, 1982), 107.

4. Maurice Merleau-Ponty, *The Primacy of Perception*, trans. James Edie (Evanston, IL: Northwestern University Press, 1964), 173 [hereafter PR].

5. Edward Conze, ed. and trans., *Buddhist Scriptures* (New York: Penguin, 1959), 162–63 [hereafter BS].

6. *The Dhammapada*, trans. P. Lal (New York: Farrar, Strauss and Giroux, 1967), 21–22.

7. Stephen Batchelor, *Verses from the Center: A Buddhist Vision of the Sublime* (New York: Riverhead, 2000), 61 [hereafter VC].

8. Jean Smith, ed., *Radiant Mind: Essential Buddhist Teachings and Texts* (New York: Riverhead, 1999), 197 [hereafter RM].

9. Michele Martin, "On the Other Side of Attachment," in *Being Bodies: Buddhist Women on the Paradox of Embodiment*, ed. Lenore Friedman and Susan Moon (Boston: Shambhala Publications, Inc., 1997), 156.

10. Martin, "On the Other Side," 160.

11. Martin, "On the Other Side," 18.

12. Nishitani, *Religion and Nothingness*, 190.

13. "Precept Study: Ethics in Action/The First Precept," *Tricycle* 1, no. 4 (Summer 1992): 10.

14. For an extended analysis of the passages referred to in Plato's *Republic* and how they deny embodiment, flux, and emotion, please see my *Emotion and Embodiment: Fragile Ontology* (New York: Peter Lang, 1994), 6–18.

15. Gadjin Nagao, *The Foundational Standpoint of Mādhyamika Philosophy*, trans. John Keenan (Albany: State University of New York Press, 1989), 8.

16. Maurice Merleau-Ponty, *Sense and Non-Sense*, trans. Hubert and Patricia Dreyfus (Evanston, IL: Northwestern University Press, 1964), 94

17. Nagao, *The Foundational Standpoint of Mādhyamika Philosophy*, 8.

18. Maurice Merleau-Ponty, *La Nature*, ed. Dominique Séglard (Paris: Editions du Seuil, 1995), 338–39. My translations throughout.

19. Merleau-Ponty, *La Nature*, 346.

20. Merleau-Ponty, *La Nature*, 271.

21. Merleau-Ponty, *La Nature*, 334–35.

CHAPTER 11

1. Maurice Merleau-Ponty, *The Visible and the Invisible*, trans. Alphonso Lingis (Evanston, IL: Northwestern University Press, 1968), 179.

2. The school of thought that claims "all exists" in terms of the dharmas understood as the "elements of existence." The Sarvāstivāda make this "positive" ontological claim with respect to the dharmas as analytically (and synthetically) explicated in the Abhidharma literature; see Herbert V. Guenther, *Philosophy and Psychology in the Abhidharma* (Boston: Shambhala Publications, Inc., 1976) and Nyanaponika Thera, *Abhidharma Studies: Buddhist Explorations of Consciousness and Time* (Pariyatti, Canada: Buddhist Publication Society, 1998).

3. These schools claim that there is a continuous self (personality or *pudgala*) that persists through the temporal impermanence (*anitya*) of one's life (or lifetimes).

4. Nāgārjuna, *The Precious Garland and the Song of the Four Mindfulnesses*, trans. Jeffrey Hopkins (New York: Harper & Row, 1975), 90 [henceforth PG].

5. *Duḥkha* arises due to (1) desire or thirst (*tṛṣṇā*) and (2) our entanglements with or attachments (*upādāna*) to both our (a) desires and (b) the objects of our desires. Such suffering relies on incorrect views that ascribe inherent self-existence (*svabhāva*) to the self (*ātman*) and worldly things or possessions.

6. The Sanskrit and Buddhist equivalent for this term is *mokṣa*, but unlike Merleau-Ponty's understanding of freedom, which is political in nature, Buddhist liberation has soteriological intent.

7. K. Venkata Ramanan, *Nāgārjuna's Philosophy* (Tokyo: Charles E. Tuttle Company, Inc., 1966), 315.

8. David R. Komito, *Nāgārjuna's Seventy Stanzas: A Buddhist Psychology of Emptiness* (New York: Snow Lions Publications, 1987), 181.

9. Nāgārjuna, *A Translation of Nagarjuna's* Mulamadhyamakakārikā *with an Introductory Essay*, trans. Kenneth K. Inada (Delhi: Sri Satguru Publications, 1993) referred to as *Mūlamadhyamakakārikā*, chapters XXIV and XVII, respectively.

10. Maurice Merleau-Ponty, *The Primacy of Perception*, trans. James M. Edie (Evanston, IL: Northwestern University Press, 1964), 11.

11. Thomas W. Busch, "Perception, Finitude, and Transgression: A Note on Merleau-Ponty and Ricoeur," in *Merleau-Ponty, Hermeneutics, and Postmodernism*, ed. Thomas W. Busch and Shaun Gallagher (Albany: State University of New York Press, 1992), 25–36, 30. Also see *Merleau-Ponty's Later Works and Their Practical Implications*, ed. Duane Davis (Buffalo, NY: Prometheus Books, 2001).

12. See Nolan Pliny Jacobson, *Buddhism and the Contemporary World* (Carbondale and Edwardsville: Southern Illinois University Press, 1983).

13. Maurice Merleau-Ponty, *Signs*, trans. Richard C. McCleary (Evanston, IL: Northwestern University Press, 1964), 35.

14. Merleau-Ponty, *Signs*, 96–157.

15. Merleau-Ponty, *The Primacy of Perception*, 26.

16. Merleau-Ponty, *Signs*, 159.

17. A. J. Steinbock's essay "Merleau-Ponty, Husserl, and Saturated Intentionality" (*Rereading Merleau-Ponty: Essays beyond the Continental-Analytic Divide*, ed. Lawrence Hass and Dorothea Olkowski [Buffalo, NY: Humanity Books, 2000], 53–74) is a fine effort to fill in the components of autochthanous organization. He identifies two general classes of what he calls *vectors*, both subjective and objective; in the first he tucks *conscious, operative*, and *global intentionality*, and in the latter *objective sense* and *affective force*. The combination of all five explains his notion of *saturated intentionality*. In terms of the ethical aspects of autochthanous organization, the relation between global intentionality ("I am/We are") and affective force ("It elicits") points to the phenomenal import of what Levinas claims as *the call of the Other*. The Other draws me into the moral sphere of responsibility that is the social world.

18. Merleau-Ponty, *The Visible and the Invisible*, 128; also see my essay, "The Hyper-Dialectic in Merleau-Ponty's Ontology of the *Flesh*," *Philosophy Today* 47, no. 4 (Fall 2003): 404–20.

19. See Sonia Kruks, *The Political Philosophy of Merleau-Ponty* (London: Ashgate Publishing, 1994); Kerry H. Whiteside, *Merleau-Ponty and the Foundations of an Existential Politics* (Princeton, NJ: Princeton University Press, 1988); and Bernard Flynn, *Political Philosophy at the Closure of Metaphysics* (Atlantic Highlands, NJ: Humanities Press, 1992).

20. Merleau-Ponty, "A Note on Machiavelli," in *Signs*, 223.

21. Merleau-Ponty, *The Primacy of Perception*, 227–28.

22. Rudi Visker, "Raw Being and Violent Discourse: Foucault, Merleau-Ponty and the (Dis-)Order of Things," in *Merleau-Ponty in Contemporary Perspective*, ed. Patrick Burke and J. Van Der Veken (Boston: Kluwer Academic Publishers, 1993), 123.

23. Hsueh-li Cheng, *Nāgārjuna's Twelve Gate Treatise* (Boston: D. Reidel Publishing Company, 1982), 14.

24. In his essay "Concerning Marxism," in *Sense and Non-sense* (Evanston, IL: Northwestern University Press, 1964), 99–124, Merleau-Ponty relativizes these laws, ideas, and principles by contextualizing them: "Justice and truth, whose source men think they possess insofar as they are consciousnesses, are in reality based upon law-courts, books, and traditions and are therefore fragile like these and, like them, are threatened by individual judgment. The individual's evaluations and his ability to think correctly depend upon his external supports, and it is essential that these be maintained" (103).

The maintenance of these external supports must resemble something like Gadamer's prejudices. Our tradition becomes the medium through which (correct) thinking happens.

25. "Merleau-Ponty in Person (An Interview with Madeleine Chapsal, 1960)," in *Texts and Dialogues*, ed. Hugh J. Silverman and J. Barry Jr. (Anherst, NY: Humanities Books, 1992), 12.

26. Merleau-Ponty, *The Primacy of Perception*, 25–26.

27. Merleau-Ponty, *Signs*, 35.

28. *Mūlamadhyamakakārikā*, chapter XXV, verses 19 and 20.

29. The self-corrective mechanism in Nāgārjuna's Buddhist approach draws upon aspects of the Eightfold Path, particularly right concentration and right understanding,

and is supplemented by the methodical application of the four-tiered logic or tetralemma. In his *Mūlamadhyamakakārikā*, the tetralemma is deployed consistently throughout the work's *prasaṅga* or *reductio ad absurdum* arguments that are designed to refute incorrect views and doctrines.

30. "Merleau-Ponty in Person," in *Texts and Dialogues*, 13.

31. Maurizio Passerin d'Entreves, *Political Philosophy of Hannah Arendt* (New York: Routledge, 1994), 72.

32. Wing-tsit Chan, *A Source Book of Chinese Philosophy* (Princeton, NJ: Princeton University Press, 1963), 22 (2:1) and 31 (6:28).

33. Eleanor Godway, "Toward a Phenomenology of Politics," in *Merleau-Ponty, Hermeneutics, and Postmodernism*, 161–70, 165 [henceforth TPP].

34. Whiteside, *Merleau-Ponty and the Foundations of an Existential Politics*, 174–79.

35. See Damien Keown, *The Nature of Buddhist Ethics* (New York: Palgrave, 2001) and his essay, "Karma, Character, and Consequentialism," *Journal of Religious Ethics* 24, no. 2 (Fall 1996): 329–50.

36. The descriptions of these virtues are generally stated as follows:

> Giving is to give away completely
> All one's wealth, ethics is to help others,
> Patience is to forsake anger,
> Effort, to delight in virtues;
> Concentration is unafflicted one-pointedness,
> Wisdom is ascertainment of the meaning of the [Four Noble] truths,
> Compassion is a mind that savours only
> Mercy and love for all sentient beings.

37. Merleau-Ponty, *The Primacy of Perception*, 30.

38. T. Serequeberhan's *The Hermeneutics of African Philosophy: Horizon and Discourse* (New York: Routledge, 1994) is an important contribution to African philosophy and philosophy in general, especially in regard to the imperialistic nature of Anglo-American and European thought.

39. Watson recognizes the violence inherent in abstract principles in his statement "No more than epistemology can ethics or politics be either simply a matter of return or a reduction to foundations"; Stephen Watson, "Merleau-Ponty, the Ethics of Ambiguity, and the Dialectics of Virtue," in *Merleau-Ponty in Contemporary Perspective*, ed. Patrick Burke and Jean Van Der Veken, 165 (see also part II of *Signs*).

40. Bernard Dauenhauer is of like mind in this regard. See his essay "Democracy and the Task of Political Amelioration," in *Rereading Merleau-Ponty*, 235–52.

41. See Michael Berman, "Nāgārjuna's Negative Ontology," *Journal of Indian Philosophy and Religion* 12 (October 2007): 115–46.

42. Burke and Van Der Veken, *Merleau-Ponty in Contemporary Perspective*, 165; see B. Watson's contribution.

43. Note that this quotation is taken from Merleau-Ponty's corpus before his critical rejection of the language of consciousness and Husserlian transcendental phenomenology.

44. Maurice Merleau-Ponty, *Phenomenology of Perception*, trans. C. Smith (London: Routledge, 1962), 453.

45. Guenther, *Philosophy and Psychology in the Abhidharma*, 19.

46. Thera, *Abhidharma Studies: Buddhist Explorations of Consciousness and Time*, 110; admittedly, Thera in this context is discussing the arising of defilements and their influence on the psyche, but since karma can be considered as wholesome, unwholesome, or neutral, such a judgment need not change the experiential import of his temporal claim.

47. Jay L. Garfield, trans., *The Fundamental Wisdom of the Middle Way: Nāgārjuna's Mūlamadhyamakakārikā* (New York: Oxford University Press, 1995), 238.

48. Garfield, *The Fundamental Wisdom of the Middle Way*, 239–40. Garfield indicates two points in this context: "[One] the consequences of actions do not cease at some point. All actions have ramifications into the indefinite future, due to dependent arising. Second, actions themselves, being empty of inherent existence, are not entities capable of passing out of existence, when passing out of existence is interpreted to mean the cessation entirely of something that once existed inherently. Since actions are not inherently existent, they are not suitable bases for inherent cessation."

49. Merleau-Ponty, *Phenomenology of Perception*, 438.

50. Merleau-Ponty, *Phenomenology of Perception*, 450.

51. Merleau-Ponty, *Phenomenology of Perception*, 455.

52. Maurice Merleau-Ponty, *In Praise of Philosophy and Other Essays* (Evanston, IL: Northwestern University Press, 1970), 31.

53. Walpola Rahula, *What the Buddha Taught* (New York: Grove Press, Inc., 1959), chapter 1.

54. David M. Levin, "Justice in the Flesh," in *Ontology and Alterity in Merleau-Ponty*, ed. Galen A. Johnson and Michael B. Smith (Evanston, IL: Northwestern University Press, 1990), 43.

55. Jacobson, *Buddhism and the Contemporary World*, 154.

56. Geraldine Finn, "The Politics of Contingency: The Contingency of Politics—On the Political Implications of Merleau-Ponty's Ontology of the Flesh," in *Merleau-Ponty, Hermeneutics, and Postmodernism*, 171–87, 171 [henceforth TPC].

57. Nāgārjuna, *The Philosophy of the Middle Way*, trans. David J. Kalupahana (Albany: State University of New York Press, 1986), 297.

58. Burke and Van Der Veken, *Merleau-Ponty in Contemporary Perspective*, 166.

59. Merleau-Ponty states in *Phenomenology of Perception*:

> Our relationship to the social is, like our relationship to the world, deeper than any express perception or any judgment. It is false to place ourselves in society as an object among other objects, as it is to place society within ourselves as an object of thought, and in both cases the mistake lies in treating the social as an object. We must return to the social with which we are in contact by the mere fact of existing, and which we carry about inseparably with us before any objectification. (362)

60. Tsenay Serequeberhan, *African Philosophy: The Essential Readings* (St. Paul, MN: Paragon House Publishers, 1991), 22.

CHAPTER 12

1. I would like to express my appreciation to Mr. Tom Downey, a friend at Temple University, for kindly going over this chapter with many insightful and valuable criticisms.

2. To name a few, "certainty" and "ultimacy" come to mind. Take the example of "certainty"—it is only a relative certainty, valid as a starting point of epistemological investigation, but not the ultimate standpoint to be reached.

3. Friedrich Nietzsche, for example, explains in *The Genealogy of Morals* how rationality came to be given the highest status of human nature in Europe by tracing the forms of punishment, an eruption of emotions. He writes "what an enormous price man had to pay for reason, seriousness, control over his emotions . . . how much blood and horror lies behind all 'good things'"; *The Birth of Tragedy and The Genealogy of Morals*, trans. Francis Golffing (New York: Doubleday and Company Ltd., 1956), 193–94.

4. Kant's solution to prevent an impulse for evil was to *suppress* the sensible desires by means of rational will. What this suggests is that there is a psychological struggle within the *ego-cogito* between its rationality and irrationality. Alternatively, this indicates an indecision of the will. (For this point, see Yasuo Yuasa, *Shūkyō keiken to shinsō Shinrigaku* [Religious Experience and Depth-Psychology] [Tokyo: Meicho Kankōkai, 1989], 202). Such a solution was aptly referred to as "hydraulic model" by Robert Solomon in his *Passions* (see *The Passion: Emotion and the Meaning of Life* [Indianapolis: Hackett Publishing Company, 1993]). Psychologically, this method creates a suppression of emotional energy. However, what is suppressed has a way of exploding once it passes a tolerable limit. It requires a natural release, which does not damage the psyche.

5. This has already been pointed out by Yasuo Yuasa in *The Body: Toward an Eastern Mind-Body Theory* (Albany: State University of New York Press, 1987) and in *Science and Comparative Philosophy* (Leiden: The Brill Publishing Co., 1989). See Maurice Merleau-Ponty, *Phénoménologie de la perception* (Paris: Gallimard, 1945), 158.

6. I propose to interpret Merleau-Ponty's "intentional arc" as a preconscious operation for the following reasons. First, his concept is inferred from a negative condition of the lived body (i.e., through the analysis of Schneider's case, who suffers from optical agnosis—that is, under normal, healthy lived body, this operation is not brought to a level of consciousness). Second, the kinetic movements, insofar as they are habituated actions, are not performed consciously.

7. The phrase "motor intentionality" is somewhat confusing, because the term "intentionality" is often associated with consciousness. Noting this possibility of confusion, Ichikawa Hiroshi uses the term "directionality of the body" in the sense that its activity can be brought to an awareness upon reflection, although it is preconscious at the time when this activity takes place. See Ichikawa Hiroshi, *Seishin toshite no shintai* [The Body as Spirit] (Tokyo: Keisei Shobō, 1976), 58.

8. The translation is taken from Maurice Merleau-Ponty, *Phenomenology of Perception*, trans. Colin Smith (London: Routledge, 1962), 138; Merleau-Ponty, *Phénoménologie de la perception*, 160–61.

9. Ibid, 130; ibid., 151.

10. Ibid.; ibid.

11. For a discussion of the variety of lived space that is generated through the body-scheme, see Shigenori Nagatomo, "Ichikawa's View of the Body," *Philosophy East and West* 36, no. 4 (October 1986): 375–91.

12. Merleau-Ponty, *Phenomenolgy of Perception*, 137; *Phénoménologie de la Perception*, 160.

13. Ibid., 136; ibid., 158.

14. The point that I wish to make here is that *ki*-energy is a necessary, but not sufficient, condition for maintaining the life of the living body.

15. "One's own body" (*le corps proper*) is not the Cartesian concept of the body that is elevated to the status of bodyness through the act of thinking. The body in question here is a lived, incarnate body.

16. Merleau-Ponty, *Phenomenology of Perception*, 101 and 117.

17. A question naturally arises here as to *what* to include. For our present concern, we shall limit ourselves to a living human body. In principle, it should extend to all the sentient beings, as well as the insentient. The recognition of the bilateral directionality discloses the possibility of going beyond the *ego-cogito* to reach the other *ego-cogito*. This is a point that needs to be developed later.

18. Merleau-Ponty, *Phenomenolgy of Perception*, 133; *Phénoménologie de la perception*, 154.

19. This interfusion of invisible energy is understood by Merleau-Ponty as a "primary meaning."

20. Husserl recognized that there is a passive synthesis, which takes place at the level of kinesthesis prior to a meaning-bestowing function of consciousness. Yet this dimension of experience has not been adequately articulated by Husserl.

21. See for an explanation of the terms "coenesthesis, kinesthesis, somesthesis, emotion-instinct," Yuasa Yasuo, *Ki, shugyō, shintai* [*Ki*-energy, Self-Cultivation, and Body] (Tokyo: Hirakawa Shuppansha, 1986), especially chapters 1 and 2. For a brief exposition of these terms, see Shigenori Nagatomo, "An Eastern Concept of the Body: Yuasa's Body-Scheme," in *Giving the Body Its Due*, ed. Maxine Sheets-Johnstone (Albany: State University of New York Press, 1992).

22. Yasuo Yuasa, *The Body: Toward an Eastern Mind-Body Theory*, trans. Thomas Kasulis and Shigenori Nagatomo (Albany: State University of New York Press, 1987), chapter 10.

23. This metaphor is found in Motoyama Hiroshi, *Toward Superconsciousness: Meditational Theory and Practice*, trans. Shigenori Nagatomo and Clifford R. Ames (Fremont, CA: Asian Humanities Press, 1990).

24. For example, Yasuo Yuasa writes in *Ki, shugyō, shintai* that "the series of images in the outer hall depicts the dark power of the unconscious that is linked to the instinctive impulses" (318).

25. I have given a little fuller treatment of this ascending process in Yasuo Yuasa and David E. Shaner, *Science and Comparative Philosophy*, 174–92.

26. Yuasa, *Ki, shugyō, shintai*, 252–53.

CHAPTER 13

1. A. C. Graham, *Disputers of the Tao: Philosophical Argument in Ancient China* (La-Salle, IL: Open Court, 1990), 85.

2. Kuang-ming Wu, *The Butterfly as Companion: Meditations on the First Three Chapters of the Chuang Tzu* (Albany: State University of New York Press, 1990), 197 [hereafter BC]. For a revised and expanded comparison of Wu, O'Neill, and Merleau-Ponty, see Jay Goulding, "Wu Kuang-ming and Maurice Merleau-Ponty: Daoism and Phenomenology," in *China-West Interculture: Toward the Philosophy of World Integration, Essays on Wu Kuang-ming's Thinking*, ed. Jay Goulding (New York: Global Scholarly Publications, 2008), 183–206.

3. Kuang-ming Wu, *On Chinese Body Thinking: A Cultural Hermeneutic* (Leiden: Brill Publishing Company, 1997), 20.

4. John O'Neill, *The Communicative Body: Studies in Communicative Philosophy, Politics, and Sociology* (Evanston, IL: Northwestern University Press, 1989), 16.

5. O'Neill, *The Communicative Body*, 16.

6. Stephen Light, *Shūzō Kuki and Jean-Paul Sartre* (Carbondale: Southern Illinois University Press, 1987), 26.

7. Maurice Merleau-Ponty, "Everywhere and Nowhere," in *Signs*, trans. Richard C. McCleary (Evanston, IL: Northwestern University Press, 1964), 126–58, 138–39.

8. Ibid., 139.

9. Maurice Merleau-Ponty, *The Visible and the Invisible* (Evanston, IL: Northwestern University Press, 1968), 151.

10. Ted J. Kaptchuk, *The Web That Has No Weaver: Understanding Chinese Medicine* (Chicago: Congdon and Weed, 1983), 256–68.

11. Gia-Fu Feng and Jane English, trans., *Lao Tsu: Tao Te Ching* (New York: Random House, 1972), poem 1.

12. Tsung Hwa Jou, *The Tao of Meditation: Way to Enlightenment* (Warwick: Tai Chi Foundation, 1983), 77.

13. Laurence Thompson, *The Chinese Way in Religion* (Encino, CA: Dickerson, 1973), 66.

14. Ninian Smart, *The World's Religions*, second ed. (Cambridge: Cambridge University Press, 1988), 115; also see Heinrich Dumoulin, *Zen Buddhism: A History Vol. 1 India and China* (New York: Macmillan, 1989), 68 and 79.

15. Roger T. Ames, "The Meaning of Body in Classical Chinese Philosophy," in *Self as Body in Asian Theory and Practice*, ed. Thomas Kasulis with Roger T. Ames and Wimal Dissanayake (Albany: State University of New York Press, 1993), 157–78, 159.

16. Hwa Yol Jung, *The Question of Rationality and the Basic Grammar of Intercultural Texts* (Niigata: International University of Japan, 1989), 11.

17. Ibid., 13–14.

18. O'Neill, *The Communicative Body*, 21–22.

19. Cited in John Hay, "The Human Body as a Microcosmic Source of Macrocosmic Values in Calligraphy," in *Self as Body in Asian Theory and Practice*, 179–211, 202.

20. Ibid., 179.

21. Nathan Sivin, "Forward," in Manfred Porkert, *The Theoretical Foundations of Chinese Medicine* (Cambridge, MA: MIT Press, 1974), xi–xvi, xiii–xiv.

22. See Jay Goulding, *Visceral Manifestation and the East Asian Communicative Body* (Cresskill, NJ: Hampton Press Inc., forthcoming); Jay Goulding, "'Three Teachings Are One': The Ethical Intertwinings of Buddhism, Confucianism and Daoism," in *The Examined Life—Chinese Perspectives: Essays on Chinese Ethical Traditions*, ed. Xinyan Jiang (Binghamton, NY: Global Publications, 2002), 249–78; Jay Goulding, "Wu Kuang-ming and Maurice Merleau-Ponty: Daoism and Phenomenology," 190–93.

23. Ames, "The Meaning of Body in Classical Chinese Philosophy," 165.

24. See Mark Elvin, "Tales of Shen and Xin: Body-Person and Heart-Mind in China during the Last 150 Years," in *Fragments for a History of the Human Body: Part Two*, ed. Michel Feher with Ramona Dannaff and Nadia Tazi (New York: Zone, 1989), 266–349.

25. Ames, "The Meaning of Body in Classical Chinese Philosophy," 165.

26. R. H. Mathews, *Chinese-English Dictionary*, revised edition (Cambridge, MA: Harvard University Press, 1944), 904.

27. Wu, *On Chinese Body Thinking*, 360.

28. Wu, *On Chinese Body Thinking*, 360.

29. William Edward Soothill and Lewis Hudous, *A Dictionary of Chinese Buddhist Terms* (Delhi: Motilal Banarsidass, 1937), 276.

30. Richard J. Smith, *China's Cultural Heritage: The Qing Dynasty, 1644–1912*, second edition (Boulder, CO: Westview Press, 1994), 169.

31. Jung, *The Question of Rationality and the Basic Grammar of Intercultural Texts*, 11–80.

32. See Smith, *China's Cultural Heritage*, 170.

33. Jing Wang, *The Story of Stone: Intertextuality, Ancient Chinese Stone Lore, and the Stone Symbolism of Dream of the Red Chamber, Water Margin, and The Journey to the West* (Durham, NC: Duke University Press, 1992), 1.

34. Wang, *The Story of Stone*, 198–99.

35. Wang, *The Story of Stone*, 199.

36. Maurice Merleau-Ponty, *The Primacy of Perception*, trans. James M. Edie (Evanston, IL: Northwestern University Press, 1964), 11; Jung, *The Question of Rationality and the Basic Grammar of Intercultural Texts*, 13.

37. See David Kherdian, *Monkey: A Journey to the West* (Boston: Shambhala Publications, Inc., 1992), vii–ix.

38. Kherdian, *Monkey*, vi–vii.

39. Merleau-Ponty, *The Primacy of Perception*, 149.

40. Maurice Merleau-Ponty, *Phenomenology of Perception*, trans. Colin Smith (London: Routledge, 1962), 431.

41. See Shūzō Kuki, "The Notion of Time and Repetition in Oriental Time," in Stephen Light, *Shūzō Kuki and Jean-Paul Sartre: Influence and Counter-Influence in the Early History of Existential Phenomenology* (Carbondale: Southern Illinois University, 1987), 43–50. For a revised and expanded comparison of Kuki, Heidegger, and Merleau-Ponty, see Jay Goulding, "Kuki Shuzo and Martin Heidegger: Iki (いき) and Hermeneutic Phenomenology," in *Why Japan Matters! vol. 2*, ed. Joseph F. Kess and Helen Landsdowne (Victoria, British Columbia: Centre for Asia-Pacific Initiatives, University of Victoria, 2005), 677–90.

42. John Haig, *The New Nelson Japanese-English Character Dictionary* (Tokyo: Charles E. Tuttle, 1997), 839.

43. Shūzō Kuki, "Iki no Kōzō (The Structure of Iki)," in *Kuki shūzō zenshū* (The Collected Works of Shūzō Kuki), eleven volumes and supplementary volume (Tokyo: Iwanami Shoten, 1981), 1–85, 16–21.

44. See Thomas Cleary, trans., *Shōbōgenzō: Zen Essays by Dōgen* (Honolulu: University of Hawai'i Press, 1986), 104–10.

45. See Makoko Ueda, "Iki and sui," in *Kodansha Encyclopedia of Japan* (Tokyo: Kodansha, 1983), 267–68.

46. Ihara Saikaku, *The Life of an Amorous Woman* (New York: New Directions, 1963), 138.

47. Shūzō Kuki, "Geisha," in Light, *Shūzō Kuki and Jean-Paul Sartre*, 87–88, 87.

48. See Matsunosuke Nishiyama, *Edo Culture: Daily Life and Diversions in Urban Japan, 1700–1868* (Honolulu: University of Hawai'i Press, 1997), 54.

49. Shūzō Kuki, "The Expression of the Infinite in Japanese Art," in *Shūzō Kuki and Jean-Paul Sartre*, 51–67, 52.

50. Kuki, "The Expression of the Infinite in Japanese Art," 53.

51. Kuki, "The Expression of the Infinite in Japanese Art," 54.

52. Yoshi Oida and Lorna Marshall, *The Invisible Actor* (London: Methuen, 1997), xvii.

53. Kuki, "The Expression of the Infinite in Japanese Art," 123.

54. Kuki, "The Expression of the Infinite in Japanese Art," 123.

55. Kuki, "The Expression of the Infinite in Japanese Art," xviii.
56. Merleau-Ponty, "Everywhere and Nowhere," 139.

Glossary of East Asian Characters

agejorō (J.)	揚女郎
ajikan (J.)	阿字観
akanukeshita (J.)	垢抜けした
akarui cogito (J.)	明るいコギト
akirame (J.)	諦め
Amidakyō (J.)	阿弥陀教
Amidakyō (J.)	阿弥陀経
bai ma fei ma (C.)	白馬非馬
basho (J.)	場所
basho no ronri (J.)	場所の論理
bashoteki ronri (J.)	場所的論理
Bashoteki ronri to shûkyōteki sekai kan (J.)	場所的論理と宗教的世界観
benshōhōteki (J.)	弁証法的
benshōhōteki sekai (J.)	弁証法的世界
biku (J.)	比丘
bitai (J.)	媚態
bodaishin (J.)	菩提心
bonnō (J.)	煩悩
bukede (C.)	不可得
bunriteki nigenron (J.)	分離的二元論
bushidō (J.)	武士道
busshin shōgai (J.)	仏身傷害
butai (J.)	舞台
Chan (C.)	禪
chin'gong myo'yu (K.)	眞空妙有
chinmoku cogito (J.)	沈黙コギト

chinyŏje (K.)	眞如諦
chongchong wujin (C.)	重重無盡
chongja saeng hyŏnhaeng (K.)	種子生現行
chūshingura (J.)	忠臣藏
daigasetsu (J.)	大我説
Dainichi Nyorai (J.)	大日如来
Dao (C.)	道
Daochuo (C.)	道綽
Dōgen (J.)	道元
dōji jōdō (J.)	同時成道
eichiteki sekai (J.)	叡智的世界
faxing (C.)	法性
fengyu (C.)	諷語
Foshuoguanwuliangshoufojing (C.)	佛説觀無量壽佛經
Fudō myōō (J.)	不動明王
fusheng (C.)	浮生
futaitenji (J.)	不退轉地
gaikaikankaku-undōkairo (J.)	外界感覚–運動回路
ganryōku (J.)	願力
geisha (J.)	芸者
Genshin (J.)	源信
geyi (C.)	格義
gō (J.)	業
gong'an (C.)	公案
goun (J.)	五蘊
guchi (J.)	愚癡
gutaiteki ippansha (J.)	具体的一般者
gyō (J.)	行
handanteki ippansha (J.)	判断的一般者
hannya (J.)	般若
Hataraku mono kara miru mono e (J.)	働くものから見るものへ
hirenzoku no renzoku (J.)	非連続の連続
hishiryō (J.)	非思量
hōben (J.)	方便
Hōnen (J.)	法然
hōshin (J.)	法身
Hōzōbosatsu	法藏菩薩
Huangdi neijing (C.)	黃帝内經
Huayan (C.)	華厳
Huineng (C.)	慧能
hun (C.)	魂
hyŏnghaeng hun chonagja (K.)	現行熏種子
Ichikawa Hiroshi (J.)	市川 浩

Igyōhin (J.)	易行品
Ihara Saikaku (J.)	井原　西鶴
iki (J.)	いき
ippansha no jikakuteki taikei (J.)	一般者の自覚的体系
jia (C.)	假
jie shi (C.)	解釋
jijuyō sammai (J.)	自受用三昧
jikaku (J.)	自覚
jikkai (J.)	十界
jiko gentei (J.)	自己限定
jinen hōni (J.)	自然法爾
jing (C.)	經
Jingangpi (C.)	金剛錍
Jingtu (C.)	浄土
jiriki (J.)	自力
jitsuzai (J.)	実在
Jōdo (J.)	浄土
jōdō–honnōkairo (J.)	情動−本能回路
jōdokyō (J.)	浄土教
Jōdoshinshū	浄土真宗
jōteki bunka wa katachi namo katachi, koe namo koe de aru (J.)	情的文化は形なも形、聲なも聲である
ju (J.)	受
Jūjū bibasharon (J.)	十住毘婆沙論
junsui keiken (J.)	純粋経験
kanji (J.)	漢字
Kanmuryōjukyō (J.)	觀無量壽經
karui cogito (J.)	明るいコギト
kayu (K.)	假有
Kazashi Nobuo (J.)	嘉指　信雄
Ken jōdo shinjitsu kyōgyōshō monrui (J.)	顯淨土眞實教行證文類
ki (J.)	気
kikō (J.)	気功
kōiteki chokkan (J.)	行為的直観
kōiteki ippansha (J.)	行為的一般者
kong (C., K.)	空
kong jia zhong (C.)	空假中
kongsang (K.)	空相
kongsŏng (K.)	空性
kongxiang (C.)	空相
kongxing (C.)	空性
Kōsō wasan (J.)	高僧和讚
kotodama (J.)	言霊

Kūkai (J.)	空海
Kuki Shūzō (J.)	九鬼 周造
Kuki Shūzō zenshū (J.)	九鬼周造全集
kurai cogito (J.)	くらいコギト
kyakkanshintai (J.)	客観身体
kyakkanteki shintai (J.)	客観的身体
Laozi (C.)	老子
li (C.)	禮
liang xing (C.)	兩行
lingqi (C.)	靈氣
Linji (C.)	臨濟
Liuzu tanjing (C.)	六祖壇經
Manyōshū (J.)	万葉集
mu (J.)	無
mu no basho (J.)	無の場所
mu no jikakuteki gentei (J.)	無の自覚的限定
muga (J.)	無我
muihō (J.)	無為法
muishikiteki junshintai (J.)	無意識的準身体
mujun no jiko dōitsu (J.)	矛盾の自己同一
mujunteki jiko dōitsu (J.)	矛盾的自己同一
mul'a ilch'e (K.)	物我一體
mumyŏng (K.)	無明
Muryōjukyō (J.)	無量寿経
myōgō fushigi (J.)	名号不思議
namu amida butsu (J.)	南無阿弥陀仏
nembutsu (J.)	念仏
neng guan zhi (C.)	能觀智
Nishida Kitarō (J.)	西田 幾多郎
Nishida Kitarō zenshū (J.)	西田幾多郎全集
Nishitani Keiji (J.)	西谷 啓治
Nishiyama Matsunosuke (J.)	西山 松之助
ōchō (J.)	横超
Ōjō yōshū (J.)	往生要集
ōjōshite jōbutsu suru (J.)	往生して成仏する
po (C.)	魄
pon'gak (K.)	本覺
pŏpsŏng (K.)	法性
qi (C.)	氣
qi (C.)	起
qigong (C.)	氣功
rekishiteki sekai (J.)	歴史的世界
ren (C.)	人

rokudai (J.)	六大
Ronri to seimei (J.)	論理と生命
sa (K.)	事
sabi (J.)	寂
saek (K.)	色
saihō gokuraku (J.)	西方極楽浄土
sammai (J.)	三昧
samurai (J.)	侍
sandoku (J.)	三毒
sanjiao heyi (C.)	三教合一
sanmitsu (J.)	三蜜
sasa muae (K.)	事事無碍
sayu (K.)	似有
se (C.)	色
Senchakuhongan nembutsushū (J.)	選擇本願念仏集
shan (C.)	山
Shandao (C.)	善導
shen (C.)	神
shen (C.)	身
shen xing ti (C.)	神形體
shen xing ti (C.)	身形體
shenxin (C.)	身心
shenxin erxiang (C.)	身心二相
shenxin yiru; K. *sinsim iryŏ*; J. *shinjin ichinyo*	身心一如
shi (C.)	事
shi jue (C.)	始覺
Shigenori Nagatomo (J.)	長友 繁法
shiki (J.)	色
shiki (J.)	識
shiki sokuze kū (J.)	色即是空
shin'i (J.)	瞋恚
shinjin (J.)	身心
shinjin datsuraku (J.)	身心脱落
shinjin gōitsu (J.)	心身合一
shinjin ichinyo (J.)	身心一如
shinjin nisō (J.)	身心二相
shinjin sōkanteki nigenron (J.)	心身相関的二元論
shinjitsu nintai (J.)	真実人体
Shinran (J.)	親鸞
shishi wuai (C.)	事事無碍
Shōbōgenzō (J.)	正法眼蔵
shobutsu (J.)	諸佛
shōmyō nembutsu (J.)	称名念仏

shugyō (J.)	修行
shukanshintai;	主観身体
shukanteki shintai (J.)	主観的身体
si'gak (K.)	始覺
sinsim (K.)	身心
sinsim yisang (K.)	身心二相
sisŏlyu (K.)	施設有
sō (J.)	想
soku (J.)	即
sokushin jōbutsu (J.)	即身成仏
sŏnggi (K.)	性起
sui (J.)	粹
Suzuki Daisetsu (J.)	鈴木 大拙
tai (J.)	対
tairitsuteki (J.)	対立的
tairitsuteki mu no basho (J.)	対立的無の場所
Taiyi jinhua zongzhi (C.)	太一金華宗旨
taizōkai mandara (J.)	胎蔵界曼荼羅
Tanluan (C.)	曇鸞
Tannishō (J.)	歎異抄
tariki (J.)	他力
Tetsugaku no kompon mondai (J.)	哲学の根本問題
ti (C.)	體
tian (C.)	天
tian di zhi jian (C.)	天地之間
Tiantai (C.)	天台
ton'gyo (K.)	頓敎
ton'yoku (J.)	貪欲
tunjiao (C.)	頓敎
uihō (J.)	有為法
ŭita'gi sŏng (K.)	依他起性
uji (J.)	有時
ukiyo (J.)	浮世
Watsuji Testurō (J.)	和辻 哲郎
wu (C.)	悟
wu (C.)	無
Wu Kuang-ming (C.)	吳光明
wuweifa (C.)	無為法
xian (C.)	仙
xiang (C.)	象
xianxing xun zhongzi (C.)	現行熏種子
xin (C.)	心
xing (C.)	形

xing (C.)	性
xing (C.)	行
xingqi (C.)	性起
xiu (C.)	修
yan wu yan (C.)	言無言
yang (C.)	陽
yi (C.)	義
Yijing (C.)	易經
yin (C.)	陰
yinyu (C.)	隱喻
yita qixing (C.)	依他起性
you (C.)	有
youweifa (C.)	有為法
yū no basho (J.)	有の場所
yū no ippansha (J.)	有の一般
yuanjiao (C.)	圓教
Yuasa Yasuo (J.)	湯浅 泰雄
yuishiki (J.)	唯識
yuyan (C.)	寓言
yuyan (C.)	語言
zang (C.)	藏
zangxiang (C.)	藏象
zazen (J.)	坐禅
Zen no kenkyū (J.)	善の研究
zenshinnaibu–kankakukairo (J.)	全身内部-感覚回路
Zenshū (J.)	禅宗
zettai (J.)	絶対
zettai mu (J.)	絶対無
zettai mu no basho (J.)	絶対無の場所
zettai mujunteki jiko dōitsu (J.)	絶対矛盾的自己同一
zhongguo (C.)	中國
zhongzi sheng xianxing (C.)	種子生現行
Zhuangzi (C.)	莊子
zixing (C.)	自性

Bibliography

Ames, Roger T. "The Meaning of Body in Classical Chinese Philosophy." 157–77 in *Self as Body in Asian Theory and Practice*, edited by Thomas P. Kasulis with Roger T. Ames and Wimal Dissanayake. Albany: State University of New York Press, 1993.

Batchelor, Stephen. *Verses from the Center: A Buddhist Vision of the Sublime*. New York: Riverhead, 2000.

Berman, Michael. "Merleau-Ponty and Nagarjuna: Enlightenment, Ethics, and Politics." *Journal of Indian Philosophy and Religion* 7 (October 2002): 99–129.

———. "The Hyper-Dialectic in Merleau-Ponty's Ontology of the *Flesh*." *Philosophy Today* 47, no. 4 (Fall 2003): 404–20.

———. "Merleau-Ponty and Nagarjuna: Relational Social Ontology and the Ground of Ethics." *Asian Philosophy* 14, no. 2 (July 2004): 131–46.

———. "Nāgārjuna's Negative Ontology." *Journal of Indian Philosophy and Religion* 12 (October 2007): 115–46.

Biyan lu. T 48.2003.139a–292a.

Brubaker, David. "Care for the Flesh: Gilligan, Merleau-Ponty, and Corporeal Styles." 229–56 in *Feminist Interpretations of Maurice Merleau-Ponty*, edited by Dorothea Olkowski and Gail Weiss. University Park: Pennsylvania State University Press, 2006.

Burke, Patrick, and Jean Van Der Veken, eds. *Merleau-Ponty in Contemporary Perspective*. Boston: Kluwer Academic Publishers, 1993.

Busch, Thomas W., and Shaun Gallagher, eds. *Merleau-Ponty, Hermeneutics, and Postmodernism*. Albany: State University of New York Press, 1992.

Buswell, Robert E., Jr., trans. *Collected Works of Chinul: The Korean Approach to Zen*. Honolulu: University of Hawai'i Press, 1983.

———. *Tracing Back the Radiance: Chinul's Korean Way of Zen*. Honolulu: University of Hawai'i Press, 1991.

Cataldi, Suzanne L., and William S. Hamrick, eds. *Merleau-Ponty and Environmental Philosophy: Dwelling on the Landscapes of Thought*. Albany: State University of New York Press, 2007.

Chan, Wing-tsit. *A Source Book of Chinese Philosophy*. Princeton, NJ: Princeton University Press, 1963.

Cheng, Hsueh-li. *Nāgārjuna's Twelve Gate Treatise*. Boston: D. Reidel Publishing Company, 1982.

Chinul. *Kanhwa kyŏrŭiron* (Treatise on Resolving Doubts about Huatou Meditation). *Hanguk Pulgyo Chŏnsŏ* (Collected Works of Korean Buddhism). Seoul: Tongguk taehakkyo ch'ulp'anbu, 1979. 4.732c–737c.

Cleary, Thomas, trans. *Entry into the Inconceivable: An Introduction to Hua-yen Buddhism*. Honolulu: University of Hawai'i Press, 1983.

———, trans. *Shōbōgenzō: Zen Essays by Dōgen*. Honolulu: University of Hawai'i Press, 1986.

———, trans. *Unlocking the Zen Koan: A New Translation of the Zen Classic Wumenguan*. Berkeley, CA: North Atlantic Books, 1997.

Clearly, Thomas, and J. C. Clearly, trans. *The Blue Cliff Record*. Boston: Shambhala Publications, Inc., 1992.

Conze, Edward, ed. and trans. *Buddhist Scriptures*. New York: Penguin, 1959.

Cook, Francis Harold. "Fa-tsang's Treatise on the Five Doctrines: An Annotated Translation." Ph.D. dissertation, University of Wisconsin, 1970.

———, trans. *How To Raise An Ox: Zen Practice as Taught in Zen Master Dōgen's Shōbōgenzō*. Somerville, MA: Wisdom Publication, 2002.

Dauenhauer, Bernard P. "Democracy and the Task of Political Amelioration." 235–52 in *Rereading Merleau-Ponty: Essays beyond the Continental-Analytic Divide*, edited by Lawrence Hass and Dorothea Olkowski. Amherst, NY: Humanity Books, 2000.

Davis, Duane H., ed. *Merleau-Ponty's Later Works and Their Practical Implications*. Buffalo, NY: Prometheus Books, 2001.

Derrida, Jacques. *La Vérité en peinture*. Paris: Flammarion, 1979.

———. *Positions*, translated by Alban Bass. Chicago: University of Chicago Press, 1981.

Descartes, René. *Discours de la méthode*. Paris: Vrin, 1637.

———. "Le Discours de la Méthode." *Œuvres philosophiques de Descartes*, volume 1, edited by Ferdinand Alquié. Paris: Édition Garnier Frères, 1963.

———. "Les meditations." *Œuvres philosophiques de Descartes*, volume 2, edited by Ferdinand Alquié. Paris: Édition Garnier Frères, 1963

———. "Les Passions de l'âme." *Œuvres philosophiques de Descartes*, volume 3, edited by Ferdinand Alquié. Paris: Édition Garnier Frères, 1963.

———. *Philosophical Writings*, translated and edited by Elizabeth Anscombe and Peter Thomas Geach. London: Thomas Nelson and Sons Limited, 1971.

Devettere, Raymond J. "The Human Body as Philosophical Paradigm in Whitehead and Merleau-Ponty." *Philosophy Today* 20 (Winter 1976): 317–26.

Dilworth, David A. "The Initial Formations of 'Pure Experience' in Nishida Kitarō and William James." *Monumenta Nipponica* 24, nos. 1–2 (1969): 93–111.

———. "The Concrete World of Action in Nishida's Later Thought." 249–70 in *Japanese Phenomenology: Phenomenology as the Trans-Cultural Philosophical Approach*, edited by Yoshihiro Nitta and Hirotaka Tatematsu. Dordrecht: Reidel Publishing Company, 1979.

Dōgen. *Shōbōgenzō 1*, edited by Kōshirō Tamaki. Tokyo: Daizōshuppan, 1993.

Dufrenne, Mikel. *Phénoménologie de l'Expérience Esthétique*. Paris: PUF, 1953.

Dumoulin, Heinrich. *Zen Buddhism: A History Vol. 1 India and China*. New York: Macmillan, 1989.

Elberfeld, Rolf, trans. *Logik des Ortes. Der Anfang der modernen Philosophie in Japan.* Darmstadt: Wissenschaftliche Buchgesellshaft, 1999.

Elvin, Mark. "Tales of Shen and Xin: Body-Person and Heart-Mind in China during the Last 150 Years." 266–349 in *Fragments for a History of the Human Body, Part Two,* edited by Michael Feher with Ramona Dannaff and Nadia Tazi. New York: Zone, 1989.

Faure, Bernard. "The Kyoto School and Reverse Orientalism." 245–82 in *Japan in Traditional and Postmodern Perspectives,* edited by Charles Wei-hsun Fu and Steven Heine. Albany: State University of New York Press, 1995.

———. *The Power of Denial: Buddhism, Purity and Gender.* Princeton, NJ: Princeton University Press, 2003.

———. *Double Exposure: Cutting Across Buddhist and Western Discourses,* translated by Janet Lloyd. Stanford, CA: Stanford University Press, 2004.

Feng, Gia-Fu, and Jane English, trans. *Lao Tsu: Tao Te Ching.* New York: Random House, 1972.

Fingarette, Herbert. *Confucius—The Secular as Sacred.* New York: Harper and Row, 1972.

Finn, Geraldine. "The Politics of Contingency: The Contingency of Politics—On the Political Implications of Merleau-Ponty's Ontology of the Flesh." 171–88 in *Merleau-Ponty, Hermeneutics, and Postmodernism,* edited by Thomas W. Busch and Shaun Gallagher. Albany: State University of New York Press, 1992.

Flynn, Bernard. *Political Philosophy at the Closure of Metaphysics.* Atlantic Highlands, NJ: Humanities Press, 1992.

Foulk, Griffith T. "Myth, Ritual, and Monastic Practice in Sung Ch'an Buddhism." In *Religion and Society in T'ang and Sung China,* edited by Patricia Buckley Ebrey and Peter N. Gregory. Honolulu: University of Hawai'i Press, 1995.

Gasquet, Joachim. *Cézanne.* Paris: Editions Cynara, 1988.

Glenn, John D., Jr. "Merleau-Ponty and the Cogito." *Philosophy Today* 23 (Winter 1979): 310–20.

Godway, Eleanor. "Toward a Phenomenology of Politics." 161–70 in *Merleau-Ponty, Hermeneutics, and Postmodernism,* edited by Thomas W. Busch and Shaun Gallagher. Albany: State University of New York Press, 1992.

Goulding, Jay. "'Three Teachings Are One': The Ethical Interwinings of Buddhism, Confucianism and Daoism." 249–78 in *The Examined Life—Chinese Perspectives: Essays on Chinese Ethical Traditions,* edited by Xinyan Jiang. Binghamton, NY: Global Publications, 2002.

———. "Kuki Shuzo and Martin Heidegger: Iki (いき) and Hermeneutic Phenomenology." 677–90 in *Why Japan Matters! Vol. 2,* edited by Joseph F. Kess and Helen Landsdowne. Victoria, British Columbia: Centre for Asia-Pacific Initiatives, University of Victoria, 2005.

———, ed. *China-West Interculture: Toward the Philosophy of World Integration, Essays on Wu Kuang-ming's Thinking.* New York: Global Scholarly Publications, 2008.

———. *Visceral Manifestation and the East Asian Communicative Body.* Cresskill, NJ: Hampton Press Inc., forthcoming.

Gregory, Peter, and Daniel Gets, ed. *Buddhism in the Sung.* Honolulu: University of Hawai'i Press, 1999.

Graham, Angus C. *Disputers of the Tao: Philosophical Argument in Ancient China.* LaSalle, IL: Open Court, 1990.

Guenther, Herbert V. *Philosophy and Psychology in the Abhidharma.* Boston: Shambhala Publications, Inc., 1976.

Haig, John. *The New Nelson Japanese-English Character Dictionary.* Tokyo: Charles E. Tuttle, 1997.

Han'guk Pulgyo Chŏnsŏ (Collected Works of Korean Buddhism). Seoul: Tongguk taehakkyo ch'ulp'anbu, 1979.

Hass, Lawrence, and Dorothea Olkowski, eds. *Rereading Merleau-Ponty: Essays beyond the Continental-Analytic Divide.* Buffalo, NY: Humanity Books, 2000.

Hatley, James, Janice McLane, and Christian Diehm, eds. *Interrogating Ethics: Embodying the Good in Merleau-Ponty.* Pittsburgh: Duquesne University Press, 2006.

Hay, John. "The Human Body as a Microcosmic Source of Macrocosmic Values in Calligraphy." 179–211 in *Self as Body in Asian Theory and Practice,* edited by Thomas P. Kasulis with Roger T. Ames and Wimal Dissanayake. Albany: State University of New York Press, 1993.

Heine, Steven, and Dale S. Wright, eds. *The Kōan: Texts and Contexts in Zen Buddhism.* New York: Oxford University Press, 2000.

Henry, Michel. *Généalogie de la psychoanalyse.* Paris: Presses Universitaires de France, 1985.

Hiroshi, Ichikawa. *Seishin toshite no shintai* (The Body as Spirit). Tokyo: Keisei Shobō, 1976.

Hiroshi, Motoyama. *Toward Superconsciousness: Meditational Theory and Practice,* translated by Shigenori Nagatomo and Clifford R. Ames. Fremont, CA: Asian Humanities Press, 1990.

Huayan wujiao zhiguan. By Dushun. T 45.1867.509a–513c.

Huineng. *The Sūtra of Hui-neng,* translated by A. F. Price and Wong Mou-lam. Boston: Shambhala Publications, Inc., 1990.

Husserl, Edmund. *Husserliana, Edmund Husserl Gesammelte Werke.* The Hague: Martinus Nijhoff, 1950.

Jacobson, Nolan P. *Buddhism and the Contemporary World.* Carbondale and Edwardsville: Southern Illinois University Press, 1983.

James, William. *Essays in Radical Empiricism.* Lincoln: University of Nebraska Press, 1996.

Johnson, Galen, ed. *Merleau-Ponty Aesthetics Reader: Philosophy and Painting.* Evanston, IL: Northwestern University Press, 1993.

Johnson, Galen A., and Michael B. Smith, eds. *Ontology and Alterity in Merleau-Ponty.* Evanston, IL: Northwestern University Press, 1990.

Jou, Tsung Hwa. *Tao of Meditation: Way to Enlightenment.* Warwick: Tai Chi Foundation, 1983.

Jung, Carl. *Mysterium Conjunctionis: The Collected Works of C. G. Jung,* volume 14, translated by R. F. C. Hull. Princeton, NJ: Princeton University Press, 1977.

———. *Two Essays in Analytical Psychology: The Collected Works of C. G. Jung,* volume 7, translated by R. F. C. Hull. Princeton, NJ: Princeton University Press, 1977.

Jung, Hwa Yol. *The Question of Rationality and the Basic Grammar of Intercultural Texts.* Niigata: International University of Japan, 1989.

———. "Merleau-Ponty's Transversal Geophilosophy and Sinic Aesthetics of Nature." 235–57 in *Merleau-Ponty and Environmental Philosophy,* edited by Suzanne L. Cataldi and William S. Hamrick. Albany: State University of New York Press, 2007.

Kant, Immanuel. *Kritik der reinen Vernunft.* Riga: Hartknoch, 1781.

———. *Kritik der Urteilskraft.* Berlin: Lagarde & Friedrich, 1790.

———. *Critique of Pure Reason,* translated by Norman Kemp Smith. New York: St. Martin's Press, 1965.

———. *Grounding for the Metaphysics of Morals,* translated by James Ellington. Indianapolis: Hackett, 1993.

Kaptchuk, Ted J. *The Web That Has No Weaver: Understanding Chinese Medicine*. Chicago: Congdon and Weed, 1983.

Kasulis, Thomas P. *Zen Action/Zen Person*. Honolulu: University of Hawai'i Press, 1981.

———. *Intimacy or Integrity: Philosophy and Cultural Differences*. Honolulu: University of Hawai'i Press, 2002.

Katz, Stephen T. "Language, Epistemology, and Mysticism." 22–74 in *Mysticism and Philosophical Analysis*, edited by Stephen T. Katz. New York: Oxford University Press, 1978.

Kazashi, Nobuo. "Bodily Logos, James, Merleau-Ponty, and Nishida." 107–20 in *Merleau-Ponty, Interiority and Exteriority, Psychic Life and the World*, edited by Dorothea Olkowski and James Morley. Albany: State University of New York Press, 1999.

Keown, Damien. "Karma, Character, and Consequentialism." *Journal of Religious Ethics* 24, no. 2 (Fall 1996): 329–50.

———. *The Nature of Buddhist Ethics*. New York: Palgrave, 2001.

Kherdian, David. *Monkey: A Journey to the West*. Boston: Shambhala Publications, Inc., 1992.

Kim, Hee-Jin. *Dōgen Kigen—Mystical Realist*. Tucson: University of Arizona Press, 1975.

———. "Existence/Time as the Way of Ascesis: An Analysis of the Basic Structure of Dōgen's Thought." *The Eastern Buddhist* 11, no. 2 (October 1978): 43–73.

Kim, Hyŏng-hyo. *Merŭllo ppontti wa aemaesŏng ŭi ch'orhak* (Merleau-Ponty and Philosophy of Ambiguity). Seoul: Ch'orhak kwa hyŏnsilsa, 1996.

———. *Haidegŏ wa Hwaŏm ŭi sayu* (Heidegger and the Huayan Mode of Thinking). Seoul: Chŏnggye, 2002.

Komito, David R. *Nāgārjuna's Seventy Stanzas: A Buddhist Psychology of Emptiness*. New York: Snow Lions Publications, 1987.

Kopf, Gereon. *Beyond Personal Identity: Dōgen, Nishida, and a Phenomenology of No-Self*. Richmond: Curzon Press, 2001.

———. "Temporality and Personal Identity in the Thought of Nishida Kitarō." *Philosophy East and West* 52, no. 2 (2002): 224–45.

Kruks, Sonia. *The Political Philosophy of Merleau-Ponty*. London: Ashgate Publishing, 1994.

Kuki, Shūzō. "Iki no Kōzō (The Structure of Iki)." 1–85 in *Kuki Shūzō zenshū* (The Collected Works of Shūzō Kuki). Tokyo: Iwanami Shoten, 1981.

———. "Geisha." 87–88 in *Shūzō Kuki and Jean-Paul Sartre* by Stephen Light. Carbondale: Southern Illinois University Press, 1987.

———. "The Notion of Time and Repetition in Oriental Time." 43–50 in *Shūzō Kuki and Jean-Paul Sartre* by Stephen Light. Carbondale: Southern Illinois University Press, 1987.

Kwant, Remy C. *The Phenomenological Philosophy of Merleau-Ponty*. Pittsburgh: Duquesne University Press, 1963.

———. *From Phenomenology to Metaphysics: An Inquiry into the Last Period of Merleau-Ponty's Philosophical Life*. Pittsburg: Duquesne University Press, 1966.

Lal, P., trans. *The Dhammapada*. New York: Farrar, Strauss and Giroux, 1967.

Lapointe, Francois H. "The Evolution of Merleau-Ponty's Concept of the Body." *Dialogos* (April 1974): 139–51.

Levin, David M. "Liberating Experience from the Vice of Structuralism: The Methods of Merleau-Ponty and Nagarjuna." *Philosophy Today* 41, no. 1 (1997): 96–112.

Light, Stephen. "The Expression of the Infinite in Japanese Art." 51–67 in *Shūzō Kuki and Jean-Paul Sartre: Influence and Counter-Influence in the Early History of Existential Phenomenology*. Carbondale: Southern Illinois University Press, 1987.

Lowry, Atherton C. "The Invisible World of Merleau-Ponty." *Philosophy Today* 23 (Winter 1979): 294–303.

Lusthaus, Dan. *Buddhist Phenomenology: A Philosophical Investigation of Yogācāra Buddhism and the Ch'eng Weishih Lun*. Richmond: Curzon, 1999.

Lyotard, Jean-François. *Discours, Figure*. Paris: Editions Klincksieck, 1985.

Madison, Gary Brent. *The Phenomenology of Merleau-Ponty*. Athens: Ohio University Press, 1981.

Mallin, Samuel B. *Merleau-Ponty's Philosophy*. New Haven, CT: Yale University Press, 1979.

Malraux, André. *Les Voix du silence*. Paris: Gallimard, 1951.

Martin, Michele. "On the Other Side of Attachment." 153–62 in *Being Bodies: Buddhist Women on the Paradox of Embodiment*, edited by Lenore Friedman and Susan Moon. Boston: Shambhala Publications, Inc., 1997.

Masao, Abe. "Dōgen on Buddha Nature." *The Eastern Buddhist* 10, no. 1 (May 1971): 28–71.

———. "Nishida's Philosophy of Place." *International Philosophical Quarterly* 28, no. 4 (Winter 1988): 355–71.

Masunaga, Reihō, trans. *A Primer of Sōtō Zen: A Translation of Dōgen's Shōbōgenzō Zuimonki*. Honolulu: East-West Center Press, 1971.

Mathews, R. H. *Chinese-English Dictionary*, revised edition. Cambridge, MA: Harvard University Press, 1944.

Mazis, Glen. *Emotion and Embodiment: Fragile Ontology*. New York: Peter Lang, 1994.

McCarthy, Erin. "Yuasa Yasuo 1925–2005: A Retrospective of His Life and Work." *Religious Studies Review* 33, no. 3 (July 2007): 201–8.

Merleau-Ponty, Maurice. *La Structure du comportement*. Paris: Gallimard, 1942.

———. *Phénoménologie de la perception*. Paris: Gallimard, 1945.

———. *Sens et non-sens*. Paris: Nagel, 1948.

———. *Éloge de la philosophie*. Paris: Gallimard, 1953.

———, ed. *Les Philosophes célèbres*. Paris: Editions d'art Lucien Mazenod, 1956.

———. *Signes*. Paris: Gallimard, 1960.

———. *Phenomenology of Perception*, translated by Colin Smith. London: Routledge, 1962.

———. *L'Oeil et l'esprit*. Paris: Gallimard, 1964.

———. *The Primacy of Perception, and Other Essays on Phenomenological Psychology, the Philosophy of Art, History, and Politics*, translated by James M. Edie. Evanston, IL: Northwestern University Press, 1964.

———. *Le Visible et l'invisible*. Paris: Gallimard, 1964.

———. *Sense and Non-Sense*, translated by Hubert and Patricia Dreyfus. Evanston, IL: Northwestern University Press, 1964.

———. *Signs*, translated by Richard C. McCleary. Evanston, IL: Northwestern University Press, 1964.

———. *The Visible and the Invisible*, translated by Alphonso Lingis. Evanston, IL: Northwestern University Press, 1968.

———. *La Prose du monde*. Paris: Gallimard, 1969.

———. *In Praise of Philosophy and Other Essays*, translated by James M. Edie, John Wild, and John O'Neill. Evanston, IL: Northwestern University Press, 1970.

———. *The Prose of the World* (1969), translated by John O'Neill. Evanston, IL: Northwestern University Press, 1973/1981.

———. *Texts and Dialogues: On Philosophy, Politics, and Culture*, edited by Hugh J. Silverman and James Berry Jr. Amherst, NY: Humanities Books, 1992.

———. "Eye and Mind." 121–64 in *The Merleau-Ponty Aesthetics Reader: Philosophy and Painting*, edited by Galen Johnson. Evanston, IL: Northwestern University Press, 1993.

———. *La Nature*, edited by Dominique Séglard. Paris: Editions du Seuil, 1995.

———. "Philosophy and Non-philosophy since Hegel," translated by Hugh J. Silverman. 9–83 in *Philosophy and Non-philosophy since Merleau-Ponty*, edited by Hugh J. Silverman. Evanston, IL: Northwestern University Press, 1997.

Morley, James. "Inspiration and Expiration: Yoga Practice through Merleau-Ponty's Phenomenology of the Body." *Philosophy East and West* 51, no. 1 (2001): 73–82.

Nagao, Gadjin. *The Foundational Standpoint of Mādhyamika Philosophy*, translated by John P. Keenan. Albany: State University of New York Press, 1989.

Nāgārjuna. *The Precious Garland and the Song of the Four Mindfulnesses*, translated by Jeffrey Hopkins. New York: Harper & Row, 1975.

———. *The Philosophy of the Middle Way*, translated by David J. Kalupahana. Albany: State University of New York Press, 1986.

———. *A Translation of Nāgārjuna's* Mūlamadhyamakakārikā *with an Introductory Essay*, translated by Kenneth K. Inada. Delhi: Sri Satguru Publications, 1993.

———. *The Fundamental Wisdom of the Middle Way, Nāgārjuna's Mūlamadhyamakakārikā*, translated by Jay L. Garfield. New York: Oxford University Press, 1995.

Nagatomo, Shigenori. "Ichikawa's View of the Body." *Philosophy East and West* 36, no. 4 (October 1986): 375–91.

———. *Attunement through the Body*. Albany: State University of New York Press, 1992.

———. "An Eastern Concept of the Body: Yuasa's Body-Scheme." 48–66 in *Giving the Body Its Due*, edited by Maxine Sheets-Johnstone. Albany: State University of New York Press, 1992.

Nietzsche, Friedrich. *The Birth of Tragedy and The Genealogy of Morals*, translated by Francis Golffing. New York: Doubleday and Company Ltd., 1956.

Nishida, Kitarō. *Fundamental Problems of Philosophy: The World in Action*, translated by David Dilworth. Tokyo: Sophia University, 1970.

———. *Nishida Kitarō zenshū dai hakkan* (Collected Works of Nishida Kitarō), nineteen volumes. Tokyo: Iwanami Shoten, 1979.

———. *An Inquiry into the Good*, translated by Masao Abe and Christopher Ives. New Haven, CT: Yale University Press, 1990.

———. *Last Writings: Nothingness and the Religious Worldview*, translated by David A. Dilworth. Honolulu: University of Hawai'i Press, 1993.

———. *Nishida Kitarō senshū* (Selected Works of Nishida Kitarō), edited by Ken'ichi Iwaki. Kyoto: Tōeisha, 1998.

Nishitani, Keiji. *Religion and Nothingness*, translated by Jan Van Bragt. Berkeley: University of California Press, 1982.

———. *Nishida Kitarō*, translated by Yamamoto Seisaku and James Heisig. Berkeley: University of California Press, 1991.

Nishiyama, Matsunosuke. *Edo Culture: Daily Life and Diversions in Urban Japan, 1700–1868*. Honolulu: University of Hawai'i, 1997.

O'Neill, John. *The Communicative Body: Studies in Communicative Philosophy, Politics, and Sociology*. Evanston, IL: Northwestern University Press, 1989.

Odin, Steve, trans. "An Explanation of Beauty: Nishida Kitarō's 'Bi no Setsumei.'" *Monumenta Nipponica* 42, no. 2 (Summer 1987): 211–18.

———. *The Social Self in Zen and American Pragmatism*. Albany: State University of New York Press, 1996.

———. *Artistic Detachment in Japan and the West: Psychic Distance in Comparative Aesthetics.* Honolulu: University of Hawai'i Press, 2001.

Oida, Yoshi, and Lorna Marshall. *The Invisible Actor.* London: Methuen, 1997.

Olkowski, Dorothea, and James Morley, eds. *Merleau-Ponty, Interiority and Exteriority, Psychic Life and the World.* Albany: State University of New York Press, 1999.

Olson, Carl. "The Leap of Thinking: A Comparison of Heidegger and the Zen Master Dōgen." *Philosophy Today* 25 (Spring 1981): 55–62.

Park, Bradley Douglas. "Ethics and Alterity: Moral Considerability and the Other." Ph.D. dissertation, University of Hawai'i, 2004.

Park, Jin Y. "Zen Language in Our Time: The Case of Pojo Chinul's Huatou Meditation." *Philosophy East and West* 55, no. 1 (2005): 80–98.

———, ed. *Buddhisms and Deconstructions.* Lanham, MD: Rowman & Littlefield Publishers, 2006.

———. *Buddhism and Postmodernity: Zen, Huayan and the Possibility of Buddhist Postmodern Ethics.* Lanham, MD: Lexington Books, 2008.

Park, Sung Bae. *Buddhist Faith and Sudden Enlightenment.* Albany: State University of New York Press, 1983.

Passerin d'Entreves, Maurizio. *Political Philosophy of Hannah Arendt.* New York: Routledge, 1994.

"Precept Study: Ethics in Action/The First Precept." *Tricycle* 1, no. 4 (Summer 1992): 10–13.

Rahula, Walpola. *What the Buddha Taught.* New York: Grove Press, Inc., 1959.

Ramanan, Krishniah V. *Nāgārjuna's Philosophy.* Tokyo: Charles E. Tuttle Company, Inc., 1966.

Rosemont, Henry. *Rationality and Religious Experience: The Continuing Relevance of the World's Spiritual Traditions.* Chicago: Open Court, 2001.

Said, Edward. *Orientalism.* New York: Vintage Books, 1994.

Saikaku, Ihara. *The Life of an Amorous Woman.* New York: New Directions, 1963.

Sartre, Jean-Paul. *La Transcendance de l'Ego.* Paris: Recherches Philosophiques, 1936.

———. *L'Etre et le néant.* Paris: Gallimard, 1943.

———. *Situations,* translated by Benita Eisler. London: Hamish Hamilton, 1965.

———. *Being and Nothingness,* translated by Hazel Barnes. New York: Washington Square Books, 1966.

———. "Existentialism." 9–51 in *Existentialism and Human Emotions,* translated by Bernard Frechtman. New York: Citadel Press, 1990.

Scarborough, Milton. "In the Beginning: Hebrew God and Zen Nothingness." *Buddhist-Christian Studies* 20 (2000): 191–216.

Schapiro, Meyer. *The Reach of Mind: Essays in Memory of Kurt Goldstein.* New York: Springer Publishing Co., 1968.

Sekida, Katsuki, trans. *Two Zen Classics: Mumonkan (the gateless gate), Hekiganroku (the blue cliff records).* New York: Weatherhill, Inc., 1977.

Serequeberhan, Tsenay. *African Philosophy: The Essential Readings.* St. Paul, MN: Paragon House Publishers, 1991.

———. *The Hermeneutics of African Philosophy: Horizon and Discourse.* New York: Routledge, 1994.

Shaner, David. *The Bodymind Experience in Japanese Buddhism: A Phenomenological Study of Kūkai and Dōgen.* Albany: State University of New York Press, 1985.

Shaner, David, Shigenori Nagatomo, and Yasuo Yuasa. *Science and Comparative Philosophy: Introducing Yuasa.* Leiden: E. J. Brill, 1989.

Sheridan, James F., Jr. *Once More from the Middle: A Philosophical Anthropology.* Athens: Ohio University Press, 1973.

Shinran. *Tannishō: A Primer—A Record of the Words of Shinran Set Down in Lamentation over Departures from his Teaching,* translated by Dennis Hirota. Kyoto: Ryūkoku University Press, 1982.

———. *Collection of Passages Revealing the True Shinjin of the Pure Land Way, The Collected Works of Shinran: The Writing,* volume 1, translated by Dennis Hirota, Hisao Inagaki, Michio Tokunaga, and Ryūshin Uryūzu. Kyoto: Jōdo Shinshū Hongwanjiha, 1997.

———. *Shinran zenshū* (Complete Works of Shinran), five volumes, edited by Mizumaro Ishida. Tokyo: Shunjūsha, 2001.

Silverman, Hugh J., ed. *Philosophy and Non-philosophy since Merleau-Ponty.* Evanston, IL: Northwestern University Press, 1997.

Sivin, Nathan. "Forward." xi–xvi in *The Theoretical Foundations of Chinese Medicine* by Manfred Porkert. Cambridge, MA: MIT Press, 1974.

Smart, Ninian. *The World's Religions,* second ed. Cambridge: Cambridge University Press, 1988.

Smith, Jean, ed. *Radiant Mind: Essential Buddhist Teachings and Text.* New York: Riverhead, 1999.

Smith, Richard J. *China's Cultural Heritage: The Qing Dynasty, 1644–1912,* second edition. Boulder, CO: Westview Press, 1994.

Solomon, Robert C. *The Passion: Emotion and the Meaning of Life.* Indianapolis: Hackett Publishing Company, 1993.

Soothill, William Edward, and Lewis Hudous. *A Dictionary of Chinese Buddhist Terms.* Delhi: Motilal Banarsidass, 1937.

Steinbock, Anthony J. "Merleau-Ponty, Husserl, and Saturated Intentionality." 53–74 in *Rereading Merleau-Ponty: Essays beyond the Continental-Analytic Divide,* edited by Lawrence Hass and Dorothea Olkowski. Buffalo, NY: Humanity Books, 2000.

The Sūtra of Immeasurable Life (S. *Sukhāvativyūha Sūtra,* J. *Muryōjukyō*). T 12.360.265c–279a.

Suzuki, D. T. *Zen Buddhism, Selected Writings of D. T. Suzuki,* edited by William Barrett. New York: Doubleday, 1996.

———, trans. *The Laṅkāvatāra Sūtra: A Mahāyāna Text.* Delhi: Motilal Banarsidass Publishers, 2003.

Taishō shinshū daizōkyō, edited by Junjirō Takakusu, Kaikyoku Watanabe, et al., one hundred volumes. Tokyo: Taishō Issaikyō Kankōkai, 1924–1932.

Takahashi, Masanobu. *The Essence of Dōgen,* translated by Yuzuru Nobuoka. London: Kegan Paul International, 1983.

Thera, Nyanaponika. *Abhidharma Studies: Buddhist Explorations of Consciousness and Time.* Pariyatti, Canada: Buddhist Publication Society, 1998.

Thompson, Laurence. *The Chinese Way in Religion.* Encino, CA: Dickerson, 1973.

Uchiyama, Kōshō. "Interdependence and the Middle Way." 195–99 in *Radiant Mind: Essential Buddhist Teachings and Texts,* edited by Jean Smith. New York: Riverhead, 1999.

Ueda, Makoko. "Iki and sui." 267–68 in *Kōdansha Encyclopedia of Japan* 3. Tokyo: Kōdansha, 1983.

Waddell, Norman, and Abe Masao, trans. *The Heart of Dōgen's Shōbōgenzō.* Albany: State University of New York Press, 2002.

Wang, Jing. *The Story of Stone: Intertextuality, Ancient Chinese Stone Lore, and the Stone Symbolism of Dream of the Red Chamber, Water Margin and The Journey to the West.* Durham, NC: Duke University Press, 1992.

Wang, Youru. "The Chan Deconstruction of Buddha Nature." 129–44 in *Buddhisms and Deconstructions*, edited by Jin Y. Park. Lanham, MD: Rowman & Littlefield Publishers, 2006.

Watanabe, Manabu. "In Memoriam: Yuasa Yasuo 1925–2005." *Nanzan Institute for Religions and Culture Bulletin* 30 (2006): 55–61.

Watsuji, Tetsurō. "Genshi bukkyō to jissen tetsugaku" (Early Buddhism and a Philosophy of Practice), in *Watsuji Tetsurō zenshū dai go kan* (The Collected Works of Tetsurō Watsuji), volume 5. Tokyo: Chikuma Shobō, 1995.

Whiteside, Kerry H. *Merleau-Ponty and the Foundations of an Existential Politics*. Princeton, NJ: Princeton University Press, 1988.

Wilhelm, Richard. *Secret of the Golden Flower: A Chinese Book of Life*, translated by Richard Wilhelm. San Diego: Harcourt Brace Jovanovich Publishers, 1962.

Wood, David. *The Step Back: Ethics and Politics after Deconstruction*. Albany: State University of New York Press, 2005.

Wu, Kuang-ming. *The Butterfly as Companion: Meditations on the First Three Chapters of the Chuang Tzu*. Albany: State University of New York Press, 1990.

———. *On Chinese Body Thinking: A Cultural Hermeneutic*. Leiden: The Brill Publishing Company, 1997.

Wumen guan. T 48.2005.292a–299c.

Yuasa, Yasuo. *Ki, shugyō, shintai* (*Ki*-energy, Self-Cultivation, and Body). Tokyo: Hirakawa Shuppansha, 1986.

———. *The Body: Toward an Eastern Mind-Body Theory*, translated by Thomas P. Kasulis and Shigenori Nagatomo. Albany: State University of New York Press, 1987.

———. *Shūkyō keiken to shinsō Shinrigaku* (Religious Experience and Depth-Psychology). Tokyo: Meicho Kankōkai, 1989.

———. *Shintairon: Tōyōteki shinjinron to gendai* (The Theory of the Body: Asian Mind Body Theory and Contemporary World). Tokyo: Kōdansha Gakujutsu Bunko, 1992.

———. *The Body, Self-Cultivation, and Ki*, translated by Shigenori Nagatomo and Monte S. Hull. Albany: State University of New York Press, 1993.

———. *Shintai no uchūsei* (The Cosmology of Body). Tokyo: Iwanami Shoten, 1994.

———. *Watsuji Tetsurō* (Tesurō Watsuji). Tokyo: Chikuma Shobō, 1995.

———. *Shūkyōkeiken to shintai* (Religious Experience and the Body). Tokyo: Iwanami Shoten, 1997.

———. "Shūkyō tetsugaku" (Philosophy of Religion). 6–267 in *Yuasa Yasuo zenshū* (The Collected Works of Yasuo Yuasa), volume 2. Tokyo: Hakua Shobō, 2000.

———. "Wasureta dekaruto" (The Forgotten Descartes), in *Yuasa yasuo zenshū* (The Collected Works of Yasuo Yuasa), volume 4. Tokyo: Hakua Shobō, 2003.

Yuasa, Yasuo, Shigenori Nagatomo, and David Edward Shaner. *Science and Comparative Philosophy: Introducing Yasuo Yuasa*. Leiden: The Brill Publishing Co., 1989.

Yusa, Michiko. *Zen & Philosophy: An Intellectual Biography of Nishida Kitarō*. Honolulu: University of Hawai'i Press, 2002.

Zaner, Richard M. *The Problem of Embodiment: Some Contributions to a Phenomenology of the Body*. The Hague: Martinus Nijhoff, 1964.

———. "The Alternating Reed: Embodiment as Problematic Unity." 53–71 in *Theology and Body*, edited by John Y. Fenton. Philadelphia: Westminster Press, 1974.

Ziporyn, Brook. *Being and Ambiguity: Philosophical Experiments with Tiantai Buddhism*. Chicago: Open Court, 2004.

Index

Abe, Masao, 160

Abhidharma, 22, 30, 52, 274n2; abhidharmic, 52, 226; criticism of, 30; and essentialism of, 22; theory of Theravada Buddhism, 58

Abhidharmakośa, 58

absolute: choice, 28, 218–19; freedom, 27, 29; relativity, 205; self-identity, 187

Acalanātha, 49

Ajikan meditation, 48, 49

ambiguity, 9, 12, 18, 20, 22–23, 26, 36–37, 51, 57, 72, 101–2, 188, 209, 221, 226, 250–51; of action, 2; and being, 260n10; of the body, 9, 86, 138–39; and double affirmation, 19; and enunciation, 109, 110; of existence, 100, 107; hyperdialectic, 246; ontological, 11; of perception, 186; structure of, 3; of subjectivity and objectivity, 51–52

Amida, 9, 113, 115–22, 125, 131, 261n20

Amitābha. *See* Amida

Amitābha-sūtra, 115

animal being, 61–62

animality, 205–7

anthropocentrism, 207

Aristotle, 145, 268n1

autochthonous, 34, 35, 212, 222

Avalokiteśvara Bodhisattva, 195

basho, 9, 10, 134, 141–53, 155, 165–66, 268nn1–2, 269n10; of absolute nothingness, 136, 142, 152; of being, 9, 134; logic of, 135, 142, 145–46, 150–51; of nothingness, 151, 155, 269n10, 271n23; of oppositional nothingness, 9, 134; philosophy of, 147

Battista Alberti, Leon, 152

being: being-for-itself, 21, 39, 85; being-for-the-other, 129; being-in-itself, 22, 85; being-in-the-world, 3, 6, 12, 19, 53–54, 137, 139, 141, 147, 260n10; being-there, 3, 260n10; being-time (J. *uji*), 89, 251; being-toward-death, 53; being-viewed-by-the-other, 76; *Dasein*, 3, 53, 134; of language, 8; and time, the unity of , 90

Being and Time, 26, 53, 251

Bernard, Emile, 148

bodhicitta, 49

Bodhidharma, 7, 246, 256n24, 265n23

bodhisattva, 6, 11–12, 24, 28, 36, 41, 49, 117, 119, 195, 198, 210, 215, 216, 218, 260n19

body, 3–10, 13, 15, 17, 19–29, 31–32, 35–38, 40–42, 45–59, 69, 71–75, 77–78, 80–81, 83–90, 92–94, 121, 125, 137–40, 146,

148, 155–59, 165, 168–69, 171–78, 183–
94, 196, 200–203, 205, 207, 210, 231–32,
234–35, 240, 241–42, 243, 244, 246–47,
250–52, 253, 254, 258n26, 260n19,
261n20, 261n24, 269n12, 272n30, 278n7;
actual, 46–47, 51, 55; biological, 139;
body-mind dualism, 6, 50–51, 56, 83,
97, 155, 230, 243; body-mind oneness,
47, 50, 55, 87; body-in-the-world, 47,
196; bodymind, 5, 46, 256n19; body-
schema, 51, 55–56, 231; body-subject,
24, 184; body-thinking, 242, 248, 254;
body-world, 79; Buddhist body of Void,
13, 242, 247–48, 253; casting off body
and mind, 47, 88, 92, 194; correlative
dualism of body and mind, 47, 50, 52;
dharma (*see dharma-kāya*); earthly, of
Daoism, 13, 242, 247–48; habit, 46, 51,
55, 231; heavenly, of Confucianism, 13,
242, 247–48; historical, 140; human, 45,
51–52, 55–56, 83–85, 87, 92–93, 128,
140, 188, 206, 253; in-betweenness,
247–49; lived, 55, 84, 86–87, 91, 134,
137–39, 173, 183, 200, 210, 225, 231–33,
237, 240, 243, 258n26, 278n6; living,
50–51, 177, 232, 258n26, 278n15,
279n17; meditative, 250; no-body
177; nonduality of body and mind,
6–7; object, 50–51, 173, 185, 231;
phenomenology of, 3; physical, 165, 174,
242, 248; physiological, 231; speaking,
139; subject, 50–51, 56, 58, 184; totality
of body and mind, 45; unconscious
quasi-body, 51–52
brute fact, 67
brute reality, 196
brute world, 104
Buddha, 1, 4, 6, 7, 9, 13, 28, 41, 98, 115–16,
118, 177, 189–91, 193, 200–201, 206,
210, 246, 260n19, 261n20, 261n24,
265n24; body, 48, 89, 118; Buddha's
enlightenment, 74; buddhahood, 5, 7,
105; buddhas, 36, 46–47, 92, 116, 215,
261n24; dharma, 87; eye, 75; nature,
7, 30, 89, 92–93, 107, 261n24, 263n34,
265n25; way, 46, 210
Buddhahood, 74, 75, 105

Buddhism, 3, 5, 7, 9, 11–12, 13, 17–19,
21–22, 27–29, 35, 38, 48, 55, 57–58,
101–2, 106, 112, 113, 125, 144, 153,
155–57, 164, 176, 183, 186, 196, 211,
213–14, 217–18, 224–25, 241–54; early,
53–55, 58–59; Huayan, 5–6, 23, 30, 36,
41, 43, 101–3, 105–7, 111, 249, 264n16,
266n26; Mādhyamika, 12, 21, 176, 196,
198, 200, 205, 209, 211; Māhāyana,
11–12, 52, 55, 58, 62, 77, 83, 115–16,
155, 160–61, 168, 203–4, 249, 259n37;
Pure Land/Jingtu/Jōdo, 113, 115–16,
121, 144, 240, 249, 261n20; Rinzai, 144;
Shingon, 40, 48–49, 55, 239, 259n38;
Sōtō, 45, 116; Tiantai/Tendai, 5, 6, 61–
71, 73–82, 115, 249, 259n10, 260n19,
261n20; Theravāda, 58, 83; True Pure
Land, 9; Yogācāra, 21, 26, 31, 259n37;
Zen/Chan, 4, 5, 7, 9, 30, 45–46, 98, 101,
103, 106, 111, 113, 116–17, 127, 142–
44, 153, 155–59, 160–61, 163–64, 177,
195–96, 204, 242, 249, 251, 256n24

care (*Sorge*), 26, 53, 137
*Cessation and Contemplation in the Five
Teachings of Huayan*, 102
Cézanne, 10, 141–43, 145–53, 185, 202,
270n15
Chan Buddhism. *See* Buddhism; Zen
Buddhism
chanting the name of Amida, 113, 115–16,
118, 121, 125, 131
chiasm, 4–7, 9, 10, 11, 13, 24–26, 33, 35–
37, 41–43, 69–72, 78–80, 95, 100–101,
105, 110, 111, 112, 153, 186, 195, 205,
209, 223–24, 242, 244, 246, 248, 249,
253
Chinese medicine, 45, 57, 245
Chinul, 9, 101, 103–8, 110, 111, 112;
dead words, 9, 110; involvement with
meaning, 110; involvement with words,
110; live words, 9, 110; on Sudden
School, 101, 105, 107, 266n26; *Treatise
on Resolving Doubts about Huatou
Meditation* (*Huatou Meditation*), 101,
103, 107, 108, 110, 266n26
clash of civilizations, 156

cogito, 2–3, 5, 9, 38, 46–47, 50, 57, 98, 105, 122–27, 131, 133–34, 136, 230, 233, 235–40, 269n8; bright, 46, 58–59; dark, 46; *ergo sum*, 57; silent/tacit, 9, 46, 57–59, 86, 121, 124–26, 128–30; spoken, 57

compassion, 10, 12, 121, 156, 184, 185, 193, 197–99, 201, 203–4, 206–8, 210–12, 214–17, 221–24

conditioned coproduction. *See* dependent co-arising

constituted language, 114

constitutive emptiness, 156, 157, 174

contingency, 12, 87, 125, 190, 221–23

conventional truth, 18, 19, 29–30, 36, 62–63

copulation, 24, 25

corporeality, 26, 30 184, 203, 234, 245, 250; of body, 36; of consciousness, 31; intersubjective, 33; quasi-corporeality, 8

Daochuo, 115

Daoism, 6, 13, 45–47, 50–52, 241–54

Dasein, 3, 26, 53, 134

dead words, 9, 110. *See also* Chinul

defilement (*kleśa*), 24, 48, 55, 58, 277n46

dependent arising. *See* dependent co-arising

dependent co-arising, 3, 4, 6, 11, 18, 20–21, 23, 27, 29–30, 32–33, 36, 41–43, 101–2, 105, 107, 111, 112, 205

dependent origination. *See* dependent co-arising

Derrida, Jacques, 8, 24, 99, 148, 270n15

Descartes, René, 25, 57, 114, 122–25, 127, 149–50, 155, 158, 190–200, 209; Cartesian, 3, 27, 38, 50, 56, 98–99, 105, 126, 127, 133–34, 136, 143, 149, 188, 230, 278n15

desire, 17, 21, 23–24, 31, 34, 49, 111, 115, 118–19, 124, 177, 183, 189–91, 194, 200–201, 211, 214–16, 220, 222, 232, 236, 274n5, 278n4

detachment, 116, 183, 273n37

dharma, 24, 30, 36, 41, 46–47, 52, 58, 72, 78, 89, 116, 118, 120, 194, 211, 226, 260n17, 260n19, 261n20, 261n24, 274n2; conditioned/*saṃskṛta-dharma*, 58; unconditioned/*asaṃskṛta-dharma*, 58

dharmadhātu, 75, 102

Dharmakāra Bodhisattva, 117, 119

dharma-kāya, 48–49, 52, 77, 194

Dōgen, 5, 6–7, 9, 45–47, 49, 52, 83–94, 116, 191, 229, 251; *Shōbōgenzō*, 46, 229

double (the), 97–98, 103, 105, 112; affirmation, 13, 18–20, 29–30; negation, 13, 18, 20–21, 29–30; walk, 13, 242

Dufrenne, Mikel, 144

Dushun, 102–3

ego, 12, 32, 133, 135, 184, 189, 191, 193, 196, 199–201, 225, 258n33; *cogito*, 46–47, 105, 233, 235–40, 278n4, 279n17; non-ego, 133, 271n10; pure, 144, 230; transcendental, 2, 3, 135

eidetic reduction, 78, 91, 108

Eightfold Noble Path, 62, 210

embodiment, 7, 48, 80, 94, 143, 146, 148, 176, 179, 183–85, 188–92, 194–201, 203–5, 207; embodied beings, 93, 94, 185; embodied consciousness, 5, 25

emptiness, 10, 11, 12, 18–21, 23–24, 29–30, 35–36, 38–39, 42, 62–63, 87, 89, 92, 103, 105, 107, 112, 125, 156–57, 159, 174, 183–87, 189, 200, 203–5, 207, 209, 214, 245, 247–49, 253; of emptiness, 62

enlightenment, 12, 72, 75, 83, 88–89, 92, 105–6, 110, 163, 178, 210–11, 227, 242; the mind of (*bodhicitta*), 49; original, 24

exclusive center, 73

Eye and Mind, 79, 138, 141, 147–48, 150, 152, 178

Fahuaxuanyi, 76

faith, 8, 25, 117–21, 155–57, 163–64, 176, 178–79, 209, 212, 218, 267n6; perceptual, 24–25, 38

Fazang, 23, 101–2, 191

felt inter-resonance, 236–37

fire sermon, 189, 191, 200

five grave offenses, 118, 120

five skandhas, 6, 45, 52–54, 59

flesh, 2,6, 9, 23–43, 70, 72–73, 78–82, 85–86, 101, 109, 112, 117, 133, 137–39,

148, 156–57, 165, 171–76, 178–79,
    181, 183–88, 191, 193, 196, 200, 202–9,
    211–13, 220–21, 222–24, 244, 246, 247,
    248, 249, 252, 270n17; philosophy of,
    30–31, 119, 148, 157, 171
For Itself, 4, 5, 12, 21, 39, 56, 69, 85–86, 88,
    124, 126, 165, 168, 172–75, 176, 232
Four Noble Truths, 62, 245, 276n36
freedom, 12, 22, 27–29, 33–34, 92–94,
    130, 169, 170–71, 185, 197–211, 213,
    218–21, 223–24
Freud, Sigmund, 52, 55, 137
functional being, 21
Fundamental Problems of Philosophy, 155,
    165, 168, 172. *See also* Nishida, Kitarō

Garbha-maṇḍala, 49, 239–40
Genshin, 115
Gestalt, 22, 25, 38 42, 172–74, 184
gestural thought, 148–49

Heart Sūtra, 189–90, 193, 195, 253
Hegel, G. W. F., 1–2, 97, 99, 144, 148, 160,
    213, 226
Heidegger, Martin, 3, 6, 8, 19, 21–23,
    25–26, 30, 35–37, 39, 40, 53, 133, 148,
    243, 251, 252, 269n15; being (*Dasein*),
    3, 53, 134; *Being and Time*, 26, 53, 251;
    care (*Sorge*), 26, 53, 137; *Fundamental
    Problem of Philosophy*, 155, 165, 168,
    172; *Introduction to Metaphysics*, 39
Henry, Michel, 56, 58, 134, 137, 268n1
high-altitude approach (high-altitude
    thinking), 41, 191, 204
Hōnen, 115–16
huatou, 9, 101, 103, 106–8, 110, 111, 266n26
Huayan Buddhism, 5–6, 23, 30, 36, 41,
    43, 101–3, 105–7, 111, 249, 265n16,
    266n26. *See also* Buddhism
Huayan wujiao zhiguan, 102
Huineng, 10, 30, 155–57, 177–78; *Platform
    Sūtra*, 30, 156–57, 177–78, 272n35
Husserl, Edmund, 1–3, 9, 53, 56, 78, 91,
    108, 135–37, 143, 144, 209, 243, 251,
    276n43, 279n20
ignorance, 30, 48, 75, 195, 250
immanence, 67, 68, 102, 137

impermanence, 62, 90, 201, 211
In Itself, 12, 21–22, 25, 39, 42, 56, 85–86,
    104, 165–66, 171, 176, 193, 201
indirect language, 108–9
indirect ontology, 37, 41, 212, 213
inexhaustibility, 101
initial awakening, 30
inner man, 98
An Inquiry into the Good, 155, 157–60,
    162, 271n12
intentional arc, 3, 5, 6, 12, 52, 56, 106,
    230–35, 278n6
intentionality, 3, 5, 9, 51–54, 56, 78, 84, 89,
    91, 111, 136, 138, 231–32, 278n7
interbeing, 193
interrogation, 9, 98, 99–101, 107–8, 110,
    111, 164, 209, 212, 219; interrogative, 7,
    92, 99–101, 107–8
intersubjectivity, 12, 32–33, 74, 110, 212,
    219, 222, 224–26, 230, 234
intertwining, 98
Introduction to Metaphysics, 39. *See also*
    Heidegger, Martin
intuition, 135, 138–39; acting, 9, 51; active,
    133–34, 137–40; lived, 135; self, 135
involvement: with meaning, 110; with
    words, 110

James, William, 158
Jesus Christ, 117, 266n5
jiriki. *See* self, power
Jung, Carl, 46–47, 49, 246, 258n21, 258n33
junsui keiken. *See* pure experience

Kamo no Chōmei, 119
Kanmuryōjukyō, 240
kansō nembutsu, 115
Kant, Immanuel, 135–36, 143–44, 158,
    161–62, 167, 170, 176, 196–97, 200,
    215, 223, 225, 230, 277
karma, 5, 27–28, 31–33, 55, 58, 75, 111,
    216, 218–19, 221, 260n17, 261n24,
    277n46; past/*shukugō*, 119
ki. *See* qi
kleśa. *See* defilement
kōiteki chokkan. *See* intuition, acting
Kūkai, 45, 47–49, 52

Kuki, Shūzō, 243, 251–53

L'Oeil et l'esprit. See Eye and Mind
La Nature, 205, 206. *See also* Merleau-
Ponty, Maurice
Lacan, Jacques, 110
lateral transcendence/*ōchō*, 121
Lebenswelt. See life-world
life-world, 1–4, 20, 22, 24, 31–32, 135, 247
live words, 9, 110
Locke, John, 114, 226
locus of beings, 10
logos, 93, 220
Lotus Sūtra, 71
Lyotard, Jean-François, 148, 270n16

Mādhyamika Buddhism, 12, 21, 176,
196, 198, 200, 205, 209, 211. *See also*
Buddhism
Mahāvairocana, 48, 49, 259n38
Māhāyana Buddhism, 11–12, 52, 55, 58,
62, 77, 83, 115–16, 155, 160–61, 168,
203–4, 249, 259n37. *See also* Buddhism
Manyōshū, 113, 266n1
meditation: *huatou*, 9, 101, 103, 106–8,
110, 111, 266n26; *zazen*, 7, 87–88, 92
meridian, 4, 56–57, 232, 243, 245, 246–47
Merleau-Ponty, Maurice: autochthonous,
34–35, 212, 222; chiasm, 4–7, 9, 10, 11,
13, 24–26, 33, 35–37, 41–43, 69–72,
78–80, 95, 100–101, 105, 110, 111, 112,
153, 186, 195, 205, 209, 223–24, 242,
244, 246, 248, 249, 253; *Eye and Mind*,
79, 138, 141, 147–48, 150, 152, 178; *La
Nature*, 205, 206; *The Phenomenology
of Perception*, 2, 4, 20, 32–33, 37, 61,
67, 72, 84, 114, 125; *The Primacy of
Perception*, 153, 208; *The Prose of the
World*, 97, 108, 114, 128; *Signs*, 11, 32;
The Structure of Behavior, 22, 38; *The
Visible and the Invisible*, 20–21, 26,
32–33, 35, 38, 40, 61, 69, 72, 84, 86,
97–99, 144, 155, 171, 174, 193–94, 202,
209, 211
Middle Way, 12, 66, 79, 183, 189, 196, 198,
200, 203, 209, 220
modernism, 147, 176

Mont Sainte-Victoire, 142–43, 146–47, 151
motor intentionality, 231, 278n7
mu. See nothingness
mu no basho. See place of nothingness
mujunteki jiko dōitsu. See self, identity
mystery of chanting the name, 114–15

nadī, 57
Nāgārjuna, 12, 21–22, 30, 62, 115, 192,
209–12, 214–15, 217, 220, 224, 226–27
namu amida butsu, 9, 113, 116, 119
nature-origination, 6, 23–24, 29–30, 36,
41, 43
nembutsu, 115–18, 120–21, 125
Nhat Hahn, Thich, 193
nirvana, 12, 161
Nishida, Kitarō, 9–10, 133–40,
142–53, 155–61, 163–71, 173–74,
175–78, 268n1, 268n4, 269nn9–10,
270nn19–20, 271n4, 271n10, 272n23;
Fundamental Problems of Philosophy,
155, 165, 168, 172; *An Inquiry into the
Good*, 115, 117–19, 160, 162, 271n12.
See also basho
Nishitani, Keiji, 187, 195, 271n10
nonexclusive center, 73
nonphilosophy, 97, 244
nonthinking/*hishiryō*, 86–87, 88, 90, 92
no-self, 10, 11, 29–30, 47–48, 58, 62, 137,
158, 178, 195, 225
nothingness, 10, 21, 35–36, 39–43, 133–37,
140, 142, 150–74, 176–79, 192, 195,
204, 244, 246, 248, 249, 253
not-thinking/unthinking/*fushiryō*, 87, 92

objectivism, 97, 98
Ōjōyōshū, 115
ontology, 33, 37–38, 40, 77, 86, 186,
200, 207–8, 211, 213, 218; of art,
141; existential, 30, 35, 37; indirect,
37, 41, 209, 211, 213; of language,
8; of nature, 207; of no-self, 29;
relational social ontology, 221–24;
transphenomenological, 36; of the
visual, 10, 269n8
Orientalism, 45, 179
other power/*tariki*, 118–21, 125, 131

overdetermination, 26–27, 33, 101

Parmenides, 114
parole parlante. See speaking words
parole parlée. See spoken words
Pascal, 119
perception, 3–4, 6, 8, 10, 13, 20, 22, 23,
    24–25, 26, 29–35, 37–38, 51, 54, 67–68,
    70–72, 80, 84, 86–88, 91, 109, 113,
    123–24, 128–30, 138, 141–44, 146–48,
    151–53, 156, 158, 161, 164, 167, 171–
    74, 176–78, 184–91, 193–208, 212–13,
    230–31, 233, 250
The Phenomenology of Perception, 2, 4, 20,
    32–33, 37, 61, 67, 72, 84, 114, 125. *See
    also* Merleau-Ponty, Maurice
phenomenology, 2–4, 6, 8, 13, 19, 23, 30,
    33, 35–38, 43, 47, 52–54, 59, 93, 104,
    106, 108, 111, 122, 125, 130, 133, 135–
    38, 146, 191, 197, 210, 211–12, 224–25,
    241, 243–44, 248, 252, 270n16, 276n43
place of nothingness. *See basho*
Platform Sūtra, 30, 156–57, 177, 178,
    272n35. *See also* Huineng
power of the vow, 117, 119–20
prajñā, 49, 178, 193, 211, 216, 271n4,
    272n35
The Primacy of Perception, 153, 208
The Prose of the World, 97, 108, 114, 128
provisional truth, 63, 64
psychologism, 137, 159–60, 271n10
pure consciousness, 22, 29, 32
pure experience, 9, 134, 138, 142–46, 148,
    153, 155–63, 166, 179, 268n4, 270n4,
    271n10
Pure Land Buddhism, 113, 115–16,
    121, 144, 240, 249, 261n20. *See also*
    Buddhism

qi, 6, 45, 47, 51–52, 56–57, 102, 229–40,
    247
qigong, 51–52, 57

reciprocity, 99, 138, 142, 186, 202
reflection, 2, 20, 22, 27, 38, 90–91, 93, 97–
    100, 102–3, 127, 133–40, 142–43, 148,
    162, 192, 197, 205–7, 209, 268n1, 278n7

relational self, 199
res cogitans/thinking substance, 122, 134
res extensa/extended substance, 50
reversibility, 27, 35, 65–66, 70, 72–74,
    76–82, 186–87, 260n17
Rinzai Buddhism, 144. *See also* Buddhism
samādhi/*sammai*, 58, 92, 216; samadhic
    awareness, 5, 50–52; self-fulfilling/
    jijuyōzanmai, 48–50
sammai. See samādhi/*sammai*
Sangha, 118, 206
Śantideva, 198–99
Sartre, Jean Paul, 21–22, 39–40, 99, 103,
    109, 144, 193, 209, 218, 235, 243, 251,
    260n19, 272n23; on Merleau-Ponty's
    language, 109–10
Schapiro, Meyer, 148, 270n15
seated mediation. *See zazen*
sedimented language, 109–10
self: contradictory self-identity/*mujunteki
    jikodōitsu*, 145; cultivation, 45–51,
    57–58, 120–21; determination, 138,
    140, 142–45, 147, 168, 170; identity,
    18, 145, 165, 168, 187, 190; identity
    of absolute contradictories/*zettai
    mujunteki jikodōitsu*, 137, 149; nature,
    10, 21, 105, 155–57, 176–77, 179, 187;
    power, 118–21
Senchaku hongan nembutsu shū, 115
Sengcan, 195
sentient beings, 11–12, 29, 36–37, 41, 46,
    47, 48–49, 73–75, 78, 92–93, 117, 178,
    260n17, 261n24
Shandao, 115
Shingon Buddhism, 40, 48–49, 55, 239,
    259n38. *See also* Buddhism
Shinran, 9, 113–22, 125, 129, 131
Shōbōgenzō, 46, 229
Signs, 11, 32. *See also* Merleau-Ponty,
    Maurice
silence, 7, 108–9, 125–26, 185, 198, 242
six elements, 48
skillful means, 21, 116–17, 121
soku, 142, 145, 153, 269n6
solitude, 35, 212
Sōtō School, 45, 116. *See also* Buddhism
speaking words, 114, 126–31

speech, 109
spoken words/*parole parlée*, 109, 114, 126, 129, 268n35; words to be spoken, 129–30, 268n35
The Structure of Behavior, 22, 38. *See also* Merleau-Ponty, Maurice
subjectivism, 97, 98
subject-object dialogue, 13, 202, 233
substantialism, 99
suchness, 10, 17–19, 21, 23, 29, 74, 77, 131, 143, 145, 156, 161, 162–63, 179, 195
Sudden School, 101, 105, 107, 266n26
suffering, 3, 11–12, 17, 19, 23–24, 36, 43, 62, 193–94, 198, 210, 214–15, 220–21, 261n24, 274n5
Sukhāvativyūha Sūtra, 116, 118, 120
śūnyatā. *See* emptiness
Suzuki, D. T., 156–57, 177

tabula rasa, 32
tacit cogito, 9, 86, 124–26, 128–30
tairitsuteki mu no basho. *See basho*
Tanabe, Hajime, 163
Tanluan, 115
Tantra, 83
tariki. *See* other power
ten worlds, 48
Tendai Buddhism. *See* Tiantai Buddhism
Theravāda Buddhism, 58, 83. *See also* Buddhism
thinking substance. *See res cogitans*
thinking: nonthinking/*hishiryō*, 86–88, 90, 92; not-thinking/unthinking/*fushiryō*, 87, 92; thinking/*shiryō*, 86–87, 92
three mysteries, 49, 55
Three Thousand quiddities, 5, 6, 70
Three Truths, 62, 67, 75, 77, 79. *See also* Tiantai Buddhism
Tiantai Buddhism, 5, 6, 61–71, 73–82, 115, 249, 259n10, 261n20. *See also* Buddhism
Treatise on Resolving Doubts about Huatou Meditation (*Huatou Meditation*), 101, 103, 107, 108, 110, 266n26
True Pure Land Buddhism, 9. *See also* Buddhism

uji. *See* being, being-time
ultimate truth, 18, 19, 21, 29–30, 36, 62–64, 67, 72–73, 79, 107, 127
unconscious, 8, 46–47, 49, 52, 58, 109–10, 126, 137, 234, 239, 250, 279n24; collective, 49
undecidability, 70, 73, 79, 80
unicentrism, 80
universal reason, 160. *See also* Hegel, G. W. F.
universal spirit, 61
upāya. *See* skillful means

Vasubandhu, 58
vijñapti-mātra, 55, 58, 259n37
virtues, 74–75, 120, 198, 211–12, 214, 216–17, 221, 223–24, 248, 251, 252
The Visible and the Invisible, 20–21, 26, 32–33, 35, 38, 40, 61, 69, 72, 84, 86, 97–99, 144, 155, 171, 174, 193–94, 202, 209, 211. *See also* Merleau-Ponty, Maurice

waka, 45
Wang, Youru, 157, 177
Watsuji, Tetsurō, 53

yang, 47, 235–39, 245, 246, 247, 248, 253, 257n10
yin, 47, 235–39, 245, 246, 247, 248, 253, 257n10
Yogācāra Buddhism, 21, 26, 31, 259n37. *See also* Buddhism
yū no basho. *See basho*, of being
Yuasa, Yasuo, 6, 45–53, 173–74, 278n5, 279n24

zazen, 7, 87, 88, 92
Zen/Chan Buddhism, 4, 5, 7, 9, 30, 45–46, 98, 101, 103, 106, 111, 113, 116, 117, 127, 142–44, 153, 155–59, 160–61, 163–64, 177, 195–96, 204, 242, 249, 251, 256n24. *See also* Buddhism
Zhanran, 5, 61, 70, 73–74, 76–79, 261n24
Zhili, 61, 78–79, 260n17, 261n20

About the Contributors

Michael Berman is associate professor of philosophy at Brock University in St. Catharines, Ontario. He specializes in comparative philosophy, and has published articles on continental and Asian philosophy. He is an associate editor for the *Canadian Journal of Buddhist Studies* and his current research focuses on phenomenology and the philosophy of religion.

David Brubaker is lecturer at University of New Haven. He earned his Ph.D. from University of Illinois at Chicago. Brubaker's research focuses on aesthetics, art criticism, the philosophy of film and video, painting, and printmaking. His recent publications on Merleau-Ponty include "Painting from the Heart: Beauty, Moore and Merleau-Ponty's Wholes of Visibility," "Care for the Flesh: Gilligan, Merleau-Ponty and Corporeal Styles," and "The Roots of Agency: Merleau-Ponty, Flesh and Foucault."

Gerald Cipriani is of Corsican-Irish origins, was brought up in France, and completed his education in the United Kingdom. He was awarded his first philosophy doctorate in Western aesthetics with a scholarship at Leeds Metropolitan University in 1998, and undertook a second doctoral research in dialogical philosophy at the School of Oriental and African Studies of the University of London. He taught aesthetics for eleven years in the United Kingdom (Birmingham), and then in Japan (Tokyo). In 2004–2005 and spring 2006, he was research fellow at the Faculty of Letters of Kyoto University, funded by the British Academy, the Japan Society for the Promotion of Science, and the Great Britain Sasakawa Foundation. He is now professor of philosophy of culture affiliated with National Taiwan University of Arts (Taipei). He has published widely on Western aesthetics and more recently on the philosophies of Gabriel Marcel and Nishida Kitarō. He is now working on a number of book publications and is conducting a research on intercultural dialogue.

Toru Funaki was born in 1952 in Tokyo. He received his Ph.D. from the Faculty of Letters at Tokyo University in 1976 and spent 1999–2000 as a research fellow at London University. After teaching at Kumamoto University, he became professor at Senshū University in 2003. Trained in eighteenth-century European philosophy, Merleau-Ponty's phenomenology, and Bentham's utilitarianism, he is currently exploring the philosophical challenges of the digital age. Among his publications are book-length introductions to the philosophies of Maurice Merleau-Ponty and Gilles Deleuze, *Lando obu fikushon* (Land of Fiction), *Miru koto no tetsugaku* (A Philosophy of Seeing), *Dejitarumedia jidai no hōhōjosetsu* (Discourse on a Method for the Digital Age), and *Shinkaron no itsutsu no mayoi* (The Five Aporias of Evolutionism). He further coauthored *Kotoba ga hiraku tetsugaku no tobira* (Words that Open the Door to Philosophy) and translated Nigel Wartburton's *Philosophy: The Classics* (Nyūmon tetsugaku no meicho) into Japanese.

Jay Goulding is professor at Atkinson School of Social Sciences, York University, Toronto, Canada, where he teaches Chinese and Japanese philosophy through hermeneutic phenomenology. He has published in *Beijing University's Gate of Philosophy*, *Journal for the Scientific Study of Religion*, *Sociological Analysis: A Journal of Comparative Religion*, *Political Theory*, *Catalyst*, *Anhui Normal University Journal of Social Sciences and Humanities*, *Dao: A Journal of Comparative Philosophy*, *Journal of Chinese Philosophy*, *China Review International*, *Asian Cinema*, and *International Journal for Field-Being*. He contributed to *Scribner's New Dictionary of the History of Ideas* (2005) with entries on East Asian philosophy. In 2006, he was visiting lecturer at Foreign Literature Studies Institute, Beijing Foreign Studies University, and Institute of Foreign Philosophy, Beijing University. He has recently edited a volume, *China-West Interculture: Toward the Philosophy of World Integration, Essays on Wu Kuang-ming's Thinking* (2008), that engages Daoism, Confucianism, and Buddhism with phenomenology and Western philosophy.

Hyong-hyo Kim is professor of philosophy at the Academy of Korean Studies, Sŏngnam, South Korea. He earned his Ph.D. at the University of Louvain in Belgium. He is the author of numerous books, including *Haidegŏ wa maŭmŭi chŏrhak* (Heidegger and the Philosophy of Mind), *Merŭlŏ ppontti ŭi aemaesŏng ŭi chŏrhak* (Merleau-Ponty's Philosophy of Ambiguity), and *Derida ŭi haechʼe chŏrhak* (Derrida's Deconstructive Philosophy).

Gereon Kopf received his Ph.D. from Temple University and is presently associate professor for Asian and comparative religion at Luther College. Generous fellowships from the Japan Foundation and the Japan Society for the Promotion of

Research have enabled him to conduct research in 1993–1994 at Ōbirin University in Machida, and 2002–2004 at the Nanzan Institute for Religion and Culture in Nagoya. He is currently involved in developing a nondualistic philosophy from the work of Nishida Kitarō and his commentators, such as Takahashi Satomi, Tanabe Hajime, and Mutai Risaku. He is also translating essays by Nishida, Mutai, and Yasuo Yuasa. His publications include *Beyond Personal Identity* and numerous articles on the religious philosophies of Dōgen and Nishida Kitarō.

Glen A. Mazis is professor of philosophy and humanities at Penn State Harrisburg. He is the author of *Emotion and Embodiment: Fragile Ontology* (1993), *The Trickster, Magician and Grieving Man: Returning Men to Earth* (1994), *Earthbodies: Rediscovering Our Planetary Senses* (2002), and *Humans, Animals, Machines: Blurring Boundaries* (2008), as well as seventy poems in various literary journals, including *The North American Review*, *Spoon River Poetry Review*, *Atlanta Review*, *Rosebud*, and so forth.

Yuki Miyamoto has held the position of assistant professor in the Department of Religious Studies at DePaul University since earning her Ph.D. in ethics from the University of Chicago Divinity School. A native of Hiroshima, Miyamoto has dedicated her work primarily to the atomic bomb discourse. Her dissertation analyzes atomic bomb discourses from the perspectives of ethics and narrative theory. Among her publications is "Rebirth in the Pure Land or God's Sacrificial Lambs: Religious Interpretation of the Atomic Bombings in Hiroshima and Nagasaki" (*Japanese Journal of Religious Studies*). In this article, she compares Buddhist and Roman Catholic interpretations of these events. She has also published articles examining Japanese ethics, the notion of marginalization, and fox imagery in narratives.

Shigenori Nagatomo is professor at Temple University. He earned his Ph.D. from University of Hawai'i. He specializes in comparative philosophy and Japanese Buddhism. He focuses on mind/body issues and approaches them from the standpoint of depth psychology and meditational experience. His publications include *Toward a Holistic Non-dualism* (2006), *A Philosophical Investigation of Miki Kiyoshi's Concept of Humanism* (1995), *Attunement through the Body* (1992), and *Science & Comparative Philosophy: Introducing Yuasa Yasuo* (1989, coauthored with Yuasa Yasuo and David E. Shaner).

Carl Olson teaches religious studies at Allegheny College. Besides numerous essays in journals, books, and encyclopedias, his latest books include the following: *The Different Paths of Buddhism: A Narrative-Historical Introduction* (2005), *Original Buddhist Sources: A Reader* (2005), *The Many Colors of Hinduism: A Thematic-Historical Introduction* (2007), *Hindu Primary Sources: A Sectarian Reader* (2007), and *Celibacy and Religious Traditions* (2007). While at Allegheny College, Professor Olson has been appointed to the following positions: holder of the National Endowment for the Humanities Chair, 1991–1994; holder of the Teacher-Scholar Chair in the Humanities, 2000–2003; visiting fellowship at Clare Hall, University of Cambridge, 2002; and elected life member of Clare Hall, University of Cambridge, 2002.

Jin Y. Park is associate professor of philosophy and religion at American University. She is the author or editor of *Buddhisms and Deconstructions* (2006), *Buddhism and Postmodernity: Zen, Huayan, and the Possibility of Buddhist Postmodern Ethics* (2008), *Comparative Political Theory and Cross-Cultural Philosophy: Essays in Honor of Hwa Yol Jung* (2009), and *Makers of Modern Korean Buddhism* (2010, forthcoming). Park also published a number of book chapters and journal articles on Zen Buddhism, Buddhist ethics, Buddhist-postmodern comparative philosophy, and Buddhist encounters with modernity in Korea.

Bernard Stevens was born in Indonesia and educated at Trinity College Dublin, the Freie Universitaet Berlin, and the University of Louvain-la-Neuve, where he is presently professor. A philosopher specializing in continental European phenomenology and, more recently, in contemporary Japanese philosophy, he has translated Heidegger ("Aristoteles: Metaphysik thêta") and Watsuji ("Introduction to Ethics"). His essays have been published in numerous French journals, including *Les Temps Modernes*, *Esprit*, *Philosophie*, *Etudes Phénoménologiques*, the *Revue philosophique de Louvain*, and *Zen Buddhism Today* (Kyoto). His main books are *L'apprentissage des signes: Lecture de Paul Ricoeur* (1990), *Topologie du néant: une approche de l'école de Kyôto* (2000), *Le néant évidé: Ontologie et politique chez Keiji Nishitani* (2003), and *Invitation à la philosophie japonaise: autour de Nishida* (2005).

Yasuo Yuasa (1925–2005) received his Ph.D. from the Faculty of the Letters at Tokyo University and taught at Tsukuba and Obirin Universities. He published extensively on Jungian analytical psychology, Watsuji Tetsurō, Japanese philosophy, and the philosophies of *ki* (energy). Three of his works have been translated into English: *The Body, Self-Cultivation, and Ki-Energy* (1993), *The Body: Toward an Eastern Mind-Body Theory* (1987), and *Science and Comparative Philosophy: Introducing Yuasa Yasuo* (1989). In December of 2005 the Japanese government bestowed on him the Order of the Sacred Treasure.

Brook Ziporyn is associate professor of religion and philosophy at Northwestern University. He earned the Ph.D. in Chinese philosophy at the University of Michigan. His publications on Chinese intellectual history, religion, and philosophy include: *Evil and/or/as the Good: Intersubjectivity and Value Paradox in Tiantai Buddhist Thought* (2000), *The Penumbra Unbound: The Neo-Taoist Philosophy of Guo Xiang* (2003), *Being and Ambiguity: Philosophical Experiments with Tiantai Buddhism* (2004), and *Zhuangzi: The Essential Writings with Selections from Traditional Commentaries* (2009).

CPSIA information can be obtained at www.ICGtesting.com
Printed in the USA
BVOW07s1121191213

339527BV00001B/3/P